The Lure of the Edge

Scientific Passions, Religious Beliefs,
and the Pursuit of UFOs

Brenda Denzler

UNIVERSITY OF CALIFORNIA PRESS
Berkeley · Los Angeles · London

University of California Press
Berkeley and Los Angeles, California

University of California Press, Ltd.
London, England

Library of Congress Cataloging-in-Publication Data

Denzler, Brenda, 1953–
   The lure of the edge : scientific passions,
   religious beliefs, and the pursuit of UFOs /
   Brenda Denzler.
      p. cm.
   Includes bibliographical references and index.
   ISBN 0-520-22432-9 (cloth : alk. paper)
   1. Alien abduction.   2. Human-alien
encounters.   3. Unidentified flying objects—
Religious aspects.   4. Religion and science—
Miscellanea. I. Title.
   BF2050 .D466 2001
   001.942—dc21   2001027670

Printed in the United States of America
08 07 06 05 04 03 02 01
10 9 8 7 6 5 4 3 2 1

The paper used in this publication is both acid-free
and totally chlorine-free (TCF). It meets the minimum requirements of ANSI/NISO Z39.48–1992
(R 1997) (*Permanence of Paper*). ∞

To Connie M.,
who allowed me to conceive of the impossible,

and to the late John Trechak,
who didn't laugh at me when I did.

The Soul of Man . . . comprehendeth all ages in a moment, and unless it perceive something more excellent, is very desolate. All worlds being but a silent wilderness, without some living thing more sweet and blessed after which it aspireth.

Thomas Traherne, *Centuries*, #62

Contents

Acknowledgments

When a long-term project is completed it is customary to express gratitude to all those who helped to make it possible. Usually the most notable supporters are named first, and apologies are extended in the end to all those contributors whose names have accidentally gone unmentioned. In a study such as this one, the unnamed "others" who merit acknowledgment are not so much forgotten as they are recognized and respected by the very fact of their omission. I mean, in particular, the men and women who constitute the UFO community, some of whom request anonymity. Their willingness to share their stories publicly in print and on film, and with me personally and privately, has made my work possible. In addition, I would like to offer my thanks —

To Greg Robbins and Mike Kalton, who helped me learn how (but not what) to think again.

To Liz Clark, for her consistent efforts to imbue my thought with greater rigor and clarity.

To Grant Wacker and Russell Richey, for daring to go where few men have gone before, and to Leigh DeNeef for being willing to help me along the way.

To Harry Partin for his unflagging belief that I had the right stuff.

To Jean O'Barr and Francesca, for Jean's commitment to this woman's studies.

To Jackson Carroll, who helped me begin to learn how to make numbers speak, and to Cheryl E., who pressed me for greater clarity.

To the St. Michael the Archangel Fund for its generous support and encouragement.

To Coralyn Bolt, who helped me nourish my dreams of learning more about religion.

To Rod K. and Katherine B., whose energizing presence came at just the right time.

To Nora Gottlieb, Melissa R., and Darlyne M. — people whose friendship is without duplication. And to Darlyne, for helping to make the tedious task of data entry fun!

To George Fawcett, for the use of his UFO library. A pioneer of ufology in North Carolina, George is a treasure trove of information and great good-will. I don't care what the geneticists say, there's no one like George!

To Gilbert G., for his critical review of, yet unqualified support for, my project.

To the Society for the Scientific Study of Religion and to The Geneva Companies, which provided me with sorely needed research funds.

To Kenneth Ring and the Omega Project, for permission to use their survey items.

To the staff at Perkins Library, particularly to Eric Smith and to those incomparable folks in the Inter-Library Loan office, without whose help my research would have been considerably foreshortened.

To the Full Story Group of North Carolina and the late Nick Summers, to the UFO Awareness Group of North Carolina, to Walt Andrus and Wayne LaPorte (and all the NC MUFON gang) of the Mutual UFO Network, to Vicki Lyons and Pat and Buddy Crumbley of Project Awareness, to Lucius Farish of the UFO Newsclipping Service, to Shannon Kluge, and to the many, many individuals who filled out surveys, sent me articles, recommended books, and were willing to share their UFO stories. I hope I have done them — and you — justice.

To my editors at the University of California Press — Doug Abrams Arava (who has since moved on to other projects and places), Reed Malcolm, and Marielle Leon for their interest in and enthusiasm for this project; Jean McAneny and Carolyn Hill for their superb attention to the details that make so much difference in the end; and to Barbara Jellow for her good-humored willingness to take a second look.

And finally to my parents and children, who provided the context and grounding that have kept my life meaningful.

Introduction

In the mid-1950s two small groups of individuals with very different histories and interests came together for a short period. Their brief interaction has had long-term effects on a third group of individuals — a larger group by far than either of the two principals. The first group consisted of a handful of people who gathered around a woman called (pseudonymously) "Marian Keech," a student of Theosophy and other esoteric teachings and a practitioner of automatic writing. The second group was composed of sociologist Leon Festinger and a handful of graduate students interested in the growth and demise of messianic movements. The groups' paths crossed after an article in a local newspaper revealed that, through her automatic writing, Keech believed she was in contact with extraterrestrial entities who had informed her that the world would end on a specific date in the immediate future. Seizing the opportunity, Festinger and his colleagues posed as believers to gain entrée to the small Keech following. The predicted date passed without incident, but Keech's predictions nevertheless bore fruit: in 1956 Festinger, Henry W. Riecken, and Stanley Schachter published *When Prophecy Fails: A Social and Psychological Study of a Modern Group That Predicted the Destruction of the World.*[1] Thirty years later it was still in print, a cornerstone of contemporary studies of messianism, new religious movements, and those who believe in UFOs.

Interestingly enough, in that same year Edward Ruppelt, who had just retired from heading the U.S. Air Force's UFO investigation (codenamed Project Blue Book), published his memoirs from that assignment.

They included much fascinating information on military UFO encounters, what was known, suspected, or speculated in higher echelons about UFOs, and the politics of the official UFO investigation.[2] Though it was not a scholarly work, it was a lengthy contemporary look at the UFO phenomenon and at official and unofficial attempts to deal with it. Ruppelt's book, however, saw only one reprint — and an attenuated one, at that.

The third group of people — those who have lived in the shadow of the Festinger book — devote time and resources to a more or less serious study of UFO phenomena. It is one of the enduring ironies of the UFO movement that the academic world has paid more attention to a book about a channeler of extraterrestrial messages than to the memoirs of a main actor in the early UFO debate. Subsequent learned treatments of things ufological have almost always focused on groups like the one that surrounded Keech. Indeed, if one were to read only the scholarly literature on the UFO movement (which would be a brief project!), one might well conclude that those who believe in UFOs are socially marginal characters whose ideas are based on the teachings of charismatic Keech-like leaders who preach a twentieth-century salvation by benevolent "space brothers" who intervene in human affairs. That is, one would have to conclude that virtually all UFO believers — or at least all serious students of the phenomenon — are contactees or their disciples.[3] Irving Hexham warned in 1986 that reports of UFO sightings and claims of meeting "visitors from outer space" are a form of pseudoscience that cult leaders can easily exploit to gain undue influence and authority. The March 1997 mass suicide of the followers of Marshall Applewhite has done nothing to dispel this scholarly impression of what it means to be interested in UFOs.

And yet this impression is mistaken, largely because of its origins in the particular interests of a small group of researchers and in the beliefs of scarcely a dozen individuals following a woman whose own beliefs were grounded in esoteric traditions. It is not an accurate representation of the larger UFO community or of the study of UFO phenomena. Still less is it an accurate representation of the place and role of religion or religious ideas within that community. This book seeks to correct this one-sided view of the UFO movement and to present a fuller, more nuanced view of the role of religion in it. That role is inextricably bound up with the UFO phenomenon itself and with the science and the politics of UFOs.

When UFO reports began to surface, the Cold War had just begun and Western leaders were not sure what kind of technology the Soviet Union might have captured from Nazi-held territories at the end of World War II. The fact that people were reporting odd-shaped aerial devices traveling at incredible speeds and making "impossible" maneuvers was cause for alarm, especially for a newly created air force that was charged with the defense of United States airspace. UFO reports were also of interest to scientists and the aerospace industry, which hoped to build aircraft with the kind of speed and maneuverability that was being described by the witnesses. Thus at the outset the UFO phenomenon was unarguably a political as well as a scientific concern. As the years passed, however, it became clear that UFOs posed no (or at least, no direct) physical or political threat to the country, and by the late 1960s most scientists had become convinced that UFOs held no promise for advancing scientific or technical knowledge. Instead, the increasingly fantastic tales of encounters with ufonauts seemed to indicate that the UFO phenomenon was primarily religious in nature. Thereafter, much popular as well as virtually all academic interest in UFOs framed the subject as a matter of belief — and uninformed belief, at that.

However, many of those who had devoted serious effort to the compilation and analysis of UFO reports did not agree with this assessment of the subject. For those investigators, UFOs were a tangible reality amenable to certain modes of scientific study, and the aerial crafts' only certain connection to religion lay in the probable impact that widespread recognition of their existence would have on religious institutions and on people's faith. On the whole, most students of the phenomena took great pains to distance themselves from religious-sounding claims about UFOs and to reiterate the essentially scientific nature of the UFO problem. The tension between science and religion as explanatory frameworks within the UFO community is the subject of this book.

MATERIALS, METHODS, AND GOALS

My first real contact with the UFO movement came in 1992 when I decided to reward myself for years of arduous graduate school labor by reading something light and entertaining.[4] Having never been particularly fond of fiction, I picked up Whitley Strieber's book *Communion: A True Story* instead. What I read both fascinated and terrified me. It was the author's first-person account of his nocturnal abduction by slender, bulbous-headed, large-eyed creatures. I slept with the lights on for several nights after that! (I am not alone in having this reaction, even in the academic world.)

After reading several more books on the abduction phenomenon, it dawned on me that I had found something I had been looking for since my undergraduate years: a segment of American society to follow through the upcoming change in the millennium. Putting this research project into action, however, entailed doing considerably more reading in the UFO literature, becoming active as a participant-observer in the local UFO scene,[5] and developing and circulating questionnaires in order to round out my qualitative assessments with quantitative data. Some of the initial results of that research are presented herein. My aim has been to unfold the literature that attests to and wrestles with — and sometimes contests — the idea of the reality of UFOs and extraterrestrial life on Earth. My sources are the written (and sometimes oral) statements of those who have figured in the dialogue on UFOs. Their testimony constitutes what I have framed in chapters 1 and 2 as the "UFO myth." I have tried to be discriminating about my source materials and to make plain to my reader where the information is based on solid evidence and where it is based on reports or personal testimony that are (so far) unverified. I have attempted to be a fair and accurate historian in both my presentation of the facts and my presentation of reports. And I have endeavored to provide numerous references so that the interested reader can do follow-up research on matters that are only briefly mentioned in this text. But as Strieber observes about UFO phenomena in general, "The conclusive evidence has not yet been gathered."[6]

If I can be accused of having a personal agenda, it is in wanting the reader to come away with a sense of the conflicting and paradoxical dimensions — and, I feel, the importance — of UFOs and the UFO movement in American society. Whatever historians of the far-distant future are able to say about the reality of UFOs in the twentieth century, I feel sure that they will look upon ufology as one of the more interesting fields of inquiry in our era. Why? Because I believe that Western thought is now at a crossroads, and part of the drama of the crossroads *zeitgeist* is being played out in the UFO community. We are daily assisted by and confronted with the achievements of science, the child of Enlightenment rationalism, which promises us a form of "salvation" in ways both practical and theoretical. Yet many of us find ourselves believing in and studying things that science rejects as at best "merely" subjective or, at worst, as serious threats to the intellectual progress and continued well-being of humanity. Such is the strength of these "irrationalities" of ours that, covertly or overtly and for a variety of reasons, many of us nevertheless hold them to be in some way true. Such is the strength of science as arbiter of Reality and thus conferrer of legitimacy that we struggle to find some point of accommodation, if not of outright confirmation, for our beliefs within a scientific framework. One manifestation of the effort to reconcile the truths of science with the truths of our beliefs can be seen in "creation science." Another manifestation is the study of UFOs — a particularly compelling manifestation because it involves not only *belief in* something but for many in the UFO community an unarguable *experience of* something.

Although its status as an experiential reality would seem to ground the UFO phenomenon in the natural, rationalized world of science, the peculiar behavior of UFOs and the unlikely events associated with them seem to push it more toward the realm of the irrational. And although many of those who believe that UFOs are real would point out that any highly advanced science might seem irrational (and thus magical and thus nonexistent) to twentieth-century scientists — yet would in fact be eminently logical — others in the UFO community have wondered if perhaps the limits of science's ability to explain reality have been surpassed in UFO encounters. For some this means that an essentially scientific approach to UFOs needs to be augmented by the insights of religious mystics and metaphysicians. For others a mystical or metaphysical understanding all by itself will suffice. For the UFO community as a whole, the challenge is to chart a path through these several ways of trying to make sense of UFO phenomena.

PLAN OF THE BOOK

There is a UFO phenomenon and there is a UFO movement. It is the latter with which I am concerned. However, because the movement is defined by its interest in the phenomenon, the first two chapters of this book present the history of UFO phenomena (primarily in the United States) and how those phenomena galvanized popular interest and led to the formation of a community devoted to their study. Chapter 3 presents the history of the scientific community's formal interest in UFO phenomena and, reciprocally, the history of the UFO community's involvement with science. The chapter covers science's rejection of the idea of UFO reality, the scientific community's attempts to dissuade the American people from belief in UFO phenomena, and ufology's attempts to win scientific respectability and also popular support. The chapter also reviews the controversial drift by some in the UFO community away from strictly scientific frameworks for understanding UFOs. Chapters 4 and 5 discuss the religious and metaphysical ideas that have emerged in ufological debates and theories, the considerable contributions of abductees and the alien abduction phenomenon to the debates, and the response of established religion to the UFO phenomenon. Finally, the appendix describes the UFO community in the mid-1990s based on information collected from two surveys I circulated at UFO conventions, among local UFO groups, and through UFO-related mailings. The appendix offers a picture of the kinds of people who hold as true parts (or all) of the UFO myth. I would also like to point out that even the cover art for this book has an educational agenda. The piece, entitled "Portal," was created especially for this volume by artist Melissa Reed. A key explaining the thirty-four UFO and UFO-related images in the work can be found at www.mreedartworks.com.

   The question inevitably arises as to whether my interest in the subject of UFOs springs from a personal encounter with them. The fact that the question is asked at all intrigues me. If it were asked mainly in the context of a learned colloquium of my academic peers, I might be able to attribute it to scholars' postmodern concern with the relative positionalities of speaker and subject in a discursive matrix in which the hegemonic "gaze" of the abstracted/-ing "other" becomes a colonizing force serving the (phal-)logocentric Word. But besides the fact that some of the questioners are scholars who have little apparent interest in postmodern theory, there is also the fact that it is asked by people from all walks of life in all sorts of contexts — from first-year college students to new acquaintances to members of the UFO community. The universality of the question is one clue to the importance of the UFO phenomenon in the unfolding history of the West. Since the Reformation depopulated the saint-filled cosmos of the Middle Ages, followed by the gradual abstraction and then elimination of God from the cosmos by rationally enlightened, scientific minds, a newly orphaned humanity has been asking, "Are we, then, alone?" The UFO experiences reported by thousands of people are one hint that the answer to that forlorn question may be, "No. We are not alone." Unfortunately, I cannot offer the hopeful reader any personal testimony from which to draw such solace. But I can offer a sympathetic yet critical look at the world of those who say that they can.

A Short History
of the UFO Myth

Our data base is overflowing. Every year we receive a vast number of current encounters to research. . . . To discard these
accounts is to stumble at the edge of some unknown and possibly dangerous event that is still in its infancy.

John Auchettl's "Foreword" to *Encounter*
by Australian abductee Kelly Cahill

UFOs and aliens are a seemingly never-ending source of amusement for
most people. A cartoon depicts two aliens visible in the bubble top of a
UFO flying away from Earth. One turns to the other and says, "It's
weird, Zork. We've been visiting that planet for years and the only ones
who believe in us are the poor white trash!" The cartoon is funny
because it plays on stereotypes about UFO believers. Those stereotypes
are, however, largely untrue. Unidentified flying objects have actually
been observed and reported by people from all walks of life — from professional astronomers, pilots, and presidents to truck drivers, homemak-
ers, and students. They are not seen only by the poor and ignorant. A
1977 survey of American astronomers revealed that 5 percent of the
respondents had made anomalous observations that they felt could be
related to UFOs.[1] In a 1979 poll of scientists and engineers, 18 percent
said that they had either definitely or possibly seen a UFO.[2] In fact, sightings reported by technical and professional people appear disproportionately often as true "unknowns" in catalogs of UFO reports.[3]

Nevertheless, according to the official conclusions of a 1969 government study, conclusions that have become a part of conventional wisdom, UFOs do not exist except in the minds of the (often deluded)
observers.[4] Therefore, UFOs have usually been relegated to the realm of
those things that are believed in by the young or the gullible — things like
Santa Claus, Big Foot, snipes, or God — on the assumption that "belief"
runs counter to empirical fact and rationality and is the undisciplined

mode of thought to which the poor and the uneducated are most prone. Because UFO belief is associated with lack of education, deficient critical thinking skills, and excessive gullibility, science educators regularly deplore the fact that despite repeated efforts to educate the public about UFOs, in the mid-1990s 12 percent of the U.S. population reported that they may have seen a UFO, and 48 percent believed that UFOs were real rather than imaginary.[5] This official association of UFOs almost exclusively with popular belief has moved the topic out of the realm of the physical sciences and into the realm of the social sciences or the humanities, where it has been studied as an artifact of personal psychology or of society and culture.[6] One name for this kind of artifact is "myth."

In common parlance and in matters of debate, the word *myth* carries the negative connotation of fiction, untruth, or deception. In the more rarified world of academic discourse, *myth* is usually viewed in more specific and positive terms, though the nature of those terms has changed over the years. A common approach for early scholars studying the myths of nonliterate cultures was to equate myth with whatever they considered to be less highly developed. For example, some proposed that myths reflected a prerational level of mental development, or were evidence of a simple observation-based protoscience.[7] Later, the trend among scholars was to study myth using criteria other than the degree of conformity to Western standards of reason. One reason for this trend was that, as field research uncovered increasing numbers of non-Western narrative traditions, it became difficult to differentiate them from myth. In order to do so, some scholars proposed substantive definitions for myth, focusing attention on typical story elements and characteristic motifs.[8] Others suggested identifying myths according to their social functions — for instance, as legitimators of the social arrangements of the cultures in which they were accepted.[9] Using these kinds of standards, scholars began to recognize the existence of myths in literate as well as nonliterate societies.[10]

Samuel and Thompson note that not all elements of a society necessarily share that society's dominant myth or invoke it in a normative way. This being so, they suggest that "myth is, or ought to be, quite central to the study of popular movements."[11] The community of individuals who believe in and study UFO phenomena is such a movement. In fact, it is one whose defining myth — that UFOs are real — is rejected by the majority of Western intellectuals on the grounds that it fails to ratify — and actually contradicts — the Western myth of rational realism. UFOs, after all, seem to defy the laws of physics and motion as we know them.

Because of this, the majoritarian mainstream insists that UFOs cannot be accepted as physically real. UFO reports must be understood as, at best, "creative interpretations" rather than as rational statements of factual experience because they involve special knowledge claims that cannot be verified by others.[12] Such reports represent an excellent example of mythic situations that are "more fabulous than realistic, more imaginative than factual, and more evocative than analytical," because they are "liberally populated with fantastic beings and impossible events."[13] Though the UFO community would deny that UFO phenomena are "more imaginative than factual," they would have no trouble agreeing with the proposition that the phenomena savor of "fantastic beings and 'impossible' events."

Throughout this book, I use the term *myth* in a specialized sense, borrowing heavily, if selectively, from the in-depth analysis of myth by William G. Doty. Accordingly, the UFO myth should be understood as a set of narratives that:

describe something that has jarred individuals "loose from their customary habits of mind"

seek to produce a similar or sympathetic effect in others

make an appeal to the audience to grant ontological validity to the account

suggest that the experiences are of universal importance[14]

Within these parameters, most people who believe in and devote time and money to the study of UFOs would feel comfortable calling UFOs a myth. But insofar as myths are typically thought to entail the use of imagery in order to convey their messages, the UFO community would protest that UFO phenomena are not just fanciful images but are, in truth, matters of literal fact.

In what follows I leave readers to form their own opinions about the validity of the real-world claims for UFO phenomena. My intention is not to resolve the tension between UFOs as empirical fact of an objective world and UFOs as images open to individual interpretation and belief. Rather, I wish to present UFOs in the context of their role in the ideas, experiences, and concerns of a group of people. I am concerned with UFOs as myth in the sense indicated. That is to say, I am interested in that set of narratives told by individuals as accounts of their personal experiences and accepted as ontologically valid descriptions of reality by a community for whom the encounter narratives form an important part of a total worldview. Some of these individuals report having had personal experiences of varying levels of intensity with UFOs or their occupants. Others have had no such experiences but grant truth status (in varying degrees) to the reports from those who have. Together with the occasional outright UFO skeptic (otherwise known as "debunkers"), these groups form what I consider to be the UFO community. It is a unique collection of individuals, united not by geography or race or socioeconomic interests, but by their participation in the UFO myth — a myth with decidedly American roots.

THE UFO MYTH IN HISTORY

The modern era of UFOs is usually dated from June 24, 1947, when pilot Kenneth Arnold reported seeing nine metallic objects flying near Mt. Rainier in a pattern "like saucers skipped over water."[15] Certainly the doppelgänger of the UFO, the "flying saucer," had its birth in that incident: Associated Press reporter Bill Bequette took Arnold's description and turned it into nine "saucer-like objects," from which a headline-writer came up with "flying saucers." The origin of the alternative appellation, "Unidentified Flying Objects," is less certain. It first appears in the title of a six-hundred-page report issued in December 1949 after an air force investigation, but there is no indication of just who came up with the name, or why. A study dated only ten months earlier referred to the same anomalous aerial phenomena as "Unidentified Aerial Objects."[16] But for the public, the term "flying saucer" caught the mood of the moment.[17]

Although the Arnold incident was a pivotal event in UFO history, later ufologists suggested that reports of unexplained aerial phenomena might have surprisingly ancient roots. The *Bhāgavata Purāna* tells the story of King Śālva's *vimāna*, a remarkable flying machine that, like twentieth-century UFOs, would appear, move rapidly and erratically in the sky, and then suddenly disappear, only to reappear somewhere else.[18] When the Hebrew prophet Ezekiel described seeing a "whirlwind from the north," some ufologists came to believe it may have been a UFO sighting.[19] In thirteenth-century Japan, strange lights that swayed and danced for hours in the night sky were officially declared to be "the wind making the stars sway."[20] Altogether, computer scientist and ufologist Jacques Vallee collected more than sixty accounts from around the world of unusual aerial events occurring before 1800 C.E. that he felt might have been reported in twentieth-century terms as UFO sightings.[21] After 1800, as the quantity and quality of sources improved, the number of reports of mysterious things in the skies increased commensurately. Based solely on notices in the scientific journals of the day and not on popular rumors, Vallee collected approximately 240 accounts of strange sightings in the nineteenth century, 84 of which occurred between the years 1880 and 1900.[22] Although many of these reported sightings occurred outside the United States, a large number of them occurred within it during the Great Airship Wave of 1896–1897.[23]

Though there were sporadic earlier reports of airships,[24] the Great Airship Wave began in November 1896 when the residents of Oakland, California, reported seeing a cigar-shaped, winged object in the sky. Over the next three weeks there were numerous sightings of strange aerial objects throughout the state. Some accounts noted solid objects; others reported distant lights that moved "rapidly" in the sky — anywhere from 20 to 150 mph. These remarkable sightings of illuminated craft that could fly "in the teeth of the wind" became national news.[25] Stories of the most recent sightings and affidavits as to the honesty and integrity of those who saw them were telegraphed regularly to major Eastern and Midwestern papers. Affidavits notwithstanding, there were doubters. The *Oakland Tribune* opined that the ships never appeared "when there was any dearth of whiskey."[26] Other newspapers attributed the sightings to misidentifications of stars or to hoaxers and a gullible public.[27] In February 1897 the airships began to appear in the Midwest. Over a four-month period, the mysterious ships were seen by single and multiple witnesses from as far south as Texas to as far north as North Dakota and as far east as Tennessee and Kentucky. Photographic evidence of the sightings was submitted and affirmed as authentic, and the secretary of the Chicago Aeronautical Association expressed no surprise that the airships existed, only that one had arrived in the city so soon.[28] Once again the newspapers printed certifications of the sighters' integrity and sobriety. And once again some doubted that heavier-than-air flying machines really existed. Though some asserted that misidentification could not account for all of the sightings, given the reported maneuvers and speeds of the objects seen, others avowed that the phenomenon was all a matter of misperception.[29] Even scientific luminary Thomas Edison was a doubter, reasoning that no man who had learned the secret of flight would be inclined to keep it to himself.[30] The problem of determining the authenticity and significance of the sightings was exacerbated by admitted hoaxes. In an April Fool's prank, two self-described practical jokers in Omaha sparked a flurry of excitement by releasing a helium-filled balloon with a lighted wicker basket suspended beneath it.[31]

But to many, burning baskets and misidentified stars could not account for all of the reported sightings, especially in view of reports in which not only airships but also their occupants were supposed to have been observed.[32] More surprising, at times the airships were said to have landed — with or without the occupants engaging the witnesses in conversation.[33] Toward the end of the sighting wave there was talk of the possibility that the airship entities were extraterrestrial visitors. "I suggest that our visitors be informed that a friendly welcome awaits them," wrote one proponent of the extraterrestrial hypothesis (ETH). "The Smithsonian Institution at Washington should take the matter in hand at once."[34]

In these early encounters the main features of the UFO myth had already begun to surface: aerial craft exhibiting properties of design and motion well in advance of anything humanly engineered at the time, mysterious occupants observed near the craft, interactions between craft occupants and human witnesses, the hypothesis that the craft originated off-planet, and the call for an official response. Also present were the main problems that plagued the later UFO myth: continuing questions about the true nature of what was seen, methodological problems of investigation because of the crafts' failure to appear regularly and on demand before interested parties, the promulgation of hoaxes and pranks, the credibility (or lack thereof) of the witnesses, and the doubt of the skeptics.

UFOS IN THE FIRST DECADES
OF THE TWENTIETH CENTURY

The years between the Great Airship Wave and Kenneth Arnold's sighting were quiet ones when compared with the furor that preceded them and the one that would follow, but by no means were anomalous aerial phenomena unknown during this period. Isolated sighting reports continued to be featured in newspapers, though undoubtedly only some of these have been uncovered by researchers to date.[35] Making up for the scarcity of contemporary written accounts from the first half of the century are the belated first-hand reports from people who came forward years after the fact, when the discussion of sightings of UFO became more acceptable. One woman remembered seeing a "cucumber-shaped" airship complete with portholes and lights on the day her younger sister was born. Her father, who also saw the object, told her then that it was "not of this world." A forty-seven-year-old man recalled an incident from 1927 when he was five years old ; he saw a disk-shaped object hovering over a neighbor's house. In telling the story, he asked for anonymity, noting that his mother had punished him when he told her what he had seen.[36]

In the 1930s and 1940s, there were two major waves of sighting reports. The first occurred in the early 1930s, mostly in Scandinavia but also in North America and Central Europe. Engine sounds came from strange lights dubbed "ghost fliers" that shone bright spotlights down onto the ground, most often during snowstorms when planes were least likely to be able to fly. Authorities surmised that they were evidence of smugglers trying to evade the law using the new technology of flight,[37] or perhaps Russian or Japanese spies. When the ghost fliers proved singularly difficult to catch, officials decided that the sightings were actually misidentifications of Venus, hallucinations, or hoaxes.[38]

The second rash of sighting reports also occurred in Scandinavia during the "ghost rocket" scare of 1946.[39] The existence of the ghost rockets should have been easier to prove because there were numerous reports of their having crashed.[40] Nevertheless, verifiable remnants were never recovered, and authorities remained uncertain about the nature of the phenomenon. Eventually the governments of Belgium, Denmark, and Britain launched formal investigations, but a Swedish military investigation was the most thorough. The Swedes not only had the benefit of hundreds of sighting reports from reliable citizens, but also tracked the ghost rockets on radar. Their initial theory was that the devices were the result of Soviet technological advances in V2 rocketry made possible by the capture of the German rocket base at Peenemunde at the end of World War II. When further research indicated that the best rocketry scientists had gone to the United States at the end of the war, and when fragments supposedly recovered from downed ghost rockets proved to be nothing more than slag metal, the Swedish committee's final (and until 1983 classified) report stated that there was no proof that the Soviet Union had been conducting rocket tests over Swedish airspace. The committee did not comment upon what the phenomenon might be instead.[41]

The Swedish military was not the only one to be stumped by these kinds of reports. During World War II, pilots and radar trackers on both sides reported seeing illuminated disks and globes that followed bombers to and from their drop sites, and warships at sea reported several instances of strange aerial craft that traversed the skies and sometimes entered the ocean. In the spirit of the war, each side suspected that the devices were the invention of the opposing side; the Allies called them "foo fighters."[42] In fact, however, the only real fighting associated with such aerial anomalies appears to have been when observers fired (or tried to fire) on them. One of the most famous instances took place in February 1942 in Los Angeles. Two days after a Japanese submarine surfaced near Santa Barbara, California, and fired upon gasoline storage tanks, a luminous object larger than an apartment house was sighted visually and by radar over Los Angeles. As powerful searchlights followed the object, antiaircraft weapons fired ineffectively on it for an hour, at which point the object vanished. During the incident, six people died — three from unexploded shells and three from heart attacks. The object itself never fired a shot. Authorities suspected that the object had been a Japanese airplane of some sort, so in the ensuing hours twenty Japanese-Americans in Los Angeles were arrested and accused of having used flashlights to signal to it.[43]

THE MODERN ERA OF UFOS

It may legitimately be asked why the modern era of UFOs began with the June 1947 sighting by Kenneth Arnold if anomalous aerial lights and structured craft had been reported from at least before the turn of the century. One reason is because it was only then that a relatively few descriptive terms began to be used consistently to refer to the objects seen, instead of changing with every new wave of reports. *Flying saucer* was a colorful shorthand way for journalists to characterize the many sightings associated with the wave that began in 1947. The term's rapid association with outer space and extraterrestrials gave it even greater popular appeal. But the promulgation of a single, colorful term had its drawbacks. As "flying saucers" entered the public arena through news accounts, the term provided not only a convenient way to designate anomalous aerial phenomena but also, very quickly, a framework for perceiving them: Numerous reports of sightings of saucer-shaped flying objects were made in the months after Arnold's sighting.[44] In contrast, *UFO*, the initially less-evocative term coined by the military, was made to order for an age of acronyms. "Unidentified Flying Object" properly indicates something seen in the sky (by definition "flying" even if the object is just hovering) for which the observer has no conventional explanation. The operative ideas here are "unidentified" — suggesting that the nature and provenance of the object is unknown, and "observer" — suggesting that the inability to identify the object may be a function of the knowledge of the observer and have nothing to do with an intrinsic unknowability of the object itself. Perhaps unavoidably, the meanings behind the terms *UFO* and *flying saucer* became conflated, which confused the issue of defining and studying the kind of problem the phenomenon presented.

A second reason for marking the beginning of the modern UFO era from the late 1940s lies in the communications industry. The growing power of the print media, the influence of radio, and the growth of the motion picture industry and television gave the UFO phenomenon more potential for public visibility than any earlier waves of sighting reports. However, the role of the media in this regard was inconsistent. After an initial bout of skepticism in which the usual explanations were offered for sighting reports,[45] national newspapers paid only sporadic attention to UFOs. Coverage increased during UFO sighting waves but waned quickly thereafter.[46] It was not until 1949 that UFOs began to be featured in popular periodicals. The first article was in *True Magazine,* which solicited a piece on the UFO phenomenon from retired marine Major Donald E. Keyhoe. Quickly following it came another article, this time solicited from a navy commander at the White Sands Missile Range who not only verified the reality of the sightings but claimed that UFOs were extraterrestrial vehicles.[47] On the whole, however, early periodical coverage of UFO sighting reports took the position that UFOs were top secret military weapons or, echoing the government's official opinion, naturally occurring phenomena.[48] It was only in the spring of 1952, as another major UFO sighting wave began, that a national periodical published an article that did not attempt to dismiss all UFO sightings with prosaic explanations. After consulting the files of Project Blue Book, the government's then-current investigation group, Robert Ginna wrote an article for *Life* magazine that, like the articles in *True* magazine three years earlier, suggested an extraterrestrial origin for the saucer sightings.[49] This kind of uneven media attention brought the topic of UFOs periodically before the public yet never addressed the situation in any depth or with any consistency from one sighting wave to another.

While the popular media vacillated in its coverage of UFO sightings, the scientific journals remained silent, no longer printing reports of anomalous aerial phenomena as they had decades earlier. This new policy reflected a hands-off attitude toward UFOs among the scientific community. A restricted-circulation 1959 newsletter from the Smithsonian Astrophysical Observatory stated, "It is exceedingly undesirable to become associated with these 'sightings' or the persons originating them. . . . On no account should any indication be given to others that a discussion even remotely concerned with UFO's is taking place."[50] Perhaps reflecting the publicly contested nature of UFOs, the theological community was likewise slow to offer any opinions or observations of its own. In fact, UFOs were largely ignored as a subject of relevance to religion until 1952 when *Time* magazine published a brief article on the "Theology of Saucers" based on astronomer Donald Menzel's anti-UFO book.[51] A year later the *Science News Letter* noted possible connections between religion and UFOs. It took three more years before any major religious periodical or journal gave the subject any attention.[52]

For the UFO community, one of the most (in)famous instances of media interest followed by complete forgetfulness occurred on July 8, 1947, just a few weeks after the Arnold sighting, when the Roswell Army Air Base in New Mexico issued a press release stating that a crashed flying saucer had been recovered by the army air force from a ranch several miles outside of town.[53] Within hours, however, military authorities pulled the story from the newswires, stating that the recovered wreckage was a "national security item." A statement and accompanying photograph released one day later claimed that the wreckage had actually been from a weather balloon.[54] The story of the New Mexico crash disappeared from the public eye until the late 1970s, when ufologists Stanton T. Friedman and William L. Moore discovered witnesses to the event and to its aftermath who confirmed the original news release and in some cases added tantalizing — but unverifiable — details. Since that time the Roswell incident has taken on epic proportions within the UFO community, for whom it serves as an example not only of the tangible reality of UFOs but also of a government cover-up (some even say a conspiracy).[55]

Despite this kind of on-again, off-again reporting, the public's awareness of UFOs was surprisingly high. A November 1973 Gallup poll indicated that 95 percent of the people in the United States had heard of UFOs — one of the highest public awareness indices ever recorded.[56] Perhaps this was because after 1947 UFOs simply became hard to ignore. Between 1947 and the dawn of the age of the abductees in the 1970s, there were at least six major UFO sighting waves.[57] To a certain extent these waves may have reflected the Cold War climate and fears about Soviet development of long-range missiles capable of carrying nuclear warheads.[58] But as had happened before, not all of the sighting reports could be attributed to mass hysteria brought on by international tensions, misidentifications of conventional objects, or hoaxes. Some were genuine unknowns.

The first major UFO wave after Kenneth Arnold's sighting began in the spring of 1952. By the time it was over, the Air Technical Intelligence Center of the U.S. Air Force (the official U.S. collection center for UFO reports) had received 1,501 sighting reports from around the country — a figure estimated by military authorities to reflect only perhaps 10 percent of the actual number of sightings made.[59] The situation went temporarily out of control in July of that year when simultaneous radar and visual sightings were made of what appeared to be a group of UFOs flying over Washington, D.C., and the Capitol building. In response, fighter jets were scrambled to intercept the objects, which disappeared whenever the planes came within range, then reappeared when the planes moved on. Calls inundated the Pentagon, tying up communication lines and seriously compromising the department's normal functioning. To deal with the flood of private and media inquiries, the air force held a press conference — the longest one since the end of World War II — to try to calm people's fears. They brought in Harvard astronomer Donald Menzel as a consultant, who explained that the sightings by radar operators, pilots, and civilians were nothing more than a well-known atmospheric phenomenon: a temperature inversion. Though an unsatisfying explanation for the many officials and agencies that had been involved in the incidents, it was this that the newswires picked up and promoted to the American public as "the" answer to the apparent invasion of the capitol's airspace.[60]

Another major sighting wave took place in 1965–1967, when nearly three thousand reports were submitted to the air force for investigation. One of the most famous incidents of this period happened on the night of March 20, 1966, when eighty-seven coeds at Hillsdale College and a civil defense director in Michigan reported that they watched for four hours as a glowing football-shaped object hovered, swooped toward the dormitory, then retreated, appearing to dim whenever cars approached and lighting back up again after they had left. Pressed on all sides for an explanation of the sightings, another air force consultant, astronomer J. Allen Hynek, offered the theory that the glowing mass might have been a pocket of methane gas created from decaying organic matter in a nearby swamp. Even for a media that had often adopted a very skeptical attitude toward the reality of UFOs, this statement proved too difficult to believe given the numbers of witnesses involved. Cartoonists and commentators lampooned the idea of UFOs as swamp gas, and public opinion about UFOs and about the military's handling of sighting reports reflected increasing skepticism of the by now official dictum that UFOs were not real.[61]

In its effort to do its job of protecting American air space, the U.S. military was adamant about finding an explanation for every reported sighting, particularly those that generated widespread media interest. This attention to duty gave the UFO myth some of its most memorable moments, the explanations becoming icons of the "official response" to UFOs and helping to spawn a series of grassroots organizations dedicated to an (ideally) less doctrinaire and more open and scientific investigation of what was going on in America's skies. In the existence of these two groups — the American military establishment and grassroots UFO investigation groups — we have a final reason for dating the beginning of the modern UFO era to 1947. During the ensuing decades, for the first time in history a small portion of the military resources of a major world power were focused on trying to understand and deal with the phenomenon, while at the same time the attention of the populace became sufficiently attuned to the issue to generate grassroots research and study efforts.

The military's involvement with UFOs began in the immediate postwar years as an outgrowth of concern over developing Soviet long-range weaponry. The Technical Intelligence Division of the Air Materiel Command, Air Force, having been assigned to collect and evaluate all reports of unidentified craft, was the natural recipient of the first wave of sighting reports in 1947. In September of that year General Nathan F. Twining, commander of the Air Materiel Command, sent a letter to the commanding general of the army air force saying that he thought people reporting "flying saucers" were seeing something real and not merely hallucinating.[62] On the basis of his recommendation a formal project code-named "Sign" began operation in January 1948. Its unofficial "Estimate of the Situation," produced at the end of that year and submitted to Chief of Staff General Hoyt S. Vandenberg, indicated that the most reasonable hypothesis about the objects being sighted was that they were extraterrestrial in origin. Vandenberg rejected the report, criticizing it for lack of evidence. The Sign report also recommended that the military continue to investigate UFO reports. As a result, Project Grudge was instituted to replace Project Sign in late 1948.[63]

From the outset the attitude behind Project Grudge was different from that of Project Sign. After the rebuke from Vandenberg, proponents of the extraterrestrial hypothesis of UFO origin found themselves increasingly in the minority, while those who denied the reality of the phenomenon gained control. Six months after beginning work, Project Grudge produced its final report on the UFO problem, stating that UFOs were misidentifications, hallucinations, or hoaxes and that they posed no threat to U.S. airspace. To the public, the report suggested that the air force would no longer be studying UFOs, and indeed after this the project more or less went on hiatus, taking in occasional sighting reports but giving them little investigation or attention. It was not until late in the fall of 1951 that the project was quietly revitalized after a simultaneous radar and visual sighting of UFOs tailing a military jet flying over Ft. Monmouth, New Jersey. The revamping of the project included the appointment of a new director, Captain Edward J. Ruppelt, and a new name and a new public mandate as Project Grudge gave way to Project Blue Book in the spring of 1952.[64]

Under Ruppelt's leadership the collection and investigation of UFO sighting reports became more systematic and less subject to official (and unofficial) ridicule. He took the UFO problem seriously enough to recommend that the Battelle Memorial Institute, a think tank in Columbus, Ohio, do a statistical analysis of existing reports.[65] When the institute's study was finally ready in late 1953 it presented an inconsistent picture. On the one hand, the statistical results indicated that sighting reports of excellent quality, a significant number of which were made by trained military observers, were more likely to remain listed as "unknowns." The objects in question in such cases had often been visible for long enough to permit identification, yet skilled observers had been unable to do so. The report also stated that the characteristics of the unknown objects were quite unlike the characteristics noted for objects that were more easily identified. On the other hand, the report summary and conclusion stated that it was unlikely that the unknowns represented anything outside the realm of possibility for that era's technology and that they almost certainly were not "flying saucers" (i.e., extraterrestrial vehicles) because there was no discernable pattern to their behavior.[66]

Before the final Battelle report was ready, however, the Central Intelligence Agency developed an active interest in the UFO problem as a national security (not a scientific) issue and arranged to have a secret official committee look into the UFO data. The Robertson Panel convened for a total of twelve hours in January 1953 and studied twenty-three UFO sighting cases. It concluded that UFOs presented little or no interesting scientific data and were only a threat to the United States insofar as sighting reports from citizens clogged communications facilities (as in the Washington, D.C., sightings in July 1952) and created a climate of uncertainty among citizens that could be exploited by an enemy before launching a real attack. Therefore the committee suggested both an active campaign of public education, perhaps using TV and radio celebrities and the services of Walt Disney Productions, and an active debunking of sightings in order to "de-mystify" UFOs in the public mind. Implicit in this education campaign was increased air force secrecy about sighting reports so as not to fan popular interest. Also, in order to monitor those who would promote public interest in UFOs, the committee recommended covert surveillance of civilian UFO groups. The panel did not recommend any scientific study of UFOs.[67]

The recommendations of the Robertson Panel were implemented in part through a series of special military regulations. Joint-Army-Navy-Air Force Publication 146 (JANAP 146) of December 1953 made reporting any UFO sighting to the public a crime under the Espionage Act, with fines of up to ten thousand dollars and imprisonment of from one to ten years. This act was considered binding on all who knew of its existence, including commercial airline pilots.[68] A 1954 revision of Air Force Regulation 200–2 (AFR 200–2) made all sighting reports submitted to the air force classified material and prohibited the release of any information about UFO sightings *unless* the sighting was able to be positively identified.[69] In February 1958 a revision of AFR 200–2 allowed the military to give the FBI the names of people who were "illegally or deceptively bringing the subject [of UFOs] to public attention."[70]

In addition to these measures the years following the Robertson Panel recommendations saw a change in the way sighting reports were handled. Project Blue Book, always severely underfunded and understaffed and with limited scientific resources, could afford to devote attention only to the most outstanding incident reports. For the rest it simply tried to find a quick explanation and then file them away. This method produced an unacceptably high percentage of "unknowns,"[71] so new categorization protocols were eventually developed. These allowed the investigator to consider as "knowns" sightings that might have been of conventional objects but were unable to be clearly identified. In addition, the new protocols allowed sightings originally assigned to one investigation category to be automatically upgraded to the next higher category. The net result was to reduce the numbers of unknowns in the Blue Book files from around 27 percent to roughly 10 percent of all reports.[72]

Despite the relatively meager demands that Blue Book made on its

resources, by the 1960s the air force wanted to be out of the UFO business altogether and tried for several years, without success, to pass the
project on to another agency.[73] Finally in February 1966 a secret ad hoc
committee that was convened to review Project Blue Book suggested that
the air force should contract with universities to conduct more scientific
investigations of selected UFO sighting reports and to make recommendations about the future of the project. Although universities willing to
conduct such studies were almost impossible to find, in October 1966 the
air force announced that a single academic institution, the University of
Colorado, had agreed to accept a contract under the leadership of Dr.
Edward U. Condon.[74]

The University of Colorado study was another of the landmark events
in the development of the UFO myth. In many ways it signaled the culmi-
nation of the government's public UFO investigations through Project
Blue Book. The study was beset with difficulties from the start. Historian
David Jacobs has identified the central problem as a confusion of the
issue at hand. Some members, responding to the official position that
UFOs were not real, wanted simply to address the question of whether
there was any "thing" out there to be studied. They were less concerned
with determining the provenance of the phenomenon than they were with
establishing its existence. Others on the committee were more focused on
the question of whether UFOs were extraterrestrial spacecraft. For them,
disproving the idea that the Earth was being visited by alien life forms
would suffice to show that UFOs were therefore not real.[75]

The causes of the difficulties on the committee went deeper than ter-
minological imprecision, however. From the early stages of the study,
Condon made both public and private statements indicating that the
project's focus as far as he was concerned was the misidentification of
natural phenomena and the psychological traits of UFO witnesses.
Indeed, the witness survey eventually prepared by the project dealt
mostly with the psychological state of the witness instead of with details
about the sighting.[76] Another indicator of Condon's orientation toward
the study lay in his fascination — and lighthearted socializing — with individuals who claimed to have taken rides to Venus or Saturn with UFO
occupants. He seemed to think that these contactees were representative
of all UFO witnesses.[77] But perhaps the most notorious indicator of the
direction the entire project would take was an early memorandum written by project coordinator Robert Low in which he stated that the
"trick" of the committee would be to make the public think that the
investigation was a completely objective one, while letting the scientific

community know that the committee was trying hard to be objective but really expected to find no evidence at all that UFOs (i.e., extraterrestrial vehicles) were real.[78]

In the end, the Condon Committee looked at ninety-one UFO sighting cases that were written up in a final report containing chapters from thirty-six different contributors. Of the ninety-one cases examined, the committee failed to identify 30 percent of the sightings — an amount three times greater than that allowed by the liberal categorization standards of Project Blue Book.[79] Despite the large number of unknowns, the summary and conclusion of the lengthy report, written by Condon himself, stated that there was no "direct evidence" that UFOs were extraterrestrial vehicles and that it would not be useful to continue to study UFO sighting reports in any systematic way. Project Blue Book could be closed with no loss to science or to national security.[80] Condon also suggested that school teachers who allowed their students to read UFO-related books for classroom credit were doing a grave disservice to the students' "critical faculties" and ability to think scientifically.[81]

As a direct result of the recommendations in the Condon Report, Project Blue Book was dismantled in December 1969.[82] For the next decade inquiries about UFOs directed to the military or to U.S. intelligence agencies produced a standard answer: The department in question had taken either no interest or else only a very limited interest in the subject, and if so, that was long ago and certainly was not an ongoing concern; the official air force investigation, Project Blue Book, had been closed, and the government was no longer in the business of collecting or analyzing UFO sighting reports.[83]

The public resignation of the air force from the UFO business meant that grassroots organizations became the only available source of information — or consolation — for the 11 percent of Americans who were UFO witnesses and for other interested parties.[84] The earliest UFO research and study groups appeared in 1952, around the time of the great sighting wave that had all of America out watching the skies. The most enduring and important of these early organizations was the Aerial Phenomena Research Organization (APRO) founded by Coral and Jim Lorenzen. Dedicated to the collection and investigation of UFO sighting reports from around the world, APRO served as a clearinghouse for many reports that never made it to the Project Blue Book files. Investigations of the better reports were carried out whenever possible by APRO members worldwide, who then sent their reports to the headquarters in Tucson, Arizona. Ten years after founding APRO, Coral

Lorenzen produce the first of a series of books based on the data in their files. The title, *The Great Flying Saucer Hoax,* was ironic.[85] APRO's data suggested that UFOs were real physical phenomena, that they had been sighted by common citizens as well as by scientific and professionally trained individuals, that a surprising (perhaps even alarming) number of sighting reports involved the flight of UFOs over sensitive military installations, and that the "hoax" of UFOs lay not in the sighting reports but in government treatment of the issue. Although critical of the military's attitude toward UFOs, Lorenzen did not necessarily believe at that time that the government knew and was hiding the truth about UFOs. "Perhaps," she wrote, "there are no facts to release — no facts upon which the Voices of Authority can agree, that is."[86]

After APRO three other important grassroots UFO organizations were founded. The first of these was the Saucer and Unexplained Celestial Events Research Society (SAUCERS) founded in 1954 by James Moseley.[87] In 1956 retired marine Major Donald Keyhoe founded the National Investigations Committee on Aerial Phenomena (NICAP), and in 1957 Ted Starrett founded Ground Saucer Watch (GSW). Since the Freedom of Information Act was passed in 1974, GSW has probably been the greatest watchdog on the government's handling of UFO information,[88] but in the mid-1950s the role of thorn in the government's side belonged first and foremost to Keyhoe's NICAP. To add legitimacy and clout to his organization, Keyhoe tried to recruit prestigious scientific, military, and political leaders for its board of directors.[89] The group focused its attention on collecting and investigating UFO sighting reports and on pressuring Congress to hold hearings in which the air force would be expected to give a public accounting for its UFO data. Based on his investigations and on "insider" information given to him through his old military connections, Keyhoe became convinced that the air force knew a lot about what was going on with regard to UFOs but was withholding important information from the public. This was the gist of his first book, *The Flying Saucers Are Real,* and of almost every book he wrote thereafter.[90] In promoting the idea that there was a governmental cover-up, Keyhoe introduced another of the fundamental themes in the UFO myth. By 1969, however, Keyhoe had begun to focus his attention on the CIA as the source of the cover-up rather than the military.[91] It was at this time that the board of directors began to take a more active role in running NICAP, which had been struggling with a series of financial difficulties. The board, then headed by Colonel Joseph Bryan III, forced Keyhoe to retire as NICAP chief. As it turns out, Bryan was a former covert CIA agent who had served the agency as founder and head of its psychological warfare division. Under Bryan's leadership, NICAP essentially disbanded its local and state affiliate groups, and by 1973 it had been totally disbanded at the national level as well.[92]

At the same time that NICAP was entering the twilight years of its existence, another small grassroots UFO research and study organization was being founded by Walt Andrus.[93] Named the Midwest UFO Network (MUFON) at its 1969 inception, the organization later changed its name to the Mutual UFO Network in order to reflect the growing scope of its investigations and its expanding membership.[94] Its monthly publication, the *MUFON UFO Journal*, had a peak circulation of over five thousand in the early 1990s, and for over a quarter of a century the organization sponsored a yearly UFO symposium. MUFON's mission was to investigate and report on UFO sightings and related phenomena in a systematic and credible manner first by using a corps of MUFON-trained members who volunteered to investigate sightings in their areas, and second by using the expertise of college-educated members willing to donate their time and talents when called upon.[95] Each month's *Journal* listed the names and specialties of professional member-subscribers who had recently offered their services. In 1996, ninety-nine of them volunteered, with almost half of these being people with advanced degrees in such fields as medical anthropology, physical chemistry, astronomy, library science, counseling psychology, education, political science, law, medicine, psychology, and various subfields of engineering. It is safe to say that many of these volunteers were never actually called upon by MUFON. Nevertheless, their very presence in the organization and their willingness to offer their expertise in UFO-related matters was an indication of the level of interest in UFOs among American professionals.

Another small measure of educated interest in UFOs was the founding in 1974 of the Center for UFO Studies (CUFOS) by astronomer and former Blue Book consultant J. Allen Hynek and some of his professional colleagues. The organization was formed to continue the work of Project Blue Book — or the work that Blue Book could or should have done — in the systematic and scientific investigation of UFO phenomena.[96] Officially, CUFOS's goal was to promote science and scholarship in ufology through the scientific collection, study, evaluation, and dissemination of information.[97] Unlike MUFON, which emphasized the field investigation of UFO sighting reports, CUFOS specialized in maintaining a library of UFO-related materials, publishing a periodical and a refereed UFO journal, and sponsoring various research projects such as the compilation of HUMCAT (a catalog of UFO-associated entity sightings) and UFO-CAT (a catalog of all then-known UFO cases). In later years, CUFOS sponsored investigation into the Roswell saucer crash. Membership numbers in this organization were not publicly divulged but were reported to be considerably less than those claimed by MUFON.[98] Nevertheless, the organization earned its share of prestige in the UFO community, partly because of its association with Hynek and partly because of its tangible contributions to the field of UFO study.

THE STUDY OF UFOS SINCE PROJECT BLUE BOOK: ALLEGATIONS AND EVIDENCE

In the years after the demise of Project Blue Book there were scores of other small UFO study and investigation groups in the United States, but none were as long-lived or as influential as APRO, NICAP, MUFON, and CUFOS.[99] Despite the proliferation and success of grassroots organizations, a large share of the development of the UFO myth came not from formally organized groups but from individual UFO researchers. Ufology became one of the few fields of intellectual endeavor in the twentieth century where a layperson willing to put in the time and effort to educate himself (most of the researchers were men) could reasonably hope to accomplish something of note. Investigations undertaken by the more sober-minded researchers were often published in the *MUFON UFO Journal,* CUFOS's *International UFO Reporter,* or the venerable British journal *Flying Saucer Review.* As in the academic mainstream, publication, whether in UFO journals or in trade-market books, helped to establish researchers as the intelligentsia in UFO circles. People such as Len Stringfield, Richard Hall, Jacques Vallee, Leo Sprinkle, Donald Keyhoe, Coral and Jim Lorenzen, and J. Allen Hynek became the voices of authority in a field that had been abandoned by mainstream science and relegated to the lunatic fringe. Yet to the researchers and their supporters in the post–Blue Book era, the study of UFO phenomena was not the lunatic fringe but the cutting edge of science, with potentially enormous implications for society. It was through telling their stories to individuals such as these that UFO witnesses could hope to get the truth of their extraordinary experiences presented to the American public.

"Simple" UFO sightings remained at the heart of ufology in the post–Blue Book era. But there were other aspects to the UFO phenomenon that gained increasing attention with the passing years. One of the most persistent was an extension of the cover-up and conspiracy theme in the UFO myth: that the government did not really abandon its interest in UFOs after Project Blue Book was closed. Members of the UFO community had several reasons for thinking so, though not everyone found all of the reasons equally credible or compelling. One indication of continuing government interest came from witnesses who sometimes said they had been visited by official-looking men in dark suits who asked questions about their sightings, confiscated whatever evidence they had, and ominously advised them to be quiet about what they had seen.[100] Although sometimes these officials were described as military personnel and seemed perfectly normal, at other times the men that UFO witnesses (and some UFO researchers) found at their front doors were rather odd in appearance and behavior. They usually came in groups of two or three, had exceptionally pale complexions, dressed in dark suits, and drove dark, early-model vehicles in mint condition. They spoke in unusual cadences and sometimes betrayed a surprising lack of familiarity with social conventions — for instance, by wearing lipstick. Their thoroughly unusual presentation led some ufologists to believe that these Men in Black (MIBs) were in fact aliens attempting to protect their covert operations on Earth by silencing too-vocal witnesses. Other MIB visitants, however, maintained that their interlocutors were certainly human and were most likely the government operatives that they claimed to be.[101]

Another suggestion that the government had a continuing interest in UFOs came from military officials and employees who leaked information to UFO researchers, usually — but not always — in exchange for a guarantee that their anonymity would be protected. The information that was received in this manner was seldom subject to outright verification and ranged from the merely believable to the absolutely incredible — even in the eyes of the UFO community. On the more easily believable end of the spectrum were reports that government agencies other than the air force had taken a covert interest in UFOs. Slightly more surprising were reports of encounters between military jets and UFOs, sometimes with tragic results. The most famous of these incidents was front-page news with the January 7, 1948, crash of national guard pilot Captain Thomas F. Mantell Jr. while chasing a reported UFO over eastern Kentucky. The official explanation for the crash was that Mantell, a veteran of the Normandy invasion and a thoroughly experienced pilot, had mistaken Venus or a weather balloon for a UFO and, in giving chase, had climbed too high and suffered a blackout from lack of oxygen. Though this particular case was widely publicized at the time, anonymous sources reported to UFO investigators in later years that numerous pilots had been lost in similar but less well known incidents.[102] More disturbing stories from publicly unnamed sources claimed that nuclear warhead storage facilities had been repeatedly overflown by UFOs and that on several occasions such incursions had knocked out all local nuclear missile control.[103]

On the still more incredible end of the spectrum of leaked information were the stories that began to surface in the 1960s concerning government retrievals of crashed disks and subsequent attempts to retro-engineer the devices in order to understand their propulsion systems and build U.S. counterparts.[104] A woman identified only as Mrs. G. claimed to have worked at Wright-Patterson Air Force Base in Dayton, Ohio, in 1955, cataloging over one thousand pieces of incoming crash retrieval material. She decided to reveal this information, she said, because she was dying of cancer and there was nothing the government could do to her any longer for breaking her security oath and telling what she knew.[105] A meteorologist visiting a friend at Wright-Patterson claimed to have been shown small space suits taken off of the dead occupants of crashed saucers.[106] In the same vein, a businessman in Tampa, Florida, told UFO researcher Raymond Fowler that he had served in military intelligence and seen with his own eyes not only parts and pieces of crashed UFOs, but alien corpses as well.[107] In 1998 a retired first lieutenant with the Army Signal Corps, known publicly only as "Kewper," revealed that during his term of service between 1957 and 1960 he had done work for the CIA during which he and several associates were taken to see — and then to talk with — a living alien being.[108] And on a UFO discussion group in 1999, a man relayed a story his father had confided to him two years earlier. The aging patriarch told his son that in 1950 he had been shown photos, movies, and the schematics for a flying disk and had been informed that it was reengineered from a crashed version.[109] At first crashed saucer stories were seriously questioned by UFO researchers. But with the 1980 publication of the first book on the incident at Roswell, ufologists began to sit up and take notice of other crash retrieval reports. By the late 1990s the list of rumored UFO crash sites ran anywhere from a dozen to eighteen or so. The wreckage from these mishaps was usually said to have been taken to Wright-Patterson Air Force Base in Dayton, Ohio, or to an extremely top secret military base in the Nevada desert known as Area 51.

Members of the UFO community were very much aware of the need for evidence to corroborate all of these stories. When the Freedom of Information Act (FOIA) was made law in 1974, ufologists acquired another tool in their search for the indisputable truth. Documents released under the FOIA since 1978 showed that some of the leaked stories were correct at least in essence, if not necessarily in all particulars. Ufologists involved in making FOIA requests reported that more than nine hundred pages of information released from the Central Intelligence Agency indicated that the organization was collecting and analyzing sighting reports from as early as 1949.[110] In 1997 the CIA came forward to admit its historical interest in UFOs and to give its own interpretation of that interest.[111] Seventeen hundred pages released from the Federal Bureau of Investigation showed that this agency had maintained an interest in the UFO phenomenon since 1947.[112] Similarly, the National Security Agency and the Defense Intelligence Agency had long been attuned to the UFO phenomenon.[113] Among these thousands of pages released under the FOIA were documents indicating that U.S. pilots continued to chase (and be chased by) UFOs, military installations were overflown on occasion by UFOs at approximately the same time that launch capability for on-site nuclear warheads was lost, and retrieval programs existed (and have been used) for the recovery of space debris of (at least initially) unknown origin.

These FOIA releases left little reason to doubt that there had been a conspiracy of silence about UFO-related phenomena on the part of the government. Whether that conspiracy hid relative ignorance or more sinister knowledge was another issue — one that was actively debated in the UFO community.[114] But the release of documents under the FOIA supported two points that ufologists had long maintained. First, many branches of the government had a serious interest in UFOs that did not end after the dismantling of Project Blue Book in 1969 — despite frequent protests to the contrary that occurred before the FOIA documents were released. Second, at least some of the rumors from anonymous sources — unsatisfactory evidence though rumors were — contained accurate information. However, careful reading of the FOIA documents that were published in the UFO literature (which presumably constituted the best available documents) showed that government agencies took the UFO phenomenon seriously as an unknown, but not necessarily as an unknown under the control of alien intelligences. Government concern with UFOs seemed to be one part of the larger picture of security concerns that each agency addressed in the course of fulfilling its duties. In many cases the paperwork that was released suggested that these agencies had no inside track on an answer to the UFO enigma but, like the grassroots UFO organizations, were largely dependent on witness reports. However, one advantage government agencies had in collecting UFO-related information lay in their ability to forbid the dissemination of sighting information that originated from within the various branches of the government, such as incidents involving military pilots and installations. In this regard, grassroots UFO organizations and independent UFO researchers were forced to rely on informants' stories that often came to the surface anonymously or at second or third hand. Researchers in the UFO community hoped that the numbers and prominence of informants who dared to come forward, future FOIA releases, or the sheer weight of other historical evidence would eventually prove the veracity of the information received from these more questionable sources.[115]

In 1989 crash retrieval stories received an important elaboration when a man named Robert Lazar stepped forward in March to state that in his capacity as a physicist he had worked at Area 51 for a week in 1988–1989. His job description, Lazar said, was to determine the theory behind the propulsion system utilized in UFOs that had crashed, but when he began his employment at the base he was also shown briefing papers on the extraterrestrial situation. These documents indicated, he claimed, that not only have crashed UFOs been retrieved, but bodies of the alien occupants were also found at crash sites, leading eventually to covert military liaisons with several different extraterrestrial races. Some of these races, as Lazar cites the report, have been involved in human history for thousands of years as genetic manipulators of human physiology and shapers of human religious traditions. Lazar stated that according to the documents he read, the U.S. government had films of the recent Earth-alien encounters and the aliens had "videos" of events that took place in Earth's history. After his public revelations, Lazar claimed that former U.S. astronauts privately contacted him to express their appreciation for his disclosure, which their security oaths prevented them from making themselves. His story received a measure of support from Command Sergeant Major Robert Dean (U.S. Army, Retired) who said that his tour of duty in Paris at the Supreme Headquarters Allied Powers Europe (SHAPE) in 1963 gave him the opportunity to read a highly classified document entitled "Assessment: An Evaluation of a Possible Military Threat to Allied Forces in Europe." According to Dean, who came forward with his story in the early 1990s, the "Assessment" was the final report from a 1961 NATO study of the UFO situation. Its conclusions were substantially the same as those in the documents Lazar claimed to have read.[116]

As usual in the community of UFO investigators, not everyone was convinced. Lazar's pronouncements elicited efforts to corroborate his story. Attempts to check his educational credentials and verify his employment history met with only limited success. Lazar's later investment in a Nevada brothel further detracted from his apparent credibility. However, journalist George Knapp reported that other individuals who had worked or currently worked at Area 51 privately confirmed many elements of Lazar's story.[117] Like so many others before them, of course, these informants preferred to remain anonymous to other researchers and to the public.

Wary ufologists were quick to point out that stories like these might not be true, not because they were the result of individual fantasies or hoaxes, but because they were the outgrowth of deliberate disinformation campaigns by government forces who wanted the truth of the alien situation to remain obscured from public view.[118] Other ufologists suggested that just the opposite was the case — that factions in the government wanted the truth to come out, and controlled leaks were a way both to test public reaction to the alien reality and to familiarize the public with the idea of the alien presence as part of a fuller disclosure yet to come. The proliferation of tabloid-style TV shows featuring regular UFO segments as well as advertisements and regular TV series episodes with a UFO or alien theme further convinced many in the UFO community that an accelerating program of desensitization to the alien presence had been mounted. The 1996 announcements of the discovery of microbial fossils in a Martian meteor fragment, followed a few weeks later by the revelation that one of Jupiter's moons had a watery surface that might be capable of supporting life, were taken as signs that the existence of extraterrestrial life would be "discovered" soon and that a UFO cover-up was about to end. When it was announced in a UFO discussion group on the Internet in early 1998 that a priest associated with the Vatican had made an officially sanctioned announcement that UFOs and alien contact were real, the reaction was mixed. Some hailed the development as the beginning of the formal announcement phase of the larger un-cover-up effort. Others expressed considerable suspicion about the reliability of the report and adopted a wait-and-see approach.[119]

Although many UFO informants were anonymous to the public, some were celebrities whose comments added weight to the idea that UFOs were real. Numerous astronauts were rumored to have had close encounters during spaceflights, the most notorious being Buzz Aldrin and Neil Armstrong who reportedly got to the moon in 1969 and found alien ships waiting for them there.[120] Few astronauts came forward to make public pronouncements on the subject of UFOs, however.[121] Among those few was Edgar Mitchell who stated on nationwide television that the government was covering up the facts of the crash at Roswell and the facts about UFOs in general. He also stated that he had met people from three countries "who in the course of their official duties claim to have had personal firsthand encounter experiences" with extraterrestrials. Mitchell did not discount their stories.[122] Another former astronaut, Gordon Cooper, reported that when he was stationed at Edwards Air Force Base in the late 1950s, a UFO landed briefly and was filmed by military cameramen.[123] In a presentation before a panel of the United Nations in 1985, Cooper said, "I believe that these extraterrestrial vehicles and their crews are visiting this planet from other planets, which are a little more technically advanced than we are on Earth."[124] Comedian Jackie Gleason reportedly named his house, built in a saucerlike shape, the "Mothership." He was said to have been taken by his friend President Richard Nixon to view alien bodies at a nearby military base late one night.[125] Political and high-ranking military figures also made public remarks that many in the UFO community found suggestive of UFO reality. General Douglas MacArthur, in a speech given to graduating cadets at West Point on May 12, 1962, stated, "You now face a new world, a world of change. We speak in strange terms, of harnessing the cosmic energy, of ultimate conflict between a united human race and the sinister forces of some other planetary galaxy."[126] Thirty years later, references to "sinister forces" from other planets found their way into speeches made by President Ronald Reagan and by Soviet Premier Mikhail Gorbachev, both of whom suggested that the presence of an alien threat would be a compelling reason for the two nations to pursue a more harmonious diplomatic situation.[127]

Media references to UFOs helped support the idea that they were real and that the government knew it. In March 1995, the Disney studios aired a program in selected markets purportedly promoting a new ride at Disney World — the "ExtraTERRORestrial." In fact, the hour-long program was almost totally devoted to a presentation of the case for UFO reality and featured Disney CEO Michael Eisner making statements such as, "Intelligent life from distant galaxies is now attempting to make open contact with the human race, and tonight we'll show you the evidence."[128] Given the recommendation by the 1953 Robertson Panel that the Disney studios be used to educate the American public *out* of its belief in UFOs, some in the UFO community wondered if this production was an attempt by factions of the military-intelligence community who disapproved of the cover-up to educate Americans *into* an acceptance of extraterrestrial reality.[129] Another media event that caused a number of raised eyebrows in the UFO community was an October 29, 1995, piece done by NBC News anchor Tom Brokaw on extraterrestrial life. Introducing a segment on radio telescopes and the government's Search for Extraterrestrial Intelligence (SETI) program, he asked, "Is there intelligent life in space? You might be surprised."[130] He followed this on November 3 by quipping at the end of a piece on the upcoming U.S. presidential election that the next officeholder, whoever he was, would have to deal with "the UFO factor."[131] Ufologists were quick to put the two statements together, but Brokaw later explained that by "UFO" he had meant that "the UnForeseen will Occur."[132] Not everyone in the UFO community was convinced by his explanation.

The 1990s saw the extension of the UFO myth into more-privileged segments of American society, segments that some social philosophers normally considered less susceptible to the fantasies and delusions likely to overtake the less-privileged masses.[133] On occasion, wealthy benefactors contributed much-needed funds to UFO-related scientific and educational projects, lending an implicit aura of high-powered endorsement to the idea of UFO reality. In 1992 Las Vegas millionaire Robert Bigelow underwrote a survey by the Roper Organization designed to determine what percentage of the American population might have been abducted by UFO occupants.[134] In 1995 he helped finance the analysis of objects that had been removed from abductees and were thought to be alien-implanted tracking or control devices. Multimillionaire Laurence Rockefeller contributed significant funds to Harvard psychiatrist John Mack's Program for Extraordinary Experience Research (PEER), an abductee support and research organization founded in 1993.[135] And in 1996 Rockefeller and Marie "Bootsie" Galbraith (wife of Evan Galbraith, former U.S. ambassador to France) sponsored the publication of a special report on the status of the UFO question, one thousand copies of which were distributed selectively to political, military, and scientific leaders around the world.[136] Finally, in early 1999 multimillionaire entrepreneur Joe Firmage made a splash in the UFO community when he resigned his position as CEO of U.S. Web in order to concentrate his attention on UFO research. His first endeavor in this direction was a six-hundred-page Internet book on the history of human-extraterrestrial contacts and the need to merge science and religion in the study of UFOs.[137]

In addition to stories from informants (publicly known and unknown), FOIA documents, and celebrity comments, there was one other category of information that contributed significantly to the UFO myth. Material artifacts allegedly related to UFO activity surfaced from time to time. If their authenticity could be established, they would provide the UFO community with its long-sought "smoking gun." But UFOs, although they were said to fall from the skies, never fell into the hands of ufologists, and undeniable physical artifacts were virtually impossible to find. When they did surface, their true nature was always subject to a great deal of controversy. In the late 1950s and early 1960s metal fragments were presented on two occasions — one from Ubatuba, Brazil, and the other from Canada. In both cases a true otherworldly provenance could not be established for the fragments, and it began to seem likely that the specimens were really only foundry slag.[138] A quirky encounter reported between UFO occupants and Joe Simonton in 1961 left the Wisconsin farmer in possession of alien "pancakes" in exchange for a jug of water. Analysis revealed them to be rather ordinary buckwheat cakes.[139] In 1996 a minutely layered metal fragment was presented to UFO researchers as a remnant of the object that crashed in Roswell in 1947. Closer inspection revealed the fragment to be a cast-off from a jewelry studio in Utah specializing in rare Japanese methods of jewelry making.[140] After decades of study the only thing that UFO groups knew for sure was that reliable people definitely reported seeing unexplainable things in the skies from time to time.

On the more puzzling side, UFO activity became associated with the phenomenon of cattle mutilations, whose cause and significance were themselves debated. As early as 1967 a horse named Snippy was alleged to have been killed and disfigured in unusual ways at approximately the same time that a UFO was spotted near the horse's pasture. Though that incident was never conclusively proven to be linked to UFOs (or to be a genuine mutilation), later cattle mutilations continued to be frequently associated with UFO sightings.[141] In a similar manner, the phenomenon of crop circles — patterns of varying complexity forming overnight in grain fields without seriously damaging the plant stalks — were also thought to be linked to UFO activity.[142] The association of these two kinds of events with the subject of UFOs had a mixed reception in the UFO community, some people feeling that marrying one anomalous phenomenon to other anomalies did little to advance the cause of scientific investigation of any of them. Others, however, viewed mutilations and crop circles as legitimate evidence of the alien presence. In this spirit, ufological benefactor Laurence Rockefeller began to sponsor crop circle research in 1999. Because of the contested relevance of mutilations and crop circles to UFO phenomena, however, these two subjects constituted only minor though important subthemes in the UFO myth.

No less controversial as UFO artifacts were documents that surfaced in circumstances that made them appear, at least on the surface, to be legitimate evidence of government knowledge about UFOs far in excess of what was formally admitted. Probably the most famous of such "unofficially released" documents were the MJ-12 papers, which came to light in 1987. Film producer Jaime Shandera said that he went to his mailbox in December 1984 and found a roll of undeveloped 35 mm film postmarked from Albuquerque, New Mexico. When processed, the film was found to contain images of a memo written apparently to apprise incoming President Dwight D. Eisenhower of the UFO situation. It described the formation of a top secret committee (mandated by an executive order of President Harry S. Truman in September 1947) to monitor and analyze UFO information. According to the document, the twelve-person committee, called "Majestic 12," or "MJ-12," initially analyzed the wreckage and bodies from the 1947 Roswell crash. At the time the memo was written, November 1952, another crashed UFO was said to have been recovered in 1950 just south of the U.S.-Mexico border.[143] After the MJ-12 papers surfaced, their authenticity was the subject of lively debate.[144] Although the preponderance of UFO researchers seemed to feel that the papers themselves were a forgery, the existence of the MJ-12 committee (or one like it) was deemed probable.[145] The ufological debate over this clandestine revelation had barely died down when in 1997 another set of documents were brought forward (not through the FOIA, but allegedly "leaked" without official authorization); these documents also purported to be official correspondence about UFO reality and the governmental cover-up. One of the first projects that Joe Firmage undertook after his public debut in ufology was an investigation into the authenticity of these papers.[146]

Contributing to the idea that MJ-12 actually existed were informants allegedly from within the intelligence community. According to these individuals, MJ-12 was a real group of people who diverted the best UFO reports that were submitted to Project Blue Book and who received information from special military and intelligence projects designed to deal with UFO crash retrievals and other human-alien interactions. (Some project code names given to researchers by the informants were verified by FOIA documents, although the releases did not usually reveal the exact nature of these projects.) In the late 1960s, the informants said,

MJ-12 decided to take government interest in UFOs entirely under-ground, and it set up the Condon Committee to facilitate that move. By the mid-1970s, the story went, the United States had entered into a for-mal agreement with at least one extraterrestrial race, and a coordinating command structure was put in place to oversee the nation's official inter-actions with aliens. Under the terms of that agreement, the government would continue to deny the alien presence in exchange for the aliens' noninterference in human society. In addition, the aliens were promised a terrestrial base of operations at Area 51 in Nevada. Other UFO researchers claimed that the terms of the agreement were more nefarious than that. According to the information obtained by these ufologists, the government agreed to allow the extraterrestrials selectively to abduct U.S. citizens for research purposes, with the proviso that only limited numbers would be taken, that they would always be returned safely with no memories of the event, and that the extraterrestrials would furnish the government with a list of the names of those so taken.[147]

If the authenticity of paper documents like the MJ-12 set could be so thoroughly questioned, the art of producing visual special effects made determining the authenticity of pictographic information about UFOs and aliens even more problematic. From the earliest years of the modern UFO era, still photos of UFOs had been offered by witnesses as proof of their encounter claims. Some photos were determined to be fraudulent, but others withstood scrutiny by critical ufologists through the years. As home movie cameras and then video cameras came into greater use, investigative groups received new evidence that they hoped would stand up to analysis and be conclusive proof of UFO reality. However, although moving pictures of UFOs were harder to fake than still photos, it was not impossible to do. The advent of home computers and increas-ingly sophisticated and accessible graphical imaging programs in the 1980s and 1990s compounded the problem of trying to separate legiti-mate UFO videos from cleverly constructed fakes. Rather than being a tool for establishing UFO reality, advances in visual communications technology meant there was a greater need for technical expertise and critical discrimination within the UFO community. It also meant greater opportunities for conflicting opinions among ufologists, conflicts that could become surprisingly acrimonious as various interpreters of the evidence tried to balance the will to believe with the need to exercise reasonably skeptical caution and the desire to maintain, as much as pos-sible under the circumstances, a respectable public image.[148]

Witness photos and films were not the only sources of visual evidence available for the UFO community to puzzle over and debate. In keeping with the tradition of "leaked" information, allegedly official or semiofficial films were occasionally offered to ufologists for public release. Film producers Robert Emenegger and Allan Sandler reported that in late 1972 air force officers offered them a chance to make a documentary film using government footage of a UFO landing and subsequent meeting with extraterrestrials that took place at Holloman Air Force Base, New Mexico, in 1971. But at the last moment permission to use — or even to see — the film was withdrawn.[149] Similarly, in 1983 an air force officer offered journalist Linda Moulton Howe film from a Holloman Air Force Base alien-human meeting for her upcoming documentary on UFOs. As with the Emenegger and Sandler offer, she was told at the last minute that permission had been withdrawn by higher authorities. She was, however, allowed to read a briefing document that discussed UFO crashes, the retrieval of alien bodies and live aliens, government projects to study the role of aliens in Earth's present and past, and information on alien manipulation of the genetics of Earth primates in order to produce the first humans. Her informant also told her that there was a group known as MJ-12 whose purpose was oversight of the alien situation.[150]

Though rumors circulated about the numbers, dates, and contents of alien encounter films that the government had classified and filed away, the only allegedly official UFO-alien film available for public perusal came to light through unofficial channels. In 1995 British film producer Ray Santilli captured worldwide attention with his story that while trying to find old footage of rock and roll superstar Elvis Presley, he was offered several canisters of old military film of an alien autopsy conducted around 1947. Santilli bought the film and showed it first to a select group of UFO insiders in Britain, but word of the film's existence spread quickly along the ufological grapevine, and soon networks in the United States and throughout Europe bought rights to show the film. The FOX network in the United States broadcast it in August 1995 and garnered a very healthy 8.1 Nielsen rating, prompting the network to rebroadcast the show scarcely a month later. The video version of the film was subsequently among the top twenty-five films rented at video stores and appeared for sale in dozens of mail-order catalogs. Needless to say, the authenticity of the film was widely debated in the UFO community. Although lab testing confirmed that the film itself was from 1947 or 1967, the images on the film were not as easy to date. Analysts focused on details in the film, such as the coiled telephone cord, in an attempt to ascertain the most likely date of the whole. Special effects experts rendered their opinions on the techniques and costs that would be involved in faking a presentation like that seen on the film. And physicians in a variety of specialties commented on the methods used by the doctors in the autopsy footage, the instruments they used, and the kinds of human diseases and abnormalities that might produce an individual looking like the one on the autopsy table. The general opinion in the UFO world was that the Santilli autopsy film was a fake, but there remained a contingent who was not so sure that the film should be dismissed.[151]

THE PEDIGREE OF THE UFO MYTH

The UFO myth is multivalent, and not all members of the UFO community agreed about which parts of it were central and which parts were an unnecessary accretion. Should "ordinary" UFO sightings be considered the core of the phenomenon, with all else relegated to the categories of fantasy, delusion, hoax, and disinformation? What kinds of sightings qualify as legitimate — high-level anomalous night-time lights? Lower-altitude, structured craft seen in the daytime? What about reports of entities sighted along with UFOs? Should ufologists trust the reports of people like Jesse Marcel, a principle player in the Roswell incident who, shortly before his death, videotaped his story about what really happened in Roswell in 1947? What about the informants who, though anonymous to the UFO community at large, were often known personally to the investigators who took their statements to a larger audience? And what about the confessions of the Robert Lazars of the UFO world, who talked about secret alien bases in the desert and clandestine government-alien liaisons? As one frustrated observer put it, "It is no secret that our government hides much from us . . . but the line must certainly be drawn somewhere."[152]

In the UFO community, there was no single legitimating structure or organization that had the resources or the status to be able to draw that line. In the 1990s the proliferation of UFO magazines for mass market consumption, the flowering of TV shows on the paranormal, and the availability of the Internet to increasing numbers of people made even more problematic any attempt at setting boundaries and legitimating some UFO themes over others. There were hundreds of small UFO study groups in the United States (and around the world), all of whom were at least potentially connected via the Internet, where any and every idea could be broached, contested, or defended. Seldom was an idea defeated once and for all in such a forum. And information gleaned from the Net

often appeared in short order in one of the UFO magazines, or on one of
the several TV newsmagazine-style shows devoted (usually) to the paranormal — or even on popular prime-time TV shows. There were dozens
of small newsletters published by individuals or by UFO study groups
who wanted to present their own research, ideas, and conclusions to the
world. And a mini-industry of presenting conferences on UFOs and
related topics gave ufologists yet another way to meet and UFO ideas yet
another way to circulate.

All of which is not to suggest that ufologists were insensitive to issues
of method and verification and would thus embrace almost anything.
Quite the contrary. A primary concern of the UFO community had
always been to make the existence of UFOs not just something that
might be believed in or not, but a demonstrable, empirical fact of life.
The most persistent problems in attaining this goal were determining the
appropriate methodology and obtaining adequate proof. But the kinds of
methodologies and proofs thought necessary to gain more widespread
acceptance of UFO reality depended, in turn, upon one's basic orientation toward the phenomenon. The primary approaches ran in three
broadly conceived veins. Some UFO students focused on the governmen-
tal-political aspects of the problem. They believed "that UFO investigators and the UFO community as a whole are only pawns in the hands of
the military." Others found the religious aspects of the UFO phenomenon to be most problematic. They were concerned that at least portions
of the UFO myth were "merely a New Age recycling of ancient messiah/
apocalypse mythologies" that were being inappropriately oversimplified
and reified in ufology. Still others were concerned with the scientific
issues in UFO investigations. They felt that the subject of UFOs was
plagued by belief systems that implicitly predisposed investigators to
arrive at certain kinds of conclusions about the phenomenon, when a
more appropriately scientific attitude — a "spirit of honest inquiry" —
would have been to assume nothing at all about the nature of UFOs and
let the evidence lead where it would.[153]

In a survey I circulated in 1995 through 1997 among participants at
UFO conferences, in UFO study groups, and among readers of UFO
periodicals, respondents were asked whether they thought the UFO mystery would ever be solved and to indicate their level of confidence in government, religion, and science as venues through which the answers
would most likely be found. Given the importance of UFO-related experiences in creating and shaping UFO history and the UFO community
itself, a fourth venue was also offered — that of "personal experience."

Although 60 percent of the respondents were reasonably certain that the UFO problem would ultimately be solved, 26 percent were unsure if it could be, and 14 percent doubted it.[154] When asked to guesstimate a date for this resolution, the median response was the year 2006. Interestingly, respondents suggested that the most likely venue through which the existence of alien life would finally become widely known was "personal experience." Fully 75 percent of survey respondents expressed a high degree of confidence that personal experience would yield the desired proof of UFO reality.[155] The next highest level of confidence was in science, with 53 percent choosing it as a likely source for further information about UFO phenomena.[156] Given the history of the relationship between the government and UFO groups, it is hardly surprising that few respondents — only 10 percent — felt they could expect answers from that quarter.[157] Similarly, only 10 percent felt that organized religion held answers to the UFO question.[158] In fact, religion fared worst among the four options in all ways: It had the highest levels of outright lack of confidence in it (77 percent of respondents), the lowest levels of positive belief that it would have anything to contribute to an explanation of UFOs (10 percent), and the lowest levels of even equivocal hope that it might be a useful source of information (14 percent). In other words, survey respondents chose personal experience as the most likely way to learn more about UFOs, were willing to give science the biggest break as a possible other source of information, and were least inclined to look to politics or institutional religion for answers. All of which bespeaks a reluctance in the UFO community to see UFOs as anything other than a tangible phenomenon lending itself to up-close — especially scientific — investigation. In view of our culture's tendency to look to science rather than to religion as the authoritative producer of knowledge, in view of ufology's historic insistence upon and efforts to live up to being considered a scientific discipline, and in view of lower rates of traditional religious affiliation among members of the UFO community,[159] this lack of confidence in religion is not terribly surprising. What is surprising is the degree of uncertainty about the ability of science to provide answers when compared with the very high levels of expectation that personal experience will be able to provide what neither science nor religion can. This response may be an artifact of the tremendous impact that abduction narratives had on the UFO community. It was an impact that shook the scientific foundations of ufology (such as they strove to be) and reopened the field to the influence of religious ideas and practices from which the larger UFO community had long sought to dissociate itself.

CHAPTER TWO

A Short History
of Alien Encounters

[Stories of] marvelous journeys [in the Middle Ages] offered
more than just pleasure, satisfaction of curiosity, amusement,
escape, terror, and enjoyment; they offered a more thorough
explanation of the whole of reality than was available anywhere else.

Pierre Mabille, *Le Miroir du Merveilleux*
(quoted in Jacques LeGoff, *The Medieval Imagination*)

In its most basic manifestation as an aerial anomaly the UFO was, to
borrow a phrase from C. G. Jung, a "myth of things seen in the sky."[1] In
its simplest form as night lights and anomalous daylight disks, it presented formidable challenges to the grassroots organizations of the
1950s, 1960s, and 1970s who were dedicated to solving the mystery.
Ideas about crashed saucers and a government cover-up conspiracy
added layers of complexity to the basic myth and siphoned time and
energy away from study of the core phenomenon while, some felt, yield-
ing little of concrete value in return. The notion of a cover-up provided
the frustrated with a partial explanation for ufology's otherwise slow
progress in discovering more about the phenomenon. But the merit of
conspiracy allegations and, as the years passed, their usefulness in
advancing UFO research were subject to dispute.[2] After the closing of
Project Blue Book, the entire public responsibility for UFO research fell
to the UFO community. It only made sense that the priority for ufology
from that point forward should be to find proof that UFOs were real
rather than proof of conspiracy. But as ufologists well knew, proving
UFO reality would be easier said than done.

A major problem in studying UFOs and proving their existence was
the ever-changing conception of just what might constitute irrefutable
proof. Project Blue Book's first director, Edward Ruppelt, pointed out
that the UFO phenomenon had in fact exhibited in increasingly sophisticated ways that it was a physical phenomenon and not just an illusion.

Simple visual sightings, prone to human error, had been followed by instrumented sightings such as radar returns, followed shortly thereafter by simultaneous radar and visual sightings, multiple-witness sightings, and reports of ground traces found after sightings.[3] But though each increase in the complexity of the reports was important, ufologists were still left with just that: reports. What was wanted was "something you could get your teeth into," not just anecdotal data.[4]

The failure of UFOs to "make predictable appearances at convenient times and places," to fly into a laboratory "for a physical and a chemical checkup,"[5] meant different things to different people. To the skeptics, it meant that UFOs were not a scientific problem because there was no physical, tangible evidence for the scientist to study.[6] Ufologists pointed out, in response, that if scientists were to wait until they could personally see a UFO or its remains before they began to take a serious interest in them, ufology could be at a standstill for another fifty years.[7] "If we had waited until we 'captured' an electron," wrote one interested scientist, "we would never even have suspected that they exist!"[8] To the ufologist, the fact that the evidence for UFO reality ultimately came down to various kinds of sighting reports meant that UFOs presented a "new kind of scientific puzzle" that might have to be studied in a slightly different manner. Jacques Vallee shared other scientists' mistrust of a "simple report" as constituting adequate proof of the existence of UFOs. He argued, however, that the data contained in many individual reports could be useful if studied and analyzed cumulatively with a view toward apprehending the phenomenon for what it was in itself, without prejudice toward making it appear to be something recognizable and ordinary.[9] Thus, as ufology approached its silver anniversary it had a clear goal in mind: to prove that UFOs were real phenomena deserving of serious scientific funding and study.

The higher level of acceptance of UFO reports within ufological circles compared to outside them led to a sort of "split personality" within the field. As the more basic questions and problems of UFO reality were answered to researchers' satisfaction (under the circumstances), other questions and problems emerged both from the analysis of the data and from the evolving nature of the phenomenon itself. Ufology slowly became a discipline divided into two separate — though related — parts. One part continued to search for the kind of evidence that would prove the reality of UFOs to the rest of the world and thereby earn intellectual legitimacy for the field. The other part proceeded to the next set of questions: Where are UFOs from, and what are they doing here?[10] When it

came to answering these questions, many ufologists became just as discriminating (others said "discriminatory") in their selection of evidence
and standards of proof as any UFO skeptic or debunker. This was especially obvious in the reception given to surprising new kinds of UFO
reports. In the mid-1950s, another type of encounter had begun to be
described: occupants sighted near hovering or grounded UFOs. It took a
decade for ufologists to take these reports seriously instead of dismissing
them, because the encounters did not seem to fit what had come to be
acknowledged in UFO studies as a "recognizable and ordinary" UFO
phenomenon.

UFO LANDINGS AND CONTACT WITH OCCUPANTS

It was a rare thing to have seen a UFO in 1947. When the first national
poll asking about UFO sightings was taken by the Gallup Organization
in 1966, almost two decades after the popular buzz created by the
Arnold sighting, only 5 percent of those queried said they had seen something that they thought might have been a "flying saucer."[11] There are no
figures for possible sightings before 1966 because "the earlier surveys virtually ignore the idea of 'visitors,' and saucer reports were something
that some other guy in some other place was claiming."[12] Given that
"simple" UFO sighting reports were at that time amazing and rare,
reports of occupants seen around UFOs were considered to be without
merit — even within the UFO community. At Project Blue Book during
the early 1950s, reports of UFO landings and occupants were put in the
"C.P." file — the crackpot file.[13] Famous French ufologist and astronomer
Aimé Michel observed in 1956 that the "numerous cases reported in the
newspapers . . . especially those in which 'little men' emerged from
saucers on the ground [broke] all implausibility records. The scientific
probability that the incidents really took place," he opined, "is infinites-
imal."[14] Although NICAP director Donald Keyhoe admitted in 1960
that "meeting a space crew wasn't impossible" and that his organization
had received reports of landed UFOs, by the mid-1960s NICAP still cautiously stated that the question of whether UFOs were intelligently controlled was one awaiting a "full-fledged investigation by scientists using
appropriate instrumentation."[15] As late as 1967 one ufologist observed
that it was "only quite recently" that serious researchers had paid any
real attention to UFO *landing* reports, and that they were still not convinced of the authenticity of *occupant* reports.[16] This despite the fact that
since the mid-1950s landing reports had become fairly common and

occupant reports were no longer unheard of.[17] In fact, a textbook used in astronomy classes at the United States Air Force Academy in 1968 devoted an entire chapter to the subject of UFOs and soberly stated that creatures had been reported near them from time to time.[18] Still, for a long time the general feeling in the UFO community about occupant sighting reports was similar to an audience comment made when one UFO lecturer tried to discuss entity sightings: "We find any conversation about 'little men' is poison. Women are tolerant of the idea but not men. Are you sure they weren't dwarfs or Singer Midgets or something?"[19]

Despite the general reluctance to countenance landing, and especially occupant, reports, some ufologists eventually felt that the sheer numbers of such reports demanded that they be given more attention.[20] One of the pioneers in this regard was Coral Lorenzen. In the 1960 edition of *The Great Flying Saucer Hoax,* Lorenzen cited seventeen such cases that she felt were reasonably reliable. When this book was revised and reissued in 1966 it included another nine cases, plus three more brief reports from individuals alleging that they had been kidnapped by UFO occupants and taken against their will aboard the flying saucers.[21] She followed this in 1967 with the first book in the field of ufology devoted exclusively to a presentation of close encounter cases, including a lengthy presentation of two landmark cases of alleged UFO abduction.[22] Also in 1967 biologist Ivan T. Sanderson presented his theories about the possible nature of the entities that were being reported by close encounter witnesses.[23] In the 1960s the British *Flying Saucer Review* declared that it would no longer automatically ignore reports of contacts with entities, because doing so was depriving ufology of important potential sources of information about the entire phenomenon. This decision was followed in 1966 by a special issue of the magazine devoted entirely to "The Humanoids," much of which was later expanded into a book-length study of landing and entity reports.[24]

In these ground-breaking publications dozens of occupant sighting reports were presented to the public for consideration. A few of these have become classics of the type. One of the most famous occurred in New Zealand on June 21, 1959, when Father William B. Gill of the Boianai Anglican Mission observed a brilliant white light coming toward the mission. Calling for others to come and see the sight, he and other mission personnel watched as three humanoid creatures emerged from an object that was by then hovering in the air about five hundred feet away. The entities entered and reemerged from the craft a number of times, then the object flew into a distant cloud bank and disappeared from sight. For an hour and a half that evening, up to four different objects flew into and out of high-altitude cloud formations, sometimes coming even closer to the mission than the first craft had done. On June 29, the UFOs returned. As "little men" once again maneuvered on the outside of a hovering craft, Father Gill impulsively raised his arm and waved to them. To the surprise of the numerous observers, one of the creatures waved back! When another observer waved both arms overhead, two of the creatures on the craft did the same, which set off a round of responsive waving that lasted some minutes. Eventually parties on both sides tired of this exchange. Father Gill went in to supper and evensong, and the entities returned to their tasks on the hovering vehicle. The sighting that night lasted almost two hours. In all, thirty-seven people at the mission attested that they had observed these remarkable events, including teachers, medical assistants, and native New Zealanders.[25]

The occupant report causing the most immediate furor in the United States was also the report that marked the turning point for many UFO investigators who had been reluctant to give much credence to such stories. On April 24, 1964, Patrolman Lonnie Zamora was chasing a speeding car out of the city limits of Socorro, New Mexico, when, he reported, he heard a loud roar and saw a blue flame coming from over the hills. Knowing that an explosives shack was located in that direction, Zamora broke off his chase and drove in the direction of the flash. As he headed down into a wash, he saw what at first appeared to be an overturned white car and two figures dressed in light-colored suits standing beside it. Zamora radioed police headquarters for help and then drove closer to the site of the "accident." As he shut off his engine and got out of the patrol car, he heard two loud sounds like metal being clapped together, followed by a roar. Then he saw a white egg-shaped object emit a blue flame and lift off the ground, tilting toward the explosives shack in the process. Zamora dove behind his cruiser, but the object's flame and roar quickly ceased, and it emitted only a high-pitched whine as it flew away toward the southeast. Zamora's reinforcement, Sergeant Sam Chavez, arrived soon thereafter and found the patrolman covered with dirt and "thoroughly disturbed." "You look like you've seen the devil," Chavez remarked, to which Zamora replied, "Maybe I have."[26] He was so frightened by his encounter that he insisted on seeing a priest before he would be interviewed about the incident by later investigators.[27]

The FBI and Army Intelligence responded to news of the Socorro sighting by sending investigators, as did Project Blue Book and several grassroots UFO groups, most prominent among them being APRO.[28]

An examination of the site revealed that brush and bushes in the wash where the object had been sitting were smoldering, and there were four rectangular marks and two sets of two circular impressions in the ground. Some suggested that the device Zamora had seen was a moon-landing test vehicle belonging to the military.[29] But the White Sands Proving Grounds were nearby, and thus it made no sense why the crew of the craft would have risked civilian discovery by landing on public land, nor why, once discovered, they would have flown off in a direction opposite to that of the Proving Grounds.[30] In his analysis of the case, Project Blue Book director Hector Quintanilla ultimately wrote that it was "the best documented" on record and that there was no doubt that Zamora was a reliable and serious police officer who had seen something that was highly unusual. It was the only landing-and-occupant report in the Project Blue Book files that was permanently classified as an unknown, and it was the first such report to be endorsed by NICAP. For many ufologists, the Socorro case was convincing evidence that the UFO mystery had taken a major leap forward.[31]

Just as remarkable in the annals of ufology was the report of French farmer Maurice Masse, who said that on July 1, 1965, he had encountered two very pale, child-sized, large-headed beings near some sort of large round vehicle that had landed in his lavender field outside of Valensole. Walking toward them, Masse got within twenty-five feet before one of the beings finally noticed him and pointed a tube in his direction. The effect of this was to paralyze the farmer. Though rooted to the spot where he stood, Masse was able to observe the entities as they looked at his plants, made strange grunting noises through mouths that appeared to be mere holes, and then returned to their vehicle, which rose from the ground and flew away to the west, making a high-pitched whistling sound as it departed. Slowly released from the effects of the paralyzing tube, Masse investigated the spot where the UFO had been sitting and discovered holes in the ground. He reported that, for many years afterward, that area of the field would not produce healthy plants, and when allowed to lie fallow, the spot where the UFO had rested reverted quickly and almost exclusively to weeds.

As for the effects upon Masse, he refused to discuss them in any detail. "One always says too much," he commented once. Physically, he was plagued with extreme exhaustion that lasted for several months. More interesting were the psychological and spiritual effects of his experience. An interview with his wife several years after the original event revealed that Masse had received some kind of intelligible communication from the visitors and that he thought of them daily. She said that he "considered his encounter with them a spiritual experience" and the ground on which they had landed as hallowed ground that should be kept in the family forever.[32]

Masse's reaction to his experience led UFO investigator Jacques Vallee to speculate that in landing-and-occupant reports ufologists might be confronting the same kind of phenomenon as in apparitions of the Virgin Mary — a phenomenon that was "masquerading through various types of entities adapted to each culture."[33] It was certainly true that, no matter what the phenomenon turned out to be in event-level reality, the psychospiritual effect of such encounters, and even of "simple" UFO sightings, was often a "dramatic change in orientation and attitude."[34] This quasi-religious dimension, which most ufologists at the time took as an epiphenomenon of the event itself, was not overly disturbing to the more nuts-and-bolts-oriented crowd of UFO researchers. But not all landing-and-occupant cases had the understated spiritual valences of the Socorro and Valensole encounters. Some occupant reports had such overstated religious valences that ufologists quickly became suspicious of the reports' reality. Such cases were so numerous during the mid-1950s through early 1960s that, rightly or wrongly, ufologists initially assumed an overt religious dynamic was at work whenever they received UFO reports involving occupants — especially interactive contact with occupants.[35]

The story of Joe Simonton of Eagle River, Wisconsin, is a case in point. Simonton, a plumber and farmer by trade, reported that on April 18, 1961, a disk-shaped UFO landed in the driveway of his farm. When he approached it, he noticed an opening in the side of the craft, in which a man stood holding a container. By means of gestures the stranger indicated that he wanted water for his jug, which Simonton duly provided. In return, one of the other occupants of the craft (for there were three) gave him some rather tasteless "pancakes." Then the door of the disk closed, and it rose into the air and flew away. The pancakes were later sent to NICAP and to the air force for analysis. Simonton himself became the temporary object of much popular interest and of considerable suspicious scrutiny by UFO investigators. However, he never appeared to have an intense spiritual reaction to his experience like Zamora and Masse had exhibited. More important, after several interviews J. Allen Hynek concluded that he was not "an Adamski type" and theorized that Simonton had probably experienced a "waking dream or delusion" while having pancakes for breakfast.[36]

Hynek's reference to an "Adamski type" was another way of saying religiously oriented "contactee" — a person who claimed to have had contact with friendly "space brothers" who, playing the role of cosmic saviors, were here to warn humanity about various dangers and in some cases to try to save us from them. The premier and prototypical contactee in American ufology was "Professor" George Adamski. In the 1950s Adamski, a Polish immigrant, tended a small hamburger stand on the slopes of Mt. Palomar, site of the famous observatory. In addition to being a short-order cook, Adamski was known locally as an amateur astronomer and a devotee of occult learning, having lectured for many years on "Universal Law" and having founded an esoteric wine-making "monastery" during the prohibition years of the 1930s. According to his own account, his first UFO sighting occurred on October 9, 1946, an event which helped to shift his attention toward the emerging UFO phenomenon and formed the basis of a new series of lectures that he gave in 1949 and 1950. But it was not until November 20, 1952, that he reportedly had his first "up close and personal" contact with not only a small UFO but its human-appearing occupant, a jumpsuited man with classically Aryan good looks. The following year the story of Adamski's encounter was published by British occultist Desmond Leslie as an addition to his book *Flying Saucers Have Landed*.[37] In 1955 Adamski published a more detailed account of his further encounters with these benevolent aliens, including trips to their homeworld on Venus and to Mars, Saturn, and the far side of the moon. He said that during these travels he had the opportunity to discuss important topics with them, most notably the nature of their religious and philosophical beliefs.[38] The two books increased Adamski's public visibility and led to lecture tours even in England and on the Continent. He taught about the Space Brothers' mission and philosophy: They had come to Earth in peace, seeking only to warn us about our warlike ways and the dangers of nuclear proliferation. The aliens themselves had learned to live in peace and harmony, and they wanted to encourage us to do the same. Adamski quickly gained a loyal following that remains active, though considerably diminished in number, to this day.[39]

But Adamski also had his detractors who accused him of everything from being a dupe of evil aliens who were in league with an international one-world conspiracy, to engaging in the outright fabrication of evidence and knowing prevarication about his alien encounters. Pictures of passing Venusian ships that Adamski claimed to have taken in December 1952 were thought by critics to be pictures of models created from chicken brooders, hats, or hubcaps — made up to look suspiciously like a prototype space vehicle whose design had been suggested by Mason Rose, Ph.D., in a February 1952 technical paper.[40] Weather conditions that Adamski reported for some of his earthly encounters were not later verified by meteorological reports for the area, and the physical conditions of Venus, Mars, and Saturn precluded their habitation by the humanlike life forms that Adamski claimed lived there, much less their visitation by any common, terrestrial human being like Adamski. Moreover, the details of his travels with the aliens sounded surprisingly like the adventures he created for his 1949 science fiction novel, *Pioneers of Space: A Trip to the Moon, Mars, and Venus.*[41] And the aliens' philosophy sounded surprisingly like the one that the occultist Adamski had been teaching for years before his UFO encounters, which a reader described as "second-rate science fiction, combined with . . . 'Theosophy and water.'"[42] In fact, one critic pointed out that entire sections of Adamski's 1936 book, *Wisdom of the Masters of the Far East,* had been republished later almost verbatim by Adamski as the wisdom of the Space Brothers.[43]

George Adamski was not necessarily the first contactee. But he was the first contactee to come forward and successfully tell — and sell — his story to the American public. Much to the dismay of the more scientifically oriented ufologists, after Adamski's revelations other contactees emerged to tell their own stories, which, if sales volume is any indication, were quite popular with the general reading public.[44] Isabel Davis, a more conservative UFO researcher, pointed out that all of the contactee stories had "a strong family likeness," much of which was set by Adamski's contact reports: The contactee was almost always a relatively obscure individual who had his experiences in private. He produced no evidence of the reality of his experiences, or, if he did, he refused to allow it to be analyzed by professionals. He encountered no communication difficulties with the aliens, who, although appearing virtually identical to terrestrial human beings, usually preferred using mental telepathy. This more sophisticated form of communication was but one of the ways in which the space beings were vastly superior to humanity. Their science and technology as well as their spirituality were so far advanced as to make their native planets virtual utopias when compared to Earth. Because of humanity's sorry condition, and sometimes also because of ancient kinship links with us, the extraterrestrials had come to show us the way toward moral and technical advancement. Nevertheless, in order not to interfere with human self-determination, they usually refused to intervene directly in Earth affairs.[45]

Truman Bethurum, a heavy-equipment operator in the Nevada desert, reported an encounter in July 1952 with the stunningly beautiful captain of a spacecraft from the utopian planet Clarion.[46] Some time later, in response to a request from the captain, Bethurum solicited funds and set up a "Sanctuary of Thought" in Prescott, Arizona. He was able to raise the necessary capital because the publication of his story in 1954 had turned him into a small-time celebrity on the UFO contactee circuit.[47] Another contactee who met a beautiful space woman was Orfeo Angelucci, who reported that after an initial meeting in May of 1952 he spent a period of seven days with the extraterrestrials in January of 1953. Unfortunately, he remembered little of his experience until something triggered his memory in September of that year. In 1955 he published his story as *The Secret of the Saucers,* an account rich with emotional detail about the beauty of his space-traveling friends and their peace-loving way of life. Although the space beings said they had an ancient kinship with humanity, Earth itself, they said, had become a purgatory because of human hate, selfishness, and cruelty. Angelucci was commissioned by the aliens to take their message of love and peace to the entire world.[48] Similarly, contactee Howard Menger appeared in the public eye in 1956 to say that he had had contacts with extraterrestrial entities since childhood. When he was ten, he met a beautiful blonde space woman who told him that her people were contacting "their own" and trying to help humanity solve its problems. When Menger was twenty-four he claimed that he saw this same apparently ageless woman emerge from a landed saucer. Some time after his entry into the public spotlight, Menger met an attractive young blonde (terrestrial) woman whom he said he immediately recognized as the sister of the space woman he had seen twice before. He divorced his current wife and married the "sister," whom he later realized had been his Venusian lover in a previous lifetime when he himself had been a Saturnian.[49]

In the long run, probably the most important person for the propagation and perpetuation of the contactee movement was George Van Tassel. In 1952 Van Tassel announced in his book *I Rode a Flying Saucer!* that he had made contact with a variety of beings aboard spaceships circling the Earth. The purpose for their interest in Earth was to help raise humanity's "vibratory level" and thus redeem us from our savage ways. In the meantime, Van Tassel was told to build the Integratron, a combination rejuvenation machine and time machine. Thanks to donations from his followers, by 1959 the large fifty-five-foot circular structure had been constructed near his desert home at Giant Rock, California. Although the Integratron was probably his most enduring legacy, his most important role in UFO history was undoubtedly as the sponsor of annual contactee conventions at Giant Rock from 1953 until 1977. These gatherings provided a way for contactees and their followers to gather and compare stories, sell books, give lectures, and form networks.[50] At the height of the contactee movement in the mid-1950s there were more than 150 flying saucer contact clubs organized in the United States alone.[51]

What motivated the widespread interest in this kind of direct contact with space-faring aliens? Consensus among the more nuts-and-bolts-oriented ufologists of the day was that the contact experience sprang from inner need rather than objective reality, from the "tragic fears" that haunted not just the contactees but their followers and supporters as well.[52] Or, less charitably, ufologists postulated that the contactees might have been motivated by the desire for public acclaim and wealth, while their followers were lured by the solace provided by the idea of protective Space Brothers, by the hope that they, too, might receive the distinction of having an alien contact, or by the desire to be in the know on a subject of cosmic importance where others expressed bafflement.[53] One writer observed that the contactee phenomenon was probably an inevitable development in the UFO world, because wherever secure knowledge and firm evidence is lacking, the vacuum seems to produce "at once a horde of goggle-eyed gullibles . . . and a much smaller group of semi-sharpies ready to satisfy the hunger for certainty of the others, at a price."[54] The one motivation that was seldom attributed by nuts-and-bolts ufologists to the contactees was the desire to further the discipline of ufology. Their stories, claimed these critics, did nothing to further the cause of establishing the reality of the UFO phenomenon, and, indeed, actually worked against that goal by making ufology in general look like the pursuit of crackpots and by diverting the resources of serious civilian UFO research groups, who found themselves constantly having to make a distinction between their own agendas and the claims of the contactees.[55]

But not all contactees fit the pattern of the more well known figures. Some remained relatively unknown on a national scale, confining their preachments and activities to a local venue. One such group, the Institute for Cosmic Research that coalesced around a Michigan contactee named "Gordon," attempted to construct a workable flying saucer.[56] Other contactees were what paranormalist John Keel called "silent contactees." These people privately claimed to have had contact experiences but did not come forward publicly to tell their stories. As contactee critic Coral Lorenzen admitted, "There seems to be . . . a considerable number of 'contactees' who are not charlatans — who, conversely, give accounts of experiences which were, to them, very real."[57] Keel believed that silent contactees formed the majority of those who had actually had contact experiences.[58]

The legacies of the contactee movement ran in two major veins, one academic and one popular. On the academic side, the contactees gained for the UFO community the attention it had sought from respectable academics, but not for the reasons or in the way the community had wanted it. Contactees, with their newsletters and meetings and networks of like-minded individuals, enabled scholars in the social sciences and the humanities to identify and study the UFO community — or at least a small subculture of it — relatively easily. Because professional rewards for UFO-related studies were very poor, any academic with a scholarly interest in ufology would have to make their investigations short, quick, and to-the-point.[59] Contactee groups facilitated this approach by providing scholars with a target population that was easy to identify and, being united by a single set of revelations and an individual leader, was relatively well integrated and easy to study. The most widely known investigation of this kind was published in 1956 as *When Prophecy Fails,* but over the years other scholars took an interest in the many contactee-oriented UFO groups and published outstanding papers describing the groups' beliefs, values, and practices, as well as their significance in terms of various disciplinary frameworks.[60] From the point of view of the larger UFO community, however, the contactees were hardly representative of that community's ideas, concerns, or methods. In the end, scholarly treatment of the subject of UFOs was disappointing in its tendency to focus on the very visible and often outrageous contactees while ignoring and obscuring the history and the nature of the UFO phenomenon itself.

A popular legacy of the contactee era appeared years later in the New Age movement, where a practice known as "channeling" became a popular form of insight and inspiration. Michael F. Brown defines channeling as "the use of altered states of consciousness to contact spirits — or . . . to experience spiritual energy captured from other times and dimensions."[61] In the early part of the twentieth century such altered states of consciousness were used by spiritualists in order to try to contact the disembodied spirits of the dead.[62] During the middle years of the century, while some contactees reported face-to-face meetings with aliens, other contactees communicated with the space brothers only by using the kind of telepathy that had been made popular by spiritualists and occultists decades earlier. George King, founder of the Aetherius Society, was such a contactee. The British taxi driver had been a student of the occult for some years when, in 1954, he allegedly learned from Cosmic Intelligences that he was to become their "primary terrestrial channel" for instructions on how to defend the Earth from destructive cosmic forces.[63] The term *channeling* appears to have originated here.[64] George Van Tassel was also primarily a telepathic contactee who made a distinctive contribution to modern New Age thought. Among the many space people with whom he reportedly communicated, one in particular has risen to prominence among New Agers and remains a source of wisdom in certain UFO circles: Ashtar, "commandant quadra sector, patrol station Schare, all projections, all waves." Today there are a small but significant number of people who claim to channel messages from "Ashtar Command" and many more who take these messages seriously.[65]

If the contactee movement left legacies for the emerging New Age movement, it did not do so as an entirely new and different offering from the pages of history. Upon closer inspection, the contactees had their roots not in UFO experience and investigation, but in esoteric groups. Many well-known contactees had been students of Theosophical and other metaphysical systems before their contact experiences began. Based on the limited evidence available from the early contactees' followers, it can be reasonably imagined that many of them had similar backgrounds. Bryant and Helen Reeve, for instance, wrote the story of their experiences investigating, following, and learning from contactees such as Adamski and Angelucci. Both of the Reeves had a long history of metaphysical interests prior to their "pilgrimage" as flying saucer enthusiasts.[66] One of the earliest groups to merge metaphysical interests with the UFO myth was the Borderland Sciences Research Associates (BSRA) of San Diego and Los Angeles, California. By 1950, members of the BSRA believed that they had established mental contact with interdimensional space travelers whom they called "Ethereans." By studying an esoteric book known as *Oahspe,* the BSRA learned that UFOs seen in Earth's atmosphere came from a ten-mile-long mothership in orbit more than five hundred miles above the Earth.[67] In short, with the advantage of hindsight, it is clear that the contactee movement was, in effect, a conduit through which established spiritualist and Theosophical ideas and practices moved into the UFO community.[68]

Although the religious background and overtones of the contactee movement were strong and tended to work against a scientific understanding of the UFO phenomenon, it was not the only reason the larger UFO community cited for rejecting contactee claims. Isabel Davis expounded at some length on the inconsistencies and absurdities of the corpus of the claims.[69] In addition, the contactees' claims failed to fit what the rest of the UFO world was reporting. One of the most obvious points of disjuncture was the complete lack of fear on the part of the contactees, whereas other kinds of UFO percipients often said that they had been quite frightened.[70] Trauma seemed logically a normal reaction to an unexpected and otherworldly event like a close UFO sighting. Coral Lorenzen highlighted this assumption in its most extreme form when she described the case of Jesus Paz of Venezuela, who was hospitalized for injuries he received when he was attacked by "hairy manlike creatures" he had chanced to discover near a landed UFO. "His is one of the first believable accounts of contact with occupants of UFOs," she observed.[71] While not an iron-clad criterion, emotional or physical trauma seemed to preclude the likelihood that an occupant sighting report was a (potentially self-serving or at least religiously motivated) encounter with quasi-angelic space brothers here to save the Earth.

Another important point of disjuncture between contactees and other UFO witnesses was the fact that contactees almost never claimed communication with anything other than thoroughly human-appearing spacefarers. Davis pointed out that other UFO occupant reports tended to describe "little men" (i.e., entities of short stature) whose appearance was humanoid but not human, whose behavior at the time seemed bizarre, and who hardly ever communicated anything at all, much less "lofty messages."[72] In 1967 Sanderson pointed out that despite the multiple alien images available from science fiction,[73] most UFO occupants were described by observers as "pygmy type entities" with disproportionately large heads, large eyes (always the most-noted feature of the entities), a slitlike mouth, either no ears or else batlike ears, hands with only four digits or else normal hands, and often claws on the ends of the digits.[74] Despite their early skepticism about entity reports, by the 1970s ufologists were sufficiently interested in the matter to undertake more systematic investigations of the types of entities that had been described. In 1974 Ted Bloecher and David Webb began HUMCAT — a catalog of all known close encounter cases, in which each case was rated in terms of its credibility.[75] In 1978 the *Flying Saucer Review* announced its intention to focus more on occupant reports (also known as Close Encounters of the Third Kind, or CE3s).[76] But this announcement was only establishing as policy what had already been the case for several years: UFO entity reports were gaining the upper hand in UFO circles, making reports of anomalous aerial night lights and distant daylight disks seem rather blasé by comparison.

Perhaps it is an indication of the inherent conservatism of "mainstream" ufology that during the very years in which this shift of focus was formally being acknowledged and approved, UFO phenomena were propelling the myth still further forward, into territory as unbelievable as it was terrifying. This new development seemed to conform itself to the general standards of credibility that had been used for separating the contactees from the more "genuine" UFO occupant witnesses. The entities in this new development were humanoid but not human. They inspired a great deal of fear in their witnesses. And they performed bizarre, seemingly inexplicable acts — like abducting human beings against their will in order to do painful and humiliating things to them.

ABDUCTIONS SURFACE

Just as the modern UFO myth as a whole can be dated from a specific event, has a prehistory, and subsequently developed numerous subthemes that both diverge and overlap at various places and to varying degrees, so too with the abduction phenomenon. The beginning of the abduction era in UFO history came in September 1961 with the abduction of New Hampshire residents Barney and Betty Hill. Unlike Kenneth Arnold's sighting, the Hills' abduction was not publicized for four years, but in the summer of 1965 the story found its way into print in a Boston newspaper. Though preferring to keep the details to themselves, when the story came out the Hills' identity became known and rumors began to fly. Soon they decided that it would be best if they came forward with the truth about their experience. In 1966 *The Interrupted Journey* was published.[77] In brief, the Hills reported that while traveling home late at night along a relatively isolated stretch of road in the White Mountains, they sighted a UFO that seemed to be following their car. When they stopped to get a better look by using binoculars, the couple could see occupants standing in the "windows" of the saucer. Barney began to walk toward it, because it had advanced and was now hovering a few feet above the ground, but he returned to the car when he finally realized that he might be in danger. As they drove away, the Hills heard an odd beeping sound and suddenly felt very drowsy, but recovered their alertness a few miles further down the road. When they arrived home and looked at the kitchen clock they discovered that the trip had taken them two hours longer than it should have.

The Hills reported their sighting to NICAP, and one month later an investigator from the organization interviewed them. During that interval, the Hills had discovered odd magnetized spots on the body of their car and Betty had experienced a series of disturbing dreams about being taken on board the UFO and physically examined by strange entities, then being shown a map of space. Intrigued by their sighting, she had devoured every UFO book she could find at the local library. Barney, however, was not as fascinated and, in fact, wanted to forget about the experience. This was the situation when NICAP investigated their case. As the months went by, Barney developed debilitating physical symptoms that no physician could successfully treat. In the spring of 1962 he was sent to see Dr. Benjamin Simon, a psychiatrist who used hypnosis as a tool for memory retrieval and stress relief. It was in this venue that a more complete story gradually emerged of what had happened during the two missing hours in September. In hypnotic sessions both Barney and Betty reported that when they heard the sound of the beeping, their car had been slowed to a stop and they were taken aboard the UFO (Barney forcibly, Betty by persuasion), where they were separated, disrobed, and subjected to physical exams by the craft's diminutive occupants. Barney had a device placed over his groin and felt that "something" was removed.[78] Betty was subjected to a large needle inserted painfully into her navel. When she cried out, one of the entities waved a hand in front of her face and the pain disappeared. He explained to her that the procedure was a pregnancy test. After being allowed to get dressed, Betty said that she was given a tour of the ship and shown a star map on which the entities' home was depicted among a constellation of lines that she was told represented "trading routes." Barney's examination took a bit longer than Betty's. It seemed that the entities were curious about the fact that he was African-American while Betty was white, and by the fact that Barney's teeth came out but Betty's did not.[79] Eventually the couple reported that they were returned to their car, where they promptly forgot their extraordinary experience as they regained their alertness and drove toward home.

Critics have pointed out that by the time the couple underwent hypnosis, Betty had done a considerable amount of reading on the subject of UFOs and may have picked up ideas that contaminated her later recall. In fact, over the years the case has been microscopically scrutinized — and argued — in regard to almost every conceivable detail. But whether the incident is considered a hoax, a manifestation of a shared psychopathology, or a truly extraordinary encounter, all agree that the Hill case set the basic pattern for the abduction subtheme of the UFO myth, the salient features of which involved missing time, physical examination while on board the UFO, a tour of the ship, conversation with the aliens, and the use of hypnotic regression to recover lost memories.[80]

As astounding as the Hill case was, it was not the first abduction claim to be brought to the attention of UFO researchers or to be presented to the UFO community for serious consideration. As early as 1955 Morris K. Jessup pointed out in *The Case for the UFO* that permanent disappearances of people had been connected with sightings of UFOs.[81] Fortunately, deadly disappearances associated with UFO sightings were never a prominent feature of the abduction phenomenon. Rather, as in the Hill case, kidnapping and return of a befuddled victim were the norm. Examination of historical records by enterprising ufologists sometimes turned up pieces of information that suggested that such things had been happening for a long time. A ninth-century French bishop related that he once had to rescue three men and a woman from a mob preparing to stone them for being ambassadors of the devil, proof of which lay in the fact that villagers had seen the four descend from a "ship" in the sky. The bishop reported that it took great effort to persuade the crowd that such things as ships flying in the sky were simply impossible and that the four accused were thus clearly innocent.[82] The oldest "contemporary" cases that ufologists thought might reflect UFO-related kidnappings came from Australia (in the 1860s) and from France (in the 1920s).[83] Both of these cases were interesting but lacked some of the details that would have fixed them firmly as a part of UFO history.[84]

The earliest modern account of a UFO-related kidnapping clearly conforming to the expected pattern came from England. Serviceman Albert Lancashire reported that, while on guard duty at a radar station on the coast in 1942, he noticed a "cloud-enshrined light" offshore that came toward him as he watched. After being drawn by a beam of light into the cloud, which then appeared to be a solid craft of some type, Lancashire was seized by very short humanoids and carried to a table where he was forced to lie down. More normally sized, human-looking figures wearing something like surgeons' caps and goggles walked into the room and began to work over an adjacent table, and at that point Lancashire's memory faded. He believed that something resembling a medical examination had been performed on him but was not sure because the next thing he remembered clearly was being back on duty at his post.[85] In a similar case, this one from 1944, a man living with his family near Rochester, Pennsylvania, reported being awakened one night by a loud noise and a flash of light. Upon opening his front door to investigate, he found himself face-to-face with five small (four-and-a-half-foot-tall) creatures with very large heads, exceptionally long arms, long thin fingers, and a slit where the mouth should have been. Accompanying the entities to a nearby craft, he then lost consciousness until he woke up back in his bed the next morning.[86] Probably the (now) most famous abduction case predating the Hill encounter was that of Brazilian farmer and law student Antonio Villas-Boas, whose story first appeared in the January and March 1965 issues of the *Flying Saucer Review* — after the Hills had completed their hypnotic regression sessions, but several months before the first publication of their case.[87]

In December 1957 Villas-Boas and his brother were out plowing a field late at night when they saw a light in the sky that seemed to change position relative to the tractor as each furrow was completed. Finally, Villas-Boas recalled, the light began to approach the field. The young men were frightened, so they left for the night, but the following evening Villas-Boas returned alone to finish the task. At about midnight the strange light returned, approached the field at great speed, and stopped about three hundred feet above it. Although Villas-Boas tried to disengage the plough from the tractor so he could leave, the tractor engine died, and the light descended to within twenty yards of where he stood. When two "people" emerged from the machine (which it now appeared to be), Villas-Boas began to run with difficulty across the soft, freshly plowed earth, but several of the beings from the craft seized him from behind and hauled him into the device. He was taken into a round room with a pedestal table in the center and subjected to what seemed to be a blood test. (The scars from this procedure, which was done on the chin, were reportedly visible for three years afterward.) Then he was undressed and taken into another room, laid upon a couch, and washed all over with some kind of liquid.

Villas-Boas was left by himself, but during this time a strange odor began to permeate the small enclosure. It made him violently ill, which was compounded by his terror in the face of his predicament. However, after about twenty minutes a door opened and two men brought in a small female with thin blond hair, no eyelashes or eyebrows, small ears, and extremely tiny, finely formed chin, lips, and nose. (The small woman's eyes were large and appeared to be "Chinese," her cheekbones prominent, and her teeth white and even.) Villas-Boas reported that his fear and nausea disappeared at once. In recounting the episode for the newspaper, he would only say that when the woman left, he was allowed to dress. He was given a tour of the exterior of the ship by means of a walkway around its circumference, after which he was allowed to leave.

He returned to his tractor, which started immediately as soon as the UFO had flown away.[88]

What Villas-Boas was reluctant to reveal to the press was that the woman who entered the room had also been naked.[89] She approached Villas-Boas "with the expression of someone wanting something. . . . Alone there, with that woman embracing me and giving me clearly to understand what she wanted, I began to get excited. . . . This seems incredible in the situation in which I found myself."[90] Nevertheless, Villas-Boas was irresistibly drawn to have intercourse with the woman and just as irresistibly felt satiated when the woman gave signs of tiring of their union. "That was what they wanted of me — a good stallion to improve their own stock. In the final count that was all it was," Villas-Boas reflected. "I was angry, but then I resolved to pay no importance to it. For anyway, I had spent some agreeable moments." But a lingering sense of shame, embarrassment, and disgust undermined Villas-Boas's resolve. "Some of the grunts that I heard coming from that woman's mouth at certain moments nearly spoilt everything, giving the disagreeable impression that I was with an animal."[91] As the woman left, he said, she stopped at the doorway of the room, pointed to her belly, toward Villas-Boas, and then toward the sky, smiling. In the immediate aftermath of the encounter Villas-Boas interpreted this gesture to mean that the woman would come back to get him again, a prospect that caused him anxiety. However, the UFO researcher in the case pointed out to him that the woman's gesture might just as well have indicated that when she returned to her home planet she was going to bear their child.[92]

The Villas-Boas story added an element to the abduction trope that became a feature of subsequent abduction reports, though not a consistent one: more or less forced sexual union between another individual — whether alien or human — and the abductee.[93] For the most part, however, the procreative element of abduction reports took the more sterile, more technological tone of the Hill encounter. The most significant aspect of the Villas-Boas case was its contribution to the on-going attempts at meaning-making by ufologists. The purpose of the alien visitations had always baffled attentive observers. Their pattern of appearances made it seem that UFOs were conducting recognizance of the planet and its societies.[94] If their intentions were hostile, why had they failed to attack in some twenty years? If their intentions were peaceful, why had they been so surreptitious, and why hadn't they landed on the White House lawn? The contactees had claimed that the aliens were space brothers here to keep us from destroying ourselves with nuclear weapons, but this seemed unlikely because the space brothers almost never offered concrete suggestions and because the individuals they contacted lacked the social status and authority to serve as effective alien-human liaisons.[95] The Hill and Villas-Boas cases supplied ufologists with another potential answer — that the aliens were investigating human reproduction and genetics.[96] Or, in a more ominous and far less altruistic light, the sexual union between Villas-Boas and the alien woman suggested that the alien race was seeking to reactivate its genes by crossbreeding with humanity.[97] It would be more than twenty years, however, before the "crossbreeding" interpretation of abduction events — and of the "alien agenda" in general — would gain real prominence.

After the publication of the Hill abduction story close on the heels of the quiet emergence of the Villas-Boas story, the mainstream UFO community was forced to sit up and take notice of an entire new class of alien encounters — a class beyond the CE3s, the plain occupant sighting reports that some ufologists already considered to be "approaching the edge of reality."[98] Bit by bit, more abduction reports filtered in to the civilian UFO research groups. Such encounters seemed quite different from the contactee reports of the 1950s. Two of the more widely publicized reports from the 1970s, the case of Pascagoula, Mississippi, fishermen Charlie Hickson and Calvin Parker (1973) and the case of Arizona logger Travis Walton (1975), were good examples of the new breed of alien contact experiences. Hickson and Parker reported their encounter to the local police, who suspected a hoax and secretly taped the two while they were alone in the interrogation room. But instead of acting as if they were engaged in a hoax, Parker and Hickson exchanged tense, fearful observations about what they claimed had happened to them only hours before. Then one of the men began to pray. Some weeks later, Parker suffered a nervous breakdown.[99]

The Travis Walton abduction case was remarkable for involving not just Walton but also several other men who were his coworkers. The men reported that as they were driving down a high-mountain logging road at dusk, they saw what they supposed was a forest fire nearby, so when they came to a clearing in the trees they stopped to check it out. Instead of a fire, they saw a huge UFO hovering near the treetops. Walton jumped from the truck and ran toward the UFO as the rest of the crew shouted in alarm for him to get back inside. Just as he turned to do so, a bright beam of light from the UFO hit him and knocked him into the brush. Terrified, the rest of the crew drove hurriedly down the mountainside in a blind panic, returning to look for Walton only after several minutes had passed and they had managed to bring their fear somewhat under control. For days search parties tried to find the missing logger, but to no avail. Meanwhile, Walton's coworkers were interrogated by law enforcement officials, who suspected foul play. Five days later, Walton "woke up" just in time to see a large, bright light moving rapidly away from him where he lay on the side of a county road.[100]

In neither the Pascagoula case nor the Walton case were good-looking humanlike captors a prominent feature, nor did any of the three return from their adventures eager to share messages for humanity from space brothers.[101] Despite the un-contactee-like nature of these men's experiences, however, general acceptance of abduction reports within the UFO community continued to be provisional for almost another decade. If CE3 reports were approaching the edge of what ufologists felt was reasonable to believe about UFOs, abduction reports (soon to be known as CE4s) were surely well over that edge.

Abductions began to be taken more seriously in 1977, when Jim and Coral Lorenzen published the first book devoted exclusively to abduction accounts.[102] This was followed in 1979 by veteran ufologist Raymond Fowler's study of the Betty Andreasson abduction report and in 1980 by a collection of abduction accounts compiled by parapsychologist D. Scott Rogo and a study of a multiple-person abduction case in Tujunga Canyon, California, cowritten by Rogo and psychologist Ann Druffel.[103] Each of these books added weight to the idea that alien abductions were really occurring, but the cases they presented also had their drawbacks in a ufological community searching for mainstream respectability and scientific legitimacy. Betty Andreasson was a Bible-believing Christian whose faith seemed to be reflected in some of the events that transpired during her abductions. Although experiencing most of the basic abduction elements reported by other abductees, including the medical exams and probings, Andreasson also reportedly experienced a vision of the death and rebirth of a phoenix while on board the UFO. In subsequent abductions, she was taken by the aliens to meet The One.[104] As Rogo observed, "Betty Andreasson didn't exactly have an alien encounter, she had a religious revelation couched *in terms* of a UFO experience!"[105]

Just as problematic as the religious overtones of the Andreasson case was the connection of ufology with parapsychology via Rogo's book. Rogo pointed out that UFO percipients, especially abductees, often had a long history of psychic events in their lives.[106] Many ufologists said in response that it was counterproductive to associate one unknown and unlegitimated phenomenon with another one suffering from the same limitations.[107] In addition, the Tujunga Canyon contacts, while an interesting case, involved a small group of lesbians. No matter how compelling the case might be as a multiple-witness encounter, ufology could not hope to advance its prospects by embracing and promoting scientific consideration of cases involving individuals who were considered socially deviant and therefore suspect by society in general. Given their flaws, none of these reports of abductions was the kind of thing that ufologists wanted to trumpet as compelling evidence for the reality of UFOs and UFO occupants. But given that the cases supported the prevailing picture of abductions as frightening and invasive experiences, they did quietly add to the drive within the ufology community to know why. Why were the aliens here, and why were they kidnapping and "examining" human beings?

ABDUCTIONS COME OF AGE

All of the books on abductions in the 1960s and 1970s helped to turn the tide even more firmly toward acceptance of the reality of the phenomenon in ufological circles, but none of them opened any floodgates of acceptance, either within ufology or outside of it. That distinction was reserved for a New York artist by the name of Budd Hopkins who in 1981 published the results of his own five-year study of the phenomenon. Hopkins rallied ufology to the cause of abduction research by suggesting that it was actually far more common than researchers had so far suspected — that, in fact, abductions constituted an "invisible epidemic" that required further study.[108] To this end, he urged ufologists to "be alert for clues in attempting to learn more about the extent of UFO abductions."[109] The most important clue, that for which his book *Missing Time* was named, he considered to be a strong indicator that something untoward may have happened to the experiencer, especially when the missing time occurred in relation to a UFO sighting. He also suggested that undue agitation over a fairly benign UFO-related event — whether reading a book or seeing a picture or even having a "simple" sighting — might be a clue to abduction, as well as finding unexplained scars or marks on the body, or having memories of odd things that could not possibly exist such as four-foot-tall white owls.[110]

In the years following the publication of *Missing Time* there were an increasing number of abduction reports, which multiplied almost exponentially after 1987 when Hopkins published his sequel, *Intruders,* and horror novelist Whitley Strieber published the first-person account of his own experiences in *Communion*.[111] The handful of researchers and therapists working by that time in the abduction field had amassed client populations of one to three hundred each, but no one knew exactly how widespread the phenomenon might really be. In order to assess this, in 1991 the Roper Organization conducted a poll sponsored by the Bigelow Foundation. Basing their calculations on responses to questions about key abduction signs and symptoms (but not on questions about abductions themselves) some ufologists estimated that the number of abductees in the United States alone might be as high as 3.7 million.[112] Less systematic surveys, such as one conducted by a New York City taxi driver on his passengers, came up with only approximately 2 million who might have been aboard a UFO.[113] And more conservative estimates suggested only hundreds of thousands to a million.[114] Perhaps the most significant indicator of the level of interest in — and identification with — the phenomenon of abduction was the fact that for seven years after the publication of *Communion,* an average of fifteen hundred letters per month flooded Strieber's mailbox. Many of them were from other abductees.[115]

Although ufologists were uncertain about the absolute numbers of abductees that might exist, abductees' increasing desire to share and explore their experiences made those who came forward a more visible part of the UFO debate and a more visible, and tantalizingly bizarre, part of the larger American culture in general during the late 1980s and throughout the 1990s. Books on alien abduction became a growth industry in the publishing field as abduction researchers reported on their more interesting cases and offered new insights into the phenomenon. A few individual abductees followed Strieber's example and wrote their own stories, although the earliest of these came out only in 1992, a full five years after Strieber's book.[116] Small companies like Wild Flower Press and Greenleaf Publishing formed to serve as publishers and outlets for UFO- and abduction-related material.[117] In 1993 *Contact Forum,* a newsletter for abductees, began publication, followed in 1997 by *The Superstition Chronicles.*[118] Interestingly, although major UFO research groups such as CUFOS, MUFON, and the Fund for UFO Research published their own UFO sighting investigation reports and materials, by the late 1990s only MUFON had published to any significant extent on the abduction phenomenon. On the Internet, both public and private discussion lists were set up to provide cyber-venues where experiencers could meet to discuss their abductions, offer coping strategies, and find solace among kindred spirits.[119] Similarly, abduction-oriented web sites were created to disseminate the latest information to the abductee community and to present abductees' stories for the elucidation (or entertainment) of web surfers. Often these sites were linked to the hundreds of UFO-related sites already on the web.

Meanwhile, in mainstream America, Hollywood producers financed several movies about UFOs and abductions, such as Strieber's *Communion* in 1991, Hopkins's *Intruders* in 1992, the Travis Walton abduction story in 1993, and the Roswell UFO crash story in 1996, not to mention overtly fictional movies such as *ID4* and spoofs such as *Mars Attacks.* Television shows such as *The X-Files,* which drew liberally and creatively on the UFO myth, were unexpected hits. It premiered in 1993 with a 7.9 Nielsen rating (meaning that it was viewed in approximately 7.4 million homes in America). By the beginning of its second season it had a 10.3 rating (viewership in more than 9.8 million homes).[120] Paranormal news magazine–type shows such as *Sightings, Unsolved Mysteries,* and *Paranormal Borderline* and late-night radio talk shows like Art Bell's *Coast-to-Coast* and *Dreamland* captured a significant share of the viewing (and listening) market. Madison Avenue capitalized on the popularity of UFOs and aliens in countless advertising campaigns both in print and on the screen, from Kodak film to AT&T cellular phones to the catalog cover for the Massachusetts Institute of Technology Press or the cover art for *The New Yorker.* In fact, UFOs and aliens became merchandising objects in and of themselves and could be found decorating coffee cups, boxer shorts, baseball caps, flower vases, silk ties, earrings, and necklaces. Alien faces were incorporated into sports designs on T-shirts, incense burners, paperweights, bumper stickers, and bongs. And full alien figures were reproduced and sold as "action figures," dolls, and puppets.

In the meantime, research into the abduction phenomenon continued among serious ufologists. As early as 1980, Scott Rogo had pointed out that an "abduction syndrome" existed, which he characterized as a prototypical experience that is "individually molded for each witness" according to their own predilections, as in the case of Betty Andreasson and the phoenix vision. Such experiences seemed to focus on people undergoing serious life problems who had otherwise shown evidence of psychic tendencies. But lest his analysis be deemed a psychologizing dismissal of the noumena behind the phenomena, he emphasized that "UFO abductions seem to be masterminded by some cosmic intelligence linked to life on this planet — perhaps some Universal Unconscious that seems clearly aware of our thoughts, lives, and actions, but which only interferes with our lives under certain rare and yet-to-be discovered circumstances."[121] Though Jacques Vallee had proposed a similar theory for the nature of UFOs in 1968, suggesting that they constituted a "control mechanism" over humanity,[122] on the whole few ufologists were prepared in the 1980s to adopt such a transpersonal approach to abductions. They focused, instead, on establishing the practical elements of a typical abduction case.

In 1987 folklorist Thomas E. Bullard analyzed the structure of abduction narratives in 270 published accounts. He found that the narrative pattern typically consisted of up to eight distinct episodes, though few narratives contained all eight. They were Capture; Examination, both physical and mental; Conference; Tour of the ship; Otherworldly journey; Theophany; Return to normal life; and Aftermath, consisting of physical, mental, and paranormal sequelae.[123] Because this pattern lacked elaboration in form or in content within the 270 accounts, Bullard felt that abduction narratives were not legends or urban myths.[124] He pointed out, however, that abductees did fit the description of the character in legends who is the hapless victim rather than the hero, someone vulnerable to external powers rather than the shaper of his or her own destiny.[125] It was this idea of the abductee as antihero that made the abduction phenomenon more palatable to the nuts-and-bolts UFO community than the contactees had been. The "typical" abductee appeared to be anything but the cosmically privileged prophet of space-age celestial wisdom.

From Bullard's study and the work done by Hopkins, a reasonably well developed picture of the abduction phenomenon began to emerge by the beginning of the 1990s. The studies revealed that abduction experiences are more prevalent at night and when the abductee is effectively or literally alone. Often this means that abductees are asleep in bed when they awaken to see a strong light and diminutive entities who walk through walls, closed doors, and shut windows to approach the bedside.[126] Abductees may try to cry out or to move, but find that they are paralyzed. The sight of the light or the entities and the ensuing paralysis often evoke a sense of panic, and often abductees think, "Oh, no! Not again!" One abductee told a friend, "I knew [then] how plants must feel before being snapped out of the ground by human beings . . . they are rooted and helpless to move."[127] The abductee is levitated out of the bed by the entities, who leave the room just as they came into it, but with the abductee in tow.[128] Any bedmates or other potential witnesses will have been "switched off" by the aliens and can render no aid to the abductee, though the process is not foolproof. In the Andreasson case, her daughter reported briefly awakening from a "switched off" state to see Andreasson conversing with the aliens.[129]

Contact between an abductee and the aliens often begins very early in life, even as young as two or three years of age. Abduction researchers report that there is a good deal of evidence suggesting potential abductees are not chosen at random, but often have been born into a family with a long history of such encounters.[130] When told the topic of her son's 1987 best-seller, Whitley Strieber's mother made the one and only comment she ever made in her life about the phenomenon: "Oh my God, Whitley's written about the little men!"[131] Another abductee reported that after a 1995 abduction experience that he managed to remember instead of forget, his father finally admitted a family history of such experiences.[132] One of the areas of greatest concern for abductee parents was how to help their children who also had experiences. Although a generation earlier such things tended not to be discussed in respectable families, greater public awareness of the abduction phenomenon helped some parents begin to deal with their own encounters so that they were able to recognize and confront the signs of abduction when they surfaced in their children. The question such parents posed to abduction researchers was, how does one offer genuine help to a frightened child without giving that child the false hope that there is anything anyone can do to stop the experience from happening again?[133]

Physical exams and manipulations are usually an important feature of abductions from the beginning, although as children abductees report that they are also invited — indeed, encouraged — to play with other children (human and alien) while on board the spaceship. Around the time of puberty the routine physical exams take on more unpleasant proportions as abductees report that they are subjected to involuntary removal of sperm and ova. The combination of the paralysis and the forcible removal of genetic material has caused many abductees and researchers to view the entire abduction experience as a series of rapes. Strieber perhaps described it best: "My initial thought . . . quite frankly, was that I had been raped; that someone had invaded my house and had attacked me, and that my mind, in its desperate attempt to escape from the fact that I, a man, had been raped, had overlaid [a] culturally induced alien phenomenon over what was actually a very human experience."[134] In some cases reminiscent of the Villas-Boas encounter, abductees report more literal rapes — that is, actual sexual intercourse being forced upon them by alien creatures.[135] As one researcher observed, it is this feature of the abduction scenario as much as any other that "stirs our deepest fears."[136]

In 1987 Hopkins suggested that not only were genetic materials being removed from abductees, they were also being combined, reengineered, and then inserted into female abductees, resulting in pregnancies that the aliens would abort at around the third or fourth month of gestation.[137] (Hopkins speculated, based on the aliens' genetic engineering prowess, that even "normal" human babies born to abductee mothers might have undergone genetic modification by the aliens.[138]) Abductees report that sometimes, during tours of the ship, they are shown rooms full of containers with very tiny half-human and half-alien babies floating inside a liquid. Although abductees are often horrified by the sight, they report being told that the infants are not dead but are completing their gestation, and in subsequent abductions some women (and some, though fewer, men) are presented with and asked to nurture tiny half-human babies. The abductees are often told that these hybrid children are their own. One abductee, a therapist, reported that her impression of the presentation of the hybrid children was that it was an effort to deal with sick infants who were failing to thrive because they were not being touched and handled.

> We spoke about the lack of touching. I told them that some animals here [on Earth] can die within a day of birth if they are not licked and touched by their mothers or other loving caretakers. . . . Strange as it may seem, I suggested their interpreting Ashley Montague's book *Touching*. I know this sounds utterly ridiculous, but [when returned to her high-rise apartment] I immediately placed the book facing out on the windowsill. This seems a strange thing to do, but I thought, "Who knows?" I don't know what else they need to know, but I feel we should help if we can.[139]

Another abductee recalled having been asked during a childhood abduction to "feed" the hybrid babies by rubbing a brownish substance onto their bodies. She was told that the process "fed two hungers" in the infants—the need for nutrients and the need for touch.[140]

Often during the medical procedures, experiencers report that some kind of implant is inserted (or removed) through a nasal passage or behind the ear or eyeball.[141] Any pain or anxiety felt by the abductee is swiftly relieved by an alien who produces a calming effect by placing its hand briefly on the abductee's forehead or by staring closely into his or her eyes. Ostensibly the implants are for tracking or communication purposes.[142] The most popular ufological analogy for this procedure is the

way humans sedate and capture wild animals, then examine and tag them
before releasing them back into their habitat. Some researchers believed
that if the alien devices could be retrieved and shown to be of nonterres-
trial manufacture, ufology would finally have found its "smoking gun."
Thus in the middle and later 1990s there was a concerted effort by some
ufologists to remove implants and subject them to laboratory analysis.
The results were curious and suggestive but did not provide abductees —
much less ufologists — with the unequivocal proof they would have liked
to have.[143] In some cases, x-rays showed strange objects, and surgeries for
their removal were planned, but experiencers reported having an abduction before the day of the surgery, and the implant could not be located
afterward.[144] Nevertheless, the search for tangible, physical evidence of
abductions in the form of implants continued.[145]

Another element of the abduction scenario worth mentioning at this
point is the small but significant number of cases in which abductees
report thoroughly human-looking military personnel working alongside
the aliens. This aspect of the abduction scenario came to light in 1993
with the publication of two books by abductees, *Lost Was the Key* and
The Alien Jigsaw. The first book described the experiences of an
Alabama certified public accountant who took the pen name of Leah
Haley. With the help of hypnotic regression to explore extraordinarily
real and disturbing "dreams," Haley said that she was able to piece
together a picture of a lifetime of abductions by various types of aliens,
some of whom seemed to be working in conjunction with military personnel. These memories, combined with a number of "waking-reality"
encounters with the U.S. military, led Haley to conclude that "there is a
great conflict going on in the universe . . . between good and evil [aliens]
in the struggle for our souls."[146] The tenor of Haley's memories left little
doubt that the military was working on the side of the evil alien forces. A
similar conclusion was drawn by virtually every abductee reporting alien-
military encounters after that.[147] Even those with no direct experience of
abductions or of military encounters did not necessarily find it hard to
believe the stories of those who claimed such experiences.[148] When psychologist and abduction researcher Richard Boylan asked participants at
the 1992 abduction research conference at M.I.T. if they trusted the
aliens or the military more, most chose the aliens.[149]

To ufologists, that the government might be interested in monitoring
individual claims of UFO contact hardly seemed surprising, given its
known history of interest in UFO groups.[150] What became a matter of

debate within the UFO community was the form that interest in individuals took. Was the government simply using traditional surveillance methods to keep abductees in sight, or was it reabducting them and subjecting them to sophisticated interrogation and memory-altering techniques in order to uncover their hidden memories of alien encounters? Were military agencies working in conjunction with alien groups, as the memories of some abductees — and the reports of some informants — suggested?[151] Or, as some researchers claimed, were "alien" abductions merely false memories implanted by military groups who had been performing the abductions all along for their own nefarious (and undemocratic) purposes?[152] The other autobiographical abduction book published in 1993, Katharina Wilson's *The Alien Jigsaw,* suggested yet another possibility. Perhaps the aliens were merely staging an illusion of human military involvement in order to deceive abductees, to make them believe that the abductions had the sanction of the government.[153] But in 1998, abduction researcher David Jacobs suggested that memories of military involvement most likely reflected the activities of alien-human hybrids.[154] Whatever the answer might be, the idea of military involvement in abductions became a standard feature of the abduction scenario by the mid-1990s and, like the subject of implants, became a specialized focus for on-going study by a small group of ufologists who formed Project MILAB.[155]

After the technical phase of the abduction experience focusing on the projects of the aliens is finished, the abductee may be treated to an informational phase that is much less traumatic. Bullard emphasizes the very different tenor of these two phases by referring to the abductee as moving from being a guinea pig to being an honored guest.[156] This part of the abduction scenario may involve conferences with the aliens or tours and descriptions of the operation of the ship. (Human military personnel seldom play a role in this phase of the experience.) Abductees report that the aliens who before seemed so emotionally cold and indifferent appear much more friendly, wise, and beneficent at this point. Although even with the aid of hypnosis abductees may not remember many details, they frequently report having had lengthy discussions with the aliens, being given instructions or a "mission" to perform, seeing scenes involving the Earth's future (often disturbingly apocalyptic), or visiting what appear to be other worlds.[157] The net result of this phase of the experience is to leave the abductee with a less negative — and sometimes an entirely positive — attitude toward their abduction experience in general and toward their abductors in particular.

In 1992 Jacobs analyzed abduction reports in finer detail, focusing a good share of his attention on the second phase of the experience in which the aliens subject their guests to a variety of mental "manipulations."[158] Although Jacobs made distinctions between several different mental procedures, his term *mindscan* has been adopted in UFO circles to refer to all of them collectively. These procedures involve removing memories and information from the abductees, imparting knowledge or information to them (knowledge that the abductees usually cannot remember afterward, but forever feel is on the "tip of their tongue"), and providing them with visions of Earth's future, or constructing a sort of virtual reality scenario in order, apparently, to observe the abductee's reactions to the events that unfold therein.[159] A direct taking and giving of information (not a true communication but more akin to uploading and downloading computer data) is often associated with very close, eyeball-to-eyeball staring reported to take place between the abductee and an alien. The focus of so much alien interest on the mental and emotional lives of human beings indicated to Jacobs that alien interest in humanity extends to more than the merely physical aspects suggested by the reproductive elements of the experience.[160] Some in the UFO community felt that the significance of this alien interest was correctly identified by Hopkins in his third abduction book, *Witnessed*, published in 1996.

According to Hopkins, aliens sometimes bring children together during abductions in such a way and with such frequency that they form deep emotional ties to one another. As the children grow, this attachment may involve anything from a very close friendship, which the abductees renew if they chance to "find each other" later on as adults, to an explicitly sexual attraction that is only allowed gratification during abduction experiences.[161] In Hopkins's opinion, this emotional bonding process is an example of "profound alien meddling in individual human lives."[162] The fact that such bonding may include sexual intimacies led him to suggest that the entire process of abduction amounts to little more than "alien-enforced copulation."[163] Another element of the abduction experience that Hopkins believed might shed light on alien interest in human mental and emotional life is what he called "human cooptation" by aliens. Not only have abductees sometimes reported seeing each other during encounters, on occasion abductees appear to be actively assisting the aliens with the processing of other abductees.[164] Hopkins views this as somewhat similar to being at least temporarily possessed.[165]

When the abduction is finished, experiencers are always returned more or less to their place of origination. A surprising number — about one-third — always manage to retain some awareness of what happened to them.[166] For most, however, there is usually little or no memory of what occurred. A bedroom visitation may seem like a strangely vivid dream or a nightmare. An abduction from a car on a country road at 1:00 A.M. may be hazily remembered as a massive traffic tie-up caused by road construction. But telltale clues often suggest to the abductee that something strange occurred — there may be mud and grass on the experiencer's feet and in the bed. A fresh wound or bruises may be discovered during the morning shower. Earrings may be found to be in backwards. One woman reported that she went to bed wearing a new Victoria's Secret nightie but woke up the next morning wearing a man's oversized football jersey that she had never seen before. (She never found the nightie. One cannot help wondering what some man may have woken up wearing!)

Eventually something happens to make abductees pay attention to their odd memories and the puzzling clues. They may read a UFO book or talk to another experiencer.[167] Most often, what happens is simply another abduction experience — one that is *not* forgotten or that cannot be dismissed or denied.[168] When memories of abduction begin to surface, they are almost invariably accompanied by a "terrible sense of self-doubt."[169] One abductee found his recently recalled, never-discussed experiences mirrored almost exactly in a story and illustrations produced by another, and he described his reaction to this evidence that his memories might be real and not just a product of a private psychopathology:

> That was the day I realized that something big was going on. Something too big. For days and weeks my head was spinning. I couldn't tell if I was going crazy or not. I would go out of the office during breaks and smoke cigarettes and weep and scream and then go back inside to my computer hoping nobody could see how terrified I was. How lost I was. How helpless I felt.[170]

"In the spring of 1988, our world ended," wrote the medieval English literature professor and abductee Karla Turner. "Life went on, but everything we had always known about reality — our trusted perceptions of ourselves, of the present and the past, of the nature of time and space — were destroyed."[171] "I will never forget when the world I know started to crumble," began Leah Haley's book about her own experiences. The discovery and eventual acceptance of the reality of one's alien experiences becomes, in effect, a personal apocalypse.

RECEIVING "COMMUNION": THE ACCEPTANCE
OF ABDUCTION STORIES IN THE UFO COMMUNITY

It was from the ranks of the traumatized, the shaken, and the confused that ufologists put together some idea of what happened to the many people who reported up-close-and-personal encounters with UFOs and their occupants. The story that emerged became a central theme, almost the dominant theme, in the UFO myth of the late 1990s — to the chagrin of some and the gratification of others. Some critics in the UFO community felt that research into abductions was a waste of energy and time.[172] Because of the incredible nature of elements of the abduction scenario and its caché in popular culture, a few ufologists feared that the focus on abductions was giving a black eye to ufology that would prove just as hard to live down as was the popular association of 1950s and 1960s contactees with serious UFO research — perhaps even harder, given the fact that the abductees' association was far more legitimate than the contactees' had been. Other ufologists were unwilling to forget about the abduction phenomenon but preferred to see it approached with greater discrimination. In general, however, legitimate one-on-one contact between human beings and aliens was still viewed as one of the best chances ufology had to obtain answers about — if not, indeed, to secure proof of the reality of — UFOs. And abductions seemed to constitute "legitimate contact" because of the overall consistency of the events related by numerous abductees and because of the nonglorious nature of the reported experiences.[173] Of course, there were debates in ufology about the degree of narrative consistency that really existed in abduction stories, and about the source(s) of whatever consistency was found.[174] More problematic, however, was the fact that one of the key features of abduction reports that at first lent authenticity to them proved to be rather ephemeral. Not all abductees were traumatized by their experiences, and not all of those who were traumatized stayed that way.

"My *Communion* experience started, let's face it, with my little men [the Visitors] ramming what looked like a telephone pole up my ass!" observed Strieber. "It wasn't the most amusing thing that's ever happened to me, but I got over it. Now it's become more interesting, and more fun."[175] As increasing numbers of traumatized abductees such as Strieber began to discuss the positive aspects of their experiences, new experiencers came forward to say that their alien encounters had always been positive. For both kinds of experiencers, repeated abductions were happy times of reunion with cherished otherworldly friends instead of intrusions of cosmic victimizers.[176] By the late 1990s those who were traumatized were no longer the sole exemplars of the abduction phenomenon for the UFO community, because those with a more optimistic perspective were finding their voice. The change-of-heart abductees together with the always-positive abductees pushed the abduction phenomenon closer to the spirit of the contactees than anyone could have foreseen in the 1970s and 1980s. Some ufologists saw this change of heart as illogical and wondered if it was a manifestation of the Stockholm Syndrome among people who had little hope of ending the experiences and could not bear to live with the anxiety any longer.[177] There was also the possibility, such researchers suggested ominously, that the aliens themselves might have taken a part in effecting such seemingly unwarranted changes.[178]

Questions about alien intentions had surfaced virtually with the birth of the UFO community. In the Cold War era, with sighting reports indicating UFO activity particularly over military bases and public utilities, a potentially hostile purpose had to be considered. As the years wore on and there was no (known) overt contact between human society and the intelligence(s) behind the disks, speculations about motive turned to more benign sociological and anthropological analogies. The emergence of the abduction phenomenon offered yet another set of possible answers. Early abductees often reported that they were told humans had no right to complain about being abducted because we were the "property" of the alien race. But some abduction researchers did not buy that idea. Instead, they focused on the events that occurred during abductions. Based on this evidence, thought some, the aliens seemed to be involved in a massive long-term breeding project, using abductees as sources for genetic materials and as short-term incubators for hybrid embryos. Jacobs suggested that the long-term goal of the hybrid project was the production of human-looking aliens — complete with a strange power to mentally manipulate humans — who could easily integrate themselves into American society.[179] Dubious researchers notwithstanding, as the abduction scenario became tempered with stories about positive experiences, abductees began to report that they believed something else that the aliens sometimes told them: "You are one of us." In a fundamental, existential way that reached far beyond the parameters of the Stockholm Syndrome, some abductees reported a sense of "alien identity."[180]

If the high strangeness of the early abduction scenario caused some researchers to worry about the image of ufology thus presented to the public, the emergence of abductees reporting positive experiences and claiming alien identities was even more problematic. Instead of providing ufologists with the evidence they sought in order to prove the reality of UFO phenomena, or even with believable information about the purpose for the alien presence, abductions increasingly seemed to endanger scientific ufology, threatening to replace it with fuzzy, mystical, quasi-religious New Age thinking.[181] Yet while some ufologists decried the field's drift not just toward the very unscientific realm of religion, but toward a flirtation with New Age religion at that, other ufologists recognized in this emerging vision of the abduction scenario an encouraging twentieth-century coming-to-terms with fundamental questions that have preoccupied humanity throughout the ages. Not who are *they* and why are they here, but "Who are we? Why are we here? Where are we going?" As one researcher observed, "The UFO phenomenon is not simply about lights in the sky, daylight disks or alien abductions. It touches on fundamental questions of our existence and the nature of the Universe."[182] The abduction phenomenon appeared to offer answers — answers that conflicted not only with the answers offered by mainstream science but also with the answers offered by most of modern American religion. But these were not the kinds of answers that a scientific ufology had hoped to get — nor, for that matter, the kinds of questions it had really intended to ask.

In the late 1990s ufology thus found itself increasingly divided into two broad camps. The camp seeking to "maximize the legitimacy" of ufology in society and in the scientific world viewed developments in the field of abduction research with increasing concern. The camp seeking to "maximize learning" about the raison d'être of UFOs viewed the experiences of abductees as one of the best ways to find answers and was often willing to follow wherever the clues seemed to lead — even if that was away from mainstream science and the dominant worldview of the West.[183]

CHAPTER THREE

Ufology: On the Cutting Edge or the Fringe of Science?

In a sense, science has become the religion of modernity; instrumental reason and technical objectivity are the core of its cult.

Stephan Fuchs, *The Professional Quest for Truth*

A discipline . . . is not essentially definable merely by the group of true statements it makes about its subject matter. It is also essentially composed of the acceptable errors it makes and makes possible. The acceptably false is what is recognizable and identifiable. . . . Outside the discipline, however, prowl "monstrosities" and monstrous statements. These seem to be outside the administration of the authoritative paradigm, outside the respectable parameters; they are wild, undisciplined statements that nevertheless seem somehow relevant.

Bernard McGrane,
Beyond Anthropology: Society and the Other

In 1968 Kevin Waters (a pseudonym) tore an article on UFOs out of *Playboy* and gave it to his son Michael to use for a school project. The article was by Northwestern University astronomy professor J. Allen Hynek, the scientific expert on UFOs during the air force's investigation into the phenomenon. Hynek had spent many hours in fieldwork and analysis of reports of strange aerial phenomena, and this was one of six pieces that he published on the subject. Five of those six appeared between 1966 and 1969.[1] Only two were in scholarly or professional journals; the rest were published in the popular press. During the symposium on UFOs held by the American Association for the Advancement of Science in December 1969, UFO skeptic Donald H. Menzel, an astronomer at Harvard, suggested that Hynek's professional position on the subject of UFOs was difficult to ascertain because he had only published in the popular press.[2] The comment was a barb, since presenting a scientific case before the public instead of to one's peers via refereed journals is commonly viewed as a hallmark of pseudoscience.[3] The reason that Hynek chose *Playboy* as publisher is revealed in a letter he wrote to Waters's son: "I am glad that your father removed my article from *Playboy* to show it to you. It is unfortunate that *Playboy* was willing to publish this article but *Scientific American* was not. This is a sad commentary on the closed-mindedness of many scientists."[4] Like other scientists with an interest in UFOs, Hynek was denied a voice in most of his profession's publications yet ridiculed for presenting his work outside of them.

Despite similar rebuffs from the mainstream scientific world, ufologists continued to claim the mantle of science for themselves and their field of study. In part this was because, in spite of assumptions to the contrary, the study of UFOs quietly attracted the sober attention of a number of qualified scientists throughout the years. But in equal part ufologists' claims to scientific status were defensive. They fought the persistent tendency of debunkers and the uninformed to conflate contactees and their cults with the study of aerial anomalies using systematic investigation and data gathering. The former was perceived as a primarily religious phenomenon; the latter was seen as a science comparable to observational scientific fields such as astronomy.

A complicating factor in the struggle for scientific acceptance was the fact that the majority of those putting in the hours and the money to do the work of data gathering were not trained scientists. To compensate for this unavoidable shortcoming, most of the major UFO research organizations stressed the importance of developing good scientific methodology for investigating UFO encounters and tried to teach that methodology to the amateur investigators. Ufology thereby became "probably the last great public investigative enterprise wherein the gifted amateur is not at any disadvantage."[5] But the effort to make scientists out of amateurs in the name of advancing scientific knowledge about UFOs, a move that might have been acceptable in the preprofessional, more democratic days of early scientific practice, was hardly acceptable to the scientific world of the late twentieth century. In part because of the nonprofessional status of most of its researchers, ufology was accounted, at best, as "one of American history's strangest and most extensive adventures in unorthodox science."[6] More pejoratively, the efforts of ufologists were considered "a substitute for religion."[7]

Suspicion, however, did not move in only one direction. From the beginning there were ufologists who questioned the ability of traditional science to provide answers to the UFO mystery. Eventually the doubts found their way into the thinking of more of the professional scientists in ufology. Such doubts were increased by the advent of the abductee era and legitimated with the popularization of the "New Physics."

SCIENCE, SCIENTISTS, AND UFOS

The modern age of UFOs was born at an important juncture in American history. With the end of World War II the practical benefits of a science that claimed to pursue knowledge for its own sake had become manifest not only to the people of the United States but also to the rest of the world. The enterprise of science ruled the day because of the benefits and the luxuries it could provide and because of the protection that it alone seemed to offer in the face of a Cold War made necessary, ironically enough, by the achievements of science. Questions about the moral valences of science emerged anew, as well as questions about just who would or should control its tangible — and intangible — products. For the most part the question of control boiled down to a question of the kind and degree of governmental (and military) control that would be exercised over scientific research. But in a democracy like the United States there was also an important popular factor in the issue of control. The people, who collectively footed the bill for government-sponsored research, needed to be persuaded to do so. And that meant public science education. It was not always an easy task.

By the beginning of the twentieth century, endeavors recognized as "science" had become embodied in a method that exalted secularity, rationalism, and naturalism. That is to say, the scientific method operated without reference to larger purposes such as human salvation or divine will. It was committed to understanding nature solely in terms of discoverable processes that operated according to abstract principles and laws. This method favored the establishment of schools to train individuals in its use and to provide them with the physical and financial means of doing so, which gave rise to the modern "research university" and the professional scientist. The days of the self-taught amateur scientist were very much on the wane by then, and drew more or less to a close by the 1920s after the famous Scopes trial effectively pitted an older view of science as a reading of God's Book of Nature against the newer view of science as the pursuit of truth based on the revelations of nature alone and uncommitted to any religious context.[8]

This professionalization of science, plus a growing tendency toward scientific specialization and an increasing abstractness in scientific discourse, tended to remove it from the intellectual grasp of the average person. Indeed, although science became increasingly successful on its own terms, it became less successful at appealing to the interests (and thus the goodwill) of the general population who were expected — nay, needed — to help foot the bill. To solve this problem an effort was made to promote wider popular appreciation not only for the practical fruits of science but also for the work itself — its purposes, methods, theories, and challenges. But because there were few or no professional rewards to scientists for doing this, the task of popularization fell largely to journalists and science educators with minimal (or no) scientific credentials. With the advent of television, the potential for science popularization reached a new high — but so did the potential for fracturing the "cultural symbolism" of science into mere bits of trivia disconnected from any substantive relationship to the practice and findings of science.[9] It was in such a time of the simultaneous apotheosis of science and fracturing of its symbols that the UFO movement came to be — and to be caught in the middle.

The role of the government in the history of ufology is a central part of the UFO myth. The role of science is equally important, but it is typically treated, by scholars who consider the matter at all, as essentially nonexistent. Ufology is cited as an example of "unorthodox" (pseudo-) science or of the lamentable failure of scientific educators to teach the American public to understand and use scientific ways of thinking. James Gilbert, for instance, in his excellent discussion of the interaction of religion and science in twentieth-century American culture, properly considers the UFO controversy as "a variant of the larger discussion about the place of science and religion in the postwar world."[10] The appearance of the contactees alone justifies that statement. But his analysis stops there. According to Gilbert, ufology's only relationship to legitimate science was, first, through its role in reiterating and deepening the problems inherent in producing a scientifically informed populace, and, second, in its threat — albeit only briefly — to "subvert the united front of mainstream science" by gaining a hearing at the 1969 meeting of the American Association for the Advancement of Science.[11] In the end, he writes, though "there was simply no scientific evidence to bolster their claims," ufologists won the day because the denials and criticisms of scientists only threw fuel on the flames of the debate about the roles of science and religion in modern life.[12] The picture Gilbert paints of ufology's relationship to science is understandable given the fact that he relied heavily for his UFO information on the writings of debunker Donald Menzel. But the actual picture of the involvement of science in the UFO movement is considerably more complex.

THE POSITIVE SIDE OF THE SCIENTIFIC INTEREST IN UFOS

When he began his job as director of Project Blue Book in 1951, one of the first facts Edward Ruppelt learned was that "UFO's were being freely and seriously discussed in scientific circles."[13] This does not mean that UFOs were the subject of funded and formalized scientific research, but rather that a relatively open attitude toward the subject prevailed in scientific circles during the early 1950s and led to the formation of an unofficial "UFO grapevine" that operated within and between major scientific laboratories.[14] Even as late as 1958 there was a UFO club at the Jet Propulsion Laboratory in California.[15] Most scientific (especially instrumented) research on UFOs was undertaken on an ad hoc basis by small groups of interested scientists whose places of employment were cooperative but formally aloof, stressing (when asked) that the investigations were strictly "the extracurricular affairs of the scientists involved."[16] One such research group, masquerading publicly as a "rock hunting" group, measured radiation emissions in UFO flap areas during the fall of 1949 and then replicated their experiments sporadically through 1950–1951 with better equipment and procedures. News of their efforts quickly made it onto the UFO grapevine and assumed the status of rumor, because almost no one knew the principals involved. Though their findings were suggestive, they were never published and made available to the larger scientific community because the researchers wanted to avoid ridicule. The one or two other "rock hunting" clubs who took inspiration from the original group also failed to publish their results, for the same reasons.[17] In 1973 a rash of UFO sightings in southeast Missouri prompted a physicist from a nearby university to set aside his fear that involvement would jeopardize his career. He began a lengthy instrumented and observational field investigation of the phenomena. Unlike his "rock hunting" predecessors, he eventually published the story of his research, though in book form and not in a traditional scientific venue or format.[18]

For most professional scientists, however, the fear of ridicule and loss of professional status prevented them from pursuing an active interest in UFOs. An informal 1952 survey of astronomers revealed that none of them would admit publicly to having an interest in UFOs.[19] But fear of public ridicule did not prevent scientists from having a privately respectful interest in the subject. In his capacity as director of Project Blue Book, Ruppelt was often called upon to provide briefings on the UFO phenomenon to groups engaged in government work.

> The one thing about these briefings that never failed to amaze me was the interest in UFOs within scientific circles. . . . Our briefings weren't just squeezed in; in many instances we would arrive at a place to find that a whole day had been set aside to talk about UFOs. And never once did I meet anyone who laughed off the whole subject of flying saucers even though publicly these same people had jovially sloughed off the press with answers of "hallucinations," "absurd" or "a waste of time and money." They weren't wild-eyed fans but they were certainly interested.[20]

Despite the reluctance of most scientists to get involved in the UFO controversy, on several occasions professional scientific (and other) organizations sponsored discussions on the subject. The American Optical Society sponsored a symposium on UFOs in October 1952; the American Institute of Aeronautics and Astronautics convened a panel in 1968 to study the UFO evidence (and found that, contrary to the Condon Committee report, the subject *did* warrant further scientific investigation). As noted previously, the American Association for the Advancement of Science made UFOs, and especially the just-released Condon Report, a focus of its 1969 meeting and later formed a special subcommittee that reiterated the need for more scientific investigation of UFOs.[21] In fact, the Condon Committee was a catalyst for a brief burst of UFO research. After the committee's creation, more scientists took up UFO investigations and, though scientific publications had refused to publish reports of aerial anomalies for two decades, the influx of scientists into the field and the legitimation of UFO research provided by the existence of the committee resulted in a temporary increase in the numbers of UFO-related papers and informational articles they accepted.[22] A survey of twenty-two scientific journals and magazines from 1953 through 1990 reveals that there was one UFO article published in 1953, three in 1966, seven in 1967, eight in 1968, fifteen in 1969, three in 1970, five in 1971, and only a few scattered through the remaining years.[23] Thereafter, scientific papers on UFO phenomena tended to be accepted (if at all) only in smaller publications with more limited readerships. A physiologist at the Ohio State University Medical School reported that between 1987 and 1990 he published five UFO-related articles in peer-reviewed scientific journals.[24] But although indeed peer-reviewed, the journals were mostly small, regionally oriented publications. This pattern for professional publication on UFOs is similar to that reported by Herbert Strentz in his survey of UFO reports in newspapers. He found that most UFO reporting was of sightings treated as local news events covered only by local newspapers. Large-circulation newspapers tended to publish only general articles about UFOs during periods of widespread UFO interest, and even then would do so only occasionally.[25]

Despite — or because of — the modest levels of formal UFO investigation made possible by the interest of scientific organizations and publications, most scientists continued to express a great deal of reserve about being publicly associated with the topic in any way, shape, or form. Surveys of engineers and scientists in 1971 and again in 1979 showed that anywhere from 18 percent to 22 percent had sighted something that could have been a UFO.[26] Most of those individuals (88 percent) had discussed it only with family and friends.[27] A 1973 poll of members of the American Institute of Aeronautics and Astronautics found that most of the group would not report a UFO sighting unless they were guaranteed anonymity.[28] In 1975 a poll of the American Astronomical Society (AAS) offered astronomers an opportunity to do just that: It revealed that 5 percent of the respondents had witnessed some kind of puzzling phenomenon in the sky.[29] The conventional wisdom among UFO skeptics, however, was that scientists (and especially astronomers) never had UFO sightings and never made UFO reports. That wisdom was wrong. Not only did a fraction of the AAS report sightings anonymously, some well-known astronomers came forward to report that they, too, had seen a UFO. Probably the most famous astronomer-sighter was Clyde Tombaugh, the discoverer of the planet Pluto. According to ufologists, his sighting on August 20, 1949, propelled him on a quest to discover whether UFOs were from another world, and he came to believe, at the least, that aerial phenomena seen by pilots might well be "related to the question of space travel."[30] According to a personal communication reported by Menzel, however, Tombaugh stated that the most likely explanation for his sighting was "some natural optical phenomenon in our own atmosphere."[31] UFO sightings were also reported by Walter N. Webb, a lecturer on astronomy at the Charles Hayden Planetarium in Boston; Seymour Hess, the chair of the Meteorology Department at Florida State University (on May 20, 1950); astronomer H. Percy Wilkins (on June 11, 1954); Bart Bok of the Mt. Stromlo Observatory in Canberra, Australia (in 1963); Robert Johnson, chief of the Adler Planetarium in Chicago; and by the Majorca Observatory in Spain.[32]

Frank Halstead, the curator of the Darling Observatory in Duluth, Minnesota, stated that he thought we should "assume that we have had space visitors."[33] And though he never claimed to have had a sighting, the father of German rocket development, Hermann Oberth, stated that he thought UFOs were interplanetary vehicles.[34]

THE QUESTION OF EXTRATERRESTRIAL LIFE

Despite the eyewitness reports of a few scientists and the interest of numerous others, the idea that UFOs really exist was never widely accepted in scientific circles. Part of the reason could be located in the term *UFO* itself. From an early date it was equated with "flying saucer," an object that was not *un*identified but, rather, was identified as a vehicle from another planet. And the question of whether extra-terrestrial life existed was not at all a settled one. Philosophers, theologians, and scientists had debated the possibility of there being a plurality of worlds for centuries.[35] By the beginning of the twentieth century the general scientific opinion was that although extraterrestrial life might exist (or have existed or come to exist) in other parts of the universe, there was no evidence that it had been or currently was a feature of our own solar system, or even a feature of our closest galactic neighbors.[36] But for the most part the subject of extraterrestrial life was not widely addressed by science during the first decades of this century. It became instead a topic for science fiction writers more than a matter for serious scientific or philosophical concern — a subject "at the very limits of science."[37]

With the technological advances achieved during World War II and its aftermath, however, and as human space travel became a reality, some scientists began to entertain the possibility of finding signs of extrater-restrial life — not in the form of UFOs but as radio signals beamed into space by other civilizations.[38] Carl Sagan, a major UFO debunker, never-theless felt strongly that humanity was not alone in the universe and that the scientific search for extraterrestrial life was an almost sacred duty.[39] Frank Drake, one of the pioneers in the radio astronomy program known as the Search for Extraterrestrial Intelligence (SETI), proposed a now-famous equation to estimate the number of technological civiliza-tions that might exist in our galaxy alone. Starting with the number of stars in the Milky Way, Drake multiplied that number by a succession of fractions representing scientists' best guesses as to what part of all stars were sunlike (neither too cold nor too hot to support life), what part of these suns might have planets orbiting them, and so on. The exact answers derived depended on the guesstimates used, but the answers never approached zero. The final results of the equation are complicated by the factor of time: How many of the possible Earth-like worlds with intelligent life would be at a sufficient level of development to have the capability of sending us a sign of their existence right now, when we are, reciprocally, advanced enough to be able to receive it? Another question was, how many advanced civilizations survived the destructive potentials inherent in their own technology? Given the Cold War climate and the justifiable concern over the nuclear arms race, such questions were not merely disinterested speculations on the part of scientists.[40]

The results of the Drake equation could be cited by ufologists as a logical reason to believe that UFOs (considered as extraterrestrial vehicles) were real. This assertion was questioned by mainstream scientists, however, because of the distances involved in interstellar travel. There was no reason to suspect that other life forms would be unconstrained by the laws that bounded our own physical existence, and no life form known to humanity could live long enough to make a round trip to an extraterrestrial neighbor — even if they were able (technologically and physiologically) to travel at the speed of light. So although it seemed likely that we were not alone in the universe, most scientists felt that it was virtually impossible that we had been visited.[41] But by the end of the twentieth century, the technological means of traveling to at least our nearest galactic neighbors was no longer impossible to envision. And if humanity could envision it, there was no reason why an alien race with only slightly superior technology might not have achieved it. Scientists then came up with a different reason for rejecting the idea that aliens had already visited Earth. The fact that no one could provide unassailable evidence of alien contact indicated that probably no intelligent extraterrestrial life existed.[42] In the end, for most scientists, UFOs qua extraterrestrial flying saucers could not exist, no matter how many people claimed to have seen them, no matter how competent those observers might have been, no matter how likely it was that life existed on other planets, and no matter how sophisticated our own plans for interstellar travel might be.

And there were other reasons for doubting the reality of UFOs. Chief among them was the fact that the UFOs' reported actions were incomprehensible. If an off-world civilization was visiting Earth, why didn't they land on the White House lawn and initiate formal contact? If extraterrestrials were here as invaders, why hadn't they quickly conquered us, given the obvious superiority of their technology as witnessed by their vehicles? The same observation applied to the idea that extraterrestrials might come here for material gain. And if something like a religious "missionary impulse" were their motive for travel, surely they would have made formal contact so as to facilitate spreading their message.[43]

If the psychology of the alleged extraterrestrials operating the UFOs remained opaque, the psychology of the individuals and the society who claimed to see them seemed less so. Scientists thought that people were victims of their own misperceptions, wishful thinking (i.e., the hope for a cosmic savior), or the desire for fame and fortune, and that society as a whole was suffering from "Cold War jitters" and an insufficient understanding of the methods and conclusions of legitimate science. For many scientists the UFO phenomenon represented, most fundamentally, a failure of science to popularize itself among the masses so as to make its own ideas and approaches to natural phenomena a part of the intellectual currency of everyday life.[44] The task of rectifying this situation, at least in regard to UFOs, was eventually taken up by a few scientists and technically trained individuals who came to be known in the UFO world as "debunkers." It was increasingly in the person of debunkers that ufology had its formal contacts with the world of mainstream science.

THE DEBUNKERS

Although Charles Mackay's mid-nineteenth-century *Memoirs of Extraordinary Popular Delusions and the Madness of Crowds* failed to mention any sort of mania resulting from UFO-like sightings,[45] by the latter part of the twentieth century similar books regularly included ufology among the ranks of "popular delusions." Martin Gardner's 1952 *Fads and Fallacies in the Name of Science* was probably the first to deal specifically with UFO sightings as one manifestation of popular pseudoscience in the modern world.[46] After that, ufology merited inclusion in most books that lamented (and hoped to correct) the scientific ignorance of the public.[47] The approach of these books tended to run in one of two different directions. Some focused attention on individual instances of pseudoscientific belief in American society and attempted to show why such beliefs were irrational and nonscientific. They cited inconsistencies internal to the belief, inconsistencies of the belief with the known facts of science, and problems with the data or the methods used to analyze the data that formed the basis for the beliefs. Other books on pseudoscience in which ufology often received mention approached the problem of irrational beliefs from the perspective of the canons of logic that through the centuries had come to inform rational thought. They described the ways in which human cognitive processes are biased toward misperceiving random events as having a discernable pattern, toward organizing events into cause-and-effect schemes, and toward seeing further events as confirming patterns and schemes that have already been mentally constructed, all of which leads most people, in short, to see what they expect to see. UFO phenomena were often cited as illustrations of these common logical fallacies. Most of the authors of these exposés of irrationality did not investigate ufology in any depth on their own, but relied for their knowledge of the subject on the writings of the few debunkers who made the crusade against ufology their special cause. These individuals thus functioned as gatekeepers between ufology and the scientific world.

At first the task of educating the public out of its belief in UFOs was undertaken on a case-by-case basis, as publicity of any particular UFO encounter made necessary (or possible).[48] But in 1953, the same year as the Robertson Panel's recommendation that UFOs be systematically debunked, the first anti-UFO book appeared in the trade market and signaled the beginning of a long scientific polemic against ufology. Written by Donald H. Menzel, *Flying Saucers* was followed in 1963 by his *The World of Flying Saucers: A Scientific Examination of a Major Myth of the Space Age* (coauthored with Lyle G. Boyd), in 1968 by Philip J. Klass's *UFOs — Identified*, in 1975 by Klass's *UFOs Explained*, in 1977 by Menzel and Ernest Taves's *The UFO Enigma: The Definitive Explanation of the UFO Phenomenon*, and in 1983 by Klass's *UFOs: The Public Deceived*. Each book attempted to address new issues raised by the ever-growing, ever-changing UFO phenomenon. Thus, after the burgeoning interest in alien abductions took the UFO world and much of the rest of the American public by storm, in 1989 Klass published *UFO Abductions: A Dangerous Game,* and in response to the growing public fascination with the Roswell UFO crash story, in 1993 he wrote *The Crashed Saucer Cover-Up.* Though there were other important contributors to the effort to educate the public out of its UFO belief, Menzel, a Harvard astronomer, and Klass, an editor for *Aviation Week and Space Technology* who some called "one of the most careful of the UFO debunkers," were the most prolific of the anti-UFO contingent.[49] When a group of concerned scientists formed the Committee for the Scientific Investigation of Claims of the Paranormal (CSICOP — pronounced like "psi cop") in 1975, Klass assumed the leadership of its UFO subsection.[50]

Together, Menzel and Klass helped to define the agenda — and set the tone — for the scientific debate with ufology.

Despite the fact that from time to time a ufologist would emphasize that the *U* in UFO stood for "unknown," at the heart of the belief in UFOs against which the debunkers battled lay the twin theories that there was other intelligent life in the universe and that it had been visiting the planet Earth.[51] Rather than flatly reject the popular belief in extraterrestrial life, UFO skeptics averred that the government and most scientists were as enchanted with the notion as the American public and, further, that they would love to be able to acknowledge the reality of alien visitation if there were any evidence for it. But, sadly, there was none.[52] In fact, the skeptics warned, the idea of aliens visiting the Earth was inextricably bound up with post–World War II science fiction and with antagonism to the intellectual and evidentiary "restrictions" imposed by the scientific method.[53] Ufologists, as scientists saw them, exhibited at best a childlike disregard for the discipline of science and at worst a spirit of scientific anarchy with their insistence on the reality of vehicles whose appearance, maneuvers, and disappearance in Earth's skies implied the "overthrowing [of] the laws of gravity and inertia."[54] Perhaps the cause of that anarchistic spirit, thought critics, was the fact that although some ufologists were "highly respected in their own professions . . . few are recognized specialists in the fields required for the analysis of most UFO cases."[55] And many were only amateur scientists at best.[56] When well-qualified scientists did take a proactive interest in studying UFOs, they were held up by the UFO community as instances of mainstream scientific validation and seen by the American public as spokespersons for science in general.[57] But critics pointed out that these scientists were not representative of the mainstream scientific community. Instead they were individuals who through the conniving and deceit of others had been led, regretfully, "through the looking glass and into the study of things that are far beyond their ability to handle rationally."[58]

The deceptive "others" in this case were the nonscientist UFO researchers and the UFO witnesses, the latter of whom seemed to the debunkers to suffer from a variety of perceptual deficits and even, perhaps, psychological problems. Skeptical psychologists speculated that it was "a population of emotionally disturbed people" who were most likely to believe in extraterrestrial visitation and have UFO sightings as a result. When under stress, these individuals supposedly fell back on the more "primal" modes of thinking characterized by magical and mythical forms of explanation that lay beneath human conscious and unconscious thought processes.[59] Other UFO witnesses, debunkers felt, were simply dishonest. "There is no doubt that a great number of alleged UFO sightings are attributable to liars telling lies,"[60] observed Menzel as a preface to a discussion of the kinds of lies that people tell and the social or psychological motivations for lying. Some UFO witnesses, he said, seemed to fit the description of the compulsive liar — a person who is able to bamboozle people with the most outlandish tales but who, when faced with proof of their lying, can only say, "I'm sorry you don't believe me."[61] Other witnesses were people who had mistaken normal phenomena for something extraordinary owing to defective vision.[62]

By far the most common reason debunkers suggested for UFO sightings was the misperception of meteorological phenomena combined with a vast overestimation of the reliability of human powers of observation.[63] Early debunkers described at considerable length the various kinds and causes of meteorological optical phenomena that were reported as UFOs, and also discussed airborne objects like weather balloons and flocks of birds that had been similarly mistaken. The relevance of these phenomena to UFO sighting reports was illustrated by case studies in which a UFO report was explainable once the phenomenon producing it was understood. But not all sighting reports, the critics admitted, were so easily solved. Sometimes accounting for all of the reported features of a UFO sighting required the critical analyst to understand that rare meteorological anomalies could, and often did, combine in such a way as to produce particularly spectacular — and particularly intractable — UFO sightings. For instance, in one case dating from 1953 a UFO was sighted by multiple ground observers, simultaneously registered on radar, and photographed by gun cameras aboard jets that scrambled to intercept the intruder. Critical analysis of the incident revealed that there had been more than one target in the air and that the visual and the radar targets had not been the same.[64] Indeed, there were many UFO cases that required a "more prosaic though complicated solution" involving such "unlikely coincidences."[65]

In the end, though, admitted the debunkers, not all features of all UFO sightings could be explained, even by recourse to theories of multiple-causation, because of one centrally important fact: Giving "exceptional weight" to an observer's statements was simply unjustified. If the extraterrestrial hypothesis (ETH) was a central organizing concept for ufology, the unreliability of witness observations was the central organizing concept of the debunkers, according to whom "most people are simply not good observers or good reporters of what they see."[66] The fallibility of the human perceptual apparatus, combined with the all-too-human tendency immediately to interpret what is perceived, meant that "even the experienced observer is easily misled."[67] Thus it felt like no defeat to debunkers to admit that there was a residuum of UFO cases that remained unexplained. These were the cases, they said, in which the data were incomplete or inadequate. But "where the sighting data are adequate, there are no unexplained cases."[68] And even if the few unexplained cases seemed compelling to some people, "A residue of unexplained cases is not a justification for continuing an investigation after overwhelming evidence has disposed of hypotheses of supernormality, such as beings from outer space. . . . Unexplained cases are simply unexplained."[69]

Despite their overwhelmingly negative appraisal of the UFO phenomenon, debunkers did not entirely shut the door on the possibility that one day alien visitation might occur. "If . . . there should occur . . . just one sighting 'with irreproachable credentials and inescapable significance,'" wrote Menzel, "the reality and nature of the UFO phenomenon would be established."[70] The issue of just what would be acceptable as "irreproachable credentials" was problematic, however. In fact, it was the crucial point of contention between ufologists and debunkers. In 1953 Menzel suggested the adoption of a five-part model for testing information. Reports should be (1) firsthand and (2) untarnished by interpretations made concurrently with the observation. They would, ideally, (3) come from a qualified observer and (4) be backed up by the observations of other independent, reliable observers. Finally, all observation statements would be written down and (5) signed "and thus backed up by the reputation of the person who makes them."[71]

By the 1960s and 1970s ufologists had offered a number of UFO encounters that seemed to fit these requirements. A classic case was the sighting in New Zealand by Father Gill. Another involved the sighting of a UFO on March 3, 1968, by multiple witnesses in Tennessee, Ohio, and Indiana. The timing of the sightings, the trajectory of the flight path, and the similarity of the object sighted in all three locations indicated that this was probably a single anomalous object. The witnesses, who included the mayor of a town in Tennessee together with two of his friends, a Ph.D. scientist from Ohio, and a group of neighbors in Indiana, observed a low-flying, structured craft with rows of "windows" around it. Appraisal of the sighting by debunkers suggested, however, that the event was caused by the Soviet Zond IV rocket reentering the Earth's atmosphere and burning up. (The windows reported by the observers were explained as misidentifications.)[72]

Clearly the standards Menzel proposed for evidence of UFO visitation were not foolproof. And they were not likely to be improved by adding instrumented observations to the criteria. As noted previously, simultaneous radar and visual sightings were not, in themselves, considered proof by debunkers, because two totally separate targets might — and often did — appear coincidentally at the same time and place. Photographs and movies of UFOs were equally troublesome, because hoaxes were easy to create but harder to spot — and in any event the vagaries of film manufacture and processing, not to mention camera function, made film a questionable medium on which to hang hopes for proof.[73] Similarly, alleged "artifacts" from UFO encounters always proved to be disappointingly mundane. Fragments of metal from malfunctioning or crashed saucers turned out to be foundry slag. Alien "pancakes" were made of thoroughly terrestrial ingredients. And "angel hair," the wispy threadlike trailings sometimes left on the ground by passing UFOs, could be caused by anything from migrating spiders spinning webs to fabric threads wafting through the air from textile mills.[74]

Some debunkers in the late 1970s felt that "the most conclusive case for the extraterrestrial origin of UFOs, if just one could be established beyond doubt, would be one in which one or more earth people went aboard an alien spacecraft and engaged in some kind of contact or communication."[75] But if the facticity of simple sightings was difficult to prove, direct contact between UFO occupants and Earth people was exponentially more so. As debunkers were wont to say, "Extraordinary claims require extraordinary evidence."[76] And contact evidence of any kind, much less "extraordinary" evidence, proved difficult to come by. One reason was because, to debunkers and their supporters in the scientific mainstream, many claims of close UFO encounters could be written off as hoaxes.[77] This included not only the legendary contactees but even the growing group of individuals known as abductees. The abduction of Calvin Parker and Charlie Hickson in Pascagoula, Mississippi, was dismissed as a giant hoax. According to Menzel, the fear that the two so obviously exhibited was because "they had just created a real whopper and were about to see what would happen in consequence of trying it out."[78]

For the most part, debunkers felt that the stories told by abductees reflected deep psychological (but not real-world physiological) events. The abduction of Betty and Barney Hill, for instance, was a case of one person's (Betty's) dreams and fantasies becoming externalized and adopted by another (Barney).[79] Indeed, one of the most oft-cited skepti-

cal theories about the etiology of abduction stories was fantasy proneness — the tendency of some people to have a very rich fantasy life, be
easily hypnotized, have vivid memories, experience "waking dreams"
(otherwise known as hypnopompic and hypnagogic hallucinations), and
report a wide variety of psychic phenomena such as out-of-body travel,
apparitions, or automatic writing.[80] The fantasy-prone were known to be
subject to nightmares, and the abduction experience as it had been popularized was nothing if not a nightmare.[81] In fact, in its basic contours it
resembled folkloric tales of being "hagged," that is, waking up with the
impression that someone has just entered the room and approached the
bed, feeling paralyzed and unable to move or cry out, and being pressed
on the chest or strangled.[82] Alternatively, some skeptics felt that abduction stories were evidence of sadomasochistic tendencies and a "flight
from the self" or manifestations of Munchausen's Syndrome or of dissociative states.[83] Other skeptics felt that some abduction narratives were
likely to be disguised artifacts of very real physical events, such as childhood sexual abuse or memories of birth trauma.[84] Or that abduction
experiences were produced from transient "electrical storms" in the
brain like those that occur in epileptic seizures or through exposure to
certain kinds of electromagnetic fields.[85]

No matter what psychological or physiological background the individual brought to their memories of abduction, skeptics almost uni-
formly agreed that the widespread use of hypnotic regression to
"uncover" abductions was a major — or *the* major — contributing factor
to the rise in claims of abduction experiences. Far from being a reliable
tool for recovering lost and repressed memories of factual circumstances,
hypnosis was a "dangerous, unreliable, and deceptive procedure" during
which subtle social and psychological pressures to perform (not to mention incompetent technique on the part of the hypnotist) could produce
"memories" of events that had never happened, a process known as
"confabulation."[86] According to debunkers, once individuals had (re-?)
constructed abduction narratives with the help of a hypnotist, they
tended to persevere in and elaborate upon their stories out of a desire to
please the therapist, who in turn reinforced the story by proclaiming
how important it was as a contribution to understanding the meaning of
the alien presence on Earth. Thus a typical abductee went from being
someone who "doesn't have much to attract people interpersonally" to
becoming "the object of interest of a significant person" (the hypnotist-
researcher) and, possibly, a celebrity in the UFO community.[87] Paralleling
earlier cautions about the accuracy of the human perceptual apparatus in

UFO sightings, abduction skeptics cautioned that "We are not fully rational creatures. Our minds are not computers. . . . Our memories cannot be trusted — not our five-minute-old memories, and certainly not our decades-old memories. . . . With or without hypnosis, we are susceptible to suggestion."[88]

As for the alleged physical sequelae of abductions, debunkers emphasized that there was no real, substantial evidence.[89] Odd patterns of scarring or bruising on abductees' bodies hardly constituted proof. Things (implants) removed from abductees' bodies only proved that something odd had gotten in there in the first place, but proved nothing about how and when it had happened, or who had put it there. And the suddenly missing pregnancies and subsequent reproductive irregularities reported by female abductees could be accounted for by any number of mundane phenomena. One skeptic pointed out that he would "sooner believe that she'd been to an incompetent abortionist than believe [an abductee's] story about alien abduction."[90] As skeptic Robert Baker observed, "The physical evidence is, and has always been, merely circumstantial and never so massive that it has ever become persuasive."[91]

In the long run, the mainstream scientific world was unable to accept UFO sightings and still less alien abductions as proof of the reality of UFOs.[92] UFO phenomena were too easy to hoax or to confabulate. Even given sincere reports, the best eyewitness testimony was still subject to distortion, illusion, and misinterpretation. Instruments used to record UFO encounters were subject to error and were often no better at detecting optical illusions than were human eyes. And memories were notoriously prone to error and manipulation. The only ones in the scientific community who failed to see things this way were, it was said, those "who believe in the existence of UFOs . . . largely because many of them have had personal experiences of sightings."[93] And indeed, that was the bottom line for the scientific community as a whole. Not only could UFO phenomena not be brought into a laboratory and studied, they could not even be expected to appear in the skies for reliably scheduled and systematic observation. What was wanted and what was lacking for the majority of those who made their living by harnessing their experiences of the natural world to the strict methods and principles of science was personal experience itself. Seeing, and only seeing, would be believing. As astronomer Alan Hale, co-discoverer of Comet Hale-Bopp, pointedly declared:

> If indeed there are alien spacecraft flying around Earth with the frequency with which UFO devotees are claiming, then I must ask how come I have never seen anything remotely resembling such an object, while at the same

time I have managed to see all these various other types of phenomena. I consider it likely that there are advanced alien races somewhere "out there," and I remain open to the possibility that, unlikely as it may seem, one or more such races could be visiting Earth. But if so, where are they? If they possess the technology capable of traveling interstellar distances, then they are so far ahead of us that there can be no reason for them to be afraid of us. If they wish to hide from us, they could do so easily; if they don't wish to, then they have no need to play games with us and only show themselves to a few unwitting individuals. Let them reveal themselves to humanity at large, to our scientists, and to me.[94]

When confronted with an experience of their own, scientists could be surprisingly receptive to the possibilities it adumbrated. Take the case of Kary Mullis, winner of the 1993 Nobel Prize in Chemistry for his invention of the polymerase chain reaction. In 1985 Mullis traveled to his isolated cabin in northern California, arriving late at night. On his way to the outhouse he met a glowing raccoon who said, "Good evening, Doctor." The next thing Mullis knew, it was sunrise and he was walking along a road near his property, uncharacteristically dry and dirt-free for someone who had apparently spent the night outdoors. When he returned to his cabin, he found the lights still burning, his solar-powered batteries almost dead, and his perishable groceries still sitting on the floor where he had hurriedly left them, unrefrigerated. Reflecting on the incident, Mullis wrote:

> I wouldn't try to publish a scientific paper about these things, because I can't do any experiments. I can't make glowing raccoons appear. I can't buy them from a scientific supply house to study. I can't cause myself to be lost again for several hours. But I don't deny what happened. It's what science calls anecdotal, because it only happened in a way that you can't reproduce. But it happened.[95]

In their high estimations of the evidentiary power of having a UFO experience of their own, scientists were actually very much like the members of the UFO community whom I surveyed. Where most of them differed was in their readiness to take seriously even the best reports of others' experiences.

SCIENCE IN THE UFO COMMUNITY

The reaction of the UFO community to the criticisms leveled by the debunkers and the rejection by mainstream science was varied. Some defended science and the scientific method as the one sure way to learn more about UFO phenomena and sought the answer to ufology's rejection by science within ufology itself. The problem preventing more widespread acceptance, they suggested, was the way in which UFO facts were presented to the scientific community, which was accustomed to certain styles and standards of presentation.[96] Others in the UFO community felt that the reason the UFO problem had not received its rightful share of attention by the scientific mainstream was because the military establishment had assumed the dominant role with regard to UFO reports from the outset, with the consequence that scientists, instead of being in charge of UFO investigations, were only employed as assistants to what was treated as a military and security issue.[97] Others maintained that the problem was just the reverse: Scientific advisors during the earliest days of the air force inquiry into UFOs had assured the military that UFOs were not unknown phenomena, which had caused all future air force investigations to be seriously deficient.[98] Still others located the main problem in the association of contactees with the UFO phenomenon or in the incredible aerial maneuvers that UFOs were reported to make—neither of which was likely to persuade scientists that UFOs were a real scientific problem, because both suggested a radical break with known scientific laws and principles.[99] Another observer pointed out that hostile reception of skeptics' arguments within the UFO community may have helped to dissuade other scientists from taking up the study of the phenomenon. "Scientists who have dared to express attitudes skeptical of alien visitations have been called liars, CIA disinformation agents, dupes, [and] incompetents. Then these same [UFO] believers demand that scientists investigate UFO's."[100]

Other critics within the UFO community located the problem more in the scientific community than in ufology. One observed, "I cannot help but be skeptical of the attitude that normal science will graciously invite ufologists into the club just as soon as they clean up their scientific act."[101] They insisted that the main problem was the debunkers who addressed themselves to UFOs but were not, in fact, scientific in their attitudes or their methods.[102] Most debunkers, ufologists claimed, were only "armchair experts" on the subject who had done little or no actual fieldwork investigating UFO sightings.[103] Debunkers based their criticisms "on the worst science, the shoddiest research, and the most inflated rhetoric" in ufology, all of which admittedly existed, given the field's necessary reliance on nonprofessional investigators.[104] When debunkers did address themselves to the better UFO reports, they took only pieces of them, twisted the facts to fit their own theories, then dismissed or ignored the rest of the report as well as other reports that tended to corroborate the first.[105] Skeptics' attitude toward witness testimony amounted to saying that witnesses were lying about parts or all of their experiences.[106] And when it came to appointing panels of scientists to consider UFO data, almost inevitably the scientists selected were those who had little or no background in the subject, instead of being from among those who were thoroughly conversant with the topic.[107] Vallee expressed the views of many in the UFO community when he observed that "the scientific method has *never* been applied to this problem."[108] In fact, ufologists said, rather than being an embarrassment to science, a truly scientific study of UFOs would be an excellent way to educate the public about how science works.[109]

Despite their disapproval of the debunkers, the UFO community did not want to reject out of hand all ideas contrary to UFO reality. Skeptical criticisms of the phenomena were welcomed, ufologists said; it was biased analyses conducted in the name of science that were not. "Opponents are valued parts of any healthy controversy," folklorist Thomas Bullard pointed out. "They keep proponents on their toes. . . . Enemies are another matter."[110] In the eyes of many in the UFO community, the evidential demands and the criticisms of the debunkers had gone far beyond the point of rational skepticism. Worse, debunkers' pronouncements were picked up and echoed by people in the scientific community who had even less direct experience with or knowledge of UFO phenomena. All of which made it difficult (and even sometimes seemingly pointless) to try to distinguish the obdurate debunker from the critical scientist whose interest might be won under the right circumstances. Yet some ufologists cautioned, "As long as we regard everyone in science, journalism and government as our intransigent enemies by definition, the more we isolate ourselves and our subject of study from the mainstream of American thought."[111]

The crux of the argument between ufologists and skeptics was the issue of proper presentation and interpretation of data. A year after the Condon Committee released its report with its 30 percent of unresolved sightings, skeptical scientists were still saying that what was required of the UFO community was just one good case. "If the proponents of extraordinary phenomena want to be taken seriously, they must pick one case which they agree is strong evidence and invite other scientists to investigate it. . . . The only way to convince the scientific community that something strange is going on is to present specific evidence concisely."[112] But therein lay the problem. Even in the early 1950s the question of what constituted "strong evidence" was a contested one. Ruppelt noted that each time the UFO evidence began to meet the requirements set forth by the skeptics, the evidential bar would be raised.

> What constitutes proof? Does a UFO have to land? . . . Or is it proof when a ground radar station detects a UFO? . . . [When] the jet pilot sees it, and locks on with his radar? . . . When a jet pilot fires at a UFO? . . . [What skeptics then demanded was] any . . . kind of instrumented data. . . . When the small group of independent scientists had gathered instrumented data suggesting that whenever there were nearby UFO sightings, background radiation rates went up significantly, the consultants called in to look over the data said "the data still aren't good enough."[113]

Despite the ever-changing standards, the response of the UFO community to this request for evidence was to supply case after case for the skeptics' consideration — so much so that Robert Low, of Condon Committee fame, called the UFO world a "revolving showcase" of sightings wherein one report said by skeptics to be mundane merely generated three more in its place.[114] To mainstream scientists the parade of UFO encounter cases offered up by the UFO community seemed the mere accumulation of a series of basically unreliable anecdotes.[115] Ufologists, in contrast, saw the accounts as having a striking homogeneity and thus as constituting a "considerable body of . . . evidence" for UFO reality.[116] They pointed out that "in a court of law, if this many credible men and women presented such intricately corroborative eyewitness testimony" it would be sufficient to send a person to jail.[117] But the skeptics rejoined that "if one is to convince the world that strange, solid objects, controlled by some unknown intelligence, are flying about in our sky, he or she must have evidence beyond common human testimony!"[118]

Some members of the UFO community felt that the "one good case" approach, with its endless series of individual reports, was never likely to be very convincing. Instead, what would be compelling was presentation of the overall pattern of information found in the variety of UFO reports.[119] But even here there was a problem with the debunkers, who were just as likely to reject UFO evidence presented in aggregate as they were to dismiss individual reports. Menzel, citing a statistical analysis of electromagnetic effects of UFOs, criticized the study in question by saying it had lumped together heterogeneous data and then tried to use mathematical methods to make sense of it.[120] Other UFO studies that looked for patterns in the data (few though such studies were) failed to attract the attention of the larger scientific community.[121] A UFO skeptic writing in the 1990s stated that no clear patterns of UFO behavior had ever emerged from UFO reports.[122]

One skeptic attempted to spell out the exact nature of the evidence that would be acceptable to scientists. "Scientific evidence," he explained, is not defined by its reproducibility, for many natural phenomena are not reproducible on demand. Nor is it defined as that which can be recorded "objectively," without the mediation of a human witness, for much good science has been done by human beings using merely observational methods. Rather, good evidence involves a "detailed and self-conscious analysis of the competence of the instrument to support the inferences drawn," meaning an analysis of the full chain of events that were involved in a particular witness having had and having reported a particular observation. "I think a witness's statement should be regarded in much the same light as the reading of a barometer or the print-out of a computer: a large number of judgments, inferences, assumptions, and hypotheses are necessary to interpret it. The analysis of that chain is the essential feature of scientific evidence."[123] For ufologists, however, the "chain of events" standard was inherently impossible to meet, because the skeptic admitted up front that "I would say that *no* witness is credible who bears a sufficiently strange story."[124] And reports of UFO encounters were the very definition of "strange stories." It was comments like these that made many ufologists feel that the scientific world was behaving in anything but a cool, dispassionate, rational scientific manner when it came to UFOs. Indeed, Vallee predicted that the scientific world's reaction to a UFO on the White House lawn would be emotional rather than professional and scientific.[125]

Of course, skeptics felt that it was the ufologists who were not being professional and insisted that they become more so, if they wanted to be taken seriously.

> If the UFO believers employed any of the recognized methods of science and they were trying to demonstrate the existence of extraterrestrial visitation, they would gather together their evidence, reduce it, analyze it, draw conclusions, and present the material in a scientific journal. They would invite other scientists to examine it and see if they confirm the results and interpretations.[126]

In other words, to gain scientific legitimacy ufologists should behave like professionals and argue their case within a peer community. Ufologists with scientific backgrounds such as Hynek, Vallee, James McDonald, and others would gladly have complied but for the fact that they were almost always denied the opportunity to publish in refereed journals because their subject matter was considered to lie outside the realm of legitimate science.[127] The effect was to exclude pro-ufological scientists from that network of citation and mutual referencing that characterizes the professional production and warranting of knowledge.[128] In addition they were denied access to the sources of funding that would have allowed more in-depth study and better research of UFO phenomena. Therefore the idea that other scientists would be able (or willing) to try to replicate ufologists' research findings was ludicrous. In fact Menzel specifically advised that "As a matter of research priority, we suggest that all scientists can spend their time to better advantage than in the study of UFOs. Taxpayers' monies, certainly, should not be diverted into this activity."[129] The track record indicates that his advice was taken; some ufologists felt that lack of adequate funding was the single greatest impediment to the progress of ufological research.[130] Finally, if the difficulty in finding a professional peer community and the difficulty in securing research funding were not sufficient incentive for most scientists to avoid the study of UFO phenomena, the problems encountered by those few who studied them anyway were no doubt instructive. Being known to hold a positive attitude toward UFO research could hurt scientists' professional reputations and cast into doubt even their nonufological work. Very early in the 1970s astronomer James McDonald testified before the House Appropriations Committee on the negative impact that the proposed Supersonic Transport (SST) would have on the Earth's ozone layer. Those who supported the SST used McDonald's interest in the UFO problem to ridicule and impugn the reliability of his cautionary remarks on the transport.[131]

If scientific persuasion is carried out by arranging "people, events, findings and facts in such a way that this array is interpretable by readers as true, useful, good work, and the rest,"[132] debunkers gradually made it clear to ufology that there were no conceivable circumstances under which students of UFO phenomena could present a convincing case. Should the evidential demands made by debunkers on behalf of the scientific community not be forbidding enough, ufology was further marginalized by having the contributions of its scientist members to peer-reviewed journals rejected and their research grant requests turned down. In the final analysis, if "our current list of pseudo-sciences is . . . defined by the Great Denials,"[133] then ufology, by virtue of its denial by the mainstream scientific community, must be recognized as one of the premier examples of pseudoscience in the twentieth century.

UFOLOGY AS PSEUDOSCIENCE

In the lexicon of the physical sciences, "pseudoscience" is the name for all that which claims to advance or to exemplify the methods and principles of science, but which in fact does not.[134] Various criteria have been proposed for distinguishing pseudoscience from the real thing. Although admitting that confusion about the difference between science and pseudoscience is a "permanent feature of the scientific landscape," Friedlander provides several clues to help with identification. He characterizes pseudoscience as observations and theories, made usually by nonscientists, which resemble science, and distinguishes it from "pathological science" (the kind of science that results from careless scientific method or the faulty interpretation of facts) and from fraudulent science (which results from deliberate manipulation of experimental or observational data). He places ufology firmly in the category of pseudoscience.[135] Pseudoscience is produced by simple assertions of fact rather than by the "internalist consensus" of the scientific community, is supported by belief rather than by rational argument and demonstration, is presented in popular rather than in professional venues, may invent its own specialized terminology, tends to lack significant mathematical support, and is more likely to gain professional acceptance only from those whose areas of specialty are not relevant to an informed analysis of the subject in question.[136]

These criteria, while useful, fail to take into account the obstacles to their fulfillment. One of the most important is that the social and technical conditions of doing science can influence whether (or to what degree) an idea gets the attention of the scientific community so as to allow "internalist consensus" through rational argument and demonstration in professional venues. There is in fact a complex series of social and technical considerations within the scientific community that can deprive would-be scientific topics of a thorough hearing. The criterion of pseudoscience being supported by scientists outside their special areas of expertise elides another important consideration. The inherent conservatism of the scientific community may make scientists in the most relevant disciplines reluctant to take an active interest in a topic deemed pseudoscience by the rest of the scientific establishment. In contrast, a nonspecialist's interest in the pseudoscientific field may be professionally safer for him or her to undertake, and nonspecialists may hope to make valuable contributions to the field because they bring to it their grounding in the general principles and methods of science. To be fair, it is nec-

essary to review the entire history of a pseudoscientific field before accus-
ing it of being illegitimate on the basis of its pursuit and promotion by
nonscientists or nonspecialist scientists. In the case of ufology, in the
early years it had several supporters from the most relevant scientific disciplines who in death or retirement were not replaced by junior colleagues, probably because of the by-then considerable professional
opprobrium attached to the study of UFOs.[137] In the final analysis,
Friedlander's criteria for pseudoscience amount to a pernicious hermeneutic circle: A field is condemned as pseudoscientific and forever outside
the fold because it does not follow the procedures accepted by recognized
fields of study, while at the same time it is denied access to the resources
that would make procedural conformity possible because it is outside the
fold.

Most attempts to define pseudoscience, like Friedlander's, begin from
a premise in which mainstream science is taken as the norm for the discovery and legitimation of knowledge, and pseudoscience is described as
a series of departures from that norm.[138] From the point of view of the
pseudoscience in question, there are always objections or rationales for·
why the field has not met the standards, and a (potentially never-ending)
debate ensues. A more fruitful way to approach the question of pseudoscience is to consider the social processes involved in the production of
both science and pseudoscience. In this way, both start on a more equal
footing, and the different processes that come to distinguish them are
equally problematized. This has been done by Nachman Ben-Yehuda in
his study of deviance as a part of social processes of stability and
change.[139]

Ben-Yehuda points out that the kinds of questions science is likely to
ask — and the answers it is likely to provide — are conditioned by the particular worldview within which they arise. That worldview contains certain assumptions about the nature of reality. But "science finds it
extremely difficult to cope with those aspects of reality that can neither
be controlled nor created at will under specific laboratory conditions."[140]
When science encounters phenomena that are consistently "irrepro-
ducible, elusive, and hard to detect or record," the scientific community
begins a process of negotiation to determine the status of the phenomena
in question. That negotiation takes place within and is "intimately linked
to the prevailing scientific paradigm," which is in turn supported by the
larger culture's worldview.[141] Ideas that get rejected in this process are
sometimes those whose time has simply "not yet come," such as the oft-
cited case of the theory of continental drift or the discovery that "rocks"

do indeed sometimes fall from the sky.[142] Others are ideas that in the end prove unable to gain the support of enough high-status scholars to win legitimation.[143] In the aftermath of a debate prompted by a would-be science, the boundaries of mainstream science become redefined and attempt to more firmly exclude the insights of the science declared deviant because those insights violate the picture of the world — of reality — that has been built over the years.[144] This is an important insight. What is at stake in the process of the scientific production of knowledge is not only the legitimacy of science but also the rationality and reliability of the larger worldview on which it is based. Most deviant science not only proposes a different view of the real world, but "a different form of rationality as well."[145]

There are benefits to the agonistic process of knowledge construction. First, having to evaluate and decide upon what is deviant and what is "legitimate" science stimulates flexibility in the cognitive categories of science.[146] Second, the process creates a group of individuals (the deviants) who can afford to explore the topic in question more freely and creatively because they are freed of the constraints that would be imposed by working within the structures dominating the scientific world.[147] Ben-Yehuda sees ufology as "a true deviant science" that has continued to thrive, in part, because "it is exceedingly difficult to persuade people who saw and experienced very strange and incredible sights or contacts that they had actually not experienced anything."[148] As a result of its marginalization by the mainstream, "the major burden . . . of developing research paradigms and investigating techniques has fallen on voluntary organizations . . . [which have] developed [their] own methodologies, hypotheses, journals, communication networks, and body of knowledge."[149] Rather than seeing the involvement of nonprofessionals and nonspecialist scientists as a problematic feature of ufology, Ben-Yehuda notes that in the field of astronomy amateurs made major advances because they were not afraid (or unable) to take risks. "One cannot help speculating," he writes, "whether the amateur activity in ufology will not prove to have played a similar role."[150]

In contrast to Ben-Yehuda's view of (at least some) pseudoscience as nonstandard scientific pursuit, another analysis of pseudoscience sees it as a form of popular activity in American culture (indeed, as a "growth industry").[151] In the best of cases, Lyell Henry points out, the more visible of the pseudoscientists are "handled roughly" by skeptical critics. More typically, however, the majority "still suffer from the oblivion that has traditionally attached to the practice of science outside the circle of orthodoxy."[152] Probing the sources of interest in deviant science in the face of such disincentives for its pursuit, Henry suggests that, just as for mainstream scientists, those pursuing less-favored sciences are drawn by intellectual curiosity and by the urge to make significant discoveries.[153] But more than that

> Their work . . . might be interpreted as efforts to *re-enchant* the world *through* science. They would bring back into science's ken the monsters, giants, wee people, dread cataclysms . . . that once upon a time were exorcised from science and by science. There is, in other words, a fascinating apparent effort to be "for" science and yet, at the same time, against its "impoverishing" impact on our modern world view.[154]

Thus the work of the unorthodox, "popular" scientist is almost foreordained "to remain forever in the zone where science, the enchanted, and even the transcendent meet. . . . In sum, science is used to establish the existence of other realms into which orthodox science can't go."[155]

These two analyses of deviant sciences — one considering them as possible protosciences, the other depicting them as a sort of "missionary arm" of science in dialog with the transcendent — accurately reflect the ideological tensions that have hounded the UFO community almost from its inception.[156]

IN SEARCH OF CULTURAL LEGITIMACY

During a real-time discussion on America Online on October 26, 1995, MUFON founder and International Director Walt Andrus was asked if one has to study science in school in order to be a UFO investigator. "No," replied Andrus, "you do not have to but it is advantageous to have a science background. This is a scientific enigma. You are better able to cope if you have a scientific background." Indeed, the themes of the annual Mutual UFO Network symposia underscored the importance that the UFO community placed on its status as a field of scientific endeavor: "A Scientific Approach to the UFO Phenomenon" (1973), "A Scientific Assault on the UFO Enigma" (1974), "UFOs: A Scientific Challenge" (1983), and "UFOLOGY: The Emergence of a New Science" (1993).[157] Though MUFON, the oldest surviving grassroots UFO group in the United States in the 1990s, was an open membership organization, it actively solicited its professional members to serve as "consultants," listing about half a dozen new ones each month in the *MUFON UFO Journal,* along with their fields of specialization. Given the fact that MUFON membership began to decline in the late 1990s, it is reasonable to speculate that perhaps the many consultants thus named did not all remain interested and involved in the subject and that the published consultant lists reflected a "revolving door" parade of professionals into and out of a major UFO organization. Because the level of scientific training differed widely among the general membership, and because UFO research had unique features requiring a distinctive methodology, MUFON sought to improve the quality and consistency of its UFO investigations by producing a manual and testing procedures for certification of field investigators.[158] Attempting to organize professional interest in another way, the Center for UFO Studies was founded by Hynek as the official arm of a community of scientists who constituted an "invisible college" interested in UFO phenomena.[159] In addition to publishing a quarterly general-interest journal, the *International UFO Reporter,* CUFOS also published the *Journal of UFO Studies,* a refereed journal. The youngest organization on the UFO scene, and the one most removed from direct popular interest in UFOs, was the Fund for UFO Research Inc. (FUFOR), a group whose raison d'être was to raise funds from private citizens for UFO research and to award grants for UFO-related projects. As of 1995 the FUFOR had raised more than five hundred thousand dollars. Though all UFO research could not be supported by this fund, ufologists continued to propose projects that could be undertaken to further knowledge and understanding both with respect to UFOs in general and with respect to abductions in particular.[160] The chronological development of these organizations indicated the seriousness of the drive toward professionalization of the discipline, a drive that was reproduced in the pages of UFO publications in the form of regular calls for a more rigorous application of the scientific method to every facet of UFO research.[161]

Another aspect of that drive for professionalization was to capture the interest and participation of scientists in the mainstream. For ufology in general, but especially for the actively proscience branch of the UFO community, it was a triumph to gain the respectful attention of credentialed scientists. However, in order for interested scientists to feel reasonably safe in taking up an overt interest in UFOs, most had to have careers that were sufficiently progressed to make them at least somewhat immune to the negative sanctions they would likely suffer from the academic community. The professional ridicule suffered by James McDonald because of his UFO interests has already been noted. Hynek cited his own status as a junior scientist and concerns for his career as one reason for his reluctance to come forward as a UFO believer long after he had ceased to be an inveterate skeptic.[162] In the early 1990s the positive attention given to abduction accounts by Harvard psychiatrist John Mack was seen as a potentially significant breakthrough in ufology's relationship with the scientific establishment. Mack's status as a Harvard scholar and as a Pulitzer Prize–winning author combined to make his endorsement of the reality of abductions a particularly exciting and compelling one to many in the UFO community. However, the professional consequences of serious study of UFO phenomena had not changed a great deal since the days of Hynek and McDonald: Ufologists' excitement over Mack's interest was not shared by many of his colleagues at Harvard, who initiated a formal peer review after the publication of his popular book on abductions.[163] Beginning with the assertion that "there is no present definitive scientific proof establishing as a scientific fact that there exists any form of intelligent life in the universe other than human life," the committee expressed its concern that Mack was "sustaining delusional behavior in his patients" instead of discouraging it and, where appropriate, medically treating it.[164] But, unable to uphold the ideal of academic freedom and still censure Mack's choice of topics to study, they ultimately censured his abduction work on the grounds of methodological weakness while reaffirming his freedom to study whatever he wished.[165]

In 1997 the UFO community noted with approval that the Society for Scientific Exploration (a skeptics' organization less doctrinaire than CSICOP) had convened an international panel of scientists to review UFO evidence with a view toward answering the question of whether the subject deserved further scientific investigation. The panel's answer in the affirmative was greeted with pleasure by ufologists.[166] Equally well received was the 1999 release of a French report by a number of scientists, military officers, and a variety of other experts. The document, a result of several years' study, stated that the numbers of reliable UFO reports from around the world that have accumulated during the past fifty years "compel us now to reconsider all hypotheses as to the origin of UFOs, especially extraterrestrial hypotheses."[167]

THE SCIENCE OF RELIGION IN UFOLOGY

Though the first decades of the modern UFO era focused on winning scientific respectability for UFO studies, ufology came to suffer from a condition common to all rejected knowledge: having an "inordinate respect and envy" for the Establishment and pointing with pride to any kind of mainstream support it received, coupled with scorn and ridicule for the "dogmatic" narrowness of an Establishment that refused to grant it recognition and legitimacy.[168]

There were always some in the UFO world who rejected science in part or in whole as an explanatory framework for UFO phenomena. This ambivalence, too, was reflected in the themes of the annual MUFON symposia, such as in "UFOs: Defiance to Science" (1971) and "UFOs: Beyond the Mainstream of Science" (1986). Some ufologists felt that the deductive method of science was simply the wrong tool to use to learn about UFOs.[169] Others felt that the tools of science worked, but the discipline itself was too narrow-minded to deal with the facts thus discovered. Science, they said, needed to enlarge its cognitive categories before it would be able to adequately address such a "complex, multifaceted" phenomenon as UFOs.[170] Some emphasized the need for more interdisciplinarity among the sciences in the study of UFOs.[171] Others suggested that scientific approaches should be augmented by insights from disciplines such as philosophy.[172]

As time passed, some scientifically trained ufologists slowly recognized that there were advantages in not being accepted by the Establishment. The most important advantage was the freedom to research whatever one felt to be significant without having to answer to a central authority whose control of research funds would determine what got studied and what got published.[173] To the general public — many of whom now believed in the reality of UFOs — the reluctance of science to fully engage the UFO question only justified their growing disenchantment with science.[174] "When an ordinary person witnesses something which lacks an obvious reference, and which science renounces both knowledge of and interest in, then he turns to the student of mystery. He may well get a rather curious response, . . . but at least he is listened to."[175] As the "purely scientific approach" appeared increasingly untenable, the path toward further ufological insight seemed to lie in other directions, such as the occult.[176]

There had been an association between UFOs and the psychic or occult from the earliest years of ufology. One of the first proponents of the occult link attempted to maintain at least a formal association with a scientific approach as well. In 1960 Trevor James claimed that inspirational contact from UFO occupants was being made not only among the contactees, but among scientists too. It was, he suggested, "a special kind of an educational programme."[177] "But," he explained later, "such men hold their tongues for fear of ridicule, social ostracism, and of being

hurled into mental institutions."[178] James pointed out that the fact that
UFO research was being conducted largely by "scientific amateurs" indicated just how fearful orthodox scientists were. Amateurs were the only
ones willing to take the risks. The proper approach to UFOs, he said, was
a "spiritually scientific" one in which the scientist would throw his entire
self into a participatory investigation of the phenomenon and then communicate his findings in a rational, scientific fashion to his colleagues.
James cautioned, however, that the entities being encountered by UFO
witnesses were both "of the anti-Christ" and of "the Christ forces," with
the agenda of the former being to enslave humanity and the agenda of
the latter to emancipate it. Attempting to pursue a fully scientific (qua
spiritually informed) investigation, he warned, was dangerous, and he
recommended that it only be undertaken by those scientists with "awakened minds." In 1962 James elaborated on the need for natural scientists
with "a working knowledge of occult science" to investigate UFOs. In
the final analysis, however, he expected most of the revolutionary knowledge to come from occult practitioners rather than from scientists,
because natural science was "a measuring science" and thus an approach
too limited for ufological study.[179]

By 1968 there was growing recognition among some members of the
UFO community that a variety of psychic phenomena seemed to occur
to people who had had UFO encounters, leading to speculation that
both might be essentially the same type of thing, or that psychic phenomena might be an aftereffect of a person's contact with tangible,
physically real UFOs.[180] At the very least, the psychic connection seemed
to indicate that an alliance between scientific studies of UFOs and of
psychic phenomena (especially manifestations) might be in order,
though there were many in both fields who were reluctant to complicate
their already marginalized status in mainstream scientific circles by associating themselves with the other field of inquiry.[181] Nevertheless, some
pressed the paraphysical issue in ufology.[182] It is an irony of UFO history
that several of the physical scientists who were actively involved in
studying UFOs eventually championed this "psychic link" hypothesis. J.
Allen Hynek, first a convert from skeptic to believer, later came to feel
that "the scientific framework, by its very internal logic, excludes certain classes of phenomena, of which UFOs may be one."[183] Wilbert B.
Smith, once director of Canada's "Project Magnet" to detect UFO activity, came to adopt a paraphysical theory of UFOs, as did biologist Ivan
T. Sanderson and numerous others.[184]

Although some saw ufology's entertainment of theories other than the extraterrestrial hypothesis as a welcome "weaning" from outgrown ideas, others defended the ETH and sought to keep UFO phenomena clearly separated from the realm of metaphysics and the occult. A comparative study of apparition reports and UFO entity reports observed that although there were similarities between the two, there were also important differences. Given the fact that the aliens' mode of transportation was obviously superior to anything of which humanity was capable, it seemed reasonable to conclude that they were "super-intelligences" whose "lofty degree of development would not be evident only in technological achievements" but would also extend to an understanding of and ability to manipulate "material and spiritual reality." Thus, argued one ufologist, it was easy to see why they might appear to be metaphysical entities yet remain conventionally, physically extraterrestrial.[185] And if they were extraterrestrial, then they were subject to investigation and ultimately to understanding via the methods and models provided by science.

THE CENTRAL PROBLEM: ARE WE ALONE?

In addition to the evidentiary and methodological issues that came between mainstream scientists and ufologists, there were political and social issues that contributed to the disinclination to accept the UFO phenomenon as real. Three of those stand out: the end of World War II, the beginning of the Cold War, and the space race. The struggles of World War II had made American intellectuals and policymakers keenly aware of the dangers of unscientific thought raised to the level of a national ideology. It was scientific illiteracy and confusion that had led the German people to support the Nazi political machine with its "insane racial theories."[186] Thus when it was decided that UFOs were not real, continued belief in their existence seemed to pose a threat to the security of the United States not only because it might be used by enemies to disguise a real attack (as the Robertson Panel suggested in 1953) but also because it was an example of the same kind of confusion that had led to the disastrous situation in Germany. In short, unscientific beliefs like UFO reality posed a potential danger to democracy on both a practical and an ideological level. To educate the public out of its belief in UFOs seemed to be not only a rational necessity but a patriotic duty.

Equally important in the worldview making it difficult to take an interest in UFO reports was the fact that the beginning of the modern UFO era coincided with the beginning of the Cold War. To meet the challenge of defending the West against possible communist aggression, the United States had brought some of the best rocketry experts of Nazi Germany into the country to assist in the development of missiles capable of delivering nuclear warheads to Russian targets. Because the Russians were assumed to have done the same, the appearance of UFOs in American air space was initially considered a security issue more than a scientific one. By the time it had become apparent that UFOs were not a physical threat, the human use of space for strategic and scientific purposes seemed a real possibility to military planners and scientists — one they were willing to invest in. But another kind of space exploration program, the SETI program using a radio-telescopic approach, was not widely or enthusiastically supported. Indeed, governmental support for SETI, which held out the hope only of long-distance extraterrestrial contact, was modest — and all too often in danger of being cut,[187] presumably because SETI did not have many obvious military applications. When it came to allocating research resources, UFO studies seemed to promise even less than SETI in the way of tangible military benefits that could be turned to fighting communist expansion.

In addition neither the SETI program nor ufology could promise to satisfy other important aspirations of the day, which were frankly Christian and missionary. In his study of the religious valences of technological development in the twentieth century, David Noble recounts the symbolic resonance of the idea of flight with the idea of the Ascension of Christ and how that symbol worked in the space race during the 1950s, 1960s, and 1970s:

> Religious inspiration, coupled with Cold War competition, fueled the manned-spaceflight effort. . . . It was God's purpose, wrote [Werner] von Braun . . . "to send his Son to the other worlds to bring the gospel to them." Von Braun had come to view spaceflight as a millennial "new beginning" for mankind, the second and final phase of his divinely ordained destiny. The astronaut, the mortal agent of this new "cosmic" era, was thus another Adam, conceived to extend the promise of redemption across the celestial sea.[188]

Von Braun's religious vision was echoed in the atmosphere (if not in the official mission statements) at NASA installations in Huntsville, Alabama, in Cape Canaveral, Florida, and in Houston. In the early years of the space program, displays of religious conviction by NASA personnel sometimes went unquestioned by NASA officials.[189] And a religious orientation was typical of the astronauts, many of whom were professing Christians who expressed their faith commitments in their public role as astronauts by reading Bible passages or reciting prayers from space, leaving Bibles on the Moon, and even performing the first lunar-based Communion service.[190] For an age that could find embodiment of its religious convictions and aspirations in a program of space exploration, the pursuit of elusive UFOs within our own atmosphere seemed far less compelling. The notion of extraterrestrial contact in this kind of religious context implied us going there — not them coming here.

It is tempting to look even more deeply into this small confluence of events and see a piece of the American psyche revealing itself. In his study of the cultural dance between religion and science in early-twentieth-century America, Gilbert saw the UFO controversy as a search for a new language and an "imaginative framework" within which to understand humanity's relationship to the universe.[191] One way of viewing the framework that ufology presented is to see it as having suggested that instead of being the explorers, the colonizers, and the missionaries of space, the inhabitants of planet Earth might instead be the explored, the colonized, and the missionized. This was, at a deep and inarticulate level, simply inconceivable to a society still intoxicated by the successes of World War II, enjoying postwar affluence and beginning to parent what would become one of the largest generational cohorts in the nation's history. The late 1940s and the 1950s were a time of large thoughts and large plans. The idea of alien vehicles circumnavigating the globe with impunity was inimical to the self-image and exploratory thrust of a country that had taken on the role of military guardian and economic savior of the world and that had its eye on the heavens.

But after all the social, political, and scientific reasons were offered for the rejection or the acceptance of the reality of UFOs, the whole issue always came down to a question of belief, and this raised the entire affair "almost to a pseudo-religious level" for all concerned.[192] Mainstream scientists and ufologists had two different cognitive maps of the world — of reality — which shared only some areas of overlap. No matter what the evidence, mainstream science just could not believe that the Earth was being visited by extraterrestrials, and could always find reasons — some better than others — for their doubt. And ufologists could always find cases — some better than others — that suggested that scientists had closed their eyes to important evidence that UFOs were real.

Some ufologists tried valiantly to shift the scientific debate away from the ETH and focus it simply on the question of whether there were anomalous aerial objects that could be usefully studied by science.[193] But questions about UFO reality and the use of the ETH to understand it were hard to separate. If you took all witness statements at face value, the reported actions of UFOs seemed to indicate that there was some kind of intelligence guiding them. The UFO community eventually came to hold a variety of views about their provenance — many of them incompatible with scientists' views. Some proposed that UFOs were from a civilization inside the Earth and accessible mainly through the polar regions, or that UFOs were visitors from time, or top secret terrestrial craft, or biological atmospheric life forms.[194] The most popular alternative to the ETH in UFO circles, the theory that UFOs were paraphysical manifestations, sounded to some ufologists and to most mainstream scientists like a reversion to prescientific occult explanations for the unknown.[195] If ufologists had to argue for UFO reality in a way that addressed the issue of UFO origins, the ETH was at least more scientifically respectable. But that was not always saying a lot.

For most of the twentieth century the idea that life might have evolved on other planets had been a popular but very contested one, even in scientific circles. Those scientists who devoted their careers to the pursuit of evidence for extraterrestrial life or in fields where the existence of extraterrestrial life was a lingering background assumption were considered by the rest of the scientific community to be on the precarious boundary of scientific legitimacy.[196] The association of the idea of extraterrestrial life with the phenomenon of UFOs merely joined one marginally acceptable hypothesis in the scientific community with another that was quite outside the community. Many scientists were not disposed to be convinced that either hypothesis was sound. The existence of extraterrestrial life — especially intelligent extraterrestrial life — was considered likely to remain a hypothesis, at best, for many years to come. For all intents and purposes, for this day and age, science said authoritatively that UFOs could not exist because humanity was alone in the universe. And even if extraterrestrial life did exist, said their more hopeful peers, what was the likelihood that such life would want to visit human beings, the "retarded cousins in the backwoods" of the Milky Way galaxy?[197] About such self-deprecating assessments, Rabbi Norman Lamm commented, "A number of scientists have become intoxicated with the sense of their own unimportance. Never before have so many been so enthusiastic about being so trivial."[198]

CHAPTER FOUR

Ufology and the Imaginal

There needs to be a large warning sign posted on the entry to UFO studies: "The study of the UFO phenomenon is NOT a substitute for religious belief; if you need emotional or spiritual fulfillment you will not find it here."

Anonymous subscriber, *Contact Forum,*
newsletter for abductees/experiencers

In any other generation, a force like this would have been called God. The religion issue will not soon go away from UFO studies.

Barry H. Downing, "The Second Coming
of Marshall Applewhite," *MUFON UFO Journal*

In many ways the study of UFOs has exemplified modernity's conflicted relationship with the "Other." In a transcendent sense, this alone qualifies ufology as having religious valences. But even in a more mundane sense, religion and ufology have been intertwined, because religious motives have so often been imputed to UFO witnesses, UFO investigators, and those who believe them. Yet although many in the UFO community struggled with mainstream science, they nevertheless tended (or intended) to use a scientific framework for understanding UFO phenomena. There was almost no room in the organized study of aerial anomalies for religion, which one theologically oriented ufologist candidly described as a "'wart' on what [ufology] hoped was a scientific hog."[1] Indeed, at the 1992 abduction conference held at M.I.T., participants were very unwilling to "deal with the spiritual and religious issues" surrounding encounters.[2]

In part this rejection of religion stemmed from the contactee phenomenon, with its salvific pronouncements about the beneficent space brothers. To most people in the UFO movement, the contactees sounded like pathetic purveyors of a quasi-religious message clad in space-age garb.

Indeed, most contactees were students of spiritualism and Theosophy who had adopted a mantle that was (at the very least) quasi-scientific and modern—the UFO phenomenon. The apparently hard-edged reality of UFOs, and the superior levels of technological achievement (and presumably of moral development) of the UFO operators, dovetailed nicely with preexisting worldviews that included infinitely wise spirit guides and Ascended Masters.[3]

The larger UFO myth did not originate in the teachings of Theosophy or spiritualism, however; it entered American consciousness as spontaneous personal experiences whose apparently real-world tangibility caused them to be reported as fact, retold as story, and eventually embraced as a veritable cultural myth.[4] Its emergence as a modern myth, combined with the psychological and spiritual impact reported by many who had a UFO experience, helped to nudge the entire subject toward the realm of religion. But if you wanted to understand a real-world event, you turned to science, not to religion, because religion in the West was no longer the Great Legitimator, the arbiter of Truth and determiner of Reality. Being reported first as factual, real-world encounters, UFO phenomena were predisposed to being studied first from a materialistic rather than a metaphysical point of view. Thus the status of UFO reports as factual claims also accounts in part for the early rejection of religion as an interpretive framework for UFO studies.

Nevertheless, religion continually intersected with UFO phenomena and those who were interested in them in a variety of ways. Donald Menzel, ufology's first official scientific debunker, was frequently vexed by correspondents who wrote to him to report sightings but who refused to accept his prosaic explanations. Sometimes these correspondents would attempt to bolster their case by pointing out UFO-like phenomena described in the Bible.[5] At other times they would simply offer biblically based barbs, as in the case of the man who, after some months' correspondence with Menzel, wrote that he could "understand better now just why Jesus Christ gathered about him relatively unschooled men, instead of trying to convince the 'learned' of his day."[6]

Within the UFO community the encounter with religion took shape most clearly in theories that aliens from other worlds—ancient astronauts—had visited Earth in the distant past and that their visits were recorded in sacred texts as divine encounters.[7] This purely evidentiary interest in the history of religions was seldom matched by any sustained discussion within the UFO community of theological or doctrinal issues that UFO reality might provoke. Most of the theologically oriented reflections that were offered stood within the ancient-astronauts frame of reference rather than within a mainstream Judeo-Christian frame and continued the ufological tradition of rejecting religion. For example, in *Past Shock: The Origin of Religion and Its Impact on the Human Soul,* Jack Barranger suggested that extraterrestrial geneticists engineered the human race as a workforce and gave us religion in order to keep us dumb and subservient and to hide knowledge of the true God.[8] In *God Games: What Do You Do Forever?* Neil Freer states that "religion as we know it is a cargo cult sublimation of the ancient master-slave relationship" for which humanity was created. In reality, he suggested, the creators of humankind endowed us with remarkable mental and spiritual abilities but discouraged the development of those gifts by means of the religious forms they gave us.[9] Outside of these critiques, more doctrinally oriented reflections on religion and UFOs were left to a handful of religious scholars and ministers in the UFO community who occasionally wrote short essays on the subject. Outside the UFO community, very few scholars and theologians took an interest in addressing the implications that contact with alien intelligence might have for religion. It was within the context of this mainstream theological silence that religion was encountered in the UFO world.

CONFRONTING THE NUMINOUS

The eventual movement by some of the UFO community in the 1980s and 1990s toward a more religious-cum-metaphysical framework for understanding UFO phenomena was primarily the result of two things: the failure to find a "home" for ufology within mainstream science and the personal impact that UFO experiences had on percipients — not to mention on many UFO investigators. Witnesses to UFO phenomena often described their experiences as extraordinary, life-changing events — and the language of awe, the language of the dumbfounded, is a religious language. "It changed my life ever since that day," one man wrote in a letter to his local newspaper. A quarter of a century earlier he had spent five minutes watching a lighted disk hover thirty yards away from where he stood.[10] Another UFO witness reported a sighting in July 1957 involving an aircraft carrier and four destroyers conducting exercises at sea. A cigar-shaped object had followed the vessels, he said, and performed incredible aerial acrobatics for more than twenty minutes. While a ship's photographer snapped pictures, "Dozens of officers and men, including both Protestant and Catholic chaplains, had assumed a genuflective position, with hands clasped in front of their faces, or raised on high, a most stirring sight indeed."[11]

The numinous quality of some UFO experiences was not lost on the scientifically minded, either. One physicist who conducted field research during a regional UFO flap described a very close, multiwitness sighting to which he was a party:

> A great wave of excitement overwhelmed me. Never had I experienced such exhilaration. UFOs really exist. And I was an eyewitness! . . . [Later that night] I slowly succumbed to sleep, believing that my life would never be the same. . . . For more than a year, as I approached that particular episode during public lectures, I had difficulty dealing with the emotion it stirred. Even now, the impact of the experience may surface without warning.[12]

This same scientist — a man who had been reluctant to become involved in UFO study because of the professional dangers it posed — later reflected on his UFO investigation:

> More was involved than the measurement of physical properties of UFOs by dispassionate observers. A relationship, a cognizance, between us and the UFO intelligence evolved. A game was played. . . . In this Project, we dealt with an intelligence equal to or greater than that of man. . . . In my opinion, this additional consideration is more important than the measurements or establishing that the phenomenon exists. This facet of the UFO phenomenon perturbed me as much as the advanced technology we observed. It is a facet I cannot really fathom — and I have thought about it every day for more than seven years.[13]

Even in the officially atheistic Soviet Union, the numinous quality of UFO sightings could not be suppressed. In one Soviet republic, a sighting flap was interpreted as a warning sign from supernatural beings, resulting in a "widespread religious revival and a return to God," much to the consternation of Soviet authorities, who pronounced witnesses to be "loonies, liars or traitors."[14]

When all was said and done, ufology's most significant encounter (or confrontation) with religion took place not in the persons of contactees, not in abstract theological speculations, and not in quests for ancient astronauts, but in the personal experiences of UFO witnesses and their subsequent attempts to make sense of those experiences. The result of these space-age theophanies on the UFO community was a form of what Phyllis Tickle has called "god-talk" — unofficial, nonsystematic theological reflections informed by the daily lives and experiences of the conversants.[15] God-talk in the UFO community, however, was often conducted using the rhetoric of science rather than religion and sought to touch base not with the verities of revealed Truth, but with the verities of empirically derived truth. As theologian Ted Peters observed, "If we are compelled to translate our spiritual concerns into naturalistic or scientific terms, then we need nothing short of the infinity of the stars to capture our specula-tions."[16] The UFO community was a place where the infinity of the stars was explicit in the everyday concerns of UFO witnesses and investiga-tors. It was a place where people could discuss "religious feelings in seemingly scientific terms."[17] It was in many respects a liminal commu-nity, poised — at first uncomfortably, but later with some degree of accep tance — between the worlds of science and religion.

The first perceptible movement toward a more metaphysical under-standing of UFOs within the larger UFO community came in the 1960s as the high-profile influence of the contactees waned in popular culture and abductions became recognized and investigable phenomena in the UFO world. By this time ufologists had gathered enough sighting reports to be impressed by the odd behavior of UFOs: sharp, right-angle turns; rapid changes of shape and size; "blinking in" and a few minutes later "blinking out" in front of astonished observers; and rapid accelerations and decelerations that no physical body could withstand. The incom-mensurability of this behavior with the laws of physics often unnerved witnesses, like the young man who, while hunting with two friends, had come upon a UFO hovering six feet above the ground. Reporting the encounter, he confessed, "If anybody comes in contact like we did and is still able to think straight, he is a better man than I am and I will admit it any time."[18]

The entity sighting reports were even more perplexing. It seemed that the aliens were forever picking up plants and rocks. When they chanced to speak to an observer, they often asked bizarre questions like "What is your time frame?" or made odd statements, as when a farmer investigat-ing an uproar in the yard one night found strange entities trying to corner one of his terrified hunting dogs. "We come in peace," he reported them saying. "We only want to take your dog."[19] As the years passed and abduction reports became more numerous, the same pattern of odd behavior associated with UFOs was reinforced: alien repetition of certain activities well beyond what seemed logical to ufologists, and, given the years of exposure the presumed extraterrestrials had had with Earth, surprising naïveté about human behavior. This lacuna in alien knowledge became apparent as increasing numbers of abduction reports surfaced and baffled many — investigators and abductees alike. One abductee try-ing to prevent another alien encounter reported that he went to bed clutching a crucifix. When he woke up one night with the familiar paralysis and sense of alien presence, he began praying. As the aliens approached his bed, one of them noticed this behavior and asked what he was doing, to which the other responded, "Oh, he's just practicing his religion," and they took him anyway. Yet another abductee reported that he had tried to prevent an abduction by winding string all around himself before he went to bed at night. This person reported that as the aliens approached his bed they stopped, stared at the string, and, not knowing what to do with a trussed victim, turned around and left without him![20]

As ufologists tried to analyze the evidence with all of its mystery and oddity, they slowly began to admit that the reported observations of UFOs and their occupants were not easily assimilable to the extant scientific worldview.[21] Investigators found themselves confronted with a series of observations that seemed incomprehensible without a new and more imaginative approach than traditional science could muster.[22] As one abductee observed, "Even when Ufology does become accepted as an authentic and necessary subject of study, I am afraid that mainstream science as it currently stands does not possess the pioneer vision to fully establish a concept encompassing the entire scope of the UFO enigma."[23] Under these circumstances, the path of inquiry that seemed to hold the most promise for illuminating the mystery of UFOs while remaining at least somewhat in touch with the scientific world was parapsychological.[24]

COMPARATIVE PERSPECTIVES IN UFOLOGY

By the mid-1960s psychic research had enjoyed a semblance of scientific respectability for nearly forty years under the leadership of J. B. Rhine, who directed a pioneering research program at Duke University. Although initially inspired by a desire to legitimate scientifically the spiritualist assertion that there is life after death, Rhine eventually focused his investigations on an attempt to find scientific proof for the existence of extrasensory perception and psychokinetic abilities.[25] But like most parapsychological researchers, he was unable to produce experimental proof that would satisfy his critics, to whom the entire enterprise looked like nothing so much as a contribution to metaphysical speculation rather than any kind of scientific research.[26] As was the case with ufology, mainstream scientists' rejection of Rhine's work was not always based strictly on the evidence. J. Allen Hynek recounted a conversation he overheard between Rhine and another man at a conference where

Rhine presented his research findings. The other man confessed that Rhine's results were impressive and that if only one-tenth that amount of data had been obtained from research in his own (more mainstream) field of study, he would not have hesitated to accept it as legitimate evidence. "But I'd have to have a hundred times more from the ESP field," he admitted.[27] Rhine's failure to win science to the cause of paranormal research induced some of his successors to look to the occult for clues on how to pursue their study, with a view this time not toward replicating the categories of thought and procedures used in modern science, but instead to correct them.[28] They came to agree with the ufologist who observed that "Our physical science, equipped to deal only with the physical, will NEVER be able to cope with the paraphysical."[29]

Like parapsychologists in the years after Rhine, some leading ufologists in the years after the Condon Committee and the closure of Project Blue Book looked increasingly often outside of science for insights into UFOs. As interest in abductions grew during the 1970s, occult teachings that depicted the universe as a place teeming with life and intelligence seemed to have more potential relevance to ufology than the scientific worldview had. But, like the parapsychologists, that did not mean that ufologists were ready to dismiss science; instead, they sought to redefine its conceptual categories. "So, we have to look for another framework. If we find that other framework then who cares about UFOs? The effect will be much greater than just explaining UFOs!" enthused Jacques Vallee, who was one of the first well-known scientifically trained ufologists to venture deeply and thoughtfully into the paranormal aspects of UFO phenomena.[30]

Disgusted by the response of mainstream science to the UFO problem, in the late 1960s Vallee, who held advanced degrees in astrophysics and computer science, began to investigate the relationship between modern UFO sighting reports and folklore describing contact with elves, dwarves, fairies, and the like. He reported his findings in *Passport to Magonia,* his third UFO book but his first to consider the problem outside of a scientific framework.[31] The approach he adopted was comparative, in which historical tales of encounters with an "aerial people" were set alongside their modern UFO counterparts. His conclusion was that

> The modern, global belief in flying saucers and their occupants is identical to an earlier belief in the fairy faith. The entities described as the pilots of the craft are indistinguishable from the elves, sylphs, and lutins of the Middle Ages. . . . . We are concerned with an agency our ancestors knew

well and regarded with terror; we are prying into the affairs of the Secret Commonwealth.[32]

Vallee's discoveries were embraced by a subcommunity of ufologists who enlarged his comparative project by looking at other sources and traditions that mentioned entity encounters. Those advocating this comparative approach to UFO research felt that the widened perspective thus achieved enabled them to be less taken in and befuddled by the oddities of the land of "Magonia" —

> the domain of the in-between, the unproven, and the unprovable, . . . the country of paradoxes, strangely furnished with material "proofs," sometimes seemingly unimpeachable, but always ultimately insufficient. . . . This absolutely confusing (and manifestly misleading) aspect . . . may well be the phenomenon's most basic characteristic.[33]

Captain Ivar Mackay, then chair of the British UFO Research Association (BUFORA), turned to the Kabalah to learn more about UFOs and their occupants. He realized that this approach would be unacceptable to those in the UFO community "suffering from the 'nuts and bolts' syndrome."[34] But, he asked, "who is there to deny that the information offered by the great Scholars, Metaphysicists and Occultists over vast periods of time is any less reliable or valuable than the postulates and dogmas of a few generations of scientists?" In fact, Mackay pointed out, recent discoveries and theories of science were likely to validate the ancient wisdom of the mystics and occultists.[35] Other ufologists compared UFO entities to descriptions of the jinn of the Moslem cosmos or the demons of the Christian one.[36] Others suggested that they might be more akin to "elementals" — the spirits inhabiting trees, water, rocks, flowers, and so on.[37]

One of the more important consequences of the comparative project in ufology was that it opened a door not just to religious and occult lore but also to textually based approaches to understanding UFO phenomena and thus to interest in ancient astronaut theories. In ufology the single most influential theorist of alien visitation in antiquity was Zechariah Sitchin, who based his ideas on texts such as the Sumerian *Epic of Gilgamesh,* the *Enuma Elish,* the Greek *Odyssey,* and the Hebrew Bible.[38] Richard Thompson, a science educator and journalist holding a Ph.D. in mathematics from Cornell University, arrived at similar conclusions based on his reading of ancient Vedic texts describing a sky-dwelling race who traveled in aerial conveyances called *vimanas.*[39] Presbyterian minister Barry Downing plumbed the Christian scriptures for possible indications of early extraterrestrial visitations.[40] F. W. Holiday, a freelance journalist, found equally compelling evidence for alien visitation in the material artifacts of the "disk" cultures of the prehistoric British Isles.[41] And astronomer Robert Temple suggested that alien visitation was the only way to explain the complex knowledge about the Sirius binary-star system possessed by the primitive Dogon tribe in Africa.[42] This kind of reading of ancient texts and of archeological and anthropological evidence was not based on a will to believe, but rather on a determination not to disbelieve. The method was to look at (some) ancient texts as records of historical events rendered in the only language available to pretechnological societies. Elements of the texts that had been interpreted by other scholars as mere metaphorical language were in fact, these new theorists suggested, instances of the use of nontechnological language to describe real technological wonders and attendant incredible events.

In some ways the comparative project in UFO studies can be seen as the filtering down into popular consciousness of elements of the historical-critical method of biblical scholarship and the comparative approach to religion, both of which heavily influenced liberal theology in the nineteenth and twentieth centuries. Advocates of the historical-critical school of interpretation reexamined the Christian scriptures with the same scholarly tools that were used to evaluate other ancient texts in order to uncover historical facts that had long been blended with (or buried by) supernatural elements. Theologians working within this framework had various ideas about the significance of these elements but generally agreed that they reflected the cosmological assumptions of the era. For the sake of credibility to modern readers, some theologians wanted to separate the supernatural from the historical parts of the biblical Christian story. Others emphasized the importance of the supernatural as an aspect of the early Christian witness. Of this latter group, some insisted that the supernatural events described in the scriptures were literal, real-world manifestations of God's actions in the processes of history. Others said it would be a mistake for modern readers to feel obligated to believe that such fantastic stories reflected real-world events. Rather, they suggested, supernatural elements in the Christian story were imaginative ways by which early Christians had witnessed to truth of the highest kind: the truth of the Christian message.[43]

Historicizers studying UFOs and ancient astronauts absorbed the historical-critical theological zeitgeist — and took it one step further. In recognizing the ancients as witnesses to real events who were trying to convey what they had experienced, ufologists not only accepted supernatural events in the text, they naturalized them. They refused to treat the "supernatural" elements differently than the "historical" based on what we currently supposed to be possible or impossible. This historical-reality approach brought so-called supernatural phenomena in ancient texts into the provenance of modernity and subjected them to more straightforward interpretation. The results of such a strategy could sometimes be quite surprising. For instance, NASA engineer Josef Blumrich, amused but unconvinced by the claims of ancient astronaut theorist Erich von Däniken, decided to apply his engineering expertise to construct a schematic for the object seen by Ezekiel in his "wheel within a wheel" vision.[44] To his surprise, the results indicated that Ezekiel had in fact observed some kind of structured craft with aerodynamic properties. In light of this, he suggested that in the future engineers should be involved in the interpretation of all archeological discoveries and ancient texts.[45]

Although some ufologists felt that the comparative enterprise contributed valuable information to the fund of UFO knowledge, others wanted to keep the study of UFOs clearly distinguished from the realm of metaphysics and the occult. Nevertheless, given the odd behavior of UFOs and UFO occupants, paraphysical theories seemed to have more explanatory power than traditionally scientific ones. For those who tried to find a rational balancing point between high-strangeness UFO phenomena, the scientific laws of motion, and paraphysical and occult theories, the New Physics offered a welcome perspective.

Quantum theory (and to a lesser extent relativity theory) were popularized in the 1970s as part of the consciousness revolution and the surge of spiritual questing that was inaugurated by the Baby Boomers who had just so tumultuously come of age. The basic insights of the New Physics are that all of reality is actually a unified whole; that the matter that makes up our experience of reality has no ontological status but is a construct of what seems to be Consciousness or Mind; that the constructions of Mind most likely include dimensions or universes that are largely (or wholly) unknowable by residents of our own space-time construct; and that Mind and its operations are nonlocal — that is, Mind is not contained or constrained by the parameters of the realities it generates.[46] Although most popularizers of quantum physics had no particular interest in the relationship of UFO phenomena to their topic, Michael Talbot proposed that the paraphysical aspects of UFOs were nicely explicable in the context of a dynamically constructed, holographic universe (a universe in which what appears is constantly being created by Mind and has as much ontological substance as a holographic image).[47] Citing the work of mythologists like Mircea Eliade and Joseph Campbell who taught that myth-making was "an organic and necessary expression of the human race," Talbot proposed that the myth-making propensity of the collective human psyche was made manifest in UFO appearances and encounters. The point, he stressed, was not that UFOs were insubstantial psychic projections (or delusions or hysteria), but that they were real, ontologically valid products of the reality-making activity of the collective human consciousness as a part of the larger, universal Consciousness or Mind.[48]

This interest in human consciousness as a reality creator linked to UFOs was taken up by philosopher Paul Davies in the context of a discussion of religious miracles:

> It is interesting to note that many of the symbols of alleged supernatural religious events have reappeared among the modern UFO cults. Take, for example, the stories of witnesses who claim to have been abruptly cured of some long-standing medical complaint after an encounter with UFO occupants, or occasionally by merely sighting a UFO itself. Levitation also plays a prominent part. . . . Clearly, aerial phenomena, levitation and healing powers are deep-rooted in the human psyche. In the age of magic they were prominent and overt. With the development of organized religion, they became refined and submerged, but the strong primeval element has never been far below the surface. Now, with the decline of organized religion, they have re-surfaced again in technological guise.[49]

Similarly, in a study of near-death experiencers and abductees, psychologist Kenneth Ring proposed that both kinds of experiences were functionally and structurally equivalent, being generated by Mind at Large and serving to induct experiencers into an "imaginal" realm — that is, a realm with form and dimension and intelligence that is usually apprehended only in altered states of consciousness.[50]

The term *imaginal* was taken from the writings of Henry Corbin, a scholar of Muslim mysticism, who in turn based the notion on the work of a twelfth-century Sufi named Ibn al-'Arabī.[51] According to al-'Arabī, the imaginal realm is an inherently ambiguous world that stands between the corporeal and the spiritual worlds and must be understood in terms of both. Manifestations from this realm can bring entities from there into contact with the corporeal world of human beings in such a way that the sensory impressions made on human observers are virtually indistinguishable from the sensory impressions made by ordinary material objects. Yet, being composed as much of spirit as of matter, entities (such as jinn) and things from the imaginal realm possess capabilities beyond those available to inhabitants of the corporeal world.[52] Patrick Harpur, in a sustained exploration of human interaction with the imaginal realm, suggested that the human faculty of imagination is the medium through which the imaginal realm — the abode of the forces classically known as daimonic — is able to manifest itself in our reality. Unlike the skeptics who see imagination pathologically and call it "fantasy proneness," Harpur presented it as an essential component of an accurate and whole-some relationship to the universe:

> People who "see things" such as phantom animals and UFOs are presumed to be "over-imaginative." Maybe the reverse is true: those who "believe in" UFOs, etc., and long to see them, notoriously do not. They have already imaginatively accommodated the daimonic. It is the people who have no conscious relation to daimonic reality who commonly "see things." If Imagi-nation is denied autonomy and recognition, it is forced, as it were, to mount a stronger display — to body forth its images not only externally but con-cretely, because no more subtle approach will impress the literal-minded per-cipient. . . . They answer our modern requirement for quantifiable effects.[53]

A similar sentiment was expressed by abductee Whitley Strieber at an early stage in his coming-to-terms with his own experiences. Our twenti-eth century, he pointed out, is "the first time that man has simply refused to respond to the ghosts and the gods. . . . Is that why," he asked, "[the Visitors] have become so physical, so real, dragging people out of bed like rapists in the night — because they must have our notice in order to somehow be confirmed in their own truth?"[54]

Although opening the door once again to a more scientifically grounded understanding of UFO phenomena, the New Physics also posed certain dangers as an interpretive framework, most particularly the danger that talk about Mind creating reality and the value of imagination was too easily collapsed into (or confused with) the simpler notion that UFOs were hallucinations and delusions. It made it easier, however, to work with the idea that parallel universes or dimensions might exist and that those dimensions might be inhabited by intelligent life forms.[55] The idea that the universe is characterized by a "creative potency" leading to life and to consciousness had been proposed by theoretical physicists such as Freeman Dyson and Frank Tipler.[56] When joined to the New Physics, theories about an intrinsically creative, multidimensional uni-verse provided a way to understand not only the provenance of UFOs but also the oddities of UFO phenomena. For instance, the sudden appearances, shape-shifting, and disappearances of UFOs could be conceptualized as the passage of an object (or being?) from another dimension through our own dimensions, the changing shapes representing only that part of the object that was intersecting with our dimensional reality at any moment.[57] Given that in other dimensions or universes the evolution of intelligence might have progressed further than in our own, it seemed reasonable to some ufologists to speculate that these intelligences had developed a dimensional technology enabling them to visit us.[58]

But science was unable to offer suggestions as to what those other intelligences might be like. Indeed, because the existence of these other dimensions was only a part of theoretical physics and not yet a proven fact, science was far from ready to tackle the question of what kinds of life (if any) might exist there and whether it could have visited us. Some ufologists had hoped that the new paradigm of reality suggested by the New Physics would "eventually lead the scientific community to embrace ufology as a legitimate science." The difficulty, however, was that in embracing these new scientific theories and linking them to UFO studies, ufologists were leaps and bounds beyond what mainstream science could or would do. And, truth be told, not everyone in the UFO community was sold on the ideas of the New Physics. Even without being associated with UFO phenomena, the New Physics seemed to some to be dangerously close to "that which [ufologists] have for so long disdained — the mystical and the paranormal."[59]

JACQUES VALLEE AND JOHN KEEL

In 1958, shortly after the launch of the first satellites by the Soviet Union and the United States, the popular theologian C. S. Lewis contemplated eventual human contact with an alien race.

> We know what our race does to strangers. Man destroys or enslaves every species he can. . . . Even inanimate nature he turns into dust bowls and slag-heaps. There are individuals who don't. But they are not the sort who are likely to be our pioneers in space. Our ambassador to new worlds will be the needy and greedy adventurer or the ruthless technical expert. They will do as their kind has always done. What that will be if they meet things weaker than themselves, the black man and the red man can tell. . . . Against them we shall, if we can, commit all the crimes we have already committed against creatures certainly human but differing from us in features and pigmentation; and the starry heavens will become an object to which good men can look up only with feelings of intolerable guilt.[60]

Lewis's statements were obviously based on the presupposition that a human-alien encounter would conform to the historical pattern of encounters between different human cultures. He failed to consider (or perhaps did not know about) the utterly bizarre kinds of encounters with the Other that came out in UFO reports. Alien abduction reports in particular made it clear to the UFO community that the ethics of first contact might be less a matter of human initiative than Lewis had considered. The real question was, what were the intentions and the ethics of the entities with whom so many reported having encounters? There were two avenues of approach to an answer. One was to return to the occult and metaphysical literature for insights; the other was to examine the reports of abductees themselves.

Jacques Vallee, the pioneer of ufology's comparative historical heuristic, soon concluded that UFOs were a genuine physical phenomenon but that they were capable of manipulating space and time in ways beyond the ken of human beings.[61] As such, he felt they might be manifestations of multidimensional or even fractal — but definitely conscious — entities who had a long history of interacting with humanity.[62] He found it most interesting that modern UFO experiences so often affected witnesses' beliefs and behavior at profound levels. Upon reflection, he also realized that "everything in [UFO] behavior seems designed to make us believe in the outer-space origin of these strange beings."[63] Given the magnitude of the psychological impact of UFO experiences, Vallee felt that associating the ETH with these encounters was dangerous, because "charlatans or dictators" could easily manipulate the UFO-ETH myth in order to gain political power and control.[64] In fact, he suspected that this had already happened. Vallee concluded that, whether or not it was intentional on the part of the UFO occupants, UFO phenomena in modern times functioned as part of a "control system" regulating humanity's development by taking advantage of our "great thirst for contact with superior minds that will provide guidance for our poor, harassed, hectic planet."[65] Drawing on the learning theory of psychologist B. F. Skinner, who found that selective reinforcement of desired behavior produced better long-term learning and retention, Vallee posited that much of the odd and paradoxical in UFO encounters was in fact the application of selective reinforcement in what were intended to be learning situations. The goal was to maximize humanity's acquisition of new concepts and beliefs that would then foster a "new cosmic behavior" — in effect "the next form of religion."[66] Vallee theorized that the agents behind this control system were

"Manipulators," by which term I mean the people who are responsible for promoting UFO contacts, for circulating faked photographs . . . , for interfering with witnesses and researchers, and for generating systematic "disinformation" about the phenomenon. . . . We may find that they belong, or have access, to military, media, and government circles.[67]

According to Vallee, not only did these Manipulators assay to unify "that enormous economic marketplace: Planet Earth" by promoting the myth of an extraterrestrial threat, they were, through their covert control of the contactee phenomenon, "undermining both religion and science."[68] The threat to science lay in the fact that the messages contactees reported receiving from the space brothers appeared to actively discourage the development and exercise of rational thought. Science, as the epitome of modern rationality, was presented by many contactees as essentially inadequate to prepare humanity for survival during an impending era of radical planetary changes.[69] In addition, the contactees depicted the signal achievements of human biological and cultural evolution as having been engineered and put in place by extraterrestrials rather than laboriously and independently worked out by a growing and developing human race. This diminished sense of the nobility of human attainment, he felt, merely set the stage for the disestablishment of traditional religious institutions and the imposition of an alternative theology in which the extraterrestrials played the role of the divinities in humanity's past.[70] The threat to religion lay in the fact that the Manipulators appeared actively to use the religious fringe — the contactees and the occult groups — as puppets to promote the idea of humanity's essential dependency on outside forces — forces that the Manipulators were conspiring to introduce. Based on the fact that the political sympathies of some contactees were very right-wing and they often painted totalitarian pictures of the "utopian" extraterrestrial homelands they claimed to have visited, Vallee feared that a government drawing its legitimation from an alleged extraterrestrial presence — the arrival of the gods (reified in the modern UFO myth as extraterrestrial supermen) — would be unlikely to safeguard or respond to democratic ideals of freedom.[71]

Despite his distaste for contactees' denigration of rational thinking, Vallee himself, in his evolving sociopolitical analysis of the UFO phenomenon, betrayed a vacillating commitment to the idea that science — the epitome of rational thinking — was a useful tool for UFO research. In *Passport to Magonia* (1969) he expressed uncertainty about whether UFOs were real physical devices subject to scientific investigation, but he stated emphatically that the idea that they were exclusively *"scientific devices having nothing to do with the mystico-religious context . . . is no longer tenable."*[72] A few years later, in *The Invisible College* (1975), he appeared to have given up on science entirely, stating his belief that, contrary to his earlier expectations that science could expand its theories of reality by studying paranormal phenomena, the dangers posed by the Manipulators of the UFO phenomenon were so serious that science could offer no useful answers. Instead, he wrote in a suitably ominous and mystical vein, "The solution lies where it has always been: within ourselves."[73] But by the time he wrote *Messengers of Deception* (1979), he had concluded that scientific analysis could after all provide a "part of the truth about UFOs; . . . [but] I no longer believe it will lead to the whole truth."[74] This was because, although UFOs were real, they were real in a way that surpassed current human understanding of physics and that could not be disentangled from "psychic and symbolic reality."[75]

For Vallee, the most problematic consequence of the essentially psychic nature of UFOs was the continuing refusal of science to take paraphysical phenomena as legitimate objects of scientific research. It was, he feared, a reenactment of the scientific dogmatism and rigidity that had helped to isolate ancient intellectuals from the masses in their day and led eventually to the overrun of science by early Christian fanatics. Vallee observed that, like the ancient Romans, increasing numbers of people in the West saw science as a spiritually bankrupt endeavor having little to do with the important issues of people's daily lives. In response, the direction that mass irrationality was taking this time was the notion that UFOs were from other planets. It was not all that different, after all, from declaring that the divine had become flesh and dwelt among us. "Receiving a visit from outer space sounds almost as comfortable as having a god," he observed.[76]

While Vallee's comparative analysis of UFO reports led him to focus on the social effects of belief in the ETH, other ufologists exploring the paraphysical connection with UFOs focused on the inhabitants of the paraphysical world. One of the more influential of these was John Keel. A professional writer with a military background in psychological warfare, Keel started his UFO investigations in 1966 as a self-avowed skeptic and atheist.[77] After reviewing the UFO literature and doing field research for four years, he was led to believe in the reality of UFO phenomena because so many people widely separated in space and time came up with the same kinds of unbelievable details about their encounters.[78] Rejecting the ETH, however, Keel concluded that "the real UFO story . . . is a story . . .

of an invisible world that surrounds us and occasionally engulfs us."[79] That world was home to a "parahuman" race of intelligent beings who effectively occupied the Earth with us — if, indeed, they had not been Earth's original occupants. He called them "ultraterrestrials."[80]

The ultraterrestrials, Keel said, were capable of manipulating objects into and out of existence on our plane.[81] They exploited human beliefs by presenting themselves to witnesses using whatever frame of reference was culturally relevant. As people looked increasingly toward science and technology as definers of reality and decreasingly toward religion, the ultraterrestrials presented themselves less often in the context of miracles and seances, and more often in the context of "hardware" such as airships and spaceships.[82] Despite their new guise, these intelligences were something that humanity had always been aware of — indeed, had frequently worshiped as gods or had revered and feared as angels and demons.[83] He suspected that the changing forms by which UFOs had presented themselves were not just convenient devices for accomplishing some noble or even just useful task, but were instead deliberately false performances designed to mislead and to control us.[84] The fact that the ultraterrestrials engaged in deception and obfuscation indicated that their intentions, far from being godly, were at best ambiguous and, given the evidence from abductions, were most likely hostile.[85]

Abductions, Keel recognized, were terrifying and coercive events for which it was difficult to imagine any redeeming rationale. The very fact that they occurred indicated that the ultraterrestrials had a need for physical human beings. Keel postulated that they had filled that need in the past by establishing religions that demanded human sacrifice. But in the modern world their methods had become more "civilized." Now they exploited humanity sexually and genetically via abductions. Using the cover story of being "extraterrestrial visitors from distant stars" who were merely exploring or who were seeking to rejuvenate their own dying genetic stock, the ultraterrestrials were in fact, suggested Keel, trying to produce a hybrid race of beings who could eventually take over the Earth.[86] Substantially the same conclusions were drawn twenty-five years later by historian David Jacobs, whose work with abductees led him to believe that the "alien agenda" (which he conceptualized within an ETH framework) was to create a hybrid race of beings who would be poised to take "complete control of the humans on Earth" within the lifetime of the next two generations.[87]

Keel felt that there were certain areas of human society where the effects of ultraterrestrial influence had already been particularly apparent. One of the most important was religion. As part of their overt control over early humans, he said, ultraterrestrials parading as gods had established the priest-king system. Later their control had been effected through intermediaries such as priests and magicians, and still later through occult societies.[88] One effect of that control had been the creation of religious factions whose constant warfare had "systematically destroyed" the true knowledge of human history — most notoriously the knowledge contained in the library at Alexandria, Egypt. The result was that "we were given a new history, generously dictated by the ultraterrestrials, and we bogged down in the Dark Ages for a thousand years. The human race quite willingly turned itself over to the ultraterrestrials."[89] In the twentieth century the continuation of ultraterrestrial control could be seen in the spread of racist propaganda, which constituted "a basic part of all the Western religions, [which are] the ancient teachings of dubious messengers [who have] kept the human race stirred up and at each other's throats for thousands of years."[90] Dominated as it was by the ETH, the UFO scene was another area in which the protean ultraterrestrials were manipulating and misleading humanity.[91] "The modern UFO scene has produced a worldwide propaganda movement of willing evangelists advocating the existence of people from another planet who altruistically intend to save us from ourselves," but whose true designs, he said, were "inimical to the human race."[92] The problem with the UFO community as Keel saw it was that despite its ostensible desire for a scientific answer to the UFO puzzle, it was unwilling to accept the "crass scientific answers" that he and other deeply perceptive researchers had discovered.[93]

In the end, Keel felt that the encounter between ultraterrestrial and human heralded "some kind of grand climax" in human history: "Our little planet seems to be experiencing the interpenetration of forces or entities from some other space-time continuum. Perhaps they are trying to lead us into a new Dark Age of fear and superstition. Or perhaps they will be guiding us upward to some unexpected destiny."[94] But he himself was not inclined to be guided anywhere — particularly by entities whose practices were so consistently deceptive. The most optimistic sign for humanity's independence in the future, thought Keel, was the fact that more people, particularly the young, were experiencing mystical illumination — an expansion of their consciousness. For some people such as the concertgoers at Woodstock, this illumination had been mediated by psychoactive drugs. One positive effect of this generational illumination was a "rapid decline" in organized religion because "people who have attained direct personal contact with the Cosmic Consciousness . . . have no need for the rites and trappings of the oldtime religions [i.e., the ultraterrestrial-inspired religions]. . . . There is no need to go to church when *your own head is your church*" and when you are aware of and in submission to "the supermind of the cosmos."[95] But spontaneous and drug-induced illuminations were not the only routes to mystical experience. It was a state also reported by numerous UFO witnesses, although Keel eventually became certain that this particular kind of illumination was a false one.[96]

The beginning of the end for the ultraterrestrials, Keel calculated, was the year 1848, when they had last attempted to use their old religious ploys to control human behavior.[97] That was the year in which "the old fairy game" the ultraterrestrials had played with humanity became passé and the new game of spiritualism had begun — a game played in the context of humanity's increasing reliance on science and its concomitantly increasing destruction of the ecological systems of the Earth upon which both ultraterrestrials and humanity relied.[98] The false illuminations produced in the twentieth century through UFO encounters were designed to draw people into an erroneous belief in benevolent space brothers, which would enable the ultraterrestrials "to interfere overtly in our affairs, just as the ancient gods dwelling on mountaintops directly ruled large segments of the population."[99] Drawing on biblical prophecies and the predictions of seers and psychics such as Edgar Cayce and Jeane Dixon, Keel felt that human history was poised on the brink of "something of cosmic proportions" involving an attempt by the ultraterrestrials to reestablish their control over humanity via an "anti-Christ" figure. The future warriors against this would-be despot, he predicted, were "sitting on floors in Greenwich Village, Paris, and Hong Kong, stoned on pot and tripping out on LSD. . . . But there are no apparent Illuminati [i.e., great leaders] on the world scene at the moment. It is certain, though, that they will appear at the appropriate moment. They always have."[100]

By the late 1980s, however, Keel felt that he had been overly optimistic about the future. At the same time that humanity had been undergoing massive illumination in the 1960s, ultraterrestrial intelligences via the UFO phenomenon and especially via abductions had produced counterfeit versions of the real thing, with intimations of direct contact in the near future.[101] "They have been leading us around by our collective noses for aeons," Keel observed. "But now, for some reason that is not yet clear, a merging is taking place. The Elders are slowly revealing themselves to us."[102] This revelation, he indicated, was to be dreaded, not anticipated.

[Historically] the arrival of the Sky People wrought great changes, often in a very short time. In some epochs these changes were for the worst. . . . The optimists among the New Age thinkers hope that we are really entering a new phase in our evolutionary progress but I'm afraid all the signs are negative. Man has ceased to evolve. . . . In a twenty-year span we became a group without any critical faculties, dedicated entirely to self-interests and to hell with everybody else. . . . We are biochemical robots helplessly controlled by forces that can scramble our brains, destroy our memories and use us in any way they see fit. They have been doing it to us forever.[103]

These foreboding evaluations of the UFO phenomenon by Vallee and Keel were not adopted wholesale by the UFO community, but some of the essential elements of their thought did take root — or find resonating spirits — among a number of people there. The first was the suspicion that the interests and intent of the entities behind the UFOs (whether ultraterrestrials or extraterrestrials) were not necessarily good for humanity. The continuing approach-avoidance dance of UFOs with human witnesses, their continued refusal to initiate direct, fully public contact, seemed more the behavior of a skulking cosmic thug than of a cosmic good neighbor. At the very least, this behavior lent itself to exploitation by unscrupulous (but unnamed) others. The second area of resonance was the skeptical evaluation of human intellectual and spiritual capabilities in the face of nonhuman manipulation. It was a pessimistic appraisal of the (fallen) human situation worthy of the great medieval Christian theologians. The third area of agreement was the lack of any clear sense of a means of release from the problems posed by the first two. In the UFO world described by Vallee and Keel, there appeared to be no plan of salvation.[104] Although Vallee held scientific debunkery in part to blame for the dangerous situation humanity faced vis-à-vis UFOs, he indicated that even in the best of circumstances only part of the answer to the dilemma could be provided through science. The other part he described, without elaboration, as being "within ourselves." Keel's answer to the problems of alien deception and human susceptibility to it was "true illumination," but he suggested no method for attaining it when confronted by a society having become "dedicated entirely to self-interests and to hell with everybody else." In short, in many ways the worldview of some of the UFO community in the later 1960s, the 1970s, and 1980s looked much like the traditional Christian one, minus any clear sense of the presence — historical, contemporary, or future — of a saving God, of a transcendent realm whence divine mercy and benevolence might be found.

In part the absence of recourse to (or even perception of) a divine answer to the threat of UFO phenomena was a function of ufology's overall embrace of science as the legitimate framework for thinking about UFOs. A cosmos understood in scientific terms demands scientific, not transcendental, answers. But it was also in part a sign of the cultural times, of a day and age when the divine had been secularized, subjected to historical-critical analysis, and rationalized to bring it more into conformity with the dominant scientific worldview.[105] As one religious scholar observed, "If contemporary religion in America seems to lack anything suggesting transcendence, it may be because it has not had much to work with."[106] More charitably, another religious scholar stated that the practical relevance of the supernatural in the late twentieth century "may have largely collapsed into the interior concerns of the self" rather than maintaining a presence as "a metaphysical, transcendent, or omnipotent being."[107] But for people confronted by experiences that seemed as highly strange and frightening as they were undeniable, recourse to a transcendent whose sphere of influence had shrunk to the confines of the interiority of the confused and frightened self was not enough. Under the circumstances, the noumena behind the phenomena of UFOs took on the mien of deviltry. "I've come away from this experience convinced of one thing," said abductee Whitley Strieber at one point. "If there aren't demons out there, there might as well be. Because these guys are indistinguishable from demons. Indistinguishable. To see them, to look into their eyes, is to be less. Forever. . . . Because then you know that that exists. And that makes you less."[108]

CHAPTER FIVE

Ufology, God-Talk, and Theology

All our most real convictions are born and brought up in . . . personal experiences.

> Robertson Ballard, quoted in
> *The Other Side* by Bishop James A. Pike

The idea that UFOs and occupant encounters were demonic, not just in their behavior but in very fact, surfaced early in the UFO community. Some UFO students with Christian convictions proposed that the aerial anomalies that had been under study since 1947 were in fact the end-time "signs and wonders in the sky" spoken of in the Bible.[1] There were a number of books and treatises published dealing with the connections between UFO phenomena and the Bible. Many of these were more readily available through Christian book distributors than through the book distributors and outlets serving the UFO community. Nevertheless, they had a readership even among ufologists. One author claimed that UFOs were not "unidentified" at all, but were *I*dentifiable as *S*atanic paranormal *A*pparitions "by their violation of the laws of nature in speed and motion and [their ability] to materialize and dematerialize at will. The coldness of UFOnauts, their sulfuric stench, and their lying also testify to Hellish origin."[2] One abductee reported that when she became a Christian, her "old friends" (the aliens) shrieked with terror the first time they came to abduct her afterward.[3] Some abductees even speculated that the intent of alien encounters was to destroy the Christian faith.[4] For these believers, ufologists and nonufologists alike, the UFO phenomenon was unambiguously malevolent and the proper human response to it was to take refuge in the Christian gospel.[5] Some believers took practical steps to make that source of refuge more visible in the UFO community. In Britain, Admiral of the Fleet Lord Hill-Norton expressed the opinion that "some UFO encounters are 'definitely antithetical to orthodox Christian belief'" and in 1996 helped to form an international group called UFO Concern to assess the UFO situation and make recommendations for appropriate action, including assessment and action with regard to the religious aspects of the phenomenon.[6] In the United States, abduction researchers in the state of Florida formed the CE4 Research Group, Inc., an organization trying to "systematically put the pieces of this puzzle together with scientific credibility" but also very cognizant of "the source [of religious insight about the aliens], i.e., the Holy Scriptures. We're going back to the original Hebrew and Greek where necessary."[7] On a smaller scale, Christians like Bill Heft, a former Baptist minister, attended local and regional UFO meetings in order to bring an explicitly Christian perspective to the proceedings.[8]

But for a number of UFO experiencers and ufologists, alien encounters, including abductions, did not seem demonic at all. Instead, UFO phenomena were spiritually uplifting experiences that reinforced their faith commitments. The most notorious of these was Betty Andreasson Luca, a lifelong abductee (as she later determined) and a born-again, fundamentalist Christian who felt that there was a direct and positive "connection between the aliens' intervention in earthly affairs [e.g., through abductions] and . . . Christian faith."[9] Luca's experiences followed the pattern of typical abduction events but also included profoundly spiritual elements.[10] During her first remembered abduction episode, several typical small gray aliens walked through the closed back door of her house. While under hypnosis Luca recalled that she had reasoned the entities must be angels, because Jesus had been able to walk through closed doors, too. And, she recalled, "Scriptures keep coming into my mind where it says, 'Entertain the stranger, for it may be angels unaware.'" When the alien leader held out his hand to her, she asked him if he wanted something to eat, and he nodded.

> And so I went and got some food from the refrigerator and a pan from the stove, and I started to cook some meat. . . . And they said, "We cannot eat food unless it is burned." And so I started to burn the meat — and they stepped back, astonished over the smoke that was coming up! . . . And they said, "But that's not our kind of food. Our food is tried by fire, knowledge tried by fire. Do you have any food like that?" [She replied in the affirmative and led the beings into the family room.] I glanced down and picked up the Bible that was on the end table. I turned and I passed it to the leader. The leader passed me a little thin blue book in exchange.[11]

After Luca was taken on board a UFO and underwent the usual medical examination, she reported that she was taken by her captors to see "The

One," who manifested to her as a giant bird that was consumed by flames. As the flames cooled into embers and finally into ashes, she witnessed a large worm take shape. Then a loud multiply vocalized voice said to her, "I have chosen you to show the world." When she asked the voice why she had been brought there, it responded that she needed to have faith in that which she trusted. "I have faith in Jesus Christ!" she asserted. To which the voice replied, "We know, child. We know that you do. That is why you have been chosen. I am sending you back now. Fear not. . . . I can release you, but you must release yourself of that fear through my son." Luca's response to the allusion to Christ was a flood of happy tears accompanied by repeated praises of Jesus.[12]

However, for most abductees the overtly religious — and more comforting — content of Luca's abduction experiences were rare. At least into the 1990s, most simply could not "make this encounter experience fly." For them, the positive aspects of encounters like Luca's were "the thing you grab onto when you're sinking."[13] But those who tried to grab onto their faith communities for support in the face of their unnerving experiences were sometimes disappointed. Being known to have on-going close encounters with UFOs and their occupants could be a mark of dubious distinction.

> I've had abductions since childhood along with at least one of my siblings and my mother. I suspect more of us were involved, but can only prove it for the three of us. Now my son is involved and possibly one or both of my daughters. I've progressed from being petrified with fear to almost totally accepting this part of my life. My religious views have not changed but I am viewed as being in contact with demons by my religious community and so they shun me like the plague. This has been the hardest aspect to deal with and has caused the most hurt.[14]

Knowing what the reaction was likely to be, some abductees did not mention their encounters to anyone in their faith community, and so quietly committed themselves to living in secret alienation. One lifelong abductee, a Southern Baptist, stated that he never mentioned his experiences to anyone in the church he attended with his family. And he admitted

> My views do not mesh with anyone that I know as they relate to religion. I do not believe in literal interpretation of the Bible. I believe much of what was originally in the New Testament has been left out, much of what would now be classified New Age. I have read a number of books on karma and reincarnation and feel much more comfortable with these beliefs than with a burning hell. I also do not feel that this belief conflicts with what is in the New Testament. When Jesus said, "In my father's house are many man-

sions," I feel he was referring to the various levels of spiritual development that we may find ourselves at when we die. . . . I believe that all religions are working toward the same goal, that of spiritual development; we each just take different paths. . . . I don't know how much the UFO experience has affected my religious beliefs. I think probably a lot more than I would like to admit. One thing these experiences have taught me are that nothing is ever as it appears on the surface. One should always be open to alternate explanations of reality.[15]

For other people in the UFO community, turning to religion for answers to or support in the face of UFO encounters was out of the question. For them, all organized religions seemed to be "irrational and rigid belief systems" that had been either instituted or else severely compromised by the aliens.[16]

Of particular interest among ufologists with religious interests was the relationship of the Christian tradition to UFO phenomena. As attention was given to the ways in which supernatural events in the scriptures and apocryphal writings seemed to parallel UFO encounters,[17] the problem arose of how to determine which events were the result of divine intervention and which the result of alien intervention. As one writer reasoned, "If we decide that ALL past incidents were UFOlogical, . . . this automatically invalidates ALL religious interpretations of such events."[18] In the end some analysts decided that the correspondences between modern UFO phenomena and supernatural events were so compelling as to suggest that alien intelligences, acting on their own behalf and not as agents of God, had been active in establishing and promoting both Judaism and Christianity. Salvador Freixedo, a ufologist who spent thirty years as a Jesuit, supported just such a contention, not only with regard to Judaism and Christianity but for all the major world religions. In writings spanning more than two decades he analyzed evidence that indicated that the religions of the world had been founded and controlled by "energy entities, intelligent and evolved to a greater or lesser degree, who interfere with human lives. . . . They have appeared and demanded to be worshiped as God. But they are not God."[19] Freixedo realized that peering behind the sacred mask that had been used to disguise alien intervention was a "demythologizing" move that could make people feel like cosmic orphans, so he cautioned that "this shouldn't undermine our faith in God but rather our faith in doctrines created by miracles."[20] Nevertheless, the idea that there were no world religions unaffected by alien manipulation effectively robbed some inquirers of any viable history or tradition of human contact with the divine to which they might turn in an attempt to address their experiences in a culturally meaningful way.

A less extreme option for understanding alien involvement in religion was to concede that while the scriptural record of supernatural events might in fact be (on the whole) a record of divine intervention, the UFO parallels in modernity were deliberate counterfeits designed to deceive.[21] *Flying Saucer Review* editor Gordon Creighton (a professing Buddhist) threw in his lot with those who felt that, although compromised by alien manipulations, the Christian scriptures were not altogether useless. In Creighton's estimation UFOs and their occupants were modern-day manifestations of entities that had been known for centuries in religious circles as angels, demons, jinn, devas, and so forth.[22] In the course of history they had influenced religion insofar as they had exerted an influence on the people who led religious organizations and transmitted religious knowledge and traditions. One possible piece of evidence in support of this idea, Creighton suggested, was the biblical verse wherein St. Paul warned the Ephesian congregation that the enemies of Christians were not flesh and blood.[23] Creighton hypothesized that the last part of the passage had been deliberately mistranslated for centuries. Instead of saying that Christians warred "against spiritual wickedness in high places," the passage should be translated, "against the spirits of wickedness in the skies."[24] Thus translated, the application of the verse to UFO phenomena was obvious.

For some in the UFO community, however, the parallels between UFO phenomena and the scriptures were less problematic if one postulated that UFOs and their occupants sometimes acted as the agents of God — indeed, as Betty Luca surmised, that they were very possibly what was meant by the term *angels*.[25] The strongest advocate for this optimistic hermeneutic was Presbyterian minister and ufologist Barry Downing. Like many others, Downing believed that alien influence was reflected in a variety of historical texts and traditions, and he was well aware of the sobering implications of that presence — even for Christianity: "Whoever they are, the alien/angelic reality already owns us and controls us. . . . It is my assumption that the alien/angelic reality was involved in the development of both the Old and New Testaments, as well as perhaps providing stimulation to other religious leaders like Mohammed, or the development of the Hindu Vedic tradition."[26] Unlike some scriptural analysts in the UFO community, Downing found cause for hope in the idea of alien-connected scriptures. He suggested, for example, that the Exodus story was an illustration of "the basic strategy of the alien/angelic reality [which] has been to create life on earth, and to guide it according to its own purposes. These purposes include the tolerance of much evil . . . but the divine reality will do us good in the end."[27]

Far from being put off by the apparent manipulation and deception associated with UFO phenomena, Downing felt that "UFOs are simply . . . giving us a course correction [by carrying out] deceptively simple actions in human society which have significant long term consequences."[28] For instance, he suggested, their appearance in the early years of the Cold War, overflying military installations and flying rings around military jets seemed to be a sort of political and military intervention strategy designed to frighten the bristling world superpowers into a more reasonable frame of mind.[29] To explain UFOs' continued reluctance to initiate overt contact, Downing proposed what he called the "Rock of Ages" principle, drawing on the story in the biblical book of Exodus wherein, for protection, Moses was hidden in a cleft of a rock on Mt. Sinai while God in all His glory passed in front of him.

> Suppose . . . that we adopt the view that UFOs are a reality so superior to humans, so powerful and complex, that it would destroy the human race if it came in direct contact with civilization as a whole. (Remember what whites did to Native Americans?). . . . A truly benevolent reality which is vastly superior to humans might realize that we need a rock to hide in.[30]

As for their behavior in the area of abductions, Downing felt that — as the abducting entities so often told their victims — experiencers were "chosen people." Chosen, said Downing, much as Moses had been chosen, to be given revelations for society while protecting society at large from being overwhelmed by the fact of the alien presence.[31]

In response to Downing's position, John White, cofounder with former astronaut Edgar D. Mitchell of the Institute for Noetic Sciences,[32] pointed out that Downing was overlooking several important facts. First, in addition to mentioning righteous angels, the Bible also talks about "fallen" angels. Second, God's messengers in the Bible did not use deception as one of their techniques but, rather, identified themselves and stated their purposes. And third, they invariably showed respect for humanity, unlike the abducting entities, and refused to overpower human will.[33] Although these points were certainly compatible with a fundamentalist Christian approach toward UFO phenomena, White's theology was far from Christian and even further from fundamentalist. Citing the convergence of physics, which studies outer space, with psychology, which studies inner space, White posed — and answered — the question to which these disciplines led: "What is reality and how do we fit into it?" The answer:

> The cosmos, then, may be conceived as having different but interpenetrating planes of existence which are space-time frameworks in their own right. The higher planes are the native realms of angels, spirit guides, ascended masters and other evolutionarily advanced beings reported throughout history as interacting with humanity to guide and protest us. Protect us from what? Protect us from harmful inhabitants of the other planes. . . . There are said to be objectively real but invisible intelligences which seek to penetrate human psyches in order to stop our evolution and enslave us to their will . . . to entice us off the spiritual path of psychobiological integrity and true evolutionary unfoldment of consciousness.[34]

In view of this, White urged caution when dealing with these entities rather than uncritical acceptance of their messages and reliance on their beneficent assistance. As he pointed out, when dealing with realms so far beyond our own conscious awareness and ability to know, "we are wholly at the mercy of whoever or whatever is out there, subject to their whims, unable to communicate except when they want to allow it, and unable to verify the information they give us about themselves unless they allow it. . . . We must beware of false gods."[35] What was needed as humanity faced contact with other intelligences, he advised all ufologists, was "a transformation of consciousness"—a deliberate movement along an evolutionary path that was, he felt, destined to lead from Homo sapiens to Homo noeticus. And to a knowledge of the True God, "the source of all transcendence."[36]

> Whether our meetings with advanced life forms seem to come from outer space or inner space, we must recognize that they principally reflect to us that which we ourselves shall eventually become, and that all time and space, all worlds and their inhabitants arise from the Transcendental Source of creation whose traditional name is God. Therefore, it is God alone to whom we should aspire in our search, recognizing that the distant goal of our evolutionary journey is also the fountainhead of our existence moment-to-moment along the path.[37]

White's endorsement of human transformation as a response to the UFO presence was not a new idea in the UFO community. It had been around, in one form or another, for decades.

CONSCIOUSNESS—OR CON?

One of the refrains heard from early ufologists studying alien encounters was a plea for caution in the face of a possible—or probable—"evil empire." Another frequent refrain was an exhortation to expedite human moral and technological development. At first such advice appeared in connection with speculation as to why overt contact by UFO occupants was not forthcoming.[38] Perhaps, some ufologists suggested, it was because humanity needed to evolve further before contact could safely occur. The concern was not for humanity's safety, but for the aliens'. Gabriel Green, of the Amalgamated Flying Saucer Clubs of America, suggested that UFO occupants may have noticed the way we slaughter animals, which indicated a "general contempt of nonhuman life [that] might clash with their ethics."[39] NICAP's Donald Keyhoe guessed that one reason for the lack of contact was because, from the aliens' aerial vantage point, the most noticeable feature of human civilization would have been warfare. And if they monitored our communications, he pointed out, talk about a human conquest of space with no thought given to the rights of other worlds, and talk of bringing back "spacemen" from other worlds as specimens, would not have inspired confidence in humanity.[40] Exhortations to increase human technological development, made using the rhetoric of science and technology that motivated the early UFO movement, were sometimes framed in terms of a larger religious obligation. In 1966 British ufologist Brinsley Le Poer Trench (later Lord Clancarty) exhorted science to learn from UFOs by watching them to see how they manipulated the Earth's electromagnetic field to produce energy. According to the biblical book of Genesis, said Trench, humanity was supposed to have "subdued" an Earth given to Adam in a "raw," unimproved condition. Before our desires to explore the reaches of outer space could be realized, it was our job to fulfill the divine mandate—to learn how to harness the energetic potentials not only of the Earth's magnetic field but also of the human bio-energetic field. "The quickest route to the stars and our neighbors throughout the galaxy," he advised, "lies right under our feet and within the development of ourselves."[41] Similarly, the "Rock of Ages" principle proposed by Downing thirty years after Trench wrote his advice was, in part, an acknowledgment of the continued need for human technological progress before overt contact between aliens and humans could be safely established, though this time the concern was for the human side of the contact equation rather than the alien.

As entity sightings became more common and then abductions became prevalent, the idea that human development was the key to establishing alien-human contact took on new dimensions. Contact—both in the present and in the future—began to be linked to human progress conceived of as an advancement of "consciousness." At its most fundamental level, consciousness indicated simple awareness — a practical and real awareness of other realms and other forms of life that were quite different from what human beings were accustomed to seeing, and a willingness to include these other life forms and their native habitats in the mental furnishings of our science, education, politics, and daily life.[42] The call to consciousness taken at this level was assimilable to the scientific spirit of the West. At a more profound level, however, the appeal for increased human consciousness was an appeal for "a redemptive form of higher consciousness at a time of crisis for the earth and its inhabitants" — an awareness of the interconnectedness of all things, corporeal and noncorporeal, and their essential unity as an expression of the Divine Mind or Godhead or The One.[43] Essentially, consciousness understood at this level was a call to mystical transcendence and, quantum physics notwithstanding, was far less compatible with normal scientific interests — whether outside or inside the UFO community. What made the call for heightened consciousness so unexpected was that it seemed to be coming, oddly enough, out of the trauma of abductions.

There was little in the initial abduction reports to indicate any sort of spiritual valence to the experiences, much less any overriding spiritual concerns. Yet paradoxically, as the abduction phenomenon unfolded, many abductees who had come forward initially with signs and symptoms of trauma not only came to terms with this aspect of their lives but embraced it and looked forward to the next experience. This development in the abduction scenario constituted an interpretive move the ultimate implications of which threatened to return UFO studies (some feared) to the era of the contactees. In the late 1960s and into the 1970s, people reported being snatched from their cars or taken from their beds at night and transported into a room where invasive medical procedures were performed on them by short, thin, gray-skinned beings with bulbous heads and large, dark, wrap-around eyes. The more fortunate reported being taken on tours of the ship after their examination ordeals, or being allowed to engage in conversation with their captors, or participating in group meetings that sometimes even included other human beings. Throughout the 1970s, however, ufologists did not pay a great deal of attention to the nonmedical aspects of abduction reports. Indeed, the communicative episodes were seldom mentioned. After all, one of the distinguishing marks differentiating abductees from contactees, according to the ufological wisdom of the day, was the fact that abductees did not appear to be (or believe they were) messengers for the aliens.[44] Besides, ufologists on the whole were mostly interested in the simple fact that abductions occurred at all and, given that they did, in discovering what factual details abductees could provide about the interior of UFOs, their propulsion systems, the appearance and behavior of the aliens, and so on.[45] In these early days of abduction research it seemed that the medical aspects of the experiences were central to the phenomenon, while the few alien communications being reported were at best an alien diversion and ruse.[46]

In the 1980s, however, an interpretive divide appeared among ufologists interested in the abduction experience.[47] Some began to pay greater attention to what abductees reported the aliens as saying and less attention to the odd physical manipulations. "It is my own feeling," wrote psychic investigator D. Scott Rogo, "that these medical examinations serve no functional purpose whatsoever" other than possibly "killing time" and "allowing the abductee to adjust to his predicament."[48] In fact, he proposed, on the whole, UFO phenomena were merely "elaborate stage settings" to help us evolve or become better educated about "metaphysical principles."[49] The idea of UFO phenomena as cosmic educational theater for the backward human species was one way to conceptualize the increasingly complex events and the warnings about an impending worldwide catastrophe being reported by abductees. Sometimes the catastrophe predicted by the aliens was to be caused by human malfeasance; sometimes it was simply to be a result of geophysical or astrophysical forces beyond human control. In either case the alien presence was tied to this future. One ufologist considered the whole scenario to be a "cosmic melodrama" complete with special effects, in which the UFO occupants showed remarkable success in "recruiting otherwise rational individuals" to play parts. Perhaps, he suggested, these performances were intended to make the UFO phenomenon "deeply meaningful and momentous" to humanity and thus grab our attention. At the very least the recurrent themes of these productions, he said, reflected the aliens' own "terminal apocalyptamania."[50]

Some researchers felt that the abduction phenomenon was not about imparting information to humanity, but getting information from humanity. Abductions, they emphasized, were really strictly one-way transactions.[51] The question was, just what did the aliens want? Some abductees reported that their abductors seemed to "take" their thoughts while they were aboard the spacecraft. Though some researchers interpreted this as an alien attempt to learn more about human science, technology, and military preparedness, the abductees themselves most often interpreted it as an attempt to learn more about human thought processes and emotions — in particular the fact that humans are all individual minds.[52] Abductees reported that the aliens seemed to have more of a group mind rather than being highly individuated, as humans are, and that they more or less lacked (and therefore did not understand) emotions.[53] The purpose of abductions, then, was framed as a quest by a highly rational, intellectually oriented species to understand emotion. "They want our love and how it is we love and care and have such compassion. They also are terrified of our anger and our ability to hate and kill," reported one abductee.[54]

The perception of the aliens as coolly emotionless and instrumentally motivated was to some extent a function of the nature of the abduction experience itself, with its coercive methods of capture and examination. But it also seemed to some as if the aliens' apparent emotional barrenness was not just a matter of circumstance or even simply a sad biological fact — the manifestation of an evolutionary dead-end for their species. Instead, it seemed like a chilling truth lying behind all alien communication and behavior. For them, reports of alien attempts to make frightened abductees feel special and loved bespoke an "enforced illusion" designed primarily to control their victims by gaining their cooperation. One abductee reported feeling that she needed to hold onto the love and peace coming from the aliens in order to overcome her fear.[55] Hopkins compared this to being "love bombed" by cult members like the followers of the Reverend Sun Myung Moon.[56] "They weren't as nice as they wanted me to think," was a common refrain among some abductees. "They were coldblooded, but they didn't want me to know it. . . . They treated me like a guinea pig. . . . They didn't care about people as people."[57]

According to Hopkins and others for whom the medical aspects of abductions rather than alien communications were central, "Information-gathering on the species [human beings] simply cannot explain all these separate [abduction] events."[58] What the aliens appeared to need from human beings, they suggested, was not our "thoughts" or an understanding of our emotions, but our genetic material for the purpose of creating a hybrid human-alien race.[59] As abduction research continued, it seemed ever more likely that these hybrid beings were to be an invasion force.[60] Abductee Karla Turner reported a dream in which the biblical story of Esau and Jacob was played out and then a voice explained to her that the aliens were attempting to produce a "variant" being that would someday supplant humanity through deception, just as in the biblical story Jacob had supplanted Esau in order to get the firstborn's birthright. By manipulating weather patterns, the dream voice told her, the aliens planned to create a false apocalyptic threat that would seem so real that "when they [the aliens] show themselves openly and offer to save us in some way, we will be willing to take their help, even if it means giving up our birthright, so to speak, which is preeminence on this planet."[61] For others, it was not just our genes and our planet the aliens seemed to want. Some feared that it was possession of the soul. "We are a resource for them," reported one abductee, "physically, emotionally, and spiritually."[62]

But for an increasingly vocal number of abductees, doubt, fear, and suspicion about the aliens became impossible to maintain. After the initial shock of remembering their experiences, abduction became one of the most profound events of their lives, something that neither religion nor psychiatry nor biology could fathom in all its depth, a "unique learning experience."[63] As one abductee commented, "I have been terrified beyond description, and have felt blessed beyond words."[64] "Now I knew a truth," wrote Whitley Strieber.

> I loved them, wanted them, needed them, chose them, and called them. I was responsible for the visitor experience becoming a part of my life. I was not being randomly oppressed by them. I saw us on our little blue planet hanging in the dark, and suddenly I felt loved and cherished by something huge and warm and incredibly terrible.[65]

"I go to bed every night now scared to death," reported another abductee, "but still wanting something to happen. I want to face whatever has entered my life."[66] "To hell with the terror," wrote another. "I miss them."[67] Harvard psychiatrist John Mack noticed that this change in attitude seemed to precipitate a change in the very nature of the phenomenon itself, which caused him to "question categorizations of the beings into constructive, good, and loving ones and others that are deceptive and hostile, bent on taking over our planet."[68] As one abductee reported being told by the aliens themselves, "There are positive and negative forces in the universe, and these forces flow freely next to one another."[69]

For "revisionist" abductees (who preferred to be called "experiencers" rather than abductees) the medical portion of their experiences made more sense when framed within the context of alien communications, a context with not only subtle religious overtones but also frankly religious content.[70] One experiencer asked her abductors if they were angels, to which she received the reply, "Yes, but not like you have been taught."[71] Others reported being told, or receiving the impression, that aliens were involved in the management of the soul after death.[72] Often it

seemed that the soul itself was the point of real interest in abduction phenomena, but not in the threatening way that some abductees and
researchers feared. "Whatever it is [that they seek]," wrote Strieber, "it is
more than simple information. . . . It seeks the very depth of the soul; it
seeks communion."[73]

In some cases the shift in the emotional and psychological valences of
the experiences was accompanied by a partial or total identification with
the goals and interests of the abductors. Many experiencers reported
having a sense of mission. Leah Haley and Whitley Strieber both felt
compelled to write the stories of their abductions.[74] Other abductees
reported being told to "tell the people outside" about their experiences
so that humanity would be willing and able to associate more openly
with the aliens.[75] But for most who felt "called" by their experiences, it
was a call that promised fulfillment only sometime and somehow in the
unknown future. Leah Haley, among others, reported being told that several groups of aliens were involved in a cosmic warfare of good versus
evil in which humanity had a coming part to play.[76] Often this warfare
was associated with a future worldwide crisis that would threaten human
existence on Earth.[77] "We were told," reported one abductee, "that we
were selected to experience the end of the world." She said that the one
conveying this information was God, appearing as "this ball of light that
looked like a little sun."[78] Another abductee reported that she felt that
she was "participating in a plan that came from a 'higher' place. 'My
feeling is it's not just them.'"[79] Sometimes abductees' identification
extended beyond promoting the goals of the aliens and became an identity with the abductors themselves. "I felt that I was one of them"
became an increasingly common observation.[80] At times this sense of
being "from elsewhere" was merely a sense of soul-level identity.[81] At
other times individuals became convinced that they were related to the
aliens even on the genetic level.[82] Sometimes, reported abductees, their
true alien identity was cited by the abductors as justification for taking
them. "You are us." "You agreed to all this a long time ago," they
reported being told.[83] In other cases, however, abductees were told that
they had been taken by right of ownership predicated on the fact of alien
genetic engineering — either of the entire human race or of the abductee
individually. When one abductee objected to her treatment as showing a
lack of respect for her, she was told, "They say they do [treat abductees
with respect] — since we're property. . . . He says I'm property."[84]

Abductees' experiences were often the stimulus for a radical rethinking of their religious as well as their physical and psychological identities.

"It was the catalyst that woke me up to my spirituality," confessed one.[85] That awakening did not always translate into new or renewed institutional affiliation, however.[86] Some 65 percent of the respondents on my abductees' survey said that as a result of their experiences their religious beliefs had changed; 55 percent reported a "decreased" or "strongly decreased" concern with organized religion; 56 percent reported that they had changed the way they practiced their religion; and 77 percent said that their concern with spiritual matters had "increased" or "significantly increased." For their part, the aliens, while seeming to encourage belief in God,[87] often discouraged an overinvestment in institutional forms of religious expression. One abductee reported being told by her abductors that churches, statues, priests, and nuns were not God and that she should not believe.[88] But that did not mean that the aliens were without a sense of the divine. One abductee reported that he asked his abductors what they thought about God and received the reply that they have the same one, but "there hasn't been a Jesus there."[89] "The beings are very spiritual," reported another abductee. "They believe all that exists is of God and is God. They believe that all material beings have a soul and a body and that the body has its consciousness just as the soul does. . . . and they believe that even the universe is in a constant state of becoming."[90] Indeed, in contrast to initial perceptions of the aliens as cold, emotionless beings, as abductees' encounters underwent a transformation they began to see the aliens as "'more advanced spiritually and emotionally than we are.'"[91]

With this change in perspective came a change in abductees' understanding about the significance of their encounters. Some reported that they were supposed to be examples for the rest of humanity, to show it how to

> awaken that part of them inside their brains that helps to communicate with the light . . . and that light is consciousness. . . . We call it God on this planet. They never mention too much about specific religions or anything like that, just universal light. It was in each of us. And all we had to do was ask for it to waken and to grow.[92]

Others received the impression that at least some abductees were among those destined to be taken off the planet during the cataclysmic Earth changes of the future, while those who were left behind—being part alien—would be better equipped to survive the catastrophe and repopulate the world.[93] Even the oft-noted reproductive program to which the aliens seemed to devote so much of their attention was reinterpreted by some abductees in spiritual terms. The hybrid children were to be used to "prepare [humans] for the changes . . . humans' spiritual transformation."[94] "We may be a doomed species," observed one abductee, "But we will not end; we will only emerge as a butterfly from a cocoon, or the Phoenix from the ashes."[95] "'Deep down inside,'" said another, "'I think that what they're doing is somehow necessary. . . . It has to do . . . with races, beings or whatever, coming together to make another creation.'"[96]

"I believe that incredible intelligence is awaiting us all," wrote one experiencer, "and I am trying to be worthy of their interest in me."[97] According to Leo Sprinkle, a former University of Wyoming psychologist and an abductee himself, the entire purpose of alien contact was exactly this kind of spiritual transformation of humanity — in essence our transformation from parochial, Earth-bound creatures to true "cosmic citizens."[98] "Perhaps the UFO display is a 'spiritual lesson' to determine which observers are willing to become witnesses," he wrote, "to demonstrate the intellectual and spiritual strength needed to speak the truth as they know it to be."[99] This sentiment was shared by Mack. Describing various experiences during abductions that seemed to foster "personal growth and transformation," Mack structured his book-length treatment of the abduction phenomenon accordingly. But his purpose was not just to illustrate progressively more adaptive individual responses to alien intrusions. For Mack the spiritually transformative implications of abductions were universally important for all of humanity.[100] They constituted, in effect, a "passport to the cosmos."[101]

Despite the increasingly warm feeling that many abductees professed for their alien abductors and the lofty spiritual lessons experiencers said they learned, not all abductees felt the same, and not all ufologists greeted this transcendent development with pleasure. Karla Turner argued that "the case is very weak for this being a primarily spiritual agenda."[102] Any spiritual growth that abductees felt they had made, she suggested, was the result of "waking up on their own," perhaps as an unintended side-effect of the alien intrusions.[103] Hopkins agreed. "We shrink the human spirit to think that all of it has to come from 'out there,'" he observed. "All of that idea, that help comes from outside, is not unlike a fundamentalist approach to traditional religious experience."[104] The aliens' suggestion that they have been involved in our existence, whether as our bodily creators or as our soul-level kinship group, Turner said, served only to bind humanity to them with a false sense of familiarity that reduced human dignity and sovereignty.[105] Jacobs shared much of that fear for human independence in the face of the aliens' machinations.

It is disturbing that the aliens and hybrids seem primarily concerned with the Earth, not with human beings; they do not comment on the preservation of life or the value of humanity or human institutions. They say they want to make a better world, but they never talk about partnership with humans, peaceful coexistence, equality. [One abductee] was told that after The Change [the coming cataclysm], there will be only one form of government: The insectlike aliens will be in complete control. There will be no necessity to continue national governments. There will be "one system" and "one goal." . . . They are engaging in the systematic and clandestine physiological exploitation, and perhaps alteration, of human beings for the purposes of passing on their genetic capabilities to progeny who will integrate into the human society and, without doubt, control it. Their agenda is self-centered, not human-centered, as would be expected from a program that stresses reproduction. In the end it is possible that it will be of some benefit to us, but if we survive as a species, the price for this charity will be relinquishment of the freedom to dictate our own destiny and, most likely, our personal freedom as well.[106]

"Never, ever get the idea that [the] bugs [i.e., the aliens] are kindly, space-age gods. They are not," advised one abductee. "Accept them for what they are, no more, no less. Do not ever trust them in word or deed."[107]

But still, to many experiencers and investigators, the new turn of events in the experiencer community was a welcome sign of evolution in human consciousness and the adumbration of a more direct, universally realized human connection with a transcendent realm of being.[108] "We participate in a universe or universes that are filled with intelligences from which we have cut ourselves off, having lost the senses by which we might know them."[109] The irony of the fact that renewal of this connection was unlikely to be welcomed by the established religions of the West, whose ostensible point was to bring humanity into relationship with the divine transcendent, was not lost on ufologists. Mack mused, "It's okay to mouth platitudes about god in churches. But to actually experience a robust intelligence operating with some stake in the fate of this earth . . . I mean. . . ."[110] The developing alien-human connection, admitted one theologian, would entail a serious "course correction" in the world's religions.[111] Freixedo felt that he could predict the direction of that correction: "In his evolution man will undo the shackles of the Holy Books and will choose to employ his own brain in transcendental affairs in the same way as he has done with the material sciences."[112] Instead of a text-based religion, he said, the word of God would be found in nature,

God's true Bible. There is no word of God beyond nature and human intelligence. . . . The rules of God and his will cannot be within any book whose words become stale or unintelligible with the passing of time. God's rules must be printed in nature itself and cannot be imposed upon us by anyone from outside its realm, nor worse yet, by anyone against nature, as has happened with many Biblical passages.[113]

A writer surveying the modern history of paranormal (including abduction) contacts observed, "There can be no doubt that human consciousness is changing; the theory [I propose] is that it is *being changed,* and that the change is a manifestation in our world of the intelligence of God."[114] For many experiencers and researchers, this was not an overstatement.

SPIRITUAL VERSUS SCIENTIFIC INSIGHTS

For some ufologists the suggestion that UFOs were a part of God's self-revelation was seen as an alarming development in a community whose grassroots beginnings had emphasized the scientific nature of the UFO problem. One frustrated UFO student had protested in 1962 that, "The problems of extraterrestrial life and its form and structure are questions for the astronomer and biochemist, and not for the parish priest."[115] In 1990, well into the period when ufologists were referencing the New Physics to shed light on UFOs and when abductions were capturing ever more attention, the same protests were still being lodged:

> I'm tired up to here with the subject of UFOs and religion. . . . Articles of this nature bring us no closer to an understanding of the UFO phenomenon, nor do they contribute to the collection, evaluation and publication of the UFO sighting reports. . . . They must also discourage the very scientists, academics and professionals we sorely need from membership and participation.[116]

As one person observed with dismay, "It seems now ufology is constantly attracted to the highest strangeness and most sensationalized cases."[117] For the more adamantly scientific ufologists, it was not just the religious-sounding abduction narratives that were disturbing. It was ufology's increasing preoccupation with encounter cases and its apparently wholesale acceptance of the entire phenomenon.[118]

> Fifties-style contactee stories are now nearly extinct, but claims of alien implants, hybridization and genetic experimentation, missing fetuses, underground alien bases, and secret cooperation of the U.S. military with aliens run rampant. No solid evidence has been found to substantiate any of these reports, just as no proof was ever found for the oldtime contactee ravings. But there is a terrible difference. Today, wild claims are accepted uncritically by many prominent UFO researchers.[119]

The abduction phenomenon, while making UFO study more visible to the public, had also in effect caused it to be judged by the public according to "its worst, not its best, evidence."[120] Difficult though it might be to question the testimony of genuine abductees — and as the abduction phenomenon grew in scope and complexity, it became increasingly difficult to reach consensus on what constituted "genuine" — the more cautious UFO investigators emphasized that it was important to subject even (or especially) abduction narratives to the scrutiny and standards of proof of scientific inquiry.[121]

But for others, the UFO phenomenon had revealed itself in such a way that there could be no going back to the days when collecting and evaluating sighting reports was the raison d'être of UFO studies.

> The challenge of understanding UFO sightings that occupied so much of my time and attention when I first began my research is now a distant memory. . . . I realized early on that the UFO phenomenon was the only physical occurrence that we have ever encountered that actively dictates the terms upon which it could be studied. I did not understand that our inability to study the phenomenon was part of a calculated program to hide its activities and purpose. . . . What researchers were hearing from those who had these experiences or even sighted low-level UFOs were merely fragments of memories, often distorted and always incomplete.[122]

Ufologists who were willing to at least countenance abduction reports urged abduction-oriented researchers not to refocus their efforts but just to reexamine their drift into New Age thought and return to the tough, hard-edged scientific orientation of early ufology.[123] "The biggest problem in ufology is the unscientific, mystical, muddleheaded, New Age element that tends to make a shambles of the enterprise with completely uncritical and illogical outpourings. As long as we passively embrace them rather than openly disown them, we deserve as a field not to be taken seriously."[124]

The call for a renewed commitment to science in the UFO community of the 1990s faced two major problems. First, in almost half a century of UFO inquiry, a suitable and adequate scientific methodology for the discipline had yet to be found. The suspicion that some ufologists had long held about traditional science's ability to address the more intractable aspects of the UFO problem had only been exacerbated by the abduction phenomenon. As Mack wrote, "It may be wrong to expect that a phenomenon whose very nature is subtle . . . will yield its secrets to an epistemology or methodology that operates at a lower level of consciousness."[125] The difficulty of the search for an appropriate scientific methodology was compounded by the postmodern spirit of the late twentieth century, which questioned all knowledge claims, including those made by science.[126] Even the notion of rationality itself — that cornerstone of scientific thinking — came under critical scrutiny. As one observer at the 1992 M.I.T. abduction conference reflected: "The threat embodied in any acknowledgment of the possibility that this [abduction] phenomenon might be true is seen as somehow reopening us to the dangers of superstition, medieval demons, witchcraft, and all of that. But I don't think it's that at all. I think it's as if we've escaped into rationality with Western science."[127] For the UFO community, close encounters tended to function as "agents of cultural deconstruction,"[128] particularly with regard to those social institutions like science that had increasingly defined and defended the collective worldview for the better part of three centuries. In the process, it also seemed to be "dissolv[ing] the great religious systems" while simultaneously "engender[ing] new forms of religious believing."[129]

The second problem with the call for a return to science was that, as one critical observer of the UFO scene pointed out, ufology appeared to have entered into a "post-secular" stage.[130] Although ufologists like Downing maintained that even the religious aspects of UFOs could and should be handled "scientifically and objectively," because the UFO phenomenon was a "confounding, monumental and earthshaking subject" it was a natural magnet for god-talk.[131] This god-talk was based on the experiences of people from a variety of religious backgrounds who sought a discourse community wherever they could find it. For the most part that place was not in the churches and synagogues. The more conservative churches were prepared only to characterize abductions as demonic, and though the experiences were frightening, many abductees were not prepared to be doubly victimized by assuming the stigma of demonic possession, particularly in light of the fact that there were redeeming features in abductions. As for the liberally inclined churches, their theology had been rationalized by the ascendancy of the scientific worldview. On the whole they failed to address themselves to a matter as exotic as alien abduction, given that abduction had not been legitimated as a feature of "reality" by science. As John E. Biersdorf remarked, "Those parts of the Judaeo-Christian tradition which deal with areas of experience denied by current scientific and cultural myths [were] neglected or forgotten."[132] In the search for a community within which to work toward integrating their abduction experiences into the private and social fabric of their lives, abductees and researchers formed themselves into loose networks of mutual support and information. "Upon meeting fellow abductees," one experiencer remarked, "you unmistakably recognize other souls who have been to the 'edge'."[133] The process of opening up to others and sharing the stories of their experiences, abductees reported, was therapeutic, not least because in doing so they broke through the isolation that remembering their abductions had forced upon them. "Here we can laugh at ourselves, joke about the aliens, speculate wildly over the phenomenon, and generally have a grand time at the gray shits' expense."[134]

In the late 1990s the various threads of religion that had found their way into the UFO community via the abductees' network and the god-talk therein were woven together into a more systematic religious tapestry of the UFO phenomenon by journalist and communications specialist Dr. Francisco J. (Joe) Lewels, himself an abductee. "Who has the best credentials to understand God?" asked Lewels. "In the end, that is exactly what ufology is all about, for it is, in fact, the study of our place in the universe and the ultimate purpose for our creation."[135] Warning against using Judeo-Christian traditions as a platform for understanding UFO phenomena, Lewels advised that it was incumbent upon "each and every one of us [to] become a theologian and a scientist [so as to] reclaim the fields of science and theology for ourselves."[136] What humanity would learn by taking up these two approaches to UFOs, Lewels called "the God hypothesis": the knowledge that UFOs and their occupants had always been here, that they had taken a hand in the creation of the human species through genetic engineering of higher primates indigenous to Earth, and that they had also been the architects of most or of all world religions.[137] Although recognizing that some ancient texts said the aliens cum gods had a basic antipathy toward the human race, Lewels nevertheless believed that the purpose of alien abductions in the modern era was to "convey the idea . . . that humans are more than just flesh and blood — that they are spiritual beings with a far greater importance and power than they, themselves, imagine."[138] Yet he did not see humanity as the "crowning glory of God's creation." Rather, he suggested, humanity was a mere prototype for a "more advanced model yet to be unveiled."[139]

It was this insight about the essential worth and dignity of humanity, Lewels said, that traditional Judeo-Christian religion had effectively suppressed. "One must recognize that religious doctrines were often molded by those who had little regard for spirituality and who held the intellectual capacity of the common people in total contempt."[140] It was such a group of people who decided to translate the Scriptures and "submit the

Sacred Word to a torturous committee process" in order to arrive at an approved version. Most recently, the heirs of these religious elitists had tried to agree upon the "true" story of the life of Jesus so as to "liberate" the historical facts from their distorting supernatural overlay.[141] Lewels suggested instead that the so-called supernatural elements of the Bible — including the virgin birth — were totally explicable as the machinations of "beings who possess highly advanced quantum technology" and who had "traveled the universe (and possibly through parallel universes) . . . for perhaps millions of years."[142] These beings, said Lewels, were the very ones described in the Old Testament as angels or intermediaries between heaven and earth.[143] Orthodox Christian theology under the influence of St. Paul reduced this angelic realm to a sphere of "weak and beggarly elemental spirits," while the cosmic role of Jesus as bringer of the saving knowledge of God through inner spirituality was transformed into the idea of Jesus as a cosmic debt-payer, with the priests and bishops of the Christian church acting as the trustees of that largesse.[144] The result, said Lewels, was a disconnection from inner knowing of the divine and from effective spiritual growth, and a general disconnection of "civilized" Western humanity from the spiritual realm combined with an ethic of unbridled growth and consumption of the physical world.[145] By way of contrast, Lewels held up the example of the indigenous peoples of the world. "These people hold the secret of how to live in harmony with nature without destroying their environment and without allowing the survival of their species to infringe upon the survival of others. Because they remain connected to God and continue to serve Him, they instinctively follow the spiritual laws that Western society has forgotten."[146]

It was a secret that some Native people were willing to share. Along with their knowledge of the aliens.

THE FIFTH WORLD (OR THE END IS NOW)

In 1996 a small group of Sioux Indians and some Anglo promoters sponsored the first "Star Knowledge Conference" on the reservation near Yankton, South Dakota. The purpose of the conference was to introduce to Western society the knowledge of the "Star People" that the Native Americans had guarded as the foundation of their cosmology.[147] The leader of the Star Knowledge Conference was Standing Elk, a Lakota Sioux who said he had been inspired to organize it as a result of a vision commanding him to share his people's knowledge.[148] Holy men, or "interpreters," from numerous tribes of the Sioux nation also participated, as did elders from the Hopi, Iroquois, Choctaw, Oneida, Seneca, Yaqui, and Mayan tribal nations, as well as shamans from the Maori tribe in New Zealand and the Sammi, a tribe living above the Arctic Circle. Other featured speakers at the conference were retired Sergeant Major Robert Dean, John Mack, Whitley Strieber, Steven Greer, Leo Sprinkle, Richard Boylan, stigmatist Giorgio Bongiovanni, and a host of other non-Natives. The conference, said the Native leaders, was a fulfillment of ancient tribal prophecies, and many of the Native elders in attendance said they had come in response to "signs" that "the time had come to speak openly about their most closely held oral traditions, including their origin in the stars, the influence of Star People on the formation of culture, spiritual beliefs and ceremonies, and the imminent return of the Star Nations" at the end of this Fourth World and the beginning of the Fifth.[149]

According to Standing Elk, the Star Nations—those whom ufologists had been calling "aliens"— "were the most crucial of all entities" for humanity to understand because knowledge of their existence and way of life would give us a new vision of how our own lives might be different. The most important difference, said Standing Elk, lay in the fact that the societies of the Star People were not based on money, but on "the mental, spiritual and universal laws with which they were too mentally and spiritually intelligent to break."[150] Another of the Native speakers, Floyd Hand, said that the Star People were avatars who would return to Earth in the latter 1990s, arriving first in Santa Fe, New Mexico.[151] Addressing himself specifically to the abduction phenomenon, Rod Shenandoah said that his people considered themselves privileged to be visited privately by the Star Nations, and Standing Elk emphasized that such visits were for the purpose of teaching humanity and nurturing our spiritual growth, as well as to help us "prepare . . . for dealing with the challenging Earth changes coming up in the next several years."[152] It was also determined through communications from the Star People that "an international, multi-racial contact team of 13 humans" was to be formed to meet with and pass along messages from "space emissaries."[153]

But according to the editor of the *Contact Forum* newsletter, throughout the conference it was already evident that "contact happened in many ways."

> Some people see UFOs. Others listen to trees or have out-of-body journeys with non-terrestrial beings. For me, the personal experiences I was fortunate to be allowed to experience during the Star Knowledge Conference and Sun Dance were as meaningful and reality-based as any other experience I can

recall. For me they constitute contact — contact with the reality that lies just below the perceived reality that most of us think we live in. Throughout the conference, and the Sun Dance, this unseen reality manifested in the see-it-and-touch-it actuality of our lives. . . . No lie. We are in contact with Great Mystery.[154]

Another participant characterized the conference as "an initiation of empowerment, the transmission of information that is sacred and secret."[155] Though that information was presented by the Anglo speakers as a "momentous discovery" about the existence of alien races and their contact with humanity, the same essential message was presented by the Native leaders with "an almost old-hat sense of normality."[156] In the pages of *Contact Forum,* an abduction-oriented newsletter, the nature and implications of that "new-old" normality found an audience that extended beyond the limited circle of those who had been able to attend the conference. Almost every issue of the newsletter printed during the year after the conference carried an article about the events that occurred there or an article by a Native leader.[157] With the November-December 1997 issue, the newsletter changed its masthead to describe itself as "a journal of the fifth world."

One of the major themes of the Star Knowledge Conference was the idea that the end of the Fourth World (this era) was imminent. Hand predicted that it would occur on January 21, 2021.[158] But during a subsequent Star Knowledge Conference, the timetable was changed. During an evening ceremony honoring the thirteen oldest grandmothers present, all of whom assumed a leading role onstage in the night's events, one of those thirteen "recited the prophecy of Crazy Horse about these very times as the Old Age (4th World) closes." Then,

After a series of moving prayers and ritual declarations, the grandmother leaders made a startling official ceremonial declaration that the old era (4th World) was ended, and that the new age (5th World) was being born! Suddenly wild cheering erupted. A tumultuous celebration broke out all over the auditorium, with women and men spontaneously grabbing instruments, drumming, and starting an ecstatic rhythmic clapping. The joyous explosion lasted over half an hour. After the attendees were finally called to order, the grandmothers explained that this new 5th World would be hallmarked by the attributes of positive feminine energy [but cautioned that] the 5th World must not be one of separatist female dominance, but rather of forming a renewed society of women and men as equals, a society shaped by the feminine paths of cooperation, nonaggression, inclusiveness, noncompetitiveness, service rather than dominance, use of psychic and spiritual gifts as well as technology, and harmonizing with nature's ways. Participants felt that an historical doorway had been opened.[159]

Those who had received visits from the Star People, whether in person, in a vision, or in a dream, said a key conference participant, became *heyokas* or "contraries" — people who behave in a way contrary to what society normally expects. Abductees as modern-day *heyokas,* he said, were "charged to live as active witnesses against the ignorance and corruption of the Fourth World, and to live as witnesses of the Fifth World which is emerging."[160]

With the blending of abduction-inspired god-talk and Amerindian religious traditions, the alien abduction movement brought to ufology its closest encounter yet with religion. But the nature of that religion was highly eclectic, idiosyncratic, and still generally amorphous.[161] Not every abductee lent support to all of (or any of) these ideas or the public activities associated with them. For most abductees, the loose network of support groups remained the most important venue for sharing their experiences, their fears, and their achievements and for promoting a sense of fellow-feeling with other abductees. In this loose association they became very much like other small groups of religious seekers whom Martin Marty described as part of the post–World War II "Second Transformation" in American religion — groups, mostly New Age, composed not of those "left behind in the [increasingly secular] culture but by those in the advance."[162]

THEOLOGY: THE FAILURE OF "THAT OL' TIME RELIGION"

In his study of the sociology of the afterlife in the modern world, Tony Walter pondered, "How to explain the remarkable invention of a society that, whatever the beliefs of some of its members, is oriented only to this world?"[163] It is a world where "the metaphysics of scientism encourages man to stop his search for inwardness at the level of psychic contents" — a world where awareness of "a conscious universe containing levels of intelligence that far exceed the highest states experienced by the ordinary, 'healthy' mind" can be psychotherapeutically defined and may be pharmacologically treatable.[164] Nevertheless, people hunger for that kind of awareness, for those experiences in life — those omens of transcendence — that leave behind a residue of meaning. They serve as a focal point for subsequent narratives of personal history.[165] When people hold those kinds of experiences up to the totalizing, reductionistic gaze of science, it can be the scientific worldview that comes up wanting, that appears "quite unbelievable" by comparison.[166] As Theodore Roszak notes in a discussion of styles of knowing, "There are disciplines of the visionary mind as well as of the rational intellect."[167] It has traditionally been the task of theologians, not scientists, to explore and legitimate the disciplines of the visionary mind.[168] But when confronted with the often life-changing phenomena of UFO sightings and alien abductions, theologians had surprisingly little to say.

Perhaps theologians' reticence to speak came from the same spirit of caution that motivated Father Georges Cottier, secretary of the International Theological Commission of Pope John Paul II in 1996. When considering the implications of scientists' discovery of a planet orbiting a distant star, Cottier advised the exercise of prudence in any subsequent theological discussions lest the Church wind up with a theory based more on "science fiction" than on science fact.[169] Or perhaps the silence of Christian theologians had its origins in an historic predilection for the Church to "react to crises rather than preempt them."[170] On the rare occasions when theologians gave thought to the matter of extraterrestrial life, most took the position that it would not ultimately be of very great consequence for Christianity. One explained that, to his surprise, his Christian faith was neither helped nor hindered by the ETH and that the verses that kept coming to mind were not from the Bible, but from the Beatles: "When I find myself in times of trouble, / Mother Mary comes to me / Speaking words of wisdom, / Let it be."[171] Surveys of Christian theological seminaries and Jewish synagogues revealed that there was little learned concern about the theological ramifications of the discovery of extraterrestrial life — much less the discovery of the reality of UFOs. A 1985 survey asked seminary deans if there had been any formal study of the relation between UFOs and Christian theology in their curricula. Out of twenty-six respondents to the question, twenty said no. Three said yes — two of those were Roman Catholic.[172] Yet when asked if they believed it was possible that UFOs might carry an intelligent life form from another world, eleven respondents said yes (a Catholic explaining that the possibility was not excluded by revelation).[173] In another survey of seminaries and synagogues conducted in 1994, 77 percent of respondents rejected the hypothesis that official confirmation of the discovery of an advanced civilization would have "severe negative effects on the country's moral, social and religious foundations."[174] A panel of theologians and scientists discussing extraterrestrial life at the Smithsonian Museum of Natural History in 1999 reached the same conclusions.[175]

But there were dissenting opinions. Presbyterian minister Barry Downing suggested that this consistent refusal to admit that UFO reality and the discovery of extraterrestrial life would have a profound impact on Christianity was a way for liberal Christians to insulate themselves from facing uncomfortable questions. Fundamentalist Christians, he pointed out, did the same thing when they automatically attributed all UFO phenomena to demonic activity.[176] In 1960 a Brookings Institute study commissioned by NASA stated that the effect of the discovery of extraterrestrial life on fundamentalists of all religious traditions would be "electrifying." It would have potentially far-reaching consequences, especially in societies where fundamentalists were a powerful social force.[177] Science fiction writer Arthur C. Clarke felt that the doctrine of the Incarnation, in particular, was a ticking time bomb for all of Christianity.[178] As one psychologist in the UFO community observed, perhaps in some ways the long battle against the UFO cover-up was not really about the public's right to know as much as it was about the public's right not to know.[179] Not only would the idea of the Incarnation itself have to come under review, as one investigator pointed out, the whole Christian idea of God's plan of salvation would be severely problematized.

> The Christian religion would be particularly compromised by the discovery [of extraterrestrial life] since it makes so much of the Incarnation as an historical event and of knowledge of the good news of Jesus Christ's Passion, Ascension, and Atonement as the *sine qua non* of salvation. It would either have to maintain that the incarnation and crucifixion of the Son of God has occurred on innumerable worlds, or embark on a vigorous missionary campaign of broadcasting the good news throughout the universe. The latter would be a vain effort, for the distant galaxies are receding from us faster than the speed of light and could never be contacted, so their inhabitants presumably would be eternally damned: a fact surely irreconcilable with any idea of Divine Providence.[180]

In order to make a more accurate assessment of the impact of the discovery of extraterrestrial life, the Brookings report advised that further studies be conducted on the position of major world religions and of "American religious denominations." Such a study was never performed, however, and for a very good reason: there *were* no articulated positions. Most theological statements on extraterrestrial life were written on an ad hoc basis. In most cases, these few writings were prompted by interests other than those surrounding UFOs.[181] For instance, an essay by Norman W. Pittenger in 1956 took as its starting point the science fiction literary genre.[182] Other reflections were inspired by the findings of natural science, especially the theories of modern cosmology, or by the early years of the space race.[183]

A very few theologians, however, found inspiration for their comments specifically in the UFO phenomenon. The author of the first American book published on the subject of UFOs (in 1950) reported that religious leaders whom he had consulted had "ridicule[d] the idea that this would upset theological concepts."[184] "God created this earth. We are descended from Adam. Other planets, other Adams. That God is almighty is best proved by the endless pattern of His creations. The more that is revealed the more almighty He becomes."[185] In 1954 Father Philipp Dessauer stated during a Bonn conference on the Christian attitude toward extraterrestrial visitors that the people from another planet who had been watching Earth for the last eight years were certainly to be considered "persons" and God's creatures in every sense.[186] A Lutheran bishop from Oldenburg stated that he believed there were visitors from another world flying around in our skies and that "Christ is their Lord in any case, whether they are aware of it or not."[187] Of course, not all theologians agreed with this. The Reverend Father Francis J. Connell, while side-stepping the issue of UFO reality, stated that although there was nothing in Catholic theology forbidding the existence of extraterrestrial intelligence, this did not mean that such an intelligent species would necessarily be partakers of Christ's grace. Although there might indeed be "other Adams," he reasoned, it could not be a foregone conclusion that these other Adams had sinned so as to require the same kind of divine intervention that Christians know as grace. If they had sinned, he wrote, God might have made other provisions for their redemption, or they might not be destined for the same kind of eternal felicity that grace made possible for Christians, or they simply might not be afforded a "second chance" at all. But, Father Connell pointed out, while the existence of extraterrestrial intelligence was speculative, what was certain was the existence of another kind of intelligence in the universe — the angels and the demons.[188]

It was in terms of angels and demons that UFO phenomena most often received theological attention in the West. Sheikh Nazim Effendi of the Nakshband Order of Dervishes remarked during a private meeting of London Muslims in 1985 that UFOs were actually operated by jinn who shared the Earth with humanity and who sought to subject and enslave us.[189] In 1997 Pat Robertson, founder of the Christian Coalition, stated that according to the Bible, abductees and anyone who believed that

UFOs were really space aliens ought to be stoned, because such individuals were in actual fact trafficking with demons.[190] In early 1998, however, it became known that Monsignor Corrado Balducci, a retired theologian, exorcist for the Archdiocese of Rome, and author of two books on demonic possession, felt that UFO entities were not demonic. In an interview granted to a German magazine, later reprinted as an appendix to a book and posted in part on the Internet (where it quickly — though erroneously — found wide distribution in UFO circles as an official Vatican announcement of UFO reality), Balducci stated that in his opinion UFOs were real and that the explanation for what they were should be pursued by science "and not in the world of angels or the Virgin Mary or the demons . . . not as a divine or demonic incident, but as a physical reality."[191] Indeed, Balducci speculated, based on the evidence of witness statements, "these extraterrestrials — if that is what they really are . . . are very good beings who aim to bring us nearer to God."[192] An important point that Balducci reiterated again and again in his short interview was that witness statements about UFOs and aliens should by and large be taken as statements of genuine fact and not as hallucinations. His reasoning was thoroughly theological. "The human testimony is a very important element. . . . If we question it, we may soon reach the point where we question the testimony of Christ's existence."[193] Ironically enough, at almost the same time that Monsignor Balducci's hopeful statement was being trumpeted around the Internet, another message was also making the rounds. This one reported the words of Joe Jordan, one of the founders of the CE4 Abduction Research Group in Florida, to the effect that "the similarity between the abduction experience and demonic possession is very, very close."[194]

Though the UFO movement worked diligently to separate itself from the claims of the contactees and did not conceive of itself as a community with primarily religious interests, it also realized from an early date that the subject of UFOs had religious implications, and it was not averse to addressing those from time to time.[195] Though not advocating as drastic a response to UFO encounters as Pat Robertson, some in the UFO community shared a negative evaluation of UFO phenomena. But there were other Christian ufologists who considered the theological ramifications of UFO phenomena very differently. Downing examined the ways in which possible UFO activity was reflected in biblical texts and sought to use the stories of the Bible as interpretive frameworks for understanding modern-day UFO activity. Based on this synthetic heuristic, Downing suggested that UFOs would never land and establish open contact because "that would be the end of God's faith game," which He was effecting through UFO phenomena.[196] Another Presbyterian minister, Jack Jennings, after outlining possible associations between biblical events and UFO phenomena, said that he "looked forward eagerly to whatever further revelations there may be" about UFOs because new knowledge was in some ways increased self-knowledge, and "the more we learn about ourselves the more mature and loving we will become. If I read my Bible correctly," he wrote, "that was God's intention for humankind from the beginning."[197]

Other theologian-ufologists were slightly less optimistic. Rather than seeing UFOs as the agents of God's work on Earth, Lutheran minister and ufologist Ted Peters saw them as potential sources of idolatry. In his judgment the UFO phenomenon had a clear religious dimension in that it evoked a sense of having encountered something transcendent, omniscient, technologically (and perhaps morally) perfect, and therefore something potentially promising assistance of such magnitude and nature that it would amount to a veritable salvation. On the positive side, he noted that UFOs as a symbol of "unconscious hope" for salvation from human ills indicated that "our religious sensibilities are still alive and well." But, he cautioned, the technological hope that UFOs represented could never cure the problems of the human heart "from which God and God alone is able to deliver us."[198] Instead of an affirmation of the Christian doctrine of unmerited grace through Christ's death and resurrection, Peters pointed out, the messages and implications of alien contact seemed mostly to recommend salvation of a gnostic-style, do-it-yourself kind. "In the last analysis, then, our UFO theologians have expressed a need for a savior but have not really found one other than ourselves. The buck still stops at home. . . . The UFO religions have not yet heard or comprehended the Christian gospel."[199]

Peters's critical assessment was reiterated by sociologist Alan G. Hill, who suggested that the UFO movement and particularly the alien abduction movement could be understood as "quasi-religious" movements serving as the functional equivalent of a religion. According to Hill the UFO movement was essentially religious in that, despite rhetoric to the contrary, in actual practice the members of the movement valued belief more than empirical evidence or critical questioning, suggested that there were universal powers greater than humanity from whom we might hope for some form of personal or collective salvation, and pictured themselves as the undeserving objects of persecution by hostile outsiders whose activities only served to ennoble the ufological quest.[200] Another scholar saw belief in UFOs more positively, viewing the UFO movement not as a substitution for traditional religion but as "an extreme example of the human quest to make [terrestrial] religion relevant to life" by giving it a more cosmic dimension while also providing it with a promise of scientific verifiability.[201] The abduction movement in particular, he said, constituted a "barely disguised grafting of . . . theological elements of America's most popular religion" onto a "technological/science fiction framework."[202]

SIC TRANSIT

Despite the attempts by a scattering of individuals to treat ufology and religion as intersecting rather than identical pursuits, in the end many theological and most scholarly treatments focused on the UFO community as a religious group in itself rather than on the theological issues that might be raised if ufologists were proven correct about UFO reality. Donald E. Ehler, president of Boothe Memorial Astronomical Society, was relieved when the Condon Report was finally released in 1969. The search for UFOs, he said, had been a "hysterical witchhunt" and was more of a "growing religion" than a scientific endeavor.[203] The director of the Smithsonian Astrophysical Observatory, when asked about UFOs, slyly offered his opinion by refusing to do so on the grounds that he would not make public comments about "the beliefs of religious cults." In response, J. Allen Hynek replied, "Neither do I."[204] He would have been pleased to know that the equation of ufology with religion was not pervasive at all levels of society. In the aftermath of the Heaven's Gate suicides in March 1997, a *Time Magazine* online poll asked respondents if they thought that belief in and study of alien life was a form of new religion. Surprisingly, given the recent publicity surrounding the suicides, more than 70 percent said no.[205]

But if not a new religion, belief in alien life was, according to philosopher Paul Davies, "at rock-bottom, part of an ancient religious quest." Davies saw public interest not only in UFOs and alien contact but also in the SETI program as stemming, in part,

> from the need to find a wider context for our lives than this earthly existence provides. In an era when conventional religion is in sharp decline, the belief in super-advanced aliens out there somewhere in the universe can provide some measure of comfort and inspiration for people whose lives may otherwise appear to be boring and futile. This sense of a religious quest may well extend to the scientists themselves.[206]

Indeed, anthropologist Richard A. Shweder offered several (mostly tongue-in-cheek) theories to account for the fact that so many of "America's best and brightest" believed in the existence of extraterrestrial intelligence. The first theory, which he attributed to "disenchanted political analysts," was that "if you can't find signs of higher intelligence on earth, you might as well search somewhere else." The second, attributed to "conservative critics of higher education," was that after leftist academics' deconstruction of "our venerable religious and scientific master narratives," anything seemed worthy of belief, so why not extraterrestrials? The third theory was simply and soberly that "a long-overdue spiritual revival is taking place in the United States in which the tired and tiresome opposition between faith and science is finally being laid to rest. . . . At the moment, all one can say with confidence is that interpretations of the cosmic inkblot are changing."[207] A part of that cosmic inkblot, according to Davies, is the image of the alien, which has become a sort of

> half-way house to God. . . . This powerful theme of alien beings acting as a conduit to the Ultimate . . . touches a deep chord in the human psyche. The attraction seems to be that by contacting superior beings in the sky, humans will be given access to privileged knowledge, and that the resulting broadening of our horizons will in some sense bring us a step closer to God.[208]

The quest to find — and to find out about — extraterrestrial life was as compelling for many scientists in the twentieth century as it was for the thousands of people around the world who reported experiencing contact with an aerial — or even a living, intelligent — unknown. If the UFO movement was motivated at heart by essentially religious impulses, they were impulses often shared by scientists. That scientists and ufologists expressed those impulses by pursuing "the alien" in such different ways is not, in the final analysis, so surprising. Some people have always had the gift of faith — an ability to believe in the existence of things they have not yet seen with their own eyes, and the determination to live their lives according to their beliefs.[209] Belief, for instance, in things like the possible existence of other intelligent life somewhere in the universe. And then again, there have always been people who have maintained that they no longer believed on faith, because they had been given a direct experience of the very thing that everyone else was still looking for.

Final Thoughts on Science, Religion, and UFOs

[In controversies] objective reality cannot yet be mobilized in support of a particular statement, for it is the very nature of reality itself that is so controversial. . . . At the time of controversy, the voices of Reason and Reality are many.

Stephan Fuchs, *The Professional Quest for Truth*

The very unwillingness of the UFO phenomenon either to go away or to come considerably closer to us in a single step has been conditioning us — initiating us, if you will — to entertain extraordinary possibilities about who we are at our depths, and what the defining conditions of the game we call reality may be.

Keith Thompson, in *Spiritual Emergency:
When Personal Transformation Becomes a Crisis,*
ed. Stanislav Grof and Christina Grof

I began this study by pointing out the problematic nature of much of the scholarship on the UFO movement, limited as that has been. In particular the equation of ufology with religion, made on the basis of studies of small groups led by people who claimed contact with aliens, goes against the self-understanding of the UFO community considered in its wider sense, for whom ufology is first and foremost a scientific quest to understand tangible, real-world phenomena. Yet I have also shown that the scientific status of ufology is in many ways problematic, even according to participants within that community, and that religion is frequently implicated in the subject. UFO witnesses often speak about their experiences in language that suggests religious awe. They often say that they feel they have been touched by something far more intelligent and powerful than anything they have ever encountered on Earth. And the reported long-term aftereffects of UFO encounters, particularly those of the more intense variety, often include profound transformations of consciousness. To the extent that reports of UFO events remain inscrutable by traditional scientific methods, the entire UFO phenomenon is often more easily understood as a modern, technological myth or legend rather than as a collection of observations amenable to scientific study. As one ufologist pointed out, "Whether or not UFOs are extraterrestrial or something else entirely, the reconstruction of religion and mythology seems to be one of its most substantial by-products, even if it's an unintended consequence of 'their' influence. . . . The ambiguous nature of the phenomenon threatens to make theologians of us all, nattering away like medieval scholastics on the nature of angels."[1]

Does this mean, then, that despite protestations to the contrary, ufology is at heart a new religious movement? If the question is construed as suggesting a reaffirmation of the traditional connection drawn between contactee groups and the UFO community, the answer would have to be no. Not only are old-fashioned contactees regarded in general with disfavor by the larger UFO community, as of this writing there are no real leaders in the community who occupy a similar role or who command a similar following (although there are several well-known abductees who function as spokespersons to the non-UFO world). In addition, groups currently coalesced around charismatic figures who claim to have had close extraterrestrial encounters, such as former French race car driver Claud Vorilhon (aka Rael), are usually insular and do not participate to any significant degree, if at all, in the larger UFO discourse community.

If the question of the religious nature of the UFO movement is posed using a substantive definition of religion, especially if the substantive definition is based on Christianity (the most familiar religious language to most people in the West), the answer once again would have to be no. The depiction of abductees in particular as individuals who have transposed Christian themes onto a technological framework fails to take into account the ways in which those themes are distorted into nonorthodox modes that are scarcely recognizable as Christian (as Peters points out with regard to soteriology, for instance). Such a depiction also fails to consider the substantial population of abductees for whom encounters remain unpleasant, uninspirational, and decidedly suspect — all traits difficult to reconcile with a positive Christian theology — not to mention experiencers who have suffered rejection by their (usually Christian) religious communities because of their experiences.

And yet there are functionally religious valences to the experiences, interpretations, and beliefs of many of those who participate in the UFO community. If the question of the religious character of the UFO movement is considered in this sense, the answer would have to be yes. However, these religious valences only find limited expression as overtly religious ideas and sentiments or in profoundly religious terminology or behavior (as, for example, in the Star Knowledge conferences). Instead, the lingua franca of the UFO community remains scientific, and the touchstone for its raison d'être is the rational, logical world of science — even when ufologists directly address the question of religion. Scientist Jacques Vallee suspected that UFO-related beliefs would prove to be foundational for "the next form of religion."[2] But, he cautioned, when offered salvation from heaven via UFOs, humanity ought to learn "something more about the helpful stranger before we jump on board." As a means to this end, he urged scientists to take UFO reports more seriously and he warned everyone against suspending their critical faculties.[3] Theologian Ted Peters also viewed the prospect of religious change brought about by UFO phenomena and beliefs as dangerous, noting that such a change "would require . . . a *sacrificium intellectus* or surrendering of common sense" that would be incompatible with a contemporary religious consciousness that sought to position itself within the "naturalistic perspective" of modern science.[4]

In the final analysis it seems reasonable to posit that the UFO community qualifies as one instance of that sort of people who, as Rodney Clapp described them in *Christianity Today,* are both scientifically enlightened and also believers "in a reality beyond the physical universe."[5] Such a people were imagined as far back as the nineteenth century, when Phillips Brooks advised Christians to "Hold fast to yourself the sympathy and companionship of unseen worlds. . . . No doubt it is best for us now that they should be unseen. . . . But who can say that the time will not come when, even to those who live here upon Earth, unseen worlds shall no longer be unseen."[6]

For many people in the UFO community, seeing previously unseen worlds in the form of UFOs and their occupants is not a matter belonging to the realm of faith and religion but is an event fundamentally consonant with a scientific worldview. If the nature and implications of their experiences ultimately require some adjustment of the traditional scientific paradigm, that does not negate the validity of the science of ufology nor discredit the scientific paradigm that would emerge under its influence. This kind of embrace and simultaneous alteration of the mantle of science is not unique to the UFO community. It is a feature of many kinds of unorthodox science.

> There are mystical and occult trappings, even distinct "spiritual" overtones, to much unorthodox scientific writing, and concrete religious ideas are built into or flow naturally out of some of it. By no means is the goal always or even usually to buttress traditional religious views; often the religious component is highly novel in content. Sometimes the spiritual or religious component may actually be unintended or even denied. . . . But often the religious component is there deliberately, as part of an effort, it would seem, to forge a new religious-scientific synthesis.[7]

A shaping effect upon science is not confined to the influence of unorthodox sciences and their quasi-religious constructions. As sociologist Eileen Barker points out, science has not only shaped the social context within which religious life is carried out, it has always been shaped in different ways and to different degrees by the ideas and practices that constitute religious life.[8] That inheritance can be seen quite easily today in the field of physics and cosmology. In the past the idea of God provided human beings with two essential pieces of knowledge: As beings in the universe, we are not alone; and, though we may be finite and subject to death, Something in the universe is infinite and eternal. Something will go on, which gives us reason to hope that, at the very least, our own brief lives lived in proper relationship to that Going On will not have been meaningless. Modern physical science, having dethroned theology as the queen of sciences, has fallen heir to the existential questions that lay behind those ancient answers. Are we alone? What is the meaning of life?

One scientific response has been the quest for the Grand Unified Theory — that schema of physics that would unite quantum theory and relativity theory into a single, overarching explanatory framework. It is, in fact, nothing less than the quest for a Theory of Everything, the foundational principles of reality upon which the universe is believed to operate. It is a quest for that which has been operative everywhere (infinite) and at all times (eternal) in the history of the universe. In a sense, it is science's quest for God.[9] Another response to the great existential questions has been the Anthropic Principle, which states that the existence of intelligence and of conscious awareness (i.e., in humanity) is part of the pattern of the universe's development and will eventually become the total, all-encompassing nature of the universe.[10] A still different response, a logical (but not necessary) corollary to the Anthropic Principle, has been the ETH — however hesitantly embraced by the scientific community. The ETH posits that there exists an independent and intelligent "other" in the universe, which implies that humanity has a relationship to that other. What kind of other and what kind of relationship? These are questions we cannot answer. Science assures us that vast interstellar and intergalactic distances preclude our knowing.

In the end, at every turn science leaves humanity essentially alone in the universe. The UFO movement, however — the sightings of UFOs and entities, the claimed interactions between ufonauts and human beings, the public and the private attempts to study the phenomena, the think-tank reports and special commissions and committees, the UFO conventions, the books and magazines and TV shows that have sprung from this fertile field of study — all these want to suggest that not only are we not alone but we have been and can be and are in contact with alien forms of intelligent life. We are not alone, and we have an ongoing relationship with that which accompanies us on our billion-year sojourn through the universe.

Science and religion, according to Needleman, are two dreams between which Western civilization presently finds itself caught.[11] No part of society finds itself more thoroughly situated at the intersection of those dreams than the UFO and alien abduction movements. If the UFO myth has done nothing else in the twentieth century, it has crystallized within itself the language and praxis of a scientific modernity along with the myths and symbols of an ancient and venerable human quest that first found a home in religion. It is a quest that in all times and ages has taken the more astute, the more persistent, or the more fortunate to the edges of reality — to the ends of our cognitive maps (and further), to the mystical margins that are said to join this world with a World Beyond. These margins and borderlands have often been suspected of being the home of witches and monsters — things alien to the world as we know it.[12] But as ufologists have learned, the margins of reality are also a provocative frontier for exploration, with potentially far-reaching consequences even for those who do not care to make the journey to the edge, themselves: "The study of UFOs is an opportunity to move toward a new reality, a means of increasing the borders of our awareness. The edge of reality is also the edge of knowledge. But beyond this edge is another science and another knowledge."[13]

It is the call of that other science and that other knowledge at the far edge of "consensus reality" that motivates many of those who become involved in the UFO community. In this sense ufology is a modern-day response to the lure of the edge — both a popular scientific inquiry teetering on the cutting edge of discovery and a manifestation of a "lunatic fringe" living at a conceptual boundary beyond which there be monsters.

A Picture of the UFO Community

The people drawn to this line of research are unusually interesting and even amusing in the diverse ways that they draw attention to themselves. "Smear" hopes to go on chronicling their activities for a long time to come.

*James M. Moseley, "Editor
and* Still *Supreme Commander" of* Saucer Smear

If the UFO's do nothing else, perhaps they will stimulate our academic friends to conduct meaningful sociological research on these matters.

Walter Sullivan, in UFO's: A Scientific Debate,
ed. Carl Sagan and Thornton Page

According to a 1996 Gallup poll, 48 percent of Americans believe that UFOs are real and not a figment of people's imaginations, and 12 percent of Americans have seen something in the sky that they could not identify as anything familiar.[1] You can meet these people when you least expect it. One day I was in a little Main Street shop admiring some alien hand puppets, and the saleswoman told me that she had had two UFO sightings. The first was in the spring of 1952 when she was in college in St. Louis. She and another student were late for class one morning and were walking hurriedly across the deserted campus, when they saw something metallic hanging in the sky ahead of them. She estimated that it was about the size of a small dinner plate held at arm's length. Puzzled, they stopped to watch it for about ten minutes. Then as she ran to the classroom to get the rest of her classmates, the UFO disappeared. Years later, when she and her husband were driving home from an opera one night, they saw a brilliant UFO as they approached a familiar toll booth. It flooded the area with light. Her husband, an engineer, had no idea what it could be, and closer scrutiny of the area next day gave them no clues. They reported the incident to the police but took the matter no further.

Of the twenty-three million people in this country who, like this businesswoman, have had an encounter with an aerial anomaly, only some become members of UFO organizations or actively study UFOs.[2] No one knows for sure how many that may be. The largest UFO organization in the world, the Mutual UFO Network, had a membership of roughly five thousand at its peak, though that number declined in the late 1990s.[3] The *UFO Newsclipping Service,* a monthly newsletter that collects and reprints UFO articles from English-language newspapers (mostly from the United States), has about six hundred subscribers. Given the numbers of UFO sightings suggested by the Gallup poll, and considering the general public fascination with the subject of UFOs and aliens, these membership and subscription figures seem amazingly small.

One reason for the lack of participation in UFO groups may be that, despite the popularity of the idea of UFOs, the UFO community remains largely invisible to the wider American culture. Few people know where to turn to report sightings or where they can learn more about UFOs. Most people who try to make reports call the police or a local military base. But even among police officers and military base personnel, few know how to access the many small but worthwhile UFO organizations and reporting centers that exist.[4] Even if sighters do know — or discover — where they can make reports about UFO encounters, many will not do so. Strentz reported that 85 percent of UFO witnesses told few or no other people about their experiences.[5] In part this was because they believed that nothing would be done if a report were made.[6] As one ufologist observed, "Most people still seem to believe that everyone else is a nonbeliever."[7] But sociologist Ronald Westrum found that failure to report a sighting may also result from a belief that one has not adequately done an "external validity check" to find plausible mundane explanations for the encounter, fear of risk to one's status and security if a report is made, or fear of ridicule by those to whom one would make the report.[8]

Given this reticence even to report UFO encounters, much less to join UFO groups, the profile of those who choose to participate in the UFO community is a matter of interest. But there have been few studies of the people involved in the UFO movement, and those studies have tended to focus on the contactee cults, leading to the perception that these groups are representative of the UFO community as a whole.[9] Yet there are a variety of agendas and organizational forms around which people with UFO interests come together. David Stupple extended the parameters of the UFO community to include neo-theosophical groups, urban discussion groups drawing upon a variety of occult traditions, religious cults adhering to the teachings of a single contactee who has exclusive access to the space brothers, isolated students of UFO phenomena who have little interest in the occult, and the grassroots research organizations who tend to be similarly disinterested in such esoterica.[10] In addition to the contactee groups and research-oriented groups, there are those whose main objective is to publish UFO-related material, local reading and discussion groups, and skeptics' groups with UFO subunits. Most large-scale studies dealing with UFO groups ignore this rich "middle kingdom" of UFO interests and focus instead on the extremes, targeting either the American population (concerning their beliefs and attitudes) as in the Gallup and Roper polls, or individuals, as with psychological studies of abductees.[11] The only attempt to present a picture of the UFO community as a whole was self-published in 1985, the result of research undertaken by Shirley McIver on the UFO movement in England.[12] McIver devoted her attention to reading groups and research groups alike, but focused a significant part of her study on the under-examined research groups.[13]

To help address this lack of information about the UFO community (broadly conceived), I conducted two surveys in the United States. By *UFO community* I mean that group of individuals who are sufficiently interested in UFOs and related topics to spend their time and money attending local meetings or regional and national conferences, or who subscribe to UFO journals and newsletters. They form the backbone of the community — the group of individuals bound together primarily by their common interest in UFO phenomena, among whom ideas and information may be expected to circulate. Each of the two surveys was designed to capture data from different segments of the UFO community. A long survey was created for abductees only. A short survey was created in order to acquire demographic data and information on attitudes and expectations from the UFO community in general. This appendix discusses data from the shorter survey.

In order to query members of this community, I attended meetings of three local study groups and six larger conferences at which I either handed out surveys to participants, included surveys in registration packets, or displayed the surveys on a literature table where attendees could pick them up.[14] Respondents were able to return completed survey forms to me via a collection box at the conferences or later through the mail. In addition I was permitted to include surveys in the June 1997 mailing of the *UFO Newsclipping Service*. Response rates were best with the *Newsclipping Service* mail-out (23 percent) and when I was permitted by conference organizers to personally hand out surveys to attendees or include survey forms in conference registration packets (29 percent).[15] At conferences where I was restricted to making my questionnaire available on a literature table (which was rather removed from the general conference traffic) the overall level of response was far less satisfactory. In total, I received completed surveys from 765 individuals.

There are two major caveats that must be made in regard to my results. First, speaking in strictly statistical terms, my surveys are not random samples; they are convenience samples. I had to seek out my subjects and prevail upon them to give me the information I wanted. Seeking them out meant attending as many local and national UFO-oriented meetings as I could, but obviously I could not attend all such meetings, or meetings in widely varying regions of the United States. Similarly, including surveys in UFO publications is a difficult (and sometimes expensive) proposition; in fact, it is usually prohibitive. The second caveat is that some of the data I have gathered is information for which there is no control group for comparative purposes. However, some of the questions are based upon the General Social Surveys (GSS), which provides me with a meaningful control.

THE UFO COMMUNITY: BASIC DEMOGRAPHICS

One of the first impressions to strike casual observers of the UFO scene is the fact that the UFO community (in the United States) is overwhelmingly white and male. This was confirmed by my survey respondents. Anglo-Americans comprise 90 percent of the UFO community, compared to 80 percent of the U.S. population.[16] There is very little information about UFO experiences and attitudes among nonwhites. I was able to locate a Boulder, Colorado, opinion poll that found that among blacks and whites in the population of that area, ideas and attitudes about UFOs were similar.[17] As far as active appropriation of the UFO myth goes, one African-American religious sect, the Nuwaubian Nation, follows the teachings of "extraterrestrial prophet" Malachi Z. York.[18] I was told by a white couple who had visited the Holy Tabernacle Church in North Carolina that it was primarily African-American and had a strong interest in "ancient astronaut" theories — the idea that the human race was contacted and possibly engineered by extraterrestrials many thousands of years ago. An African-American informant in the UFO community told me about a similar church in the Philadelphia area.

There are very few African-Americans who have come forward to report contact experiences. Beside Barney Hill, who with his Anglo-American wife, Betty, experienced the first publicly acknowledged abduction in the United States, older UFO books mention only one other black abductee, Harrison Bailey, who had his encounter in the 1950s. According to his report, shortly after he had seen a UFO and experienced a period of missing time, an upset mob of whites approached him because they thought they had seen him emerge from a UFO that had been flying around their town. He was saved from their threatened violence, however, when they got closer to him and realized that he "couldn't have" come from the UFO because he was black.[19] The only other African-American who has gone public with UFO experiences, Riley Martin, appears to be a cross between a contactee and an abductee.[20] In general, UFO books almost never feature an African-American abductee's story, though nonblack abductees have occasionally said that during their own abductions they saw other abductees who were black.[21] When I questioned one African-American conference-goer about the lack of active interest in UFOs shown by the black community, he gave a short chuckle and said that he supposed the reason was that black people had enough trouble in their lives already without getting involved in something "crazy" like UFOs.[22]

Just as the UFO world is overrepresented by white Americans, it is also overrepresented by men, though in some ways to a lesser extent: 56 percent of the UFO community are men, and only 44 percent are women, compared to 49 percent men and 51 percent women in the United States.[23] This small predominance of men in the UFO community in general is more pronounced where organizational leadership and UFO research are concerned. At a by-invitation-only abduction conference held at M.I.T. in 1992, only 24 percent of the presenters were women.[24] In fact the vast majority of speakers at UFO conferences or contributors to UFO publications are men. At twenty-one UFO-oriented conferences open to the general public during 1995 through 1997, 80 percent of the invited speakers were men. In the most highly regarded UFO periodicals, 87 percent of the articles are by men.[25] In only one area of the UFO community do women predominate: According to my surveys, 58 percent of abductees are women.[26] The increased visibility of women as abductees has led some critical observers of the UFO community to comment that the movement has been taken over by "lots and lots of people, mostly women, who think they've been abducted by aliens."[27] Be that as it may, of those who write books about abductions, the most well known are men who write about other people's experiences or cumulative studies of experiences.[28] When women write about abductions, they tend to write their own stories rather than tell the stories of others, and they are more likely to be published by small, private presses than by larger, recognized publishing houses.[29]

Despite the gendered dynamics of the UFO movement, gender is not an issue that gets much explicit attention from students of UFO phenomena. But there are occasional exceptions. Robert Girard, a bookseller specializing in UFO materials, pointed out the gendered nature of much of the abduction literature in his review of a new book by a female abductee:

> Someone should do a study on the emerging pattern of nice, articulate, well-intentioned women who write abductee books. Are we watching the birth of the successor to Harlequin novels here? Could be. Anyway, this one contains the usual female perspective toward abduction, motherhood, hybridization and awakening spiritual consciousness — but also contains a very unfortunate mess of alien gobbledygook — completely unintelligible technical stuff reminiscent of [a recent set of UFO] fabrications.[30]

One of the few female UFO researchers active in the field advised me to have nothing to do with certain grassroots UFO organizations.

> They hate women and are disgusting people. I'm sorry. I don't know anything about you but you need to know there are only a handful of women "researchers" and I use the word loosely. Most women are put into the victim/abductee position only. If you watch UFO/TV shows, the only place women show up are in the victim's position; 100% of all researchers and people questioned as being "authorities" are men — 100%. I've been on many [TV] shows [about UFOs] . . . but not on any UFO special. . . . All the deals being made for movies are by men for men. It's a shut out.[31]

When confronted with allegations like the preceding, the editor of the *MUFON UFO Journal* responded by saying that any gender biases exhibited in that organization were strictly a function of "a lack of time and resources rather than . . . any ingrained attitudes toward gender." He pointed out that few people had ever "complained openly" about gender-based problems, and he went on to list the names and contributions of several well-known women UFO researchers.[32] Nevertheless, subsequent issues of the *Journal* carried letters from two women serving MUFON in state-level capacities who pointed out that "Discrimination is usually not expressed in major and obvious acts. It is located in the innumerable small, barely noticeable, always ambiguous acts. . . . And [it is] not even a conscious process."[33] One ufologist suggested that there should be a task force on racism, sexism, and ageism in ufology.[34] It should be

pointed out, in all fairness, that while gender is not usually an explicit category of analysis and may exist as an issue only implicitly or as an under-
current of dissatisfaction among some ufologists, many people in the
UFO community hold views that could be seen as woman-oriented in the
sense that many seem to have — or to develop — an ecological consciousness similar to that discussed in and supported by feminist spirituality and
eco-feminism.[35] Nevertheless, in the face of the "other" qua alien life
form, the "otherness" of women — and of different races — is not a way
of looking at the world that garners much attention in ufology.[36]

If the UFO community is distinctive in terms of race and gender, it is
also distinctive in terms of the income and educational levels of its members. The median income of the typical inquirer into things ufological is
between $36,000 and $50,000 per year and the median level of education is a bachelor's degree. In the United States in 1993 the mean household income was $41,428, while the average level of education in 1995
was a high school diploma.[37] Among those households in the United
States whose primary wage-earners hold bachelor's degrees, the median
income in 1994 was $52,370.[38] Although the median income level
among UFO buffs with bachelor's degrees is $36,000 to $50,000 and
thus appears at first sight to be near the national norm, the overall distribution of responses shows a slight skew toward the lower end of the
scale,[39] indicating that on the whole members of the UFO community
may not enjoy quite as high a standard of living as do their peers with
similar levels of education. But if their economic status is slightly below
the national average, their educational attainments are above average.
Those holding a bachelor's degree comprise 19 percent of the UFO community, compared to anywhere from 13 percent to 16 percent of the U.S.
population in general.[40] Further, 33 percent of the UFO community has
done some graduate-level study, whereas in 1993 only 11 percent of the
U.S. population had done graduate-level study.[41] To make finer distinctions, 18 percent of the UFO community have earned masters' degrees,
and another 7 percent have earned doctoral degrees. In the United States
as a whole, the combined numbers of those having earned masters and
doctoral level degrees is only 7 percent to 8 percent of the population.[42]

STATUS, SOCIETY, AND UFOS

In 1970 Donald I. Warren published an influential article suggesting that
"UFO sightings are linked to status frustration and, especially, to perceived status deprivations relative to one's position on the social lad-

der."[43] His analysis of data from a 1966 Gallup poll indicated that low-income white males who have moderate to high educational levels or occupational status are the most likely to report sighting UFOs, and that these sightings, insofar as they are interpreted by the observers as extraterrestrial craft, reflect a "rejection of the established society and its values" (i.e., social alienation) by the status-inconsistent observers.[44] In a figure heading he noted that, in general, few sightings were reported by individuals with low and moderate levels of education, no matter what their occupational and income status.[45] A higher educational level among UFO sighters in general agrees with my own survey results about the UFO community in particular. Insofar as my data suggest the possibility of a slightly lower income level for UFO community members relative to their educational levels (when compared to the U.S. population), Warren's finding of a correlation between status inconsistency and UFO sighting reports is also supported.

Warren ends his article with the statement that "nothing in the data rejects the possibility that some individuals have, in fact, seen objects" of some nature, although his primary position is that the very *sighting* of a UFO occurs in response to status inconsistency and social alienation.[46] However, from the UFO community's perspective, there are alternative interpretations for the correlations Warren observed. Westrum points out that status-inconsistent individuals are less likely to be as thoroughly integrated into their society and thus into the cognitive set(s) that it promotes, which may enable them to perceive that which the dominant cognitive set does not allow for — in other words, status inconsistent individuals may be more psychologically free to admit to themselves (and others) that they are unable to identify what they have seen.[47] Thus, while Warren sees status inconsistency as a deficit, Westrum posits it as a potential advantage enabling individuals to think (and see) "outside the box." Another pro-ufological critique of Warren's study would highlight the distinction between sighting reports and sightings themselves. Warren's data may be read as indicating that status-inconsistent individuals, having less to risk by admitting a UFO sighting, feel the freest to do so. This would be consistent with the observation that one reason for failure to report a UFO encounter is fear of risk to one's social status and security.[48]

The weakest part of Warren's argument is his assumption that an extraterrestrial interpretation of a UFO sighting is a result of social alienation caused by status inconsistency. According to Warren's reasoning, the alienated UFO observer interprets the experience in terms of a hypothetically different society and different social situation (an extraterrestrial one) in which he or she might "escape the [earthly] system without threatening [his or her] gains in the immediate social environment."[49] It is equally reasonable to suggest, however — and many in the UFO community would do so — that resort to the ETH occurs because the relatively well-educated observer has done a reasonably thorough reality-check and cannot find any more conventional and logical explanation for the observation.[50] A psychological study of the causes of UFO belief found that the "cultural rejection" thesis was not supported. Nor did believers manifest psychological disturbances suggesting inappropriate patterns of thought or delusions. Instead the data showed that believers in UFOs were "simply . . . caught up in the awe and excitement of possible extraterrestrial life."[51]

Despite these considerations, Warren's theory that UFO sighters tend to be socially alienated individuals, and that this is the source of their propensity to see UFOs, is a popular one. To test the idea that those with UFO interests have a higher incidence of social alienation, my short survey of the UFO community included two questions on anomie based on the GSS and also collected data on levels of participation in three social arenas: religion, politics, and charities. In other words, instead of inferring social alienation on the basis of a theory that describes conditions under which it may occur (such as high educational attainment but lower economic status), I have tried to use more direct measures of alienation. The questions based on the GSS asked respondents to what extent they agreed, first, that the lot of the average person is getting worse, and second, that most officials are not interested in the average person. UFO survey respondents were less inclined than GSS respondents to say that the condition of the average American is getting worse. Although 53 percent from the UFO survey agreed with the statement, 24 percent disagreed, and an impressive 23 percent were unsure. By comparison, 66 percent of GSS respondents agreed, 30 percent disagreed, and only 4 percent were uncertain. Similarly, UFO survey participants were inclined to think more positively about government officials than GSS respondents. When asked to assess the interest of officials in the condition of the average person, 64 percent of UFO survey participants tended to feel that officials were not very interested, compared to 76 percent of the GSS respondents. Only 20 percent of respondents from the UFO survey felt that officials were interested in the condition of the average person, compared to 24 percent on the GSS, while 16 percent of the UFO group availed themselves of a response option not available on the GSS, declaring that they simply weren't sure how interested officials were. These measures of anomie, which reflect confidence levels in public officials and general attitudes toward the conditions of everyday life, do not support Warren's status-inconsistency theory about those who admit having had UFO experiences.[52]

Another way of examining the degree of social alienation is to look at the levels and kinds of participation in basic social institutions reported by respondents. The UFO survey asked questions about political affiliation and participation, involvement with charities in the form of providing labor or making monetary contributions, and religious identification and participation. As political actors, people in the UFO community are almost equally divided between Democrats and Republicans (25 percent and 27 percent), though on the whole they tend not to fall into an easy two-party grouping: 24 percent call themselves independents, while 13 percent identify their political affiliation as "Other," and 11 percent as "None." (One participant simply wrote "Disgusted" as a political affiliation.) According to the GSS data for 1993, 34 percent of Americans are Democrats, 30 percent Republicans, and 35 percent independents, with only 1 percent choosing "Other" as their political affiliation.[53] Although political identity within the UFO community is diffuse, participation in the political process is comparable to or better than the national average on some measures. Among survey respondents, 83 percent have supported their political candidates by voting (in any type of election), and 22 percent have contributed money to campaigns. Nationally, 55 percent of Americans voted in the 1992 presidential election (and far fewer in nonpresidential elections), and 22 percent have contributed money to political campaigns.[54] When it comes to hands-on work in campaigns, however, the UFO community participates at considerably more modest levels (11 percent) than the national average (26 percent).[55] The significantly higher rates of voter participation among the UFO community may need to be nuanced: The UFO survey did not ask about voter participation in a specific election but instead asked a general question about habits, whereas national data is keyed to specific election participation but does not reflect general or habitual behavior. Despite these inconsistencies between the two data sets, it seems reasonable to suggest as an hypothesis that the participation figures for the UFO community are at least comparable to national figures and may indeed be higher because the UFO community has a significant focus on the role of government in the UFO mystery. Political participation through exercising voting rights may be one way in which ufologists seek to influence the government, with an ultimate view toward encouraging full disclosure of the UFO secrets that many believe the government hides.

Figures for participation in charitable activities are similar to those for political activity: 80 percent of the UFO community gives money to charities (compared to 73 percent nationally), but UFO enthusiasts are less likely to give their time to charitable causes — only 36 percent do volunteer work (compared with 48 percent nationally).[56] One reason for these lower levels of volunteer work may be that activities and interests in the UFO community consume the discretionary time of UFO survey respondents: 63 percent of respondents said that they pursued their interest in UFOs by attending local meetings on the subject, and 94 percent reported that they pursued their interest by reading UFO-oriented books and periodicals. The somewhat higher levels of monetary contributions made to charities may reflect ufologists' attempts to "make up for" their inability to give their time.

The picture of UFO enthusiasts as more diversified than the national average in terms of their political identification is echoed in their religious profile. Less than half of the UFO survey participants identify themselves as Protestant Christians (44 percent), while 15 percent are Roman Catholic Christians, and 3 percent are Jewish. In the 1993 GSS these breakdowns are 64 percent Protestant, 22 percent Roman Catholic, and 2 percent Jewish.[57] The religious categories between the UFO survey and the 1993 GSS are not alike in every respect, however, because the UFO survey included a category "Agnostic/Atheist" and did not provide a "None" category, while the GSS did just the opposite. If the "Agnostic/Atheist" category in the UFO survey can be compared to the GSS category of "None," then the two samples are very close on this item (UFO survey is 10 percent; GSS is 9 percent). The most extreme difference between the two populations lies in the numbers who choose to identify themselves as "Other." In the GSS this catch-all category comprised 3 percent of respondents, whereas in the UFO community it was 29 percent. A blank after the "Other" choice enabled UFO survey respondents to specify their religious tradition. People identified themselves as anything from Druid to Pentecostal to Hindu to Lutheran. In its higher rates of rejection of mainstream religion in favor of nonconventional paths, the UFO community shows its generational bias: 33 percent of the survey respondents are in the thirty-one to forty-five age group, and another 36 percent are in the forty-six to sixty age group. The former lies solidly within the accepted parameters of the "Baby Boom" generation, and the latter contains a number of its older members — a generation noted for their mistrust of institutions of all kinds and their drift away from denominational commitment.[58]

The high proportion of respondents who chose the "Other" category as their religious affiliation may have a bearing upon another survey item — religious participation. Whereas only 21 percent of GSS respondents said that they seldom attended religious services, 47 percent of UFO survey respondents said the same. Similarly, those who said they participated in religious activities weekly comprised only 17 percent of the UFO community, compared to 27 percent of respondents nationally.[59] I suspect that the low levels of reported religious participation in the UFO community may be explained by two facts. First, the community has a relatively high percentage of people who identify themselves as being on a spiritual path lying outside the mainstream. What does "religious participation" mean if you're part of an extreme religious minority, such as being a Druid or a member of a Wiccan circle? Do you participate in your "religious group" only by meeting with other believers like yourself? Or do you consider, for instance, a daily meditation practice as participation in your religious tradition? Second, the lower levels of religious participation may also indicate that for some ufologists, their UFO activities are effectively a substitute for religious activities, and that the UFO community therefore functions as a quasi-religious association for them.[60]

The figures on religious identification suggest a higher-than-average level of disaffection with mainstream religion in the UFO community, which, when combined with their tendency to have more diverse political identifications and do less political and charitable volunteer work, lends some weight to the theory that UFO "believers" live more toward the margins of mainstream society. This picture is offset, however, by the strong data that present the UFO community as being comprised of well-educated, middle-income white Americans who are less pessimistic about the human condition, and officials' interest in it, than most other Americans. A significant number of UFO community members participate in the social arena when compared to the national average, as long as that participation does not mean "hands-on" time and energy. In this they are unlike their peers nationally, among whom higher levels of education tend to correlate with higher levels of volunteer work, but once again they are more like the Baby Boomers, who are the peers of many in the UFO community.[61] It is also worth noting that when it comes to doing charitable work, the discrepancy between the UFO community and the U.S. population in general is narrower than when it comes to doing political campaign work — an indication that members of the UFO community, while abstemious with their time and energies, may be more likely to contribute them to humanitarian and social-welfare causes than to causes involving political institutions.

So what accounts for the disparities between Warren's data and my own? One obvious answer is that we have measured different populations. The strength of the UFO survey over Warren's research data is that the survey measures a more well-identified community of individuals with explicit UFO interests. Warren's data was taken from a 1966 Gallup poll of the American public; from that group he isolated individuals who, when asked, said that they had seen something in the sky that they could not identify and that might be a UFO. These were not necessarily "UFO buffs" — they had not necessarily reported their sightings to authorities or to UFO organizations, nor had they necessarily joined such an organization or pursued an interest in the subject in any other way. They simply confessed, when asked, that they had seen something anomalous. In addition, the UFO survey measures alienation from society not on the basis of a theory predicated upon finding certain relationships between demographic factors, but on the basis of direct questions — questions that have also been presented to the U.S. population in general. Warren's survey group, in contrast, were individuals whose demographics made them likely candidates for suffering feelings of social alienation, which he postulates as the cause of their UFO sightings.

Though Warren's social deprivation hypothesis does not accurately describe the UFO community in general, could it simply describe individuals who sight UFOs? On a gross level, that seems unlikely. Among the UFO survey respondents, 53 percent report having had some kind of UFO experience. Data on this subset of the UFO community shows somewhat higher levels of anomie than for the community as a whole, but still not quite matching the levels for the U.S. population.[62] Compared to the larger UFO community, they are equally well educated (in fact, slightly more so), and they fall into the same income bracket.[63] In addition, they participate in the social arena at approximately the same levels as their UFO peers.[64] In short, experiencers in the UFO community do not fit the profile of individuals prone to see UFOs as compensation for their marginal status. The slight rise in measures of anomie among experiencers when compared to the UFO community may be an effect of their sightings rather than a cause of them. Perhaps what Warren's analysis and my UFO survey highlight is the difference between the many UFO experiencers who never follow up on their encounters, and experiencers who go on to become more or less actively involved in the UFO community. Perhaps those with higher levels of status inconsistency are *less* likely to follow through on their sightings by taking steps to learn more about what they saw. It may be postulated that the material circumstances of their lives might preclude their having the time, educational background, or money to accurately pursue explanations for their UFO experiences.

THE UFO COMMUNITY: EXPERIENCES, ATTITUDES, AND EXPECTATIONS

In addition to basic demographic and social participation data, the UFO community survey is designed to determine what kinds of UFO experiences individuals in the community may have had and their interest in the subject prior to their experiences.

TYPES OF UFO EXPERIENCES REPORTED

In 1972 J. Allen Hynek suggested a typology of UFO reports that, though later elaborated, has become the standard shorthand for describing a UFO encounter. In this scheme a CE1 (Close Encounter of the First Kind) is a sighting of a UFO at close range (approximately five hundred feet or less) in which there is no effect of the UFO upon the environment. A CE2 (Close Encounter of the Second Kind) occurs when the UFO also affects the surrounding environment, for instance, by crushing or burning nearby vegetation, or by stalling the engines of nearby automobiles. A CE3 (Close Encounter of the Third Kind) involves the witness(es) seeing what appear to be occupants around the UFO.[65] Since Hynek developed his schema a fourth category has been added. A CE4 (Close Encounter of the Fourth Kind) involves direct interaction between the UFO occupants and the witness(es).[66] The survey of the UFO community asked participants about their encounter experiences, basing encounter categories loosely on Hynek's classification system, namely:

I have personally:

☐ Never seen a UFO, and don't know anyone who has (Level 0)

☐ Never seen a UFO, but do know someone who has (Level 1)

☐ Had a sighting of a UFO (Level 2)

☐ Had a sighting of a UFO in which there were physical effects or traces (Level 3)

☐ Had a sighting of a UFO in which I saw occupants or entities (Level 4)

☐ Had a sighting of a UFO during which the reality around me seemed altered (Level 5)

☐ Had a sighting of a UFO from which I have sustained permanent physical effects (Level 6)

☐ Actively attempted to contact UFOs (for example, through work with CSETI) (Level 7)

Levels 2 and 3 correspond to CEs 1 and 2, respectively. Level 4 corresponds to a CE3, and Levels 5 and 6 reflect characteristics often ascribed to CE4s. (A related question on the survey directly asks respondents whether they consider themselves to be abductees, a type of CE4, giving them a five-point scale ranging from "no" to "yes" for their response.) Level 7 reflects the active attempts of some UFO enthusiasts to contact UFOs and establish communication with the occupants. The most notable example of this type of endeavor is Dr. Steven Greer's Center for the Study of Extraterrestrial Intelligence (CSETI), based in Asheville, North Carolina.[67] A small group of individuals under the guidance and leadership of California psychotherapist Richard Boylan and Standing Elk, a Lakota medicine man from South Dakota, has also been attempting to establish contact.

One of the more surprising findings from the UFO survey is the number of those who have become involved in ufological studies but have not had their own sightings: 9 percent said they had never had a sighting and did not know anyone who had (Level 0); 38 percent said they had never had their own sighting but knew someone else who had (Level 1). Together, these nonexperiencers constitute nearly half of the UFO community. In retrospect the Level 0 response is actually rather problematic to interpret. If a respondent does not know anyone who has had a UFO sighting, they certainly could not be a regular participant in any local UFO group, where there are usually a number of individuals who have sighting stories to tell. Perhaps those who marked this response based their answers on their situation before becoming involved in the UFO community. Or perhaps the answers reflect those individuals who come to UFO conferences or attend a local UFO meeting out of curiosity but may not have (yet) become regular attendees. Or they could reflect the responses of spouses attending conferences or meetings with their more actively interested partners. Whether they are newcomers to the UFO scene, however, or just participating out of curiosity, they, too, form a part — if a transient part — of the UFO community.

Those who have had a UFO experience have encountered them in a variety of ways. Fully 44 percent of those survey respondents who reported experiences said that they had had a "simple" UFO sighting (CE1). The number of those reporting more complex (more strange) UFO experiences was significantly smaller: Only 6 percent had had a sighting in which there were physical traces of the event in the environment (a CE2), and only 8 percent had seen entities in association with their sighting (a CE3). The two statements designed to reflect possible CE4 experiences, asking about sightings in which the reality around the percipient seemed altered (the "Oz" effect) and about whether the witness had suffered any permanent effects from a UFO encounter, produced positive responses among 11 percent and 6 percent of the population, respectively. But when asked outright if they considered themselves to be abductees (one type of CE4 experiencers), 21 percent said that they felt reasonably or absolutely certain that they were, 65 percent of respondents said they were not, and 14 percent said they were unsure.[68]

The disparity between the numbers of self-identified abductees and those who responded positively to the "altered reality" and the "permanent effects" questions indicates that although these two markers are commonly considered by abduction researchers to be indicators of a possible CE4, they are not strong indicators. Among those who feel they are abductees, only 45 percent reported that at some time during their experience the reality around them seemed to be altered, and only 29 percent reported that they had sustained permanent physical effects from their experiences. Furthermore, some individuals who report these two kinds of UFO experiences nevertheless do not consider themselves abductees (19 percent of those who report "Oz effect" encounters, and 4 percent of those who report permanent effects after sightings).

THE ROLE OF PRIOR INTEREST
IN GENERATING UFO EXPERIENCES

One button I picked up at a UFO conference said, "If I hadn't believed it, I never would have seen it." Though a simple bit of facetiousness — the UFO community laughing at itself — the question is, does a chuckle hide the truth? Are those who believe that UFOs are real more inclined to actually see one? When asked whether they had any interest in UFOs before their encounter experiences, 68 percents of percipients said yes. Only 32 percent said no. The question did not specify what kind of interest the percipients may have had — whether it was a passive interest sufficient to cause them to tune in to television programs on the subject or a more aggressive interest sufficient to cause them to buy books and magazines on the subject or to attend local UFO group meetings. Although more than two-thirds of UFO experiencers in general report having had a prior interest in the subject, having a prior interest is inversely associated with the more high-strangeness types of UFO experiences (CE2, CE3, or CE4). Only in the case of simple sightings (CE1) is there a slight advantage to having a prior interest: 71 percent of experiencers with no prior interest in UFOs reported having had a simple UFO sighting, while 77 percent of those with a prior interest reported the same. Percipients with no prior UFO interest were more likely to report sightings with traces left behind (14 percent compared to 6 percent of those with prior interest), sightings with occupants (again 14 percent compared to 6 percent), sightings in which reality has seemed to be altered (23 percent compared to 13 percent), and sightings in which permanent effects have been sustained (12 percent compared to 3 percent).

The pattern revealed by this data is interesting on two counts. First, having a UFO experience, especially an experience of the more bizarre type, is not necessarily a matter of wish fulfillment predicated on a prior interest in the phenomenon. Indeed, those with prior interest in the subject, who might be most likely to wish for a spectacular UFO encounter, report fewer such encounters than those with no prior interest. This holds true even for abductions — the most bizarre kind of UFO encounter. Among respondents with a prior interest in UFO phenomena, 25 percent indicated that they were probably or definitely abductees, compared with 43 percent of those who lacked a prior interest. Whatever may be the cause(s) for having a UFO encounter, wish fulfillment based on a prior interest in the subject is probably an inadequate theory.

Second, the data tell us something about the nature of the experiences people report having. Although there are a large number of individuals who have had a simple UFO sighting (44 percent), the next kind of sighting, in which the level of strangeness increases, shows a radical drop in numbers (only 6 percent). But instead of increasingly strange UFO events being increasingly rare, as we ascend the experience scale just the opposite occurs. Positive response rates slowly increase with every incremental increase in "strangeness," peaking at the level where the UFO experience is accompanied by an apparent change in the surrounding reality: the Oz Effect in which birds quit singing, the wind can no longer be felt or heard, and so on (11 percent). The statement about the percipient suffering permanent physical aftereffects from their encounter, however, once again drops to only 6 percent. In short, the percentage of high-strangeness UFO encounters is small, but instead of each increase in strangeness producing a decrease in reported frequency, increases in strangeness produce slight increases in frequency. The limits to this "strangeness" effect are reached when it comes to encounters leaving permanent effects.

An analyst with staunchly pro-UFO sentiments might see this pattern as an indication that, whatever the nature of UFO and particularly CE4 encounters, and however much psychological trauma or confusion they may cause, the experiences do not often cause bodily harm. It should be pointed out, though, that the physical effects that people report are not necessarily always bad. A number of UFO witnesses have reported inexplicable healings of anything from minor abrasions to life-threatening conditions after their encounters.[69] An alternative pro-UFO interpretation would see the lower reports of permanent effects as evidence of the care taken by aliens to conceal their activities. A more skeptical analyst, however, might point out that this pattern, with its sudden drop-off when it comes to permanent physical effects, suggests that those who claim UFO experiences are reluctant (or unable) to provide solid proof of what they claim, so they avoid "having" the kinds of experiences that might lead one to expect such proof. While this is certainly a valid critique, an attempt to avoid providing scientific evidence of encounters runs contrary to the stated interests (at least) of the UFO community. In fact there are a number of UFO percipients who have attempted to furnish proof of their experiences, including CE4 experiences.[70] Until incontrovertible evidence is forthcoming, much of the UFO community would insist on the principle that "Absence of evidence is not evidence of absence."

Still another way of looking at this sighting pattern is that the reporting of high-strangeness experiences whose nature falls just outside the parameters of being susceptible to empirical proof suggests that the UFO phenomenon may lie in a realm that Huston Smith calls the "middle kingdom" — a different realm than the terrestrial but related to it, where "enigmatic energies of some kind seem to be at work, but . . . it is the very mischief to verify them or identify what they are."[71] The controversial association of UFO phenomena with the idea of this scientifically unverifiable middle kingdom is the subject this volume has addressed.

Notes

INTRODUCTION

1. Festinger, Riecken, and Schachter 1956.
2. Ruppelt 1956.
3. Hexham 1986, 14.
4. In retrospect I remember reading one or two of Frank Edwards's books on UFOs when I was in my preteen years. I remember, in particular, hot summer days spent exploring the cool, musty stacks of books in the "adult" part of our small-town library.
5. Unlike the Festinger-Keech researchers, I have not gone in "under cover," but have informed my fellows in the UFO community (at appropriate junctures) of my sociological and religious interests in the movement and of my self-identification as a participant-observer in it.
6. Strieber 1998, 255.

1. A SHORT HISTORY OF THE UFO MYTH

1. Sturrock 1994a, 8.
2. Anon. 1979, 139–40.
3. Richard Hall 1964; Hynek 1977.
4. Condon and Gilmore 1969.
5. Gallup poll, 1996; reported at www.nacomm.org and cited in *AUFORA News Update*, 5 May 1997, at <www.aufora.org>. The public education campaign has, in the long run, had more of an impact upon those technical and professional people who once freely reported anomalous sightings. For an example of this, see Cordova 1999, 13–14; Reid 1999, 14–15; and Eberhart 1999, 15, 32.

6. For excellent treatments of UFO belief in this context, see J. Dean 1998 and Lieb 1998.

7. For the prerational, see Lévy-Bruhl 1966, or, in a slightly different vein, Müller 1885. For protoscience, see Tylor 1883.

8. For instance, see Bascom 1965, 3–20.

9. Brief surveys of the history of the study of myth and major interpretive traditions can be found in Eliade 1987. A more extended discussion of myth can be found in Doty 1986.

10. See Samuel and Thompson 1990 and O'Flaherty 1988.

11. Samuel and Thompson 1990, 4–5.

12. Winthrop 1991, 192–93. Of course, it is Samuel and Thompson's contention that such an argument constitutes a rejection of one mythic system on the basis of the tenets supported by another mythic system.

13. Schmidt 1988, 185.

14. Doty 1986, 10–40. On producing a similar or sympathetic effect, see Bolle 1987, 266.

15. Among the numerous examples, see Spencer 1991, s.v. "Arnold, Kenneth; Sighting By"; and Maccabee 1995a, 1995b, and 1995c. For the skeptical point of view, see Menzel 1953, 7–10, 19, 41–42. Arnold wrote his own account of the sighting. See Arnold and Palmer 1952.

16. Stacy 1993a, 3. See also Heiden 1996, 11–12, and Lagrange 1998, 15, 20.

17. David Michael Jacobs 1975, 3–4.

18. *Bhāgavata Purāna,* Canto X, quoted in R. Thompson 1993, 224–25.

19. Ezekiel 3–4. Ironically, one of the first people to suggest the connection between UFOs and Ezekiel's visions was debunker Donald Menzel. (See Menzel 1953.) His rhetorical strategy of linking UFOs to biblical stories in order to show the absurdity of UFO belief backfired. The schematics of Ezekiel's chariot were puzzled out in the late 1960s and early 1970s by NASA engineer Josef F. Blumrich (Blumrich 1974).

20. *Bulletin of the C.B.A. Association,* III, I (Yokohama: n.p., 1964), cited in Vallee 1969, 4–5. For other possible reports of sightings from the past, see W. R. Drake 1963, 11–13, 1964a, 21–23, and 1964b, 10–12; Paris 1965, 22–23; and Ferris 1963, 26. Ufology even touches the field of art history with reference to several paintings and woodcuts depicting unusual aerial displays. See Daniels 1987, 8–27, and Brookesmith 1995, 11–19.

21. Vallee 1965, 7.

22. Ibid., 7, 14, 18.

23. For sightings outside the United States, see Rojas 1996. For more in-depth discussion of the Great Airship Wave of the late nineteenth century, see Hanlon 1970; Neeley n.d.a and n.d.b; and Clark 1998b, s.v. "Airship Sightings in the Nineteenth Century."

24. Clark 1992, 17–19.

25. *The Oakland [California] Tribune,* November 1896, cited in Menzel and Taves 1977, 60. The following citations taken from newspaper accounts mentioned by Clark and by Menzel have been checked for accuracy as far as possible, given the microfilm resources available to me. Specifically, references to *The New*

York Herald were tracked down and examined. All citations were found to be accurate. Given that one of the sources for these citations (Menzel) did not believe in UFOs, and the other author (Clark) concluded that the airship wave was largely the product of creative writing in an age when journalistic standards were less rigorous, it seems reasonable to assume that the citations I have not been able to verify are as accurate as those that I did verify.

26. *The Oakland [California] Tribune,* November 1896, cited in Clark 1992, 20.

27. *The San Francisco Chronicle,* 19 November 1896, cited in Clark 1992, 19.

28. *The New York Herald,* 12 April 1897, cited in Menzel and Taves 1977, 65. *The New York Herald,* 11 April 1897, cited in Menzcl and Taves 1977, 63.

29. *The Kansas City Times,* 29 March 1897, cited in Clark 1992, 25. *The Kansas City Star,* 28 March 1897, cited in Clark 1992, 24.

30. Note, for instance, *The New York Herald,* 16 April 1897, cited in Menzel and Taves 1977, 74. Regarding Edison, *The New York Herald,* 20 April 1897, cited in Menzel and Taves 1977, 78–79. Of course, as Jerome Clark observes, Edison also thought that heavier-than-air flying machines would be, at best, toys with no commercial value (Clark 1992, 34). As a further footnote in the history of educated opinions on anomalies, it may be noted that although Edison protested that he preferred spending his time on things with more commercial value than flying machines, in the 1920s he tried to invent a device for communicating with the spirits of the dead (R. Moore 1977, 176).

31. *The New York Sun,* 11 April 1897, cited in Menzel and Taves 1977, 69.

32. *The Des Moines Leader,* 13 April 1897; *The Quincy [Illinois] Morning Whig,* 11 April 1897; *The Cincinnati Enquirer,* 16 April 1897; *The Minneapolis Tribune,* 13 April 1897; *The Bloomington [Illinois] Pantagraph,* 17 April 1897; *The Louisville Evening Post,* 13 April 1897; and *The Logan Valley Sun* (Lyons, Nebraska), 21 April 1897, cited in Clark 1992, 28–29.

33. *The Burlington [Iowa] Hawk-Eye,* 16 April 1897; *The Galveston Daily News,* 18 April 1897; *The Saginaw Courier-Herald,* 17 April 1897; *The Indianapolis Journal,* 17 April 1897; *The St. Louis Post-Dispatch,* 19 April 1897; *The Kokomo Daily Tribune,* 4 May 1897, cited in Clark 1992, 28, 32–33.

34. *The Clarksville [Tennessee] Daily Leaf-Chronicle,* 17 April 1897, cited in Clark 1992, 33. Lucius Farish discusses other appeals to the extraterrestrial hypothesis during the airship wave (Farish 1973).

35. Clark 1992, 361–85. The *U.F.O. Historical Revue,* dedicated to uncovering more of the early UFO reports buried in newspaper and magazine archives, began publication in 1998. For more information, write to PO Box 176, Stoneham, MA 02180.

36. Clark 1992, 362, 373–74, 376. For another account of a sighting from the "interim" period of UFO history, see Shirley 1997–1998.

37. "Paris Interested in the Airship," in *The New York Herald,* 15 April 1897, cited in Menzel and Taves 1977, 75.

38. Clark 1992, 376.

39. Ibid., 168–76, 375–76, 381.

40. For information on early claims about crashes involving aerial anomalies, see Clark 1993a.

41. Clark 1992, 170–72. Also see Aldrich 1998b.

42. Clark 1992, 153–56. Menzel and Taves observed that the foo fighters were probably light effects from the wing surfaces caused by a slight loss of aerodynamic trim because the wings were damaged and patched so often during the war (Menzel and Taves 1977, 56).

43. Bruce Henstell, "Bombed!" *Los Angeles Magazine* (March 1991): 70–75, and "Japanese Carry War to California Coast," *Life* (9 March 1942): 19–23, both referenced in Clark 1992, 378–79; Marvin Miles, "Chilly Throng Watches Shells Bursting in Sky," *Los Angeles Times,* 26 February 1942; "Army Says Alarm Real: Roaring Guns Mark Blackout," *Los Angeles Times,* 26 February 1942. See also Good 1988, 15–18.

44. Spencer 1989, 19.

45. David Michael Jacobs 1975, 38, 41.

46. Ibid., 237–38, 258. For a more detailed treatment of the press's role in UFO reporting, see Strentz 1970.

47. David Michael Jacobs 1975, 56–58.

48. Lawrence 1950.

49. Darrach and Ginna 1952, 80–82, cited in David Michael Jacobs 1975, 69–70.

50. Vallee 1965, 129, 130n.

51. Anon. 1952, 62.

52. "Biblical Flying Saucers," *Science News Letter* 63 (7 March 1953): 148. For the first religious periodical to deal with the question of extraterrestrial life, see Pittenger 1956.

53. "RAAF Captures Flying Saucer on Ranch in Roswell Region," *Roswell Daily Record,* 8 July 1947.

54. "Suspected 'Disk' Only Flying Weather Vane," *Dallas Morning News,* 9 July 1947; "Ramey Says Excitement Not Justified," *Roswell Daily Record,* 9 July 1947; "'Disk' Near Bomb Test Site Is Just a Weather Balloon," *New York Times,* 9 July 1947. Modern photographic and computer enhancement techniques allowed researchers in 1999 to reexamine the photos taken at the 1947 press conference. Of particular interest was a piece of paper held by General Roger Ramey in one of the photos. Analysts felt that they could make out words and phrases suggesting that the balloon explanation was a cover story. See Filer 1998; Burleson 1999; Randle 1999; message from Bruce Fleming, "Text of Concealed Roswell Memo and Others," on <iufo@world.std.com> on 2 May 1999; and for a copy of the photo in question, see <www.angelfire.com/co2/4reesearch/images/roswellmemo.jpg> and <www.angelfire.com/co2/4reesearch/images/ memomessage.jpg>.

55. For the UFO community's research, see Berlitz and Moore 1980, and Randle and Schmitt 1991 and 1994. For brief accounts, see Good 1998, 254–57, and Clark 1992, 113–15.

Preempting a GAO investigation report, in September 1994 the air force released its own report on the so-called Roswell Incident. Their conclusion was that the debris found near Roswell was from a top secret military balloon project. The GAO report was released in July 1995 and stated that many of the air force records from this period had been destroyed, though, contrary to accepted practice, no records could be found as to who had authorized the destructions or when. A second air force report addressing additional features of the Roswell case was released in 1997. (See General Accounting Office 1995; Weaver and McAndrew 1995; and McAndrew 1997.)

This entire matter was the occasion for great debate and comment in the UFO community. Major critiques of the air force reports and commentary on the GAO report can be found in Rodeghier and Chesney 1994, 1995a, and 1995b; Pflock 1994; Randle 1994; Galganski 1995; Anon. 1995; and Richard Hall 1995.

For a critical perspective on the Roswell case, see *The Skeptic's UFO Newsletter,* January 1995, March 1995, and May 1995 (available from 404 "N" St. SW, Washington, DC 20024); Jeffrey 1997; and Randle 1997. The Jeffrey article prompted one MUFON member to write:

> I do not believe that *my* Journal should be used to debunk the UFO phenomenon generally nor the Roswell crash specifically. I was astounded and irate that the editor would give Kent Jeffrey fifteen pages. . . . This is not the first time you have given over *my* journal to debunkers, but if it is not the last, you no longer represent my thinking and have no further need of my membership dues or my services. . . . MUFON is not a debating society which presents both sides of the question of UFOs and aliens. MUFON is an advocacy organization. (Schoen 1997, 16–17)

56. Gallup Organization, Question USGallup.883 Q05A, survey of 5 November 1973. See also the *New York Times,* 29 November 1973, 41.

57. Dating UFO sighting waves is to some extent a subjective matter depending on how one views periodicity. This is especially the case in the early 1950s, when one flurry of sightings seemed to be followed by another within less than a year. This being the case, I have lumped together periods that ufologists tend to separate into finer categories. The major waves to which I refer occurred in 1947, 1952, 1954, 1956–1958, 1965–1968, and 1973–1974, after which this study becomes less concerned with sightings per se and focuses instead on occupant and contact reports. For more detailed information on sighting waves, see Vallee and Vallee 1966; Randles 1986; C. Lorenzen 1969; Ritrovato 1995; Jeffers 1996; and Richard Hall 1998.

58. Ufologists have downplayed the social factors that might contribute to sighting waves, because the implication behind such theories is that *all* sightings are reducible to social factors such as mass delusion and hysteria. In rejecting this correlation they have discovered other factors such as astronomical alignments, tectonic activity, and geomagnetic fluctuations that they say positively correlate with sighting waves. See Kottmeyer 1995–1996; Vallee and Vallee 1966; Ritrovato 1995 and 1996.

59. David Michael Jacobs 1975, 63, 87; cf. Ruppelt 1956, 149.

60. Clark 1992, 396–403; David Michael Jacobs 1975, 77–78. Also see Ruppelt 1956, which deals extensively with that time period and the events surrounding the Washington flap.

61. David Michael Jacobs 1975, 201–202; Vallee 1992a, 173–77.

62. Memo of General Nathan F. Twining to the Commanding General of the Army Air Forces, 23 September 1947, "Subject: AMC Opinion Concerning 'Fly-

ing Disks.'" For a copy of the report filed by Twining and a discussion of it, see Good 1988, 476–78, 260–62; Fawcett and Greenwood 1984, 213–14; and Bourdais 1998a. Despite the official military position that UFOs are not real, the opinion that people, including personnel at military bases, are seeing something genuinely anomalous has been found in numerous documents released from government and military agencies under the Freedom of Information Act. See Fowler 1981, 186–92, and Fawcett and Greenwood 1984, esp. 1–56 and 468–69, 485ff. For photocopies of FOIA-released sighting reports from around military installations such as air force bases, NORAD defense posts, nuclear weapons storage facilities, and so on, see Stone 1991.

63. David Michael Jacobs 1975, 41–48; Ruppelt 1956, 41, 45; Clark 1992, 282–84. In the 1990s large numbers of documents from Project Sign and Project Grudge were released under the Freedom of Information Act. See "Projects Sign and Grudge Records Released," *Just Cause* 49 (December 1996), downloaded on 8 January 2000 from <www.ufomind.com/ufo/updates/1997/jan/m23–022.shtml>. For a copy of the original Project Sign report as released under the FOIA, see Stone 1991, 13–41. Also see Swords 1995, and Aldrich 1998a. In 1991 a small group of ufologists began the Project Sign/Grudge Research Center to investigate the "historical aspects of the first official and secret investigation of UFOs by the U.S. Air Force." See their web site at <www.geocities.com/~pjct-sign/>.

64. Clark 1992, 280–82.

65. David Michael Jacobs 1975, 50–66, 86; Anon 1994a; and Zeidman and Rodeghier 1993.

66. Maccabee 1979 and 1983; Zeidman and Rodeghier 1993. On the tendency of the best "unknowns" to come from qualified observers, note W. Johnson and Thomas 1998, 77–78.

67. David Michael Jacobs 1975, 89–90, 91ff, 94, 99; Fowler 1981, 16–18, 172. For the story of Ruppelt's involvement in Project Blue Book, see Ruppelt 1956. For another look at Ruppelt's involvement, see M. Hall and Connors 2000, which is based on Ruppelt's unedited papers and private notes as well as on interviews with those who knew him.

68. Commercial pilots objected to being required to report all UFO sightings yet being treated like "incompetents and told to keep quiet" when they did. They published a protest petition in the December 22, 1958 *Newark Star Ledger*. See Fowler 1981, 183.

69. David Michael Jacobs 1975, 104–105. For a discussion of the locus of control in the air force's study of UFOs, see Skow and Endres 1995, and Cybulski 1995.

70. David Michael Jacobs 1975, 151.

71. Ruppelt reported that as of January 1953, 27 percent of all sighting reports filed with Blue Book had remained unexplainable. See Ruppelt 1956, 211. Even that number was an improvement, however. A 1949 article in the *Air Force Times* had stated that 40 percent of early UFO reports remained unexplained after investigation. See "Many Flying Saucers Incidents Remain Unsolved, AF Reports," *Air Force Times* (7 May 1949), 6.

72. David Michael Jacobs 1975, 134–35, 144, 253.

73. Ibid., 168–69. NASA was one of the agencies that seemed like a logical "home" for the Blue Book project. They declined, however. For this story, see R. Henry 1988.

74. David Michael Jacobs 1975, 209.

75. Ibid., 230, 246, 297, 301, 302.

76. Ibid., 212, 226–27.

77. Ibid., 227, 243.

78. Ibid., 228–29.

79. Ibid., 239–40, 246. Note that in *The UFO Enigma,* Menzel and Taves provide their own explanations for these obstinate cases and claim to bring the percentage of unknowns down to zero (Menzel and Taves 1977).

80. David Michael Jacobs 1975, 242, 238, 255.

81. Ibid., 243.

82. For a fuller discussion of the Condon Committee, its work and results, see the following books by two principals in the matter: Saunders and Harkins 1968, and Craig 1995. A very thorough analysis of the Condon Report is found in Sturrock 1999, 18–56.

83. Fawcett and Greenwood 1984, 1–2. For examples, see the letter from the Department of the Air Force reproduced in Stone 1991, 74; from the Defense Intelligence Agency, reproduced in Stone 1991, 97; and from the Central Intelligence Agency, reproduced in Stone 1991, 172. Also see Fawcett and Greenwood 1984, 7 and 113 regarding the CIA; 7–8, 147 and 159 regarding the Federal Bureau of Investigation; 180–82 for the National Security Agency; 193 for the State Department; and 226–27 on the air force's continuing involvement with UFO sighting reports.

84. Gallup poll, 5 November 1973 (Roper Center for Public Opinion Research), Question US Gallup.883 Q05B.

85. C. Lorenzen 1962. This book was reissued in 1966 in expanded form under a new title; see C. Lorenzen 1966.

86. C. Lorenzen 1966, 277. APRO folded in the late 1980s with the deaths of their founders. The organization's records then disappeared until researchers unearthed microfilmed copies of many of the original records in 1999. See Aldrich 1999.

87. Sachs 1980, s.v. "Saucer and Unexplained Celestial Events Research Society." By the late 1990s, SAUCERS as an organization was long since defunct, but its founder was the author and editor of *Saucer Smear,* an irregular UFO newsletter "dedicated to the highest principles of ufological journalism" and wryly billing itself as "Shockingly Close to the Truth." Moseley and *Saucer Smear* can be reached at P.O. Box 1709, Key West, FL 33041.

88. GSW has specialized in photographic analysis of UFO pictures and in filing legal suits against the CIA for their failure to fully comply with Freedom of Information Act requests (see Spencer 1991, s.v. "Ground Saucer Watch"). In 1978 Todd Zechel founded Citizens Against UFO Secrecy (CAUS) to file such requests and to push the government to release ever greater portions of its information on UFOs (see Spencer 1991, s.v. "Citizens Against UFO Secrecy"). Though such FOIA efforts have been remarkably successful, sometimes the information released has been censored with a black marker so heavily that little is left

to read. Even this has been useful information, however, for the release of such highly censored documents has shown that, contrary to official pronouncements, the U.S. government still has an active interest in UFOs, the issue is considered important to national security, and there are many more files on the subject that have not yet been released.

89. Among the first members of the board were the first director of the CIA, Vice-Admiral R. H. Hillenkoetterr; retired Rear Admiral Delmer S. Fahreny, the former head of the navy's guided missile program; a professor of religion; a minister; a professor of physics; popular columnist Earl Douglass; and radio-TV commentator Frank Edwards. See David Michael Jacobs 1975, 145–48; 183–84.

90. Donald Keyhoe 1950, 1953, 1955, 1960, and 1973.

91. Fowler 1981, 62.

92. Ibid., 57–62; Spencer 1991, s.v. "NICAP"; Good 1988, 346–52; Fawcett and Greenwood 1984, 206–207, 231–34. The files from NICAP were eventually turned over to the Center for UFO Studies for safekeeping.

93. David Michael Jacobs 1975, 257.

94. Clark 1990b, 163–64.

95. For MUFON's statement of purpose, see Andrus 1992, 3.

96. Spencer 1991, s.v. "CUFOS." For more of the story of the founding of CUFOS, see also Craig 1995, 189–90.

97. Personal communication, Mark Rodeghier, 12 October 1996.

98. Ibid.

99. Interestingly enough, in the late 1950s even the Jet Propulsion Laboratory in Pasadena, California, had a UFO Club. See Anon. 1958. For an up-to-date listing of UFO organizations, see Blevins 1996.

100. Fowler 1981, 165; Fawcett and Greenwood 1984, 196–99, and the copy of a Department of the Air Force memo on the subject on 237.

101. The earliest promoter of the reality of Men in Black was Gray Barker. See G. Barker 1956; Bender 1962; Clark 1992, 71–73, 73–76; Spencer 1991 s.v. "Men in Black." Most recently the subject has been taken up again by Jim Keith (Keith 1997) and by Jenny Randles (Randles 1997).

102. Clark 1992, 240–44; Fowler 1981, 185; Fawcett and Greenwood 1984, 64; W. Johnson and Thomas 1998, 90–93; and Allan 1998. For information on alleged attacks on aircraft by UFOs, see Good 1993, 25–28.

103. See Fawcett and Greenwood 1984, 1–56. Also see Fowler 1981, 186–94; Salas 1997; and Craig 1995, 170–72.

104. One anonymous informant, an air force colonel, told Roswell researcher Kevin Randle that the original report submitted by Project Sign in late 1948 contained two paragraphs about physical evidence recovered from a crashed disk near Roswell. General Vandenberg is said to have refused to accept the report until the two paragraphs were removed (Clark 1992, 138–39). Abduction researcher Richard Boylan believes that this retro-engineering project has been in progress for a number of years and is supposed to prepare the United States for a hostile alien invasion "by seeking to have equivalent spacecraft on 'our side'" (Boylan 1992). For a general discussion of the reports of saucer crashes, see Randles 1995 and Stringfield 1977, 1978, 1980, 1982, 1991, and 1994.

105. Fowler 1981, 212. As an example of the circuitous route such stories may travel before reaching the light of day in the UFO community, the story of Mrs. G. reached Fowler via ufologist Charles Wilhelm, who heard it from Mrs. G's friend, who originally heard the story from Mrs. G.

106. C. Lorenzen 1966, 193.

107. Fowler 1981, 196–217; Richard Hall 1988, 73–87.

108. Interview of Linda Moulton Howe with "Kewper," on Art Bell's *Coast-to-Coast* radio show (1 June 1998).

109. Norlandar@aol.com, post of 26 October 1999 to <ufolist@egroups .com>. For other instances of military insiders revealing information about UFO matters, see Howe 1998, 1–144.

110. Fawcett and Greenwood 1984, 112–46; Good 1988, 326–65.

111. See G. Haines 1997, also available at </www.odci.gov/csi/studies/ 97unclas/ufo.html>. For discussion of this article, see Rodeghier 1997 and Maccabee 1997.

112. Fawcett and Greenwood 1984, 147–79; Good 1988, 253ff.

113. Fawcett and Greenwood 1984, 180–91; Good 1988, 306–25.

114. For a European perspective on the FOIA releases, see Gildas Bourdais 1998a.

115. Indeed, physician and ufologist Steven Greer has engaged in an active campaign to locate important or well-placed informants, to secure their testimony, and to make it possible for them to speak publicly without retribution for violating security oaths. See <www.cseti.org>.

116. Rayl 1994; B. Anderson 1995–1996; Hesemann 1992; King 1996; and Anon. 1996a. For a skeptical review of Dean's claims, see Klass 1997.

117. Good 1991, 150–213; Basiago 1992; Kirby 1993; Campbell 1994.

118. An interesting essay on cover-ups in general as a normal function of government appears in Stacy 1992c.

119. The discussion in question began on the I-UFO list <iufo@world.std .com> on 3 April 1998 with a post from Richard Boylan, a psychologist, abductee, and UFO investigator. By 6 April 1998, Citizens Against UFO Secrecy (CAUS) had issued a statement to the effect that "the motivation and credibility of the original source of this story is questionable and highly suspect. None of the information, other than there being a Monsignor Balducci, can be substantiated" (Peter A. Gersten, Esq., Executive Director, Citizens Against UFO Secrecy, Inc., posted to I-UFO on 6 April 1998). On that same date a list member cited an English-speaking Italian ufologist he knew, who said that the monsignor was a regular guest on Italian TV talk and opinion shows, but he was not aware of any close Vatican connections (Mike Spitzer to I-UFO on 6 April 1998). A second post forwarded from yet another Italian ufologist added that Balducci was not a Vatican theologian and that whatever opinions he (Balducci) expressed were private ones, not official. The poster also noted that the opinions of the monsignor had been given over the course of the past two years, thus negating the idea that this was a "sudden" development in a UFO un-cover-up program (<Doc-Bulletin@webtv.net> to I-UFO on 8 April 1998). Abductee Whitley Strieber entered the fray to inform the I-UFO list that Balducci had given him a personal interview. Noting that Balducci was an exorcist for the Archdiocese of Rome, Strieber

commented that the monsignor's expertise in that field lent "authority" to his views on the question of whether the Visitors (as Strieber calls the aliens) are demons (post forwarded by Richard Boylan to I-UFO on 11 April 1998). Strieber's interview with the monsignor is appended to his book *Confirmation* (Strieber 1998).

120. Whitehead 1996. See also B. Anderson 1995–1996. The idea that astronauts in space saw UFOs became a part of the UFO myth at an early stage. For a summary of alleged astronaut sightings, see Hynek and Vallee 1975, 63–65, and Menzel and Taves 1977, 115–16. For the skeptical view of the alleged encounters of astronauts with alien craft, see Oberg 1977.

121. A group of UFO researchers formed a coalition in 1996 to get more high-ranking officials who have knowledge of the UFO situation to come forward with what they know. North Carolina physician and ufologist Steven Greer stated that, in his opinion, security oaths in the matter of the alien presence are invalid. See "On the Validity of National Security Oaths Related to the UFO/Extraterrestrial Subject," *CNI News* 2, no. 16 (1 November 1996); and "Steven Greer Calls for Congressional UFO Hearings," *CNI News* 2, no. 21 (1 February 1997) at <CNINews1@aol.com>.

122. *Dateline*, National Broadcasting Company, 19 April 1996.

123. Good 1991, 76–77; also see an interview with Cooper broadcast on UPN's *Paranormal Borderline* on 7 May 1996, and Geremia 1997.

124. *UFO Universe* 1:3 (November 1988); also see *Dateline* interview, National Broadcasting Company, 19 April 1996.

125. Sheaffer 1987–1988, 134; Beckley 1993.

126. Quoted in Keyhoe 1973, 50–51; also quoted in Anon. 1994b. Also see "Duty, Honor and Country," *Vital Speeches* 58 (15 June 1962): 519–21; *U.S. News and World Report* 52 (4 June 1962): 78–79; and MacArthur 1964.

127. Especially in light of Reagan's comment, his support for the Strategic Defense Initiative was seen by some ufologists as a response to fears of invasion from outer space. The collapse of the communist regime in the Soviet Union added fuel to this speculation, it being reasoned that the collapse was deliberately engineered or embraced by major power-brokers because a unified Earth would be better able to repulse an attack from outside. Vallee cites this belief as one of several unfortunate accretions to the actual UFO evidence (Vallee 1991a, 18). For the idea that several presidents have had meetings with aliens, see Creighton 1999; Rivas 1999; and Freixedo 1994 and 1995.

128. "Alien Encounters from Tomorrowland," broadcast on 18–19 March 1995. See also Vick 1995 and "Disney Encounter Lifts UFO Believers," *The Orlando Sentinel*, 3 May 1995.

129. For the Robertson Panel recommendation, see note 67. For the UFO community's reaction to the Disney piece, see Bartlett 1995 and "UFO Reality Is Breaking Through" by Richard J. Boylan, posted 14 January 1996 on I-UFO <i_ufo-l@europe.std.com> and originally published in *Perceptions Magazine* (January–February 1996). In contrast, some UFO students have been suggesting for many years that "they" are trying to undo the cover-up. See Kor 1977.

130. Tom Brokaw, "In Depth," *NBC Nightly News*, 29 October 1995.

131. Tom Brokaw, *NBC Nightly News*, 3 November 1995.

132. *NBC Nightly News,* 6 March 1996.

133. Though pejorative, this idea is implicit in criticisms of UFO percipients and ufologists that suggest that people come up with UFO stories to enliven their otherwise dull and uneventful, working-class lives. See Rae 1993.

134. The results of the survey were published in Hopkins, Jacobs, and Westrum 1992. For critiques of and reflections upon the Roper survey, see Robert Hall, Johnson, and Rodeghier 1993; Hopkins 1994; and Donderi 1994.

135. PEER, P.O. Box 398080, Cambridge, MA 02139, or at <www.peer-mack.org>.

136. "Rockefeller to Send New Roswell Study to Congress," *CNI News* 13, no. 5 (18 December 1995) at <CNINews@aol.com>; Anon. 1996c. "Prez' Hunt for Campaign Cash May Turn Up UFOs First," *ISCNI Flash* 1, no. 13 (16 September 1995) at <CNINews@aol.com>; and Richard J. Boylan, "UFO Reality Is Breaking Through," posted to I-UFO <iufo@alterzone.com> on 8 September 1996. For an analysis of the document and a look at its table of contents, see Paul B. Thompson, "The Rocky Report," on the ParaScope web page <www.parascope/com/nb/ rockyufo.htm> on 9 February 1997. Webster Hubbell, a former deputy attorney general in the Clinton Administration, indicated that Clinton asked him to find the real answers to two questions: who killed JFK, and were UFOs real? (See Hubbell 1997, 282.)

137. See "The Truth," Press Release, 25 November 1998 at <mmattei@earthlink.net>; Joe Firmage's biography at <www.meaningoflife.com/Firmage.html>; The Kairos, "The Truth," e-mail from <thekairos@the-word-is-truth.org> on 16 January 1999; and Anon. 1999b.

138. Spencer 1991, s.v. "Ubatuba, Brazil"; Craig 1995, 105–13 and 121–28; Menzel and Boyd 1963, 235–37; Swords, Walker, and Johnson 1992; and Howe 1993, 18.

139. Clark 1996b.

140. M. Johnson 1996.

141. Howe 1989 and 1992, 3–9; Spencer 1991, s.v. "Cattle Mutilations"; Stainic 1993; Lamarche 1996; Wolverton and Danenhower 1995; Craig 1995, 117–21; Fawcett and Greenwood 1984, 32–33, 102–105; and Good 1991, 147.

142. Chorost 1993; Delgado and Andrews 1991; Hesemann 1995; James Schnabel 1992; Jim Schnabel 1994c; Stacy 1993b; Deetken 1993; Rutkowski 1993; Clark 1994c; Wingfield 1995a; Rydeen 1995. For excellent presentations of both crop circles and cattle mutilations in one location, see Howe 1993 and 1998.

143. For copies of the original memo as received by Shandera and for a transcription of its contents, see Richard Hall 1988, 366–79. The document is famous in UFO circles and has been reproduced in a variety of locations. It may also be seen as a part of Stone 1991, 126–32.

144. The most thorough treatment of the controversy surrounding the MJ-12 papers can be found in Friedman 1996. Also see Jon Elliston, "The MJ-12 UFO Documents Hoax," on the ParaScope web site <www.parascope.com/ds/0996/ maj1.htm> on 9 February 1997. Even the Government Accounting Office was drawn into the debate when Representative Schiff of New Mexico asked that

office to check on the authenticity of the MJ-12 material. See "GAO Letter to Rep. Schiff Regarding Majestic 12 Documents" on the ParaScope web site <www.parascope.com/articles/1296/mj12gao.htm> on 9 February 1997.

145. See, for instance, Blum 1990.

146. Joseph Paramore Firmage, *The Truth* (1998) at <www.thewordis-truth.org>.

147. The gist of the MJ-12 myth is spelled out in Good 1988, 257–60, 544–51, and Good 1991, 123–37. The story has undergone further elaboration in a decidedly conspiratorial vein in books such as Cooper 1991 and William F. Hamilton 1991. In early 1996 a continuation of the MJ-12 myth developed as copies of a document entitled "Extraterrestrial Entities and Technology Recovery and Disposal: Majestic-12 Group Special Operations Manual" circulated in UFO circles. Many ufologists consider this document, like its predecessor, to be a fake. See Randle 1996b. For the skeptics' view of the MJ-12 papers, see Klass 1987–1988.

148. For a discussion of the best UFO photos, movies, and videos, see Strieber 1998, 9–82. For a skeptical perspective, see Klass 1975, 138–66.

149. Good 1991, 111–13. For information on another alleged film of alien encounters, see Maccabee 1996.

150. Good 1991, 114–17. Also see Howe 1993, 278, and 1989, chapter 7.

151. Andrus 1995a; Mantle and Friedman 1995; Jeffrey 1995 and 1996; Mantle 1995; Wingfield 1995b; Tobin 1995a and 1995b; and J. Carpenter 1995b, 1995c, and 1996.

152. Letter by John William Lopez (Lopez 1992).

153. See ibid. For an excellent presentation of the "ufology as military pawn" orientation toward the UFO myth, see Kanon 1997.

154. N = 742.

155. N = 738. Respondents were asked to evaluate the venues for UFO discovery by assigning each a value of 1 (not likely) to 5 (most likely). Not all respondents offered an opinion for each of the suggested venues.

156. N = 727.

157. N = 676.

158. N = 685.

159. See the appendix.

2. A SHORT HISTORY OF ALIEN ENCOUNTERS

1. Jung was very interested in the UFO phenomenon. He began collecting references to aerial anomalies by at least 1946 and published *Ein moderner Mythus von Dingen die am Himmel gesehen werden* in 1958 (published in English in 1959). At the same time, he wrote an article for the monthly bulletin of APRO, which caught the attention of an Associated Press correspondent in Alamogordo, New Mexico, site of the White Sands Missile Range and several unexplained UFO sightings. In a wire dispatch dated July 30, 1958, the journalist reported that the eminent psychologist had said that "'Saucers' Exist," that they could not be explained as mere psychological phenomena, and that they seemed to be intelligently guided ("Dr. Jung Says 'Saucers' Exist; Bars Psychological Explanations,"

The New York Times, 30 July 1958). Other readers of Jung's UFO monograph have questioned whether he truly believed in their objective reality, emphasizing instead his analysis of them as modern-day expressions of archetypal symbols of wholeness. In fact, the monograph makes several statements about UFOs that, taken singly, seem to be contradictory and that have been used by UFO realists and by UFO debunkers to support their conflicting points of view. I believe he did the only intellectually safe thing: He analyzed the psychological significance of UFOs, leaving the question of their ontological status for others to debate, but bowed to the possibility of UFO reality with the observation that archetypes were seldom known to leave ground traces and give radar returns.

2. Even in the late 1990s Bob Pratt devoted a chapter of his book on UFO contacts in Brazil to an admonition against the conspiracy mindset in ufology, noting that for many the whole scenario served "egos starved for recognition" but added little to our knowledge of UFOs. (See Pratt 1996, 307.) Similarly, veteran ufologist David Jacobs urged the field to abandon its concentration on cover-ups and conspiracies in favor of more profitable lines of inquiry. He sagely pointed out that cover-up theories may serve as a psychological comfort for "those who would like the phenomenon to be controlled in some way" by *someone,* when in fact the UFO phenomenon has remained obdurately unpredictable and uncontrolled. See David M. Jacobs 1997.

3. Ruppelt 1956, iv, 45–46, 144, 167, 170, 195.

4. Ibid., 5, 18, 195, 201, 209, 224.

5. Stanton 1966, 41.

6. Vallee 1965, 108.

7. Michel 1956, 227.

8. Sanderson 1967, 6–7.

9. Vallee 1965, 152, 109, 112, 113, 125.

10. As late as 1983 J. Allen Hynek was urging ufologists not to get caught up in dogmatic statements about the origins and purposes of the intelligences controlling UFOs. He emphasized that the *U* in "UFO" stands for "unidentified," and that a too-facile and too-precipitous attempt to answer second-tier questions would only hurt the standing of ufology among the few mainstream scientists who were willing to consider the subject valid for study. In order to bridge the gap between the advancing research interests within ufology and the still-open question of UFO reality among mainstream scientists, Hynek urged ufologists to remember that they were still only studying UFO reports and their surrounding circumstances — not UFOs, or UFO occupants, themselves. See Hynek 1983.

11. The Gallup Organization, 1966, reported in Durant 1993. Since 1966, random national surveys asking about sightings have yielded "yes" responses ranging from 8 percent to an all-time high of 14 percent in 1990. Nonrandom survey responses have run as high as 33 percent "yes." (For the latter, see Anon. 1997.)

12. Durant 1993, 11.

13. Ruppelt 1956, 10.

14. Michel 1956, 99.

15. Keyhoe 1960, 123; Richard Hall 1964, 4.

16. Sanderson 1967, 82, 100.

17. Vallee 1965, 183.

18. See D. Carpenter 1968, 461ff. See also Creighton 1997a.

19. Scully 1950, 181.

20. Interestingly, most of the reports of entity sightings from the mid-1950s came from Europe and South America. See C. Lorenzen 1966, 192. Although at least some UFO investigators from all nations entertained such reports with great reserve, one does wonder to what extent this reluctance of ufology in general reflected the leadership role of the United States in the field.

21. The landing and occupant cases in question can be found in ibid., 38, 40–42, 46, 48, 49, 49–50, 50–51, 52–53, 55–56, 57, 57–58, 60–64, 74–77, 77, 102–103, 200, 215–17, 218–22, 229, 229–33, 233–34, and 244–45. The early abduction cases mentioned for the first time in the 1966 edition of the book are found in ibid., 64–74, 80, and 213–15.

22. C. Lorenzen and J. Lorenzen 1967.

23. Sanderson 1967.

24. Bowen 1969b.

25. C. Lorenzen 1966, 175–77. Of course, not all those interested in UFO matters considered this case to be reliable. Donald Menzel, whose professional sideline seemed to be serving as a debunker of all things ufological, offered the theory that Father Gill was myopic, probably severely so, and had simply not had his glasses on at the time of the sighting (Vallee 1992a, 346–47). Later he suggested that what Gill and the others had seen was the planet Venus. In addition, although many people from the mission signed the report that Gill wrote about the sighting, Menzel felt that Gill himself was not necessarily a reliable witness and that those who signed his report may not have really known what they were signing. "All of them, undoubtedly, saw something bright in the sky. And if that bright thing, whatever it was, so impressed their priest, they would certainly have signed and attested to anything. One can hardly term them independent, unbiased observers." (See Menzel 1972, 146–53.) For Father Gill's response to his critics, see Anon. 1977.

26. Clark 1996a, 454.

27. Vallee 1992a, 102.

28. It is interesting to note that the army captain from White Sands who was assigned to investigate the case quickly received a secured-line telephone call about it from a colonel serving the Joint Chiefs of Staff at the Pentagon. The captain was ordered to give his report on the case orally, at that moment, to the inquirer, leading him to wonder why there was such interest in such high circles (Clark 1996a, 457).

29. Notably, Project Blue Book astronomer J. Allen Hynek. See Vallee 1992a, 111: "He would like to be able to explain away Socorro because of its implication that the diminutive pilots are a real factor in the phenomenon. It is true that there is something absurd, even ludicrous, about the humanoids. Yet they are real." Still, Vallee had his doubts about the sighting as well, and wondered in his diary if it might not be an experimental device that the government was working on (1992a, 286–87). Ultimately, Hynek was convinced by the sincerity of the witness and the physical evidence in the case, expressing the opinion that it could in fact be the "Rosetta Stone" of ufology (quoted in Clark 1996a, 458).

30. Vallee was unconvinced by the arguments against the Socorro sighting being an experimental moon device; he found reason to believe the sighting to be genuine because it was part of a worldwide wave of sightings that was then occurring (Vallee 1992a, 111).

31. Quintanilla 1966, 95–100, cited in Clark 1996a, 462. For lengthier treatments of the Socorro sighting, see C. Lorenzen and J. Lorenzen 1967, 26–28, 132–33; Clark 1996a, 452–65; and Powers 1969 in Bowen 1969b, 130–42. For a more skeptical presentation of the case that suggests that the sighting was a hoax perhaps perpetrated in order to create a tourist attraction for the town, see Peebles 1994, 148–53, and Klass 1968.

Though it would perhaps be easier if the UFO myth consisted of clearly distinct tropes and trajectories, such is not the case. There is always some overlap of tropes and surprising convergences of seemingly disparate trajectories in the UFO story. For example, as an interesting aside to the Socorro case, when ufologist Linda Moulton Howe was shown the "briefing paper" by air force Sergeant Richard Doty, as mentioned in chapter 1, it was explained to her that the Socorro landing had been the result of a mix-up in a scheduled military-alien "foreign exchange" meeting. See Peebles 1994, 261.

32. C. Lorenzen and J. Lorenzen 1967, 101–02; Bowen 1969b, 239–48; Vallee 1990a, 96–100; Clark 1996a, 534–37.

33. Vallee 1992a, 152. See also the study by Antonio Ribera of the miracle at Fatima in which he too suggests that the reality behind UFO occupant sightings strives to present itself in terms congenial to the percipients (Ribera 1964). Finally, see Clark 1965.

34. C. Lorenzen 1966, 9.

35. Bowen 1969b, 9.

36. Clark 1996a, 168–75; and for a slightly more skeptical view of the incident, though short on thorough explanation and analysis, see Menzel and Boyd 1963, 226–27.

37. Leslie and Adamski 1953.

38. Adamski 1955.

39. Moseley 1997, 4.

40. W. Moore 1985, 1, 3–4, cited in Clark 1992, 6–7; Menzel and Taves 1977, 193.

41. Blomqvist 1988, and Stupple 1979a and 1979b, all cited in Clark 1992, 1.

42. Cleary-Baker 1965, cited in Clark 1992, 9.

43. Honey 1964, cited in Clark 1992, 4.

44. Jacques Vallee recorded in his diary for April 1964 that the only books on UFO matters that had been consistently commercially successful during the previous ten years were contactee accounts and "arch-skeptical" debunkery. Publishers had a hard time understanding that there could be any other approach to the subject, the more wary shying away from all UFO books, while the less discriminating sought to cash in on popular interest by producing only books that catered to the sensational. See Vallee 1992a, 98–99, 110.

45. I. Davis 1957; C. Lorenzen and J. Lorenzen 1967, 40.

46. This captain may be the first extraterrestrial ever to have been named in a lawsuit. In 1956 Bethurum's wife filed a petition for divorce. She claimed that

her husband had "neglected marital duties" because of Aura Rhanes, the beautiful captain of the saucer. (See I. Davis 1957, 35, and C. Lorenzen and J. Lorenzen 1967, 39.)

47. Bethurum 1954; also see Clark 1992, 76–79.

48. Angelucci 1955; see also I. Davis 1957, 34–35, and Clark 1992, 47–49.

49. Menger 1959; Clark 1992, 246–49. Menger's new wife, Connie, wrote her own book — under a pseudonym — about their relationship. See Baxter 1958.

50. Van Tassel 1952; see also Clark 1992, 390–92 and 176–77.

51. David Michael Jacobs 1975, 123, 126–27.

52. C. Lorenzen and J. Lorenzen 1967, 40; I. Davis 1957, 40.

53. I. Davis 1957, 57–58. In this light it is interesting to note that, at the request of an alien from Alpha Centauri, contactee Gabriel Green ran for President of the United States in 1964 on the Flying Saucer ticket. (For Green's take on the UFO subject, see Green 1967, esp. 122–27. Green was also the founder and president of the Amalgamated Flying Saucer Clubs of America.)

54. Stanton 1966, 85.

55. Sanderson 1967, 9; David Michael Jacobs 1975, 124, 125, 131. An infamous example of the way that contactee stories could be used to make the entire subject of UFOs look ridiculous occurred during the Armstrong Circle Theater debate on UFOs between NICAP's Donald Keyhoe and the air force's Lieutenant Colonel Spencer Whedon in January 1958. While Keyhoe tried to focus attention on the many good sighting reports in NICAP's files, Whedon spent more than half of his own allotted air time talking about contactee claims. (See Keyhoe 1960, 158.)

56. In the end the project — and the group — failed, in part because the members really constituted three subcultures with quite different interests and agendas. See Stupple and McNeece 1979.

57. C. Lorenzen and J. Lorenzen 1967, 36.

58. Keel 1970, 162, 179, 190–91. There is some evidence in the extant literature to support Keel's claims. The March 1963 issue of *Flying Saucer Review* carried a brief article summarizing contact claims dating from 1955 through 1962. Most of those listed are individuals who otherwise never made a noticeable impact on the contactee scene.

59. For a discussion of the lack of professional and funding rewards for UFO-related studies and the effect of that situation on ufology, see Emmons 1997, 13–71.

60. Festinger, Riecken, and Schacter 1956. Scholarship since the Festinger study has criticized it for methodological flaws, the most important being the fact that there were so many incognito participant-observers in the small group that their presence may have seriously affected the dynamics of the group. Furthermore, subsequent studies of prophetic disconfirmation have either modified or rejected the concept as presented by the Festinger study. See Hardyck and Braden 1962; Halford, Anderson, and Clark 1981; Balch, Farnsworth, and Wilkins 1983; and Singelenberg 1988. For an example of various scholarly papers and a bibliography leading to others, see J. Lewis 1995.

61. M. Brown 1997, viii.

62. For the best general discussion of the development of spiritualism in the

United States, see R. Moore 1977. Brown's study of channeling (Brown 1997) draws out more of the connections between spiritualism and modern-day channeling in the New Age movement.

63. Abrahamson 1965; see also Clark 1992, 15–16.

64. See Melton 1992.

65. See Commander Lady Athena through Ashtar-Athena, "The Ashtar Command: Our Mission, Purpose and Directive," published in *Sedona, A Journal of Emergence* and distributed by John Winston at <johnfwin@sonnet.com> on 1 August 1995.

66. Reeve and Reeve 1957, esp. 233–49 and 284.

67. Scully 1950, 45, 56–59, 61–62. See also Clark 1990b, 27–28.

Oahspe is a set of automatic writings that were transmitted in the 1880s by physician, dentist, and paranormal enthusiast John B. Newbrough. Newbrough had become disgusted with the low-level quality of nonphysical entities he was contacting through regular mediumistic channels, so he sought a higher level of intelligences with whom to communicate. After ten years of spiritual self-purification, he obeyed a spirit voice telling him to buy a typewriter (then a new invention) and sit at it for one hour each morning with his hands covered by a towel. The resulting book, called *Oahspe, A New Bible,* states that the world entered a new era in 1848. Coincidentally or not, that was the year in which the Fox sisters of upstate New York first created a sensation with their spirit rappings.

68. The juxtaposition of the idea of space exploration with metaphysics and the occult was not new even in the case of the contactees. Psychologist Robert A. Baker, a long-time skeptic in matters ufological, presents a fascinating, if jaded, summary of the history of telepathic planetary voyages claimed by spiritualists and metaphysicians of the eighteenth and nineteenth centuries, starting with famed seer Emmanuel Swedenborg. See Baker 1996, 111–40. Also see Stupple 1994.

69. I. Davis 1957, 40–43.

70. C. Lorenzen and J. Lorenzen 1967, 40; I. Davis 1957, 45. After a 1967 sighting in Butler, Pennsylvania, the percipients drove directly to their minister's house because they were terrified by the thought that perhaps they had seen a demon. (See Clark 1996a, 99.) For further examples of this kind of reaction, one can read almost any of the early UFO books, whose format tended to include the citation of numerous exemplary cases.

71. C. Lorenzen 1966, 55.

72. I. Davis 1957, 44–45. See also C. Lorenzen and J. Lorenzen 1967, 40. Jerome Clark points out that in 80 percent of the occupant reports, the entities described were humanoid, not human. See Clark 1996a, 92, 102.

73. The issue of the role of science fiction in creating UFO — and particularly entity — encounter reports has been a matter of long-standing debate. Jacques Vallee points out that between 1914 and 1946, during the flowering of science fiction in the United States, there are very few sighting reports on record. In particular he points out that sighting waves did not follow such cultural science fiction adventures as Orson Welles's 1938 broadcast of *The War of the Worlds.* (See Vallee 1965, 37–39.) However, he reports the research of Bertrand Meheust, who gathered "an enormous textual and pictorial database" on abductions in

science fiction literature predating World War II. (See Vallee 1990a, 161–62, and Meheust 1978 and 1985.) Phil Cousineau suggests that science fiction, particularly in the movies, *followed* the UFO phenomenon as it had taken root in the imagination of the times, though Jenny Randles points out that the image of alien contact presented in science fiction movies of the era was decidedly different from that presented by contactees (Cousineau 1995, 59; Randles 1993, 21). Menzel and Boyd, however, equate UFO reports with science fiction itself—except for contactee accounts, which they esteem as "fiction of such poor quality that they would be rejected by even the most hard-pressed editor of fantastic tales." (See Menzel and Boyd 1963, 9–10, 16–23, and 200.) For other advocates of the influence of popular culture on the UFO myth, see Kottmeyer 1990; Peebles 1994, 287–88; Randle 1996a; and Spencer 1989, 176–85. Also note Strentz 1970, 113–14; and for the role of the belief in extraterrestrial life in the emergent science fiction genre, see Dick 1996, 222–66.

74. Sanderson 1967, 166, 147, 149. This description was remarkably like that provided by Leonard Stringfield, who in 1980 constructed a composite portrait of the entities that had reportedly been recovered from crashed UFOs. They were, he said, 3.5 to 4.5 feet tall, with relatively large, hairless heads; large, deep-set, slightly slanted eyes; no external ears; only a vague nose; and a mouth that was a mere slit or fissure. They had very thin necks and very thin torsos, with long, thin arms and digits to match—only four, however, and no opposing thumb—and no visible sexual organs. Their skin was reported to be either gray or else beige, tan, or brown. See Stringfield 1980.

75. The nature of the information derived from the study concerned the apparent relationships between the entities reported and the UFOs associated with them (such as whether the entity was standing near the UFO, entering it, and so on). The results of this study were published at various points in time. See Bloecher 1975 and 1978, and Webb 1976a and 1976b.

76. For a complete description of the "Close Encounters" classification system, see Hynek 1972b.

77. Fuller 1966a, 11–15.

78. Modesty prevented him from elaborating at the time, but later he privately admitted that the "something" was sperm. See D. Scott Rogo, "Current Research on UFO Abductions, 1978–1988," in Druffel and Rogo 1980, 303.

79. Although occasionally abductees report seeing groups of humans that include African-Americans and other minorities on board a UFO during a mass abduction event, both these events and the presence of minorities are rare. Nor do many people of color come forward to report abduction experiences. Besides the pioneer abductee Barney Hill, Harrison Bailey and Riley Martin are the only exceptions. (See Druffel 1980a, and Martin and Wann 1995.) On a collective level, there are at least two independent African-American religious groups whose teachings include UFO and alien material. One is the Holy Tabernacle Church in Greensboro, North Carolina. The other is the Nuwaubian Nation of Moors, a group headquartered in Eatonton, Georgia, which "combines African-American self-determination, Egyptian symbolism and a belief in UFOs" (Alan Scher Zagier, "Durham Wreck Writes Tragic End to Outing," *The Raleigh News and Observer* [2 July 1997]). From these very limited examples it seems safe to

suppose that minority experiences of UFO phenomena are similar to what is reported in the larger UFO community. However, one can only speculate on the interpretive differences that may reveal themselves between racial subgroups in America . . . if and when more nonwhite experiencers come forward.

80. Rodeghier 1994a. For a skeptical interpretation of the Hill encounter, see Klass 1989, 7–24, and Peebles 1994, 160–66. It should be noted, however, that especially in the early years and even to this day, not all of the UFO community was any more convinced by abduction reports than were the UFO skeptics. See, for instance, Spencer 1989, 47–72.

81. Jessup 1955, 18–19, 103, 112, 119, 121, 139–43.

82. St. Agobard, "Contra Insulam Vulgi Opinionem: De Grandine et Tonitruis," *Patrologia Cursus Completus,* Series Latina Prior, ed. J. P. Migne, Vol. 104 (1864), ¶ ii, col. 148. Referenced and translated in Vallee 1969, 9–10.

83. For Australia, see "Abduction," from <www.ipacific.net.au/%7Epavig/abduction_451.shtml>, downloaded on 3 April 1997. For France, see Vallee 1965, 32.

84. Of course, this is to ignore for the moment those cases from the ancient scriptures of several different faiths that record incidents that some believe may reflect UFO activity — including abductions. This topic is more properly considered under the rubric of "ancient astronauts" theories, which will be taken up briefly in chapter 5.

85. Anon. 1976.

86. Clark 1992, 92.

87. For a comparison of the Villas-Boas case, the Hill case, and the Masse case with regard to common features and the timing of publicity about each case, see Bowen 1969b, 239–48.

88. Creighton 1965a.

89. For a complete English translation of Villas-Boas's statement, as well as statements from the investigating UFO consultant and physician, see C. Lorenzen and J. Lorenzen 1967, 42–72, or Creighton 1969.

90. Creighton 1969, 217.

91. Ibid., 218.

92. Ibid.

93. The most notorious case of this was reported by Karla Turner in Turner 1994a, 44–50, 229–38. See also the episode reported by David Jacobs in David M. Jacobs 1992, 149–50, and 1998, 76–88; and Strieber 1998, 207–8.

94. C. Lorenzen 1966, 21, 36, 47–48, 54, 179, 190–91, 198, 258–59, 261, 278. Also see David M. Jacobs 1998, 14–15, 18–19, 103–111.

95. I. Davis 1957, 49–50; Sanderson 1967, 166.

96. Sanderson 1967, 124–25, 152.

97. Creighton 1965b. As a further development on the crossbreeding speculation, the editor of the *Flying Saucer Review* reported that according to a private communication from General George Marshall, U.S. authorities had determined as early as the mid-1950s that the aliens were trying to figure out how to breathe and stay alive in Earth's atmosphere. Crossbreeding might be one response to that problem. Other interpretations offered for the abduction were that the aliens wanted to make a physical check-up on humans, that they wanted to indicate to

humanity that physical conditions on Earth and on their own planet were not vastly different, that they wanted to establish an interplanetary kinship with humanity as a basis for future cultural exchange, and that the encounter took place simply because the female wanted it (suggesting that their society might be matriarchal).

A dissenting opinion was published in the next issue of *Flying Saucer Review* from Henk J. Hinfelaar, editor of *Spaceview*, the *Journal of New Zealand Scientific Space Research*. He stated that in his files there was another case very much like the A. V. B. case and that the facts he had uncovered about that case suggested that the craft and crew were of human, earthly origin. This, too, has been a minor but noticeable feature of the abduction trope. (See Hinfelaar 1965.) For more on the idea that UFOs are thoroughly terrestrial inventions, see Lawrence 1950 and Vesco 1971. For the incorporation of the abduction trope into such a terrestrial scenario of UFO origin, see M. Cannon n.d. and Kanon 1997.

98. See the chapter titled "Approaching the Edge of Reality: Close Encounters of the Third Kind" in Hynek 1977.

99. C. Lorenzen and J. Lorenzen 1977, 132–36. The Hickson and Parker abduction was detailed mostly in the popular press and, more extensively, in UFO periodicals. In 1983 a Michigan college professor, William Mendez, along with Hickson, self-published the results of his extensive investigation of the case. See Mendez and Hickson 1983. For a brief synopsis of the events in both cases, see Clark 1996a, 389–96 (on the Pascagoula case) and 545–64 (on the Walton case). See also Heiden 1975 and Gills 1998.

100. Walton wrote about his experience in Walton 1977 and 1996. The 1996 version is an expansion of his original story with information about the long-term aftermath of the incident and about the making of a movie about his encounter called *Fire in the Sky*, which was released in 1993. Also see the treatment of the incident in C. Lorenzen and J. Lorenzen 1977, 80–113, and the skeptical evaluation of the case in Klass 1989, 25–37.

101. Neither of these cases contributed appreciably to the abduction trope of the UFO myth. As for their conformity *to* the trope, in both cases there was "missing time," but the fact that the encounter had occurred was never forgotten by any of the experiencers, and subsequent hypnosis failed to reveal significant details that were not already remembered by all parties. The most outstanding thing that separated these accounts from contactee stories was the fact that all of the parties were absolutely terrified and thoroughly traumatized after their experiences. Like a number of the 1990s close encounter experiencers, however, these men later came to believe that, while they had indeed been initially traumatized by their UFO experiences, they were also given important information and messages by their captors, who ultimately meant them no harm.

102. C. Lorenzen and J. Lorenzen 1977.

103. Fowler 1979; Rogo 1980; Druffel and Rogo 1980.

104. Fowler 1982.

105. Rogo 1980, 15.

106. Ibid., 15, 17.

107. For instance, see Davenport 1994, 11. For a discussion of the relation-

ship of parapsychology to ufology, see Emmons 1997, 187–88, 194–95. Also see chapter 4, this volume.

108. Hopkins 1981, 224. Indeed, abductee Betty Andreasson was told by her captors that "many, many, many, many, many. Many, many" people had already been taken aboard the aliens' craft and examined. See Fowler 1979, 146, 122, 183.

109. Hopkins 1981, 225.

110. Ibid.

111. Budd Hopkins 1987b; Strieber 1987.

112. Hopkins, Jacobs, and Westrum 1992. For insightful reporting on the reception of this survey within the community of UFO abduction researchers, see C. D. B. Bryan 1995, 46–47, as well as David M. Jacobs 1998, 121–25; Hopkins 1994; Nyman 1994c; and Donderi 1994. See also Robert Hall, Johnson, and Rodeghier 1993, which points out that the symptoms selected as indicative of abduction experiences might just as plausibly reflect other situations totally unrelated to abductions, and makes the critique that flaws in the Roper survey make ufology in general lose credibility among those individuals with training and education whom most UFO groups would like to attract to the field. For a discussion of the signs and symptoms of abduction, see J. Carpenter 1994.

113. Bryan 1995, 235–36.

114. Ibid., 256.

115. Strieber said that as of 1994 only eighty-two of the letters had been critical, most of them from people with religious objections to the idea of alien contact. Another two hundred of the letters were "disorganized" and indicated possibly significant psychological difficulties on the part of the writers. The rest, he reported, were "articulate" communications from people concerned about their experiences. See Strieber 1995, 96, and Strieber and Strieber 1997, 3.

116. The three autobiographical abduction accounts published in 1992 could not have been more different in tone and direction. Royal and Priest 1992 took a very positive approach to the phenomenon and Lyssa Royal's involvement in it. She later found it unnecessary to rely on abduction experiences in order to make contact with the extraterrestrials, becoming instead a channeler of extraterrestrial information. Turner 1992 was written by a professor of medieval English literature at a southwestern university when she and her husband began to uncover their abduction experiences in 1988. The title, *Into the Fringe,* reflected a keen appreciation for what their situation meant: They were leaving behind the respectable lives of a computer consultant and a college professor and going into the fringes of American society. The experiences they reported were not altogether pleasant, and in subsequent years Karla Turner became convinced that at least a part of her experiences involved American military personnel. Because the nature of what happened during abductions was so invasive and unpleasant, Turner felt that the military were working in league with malevolent aliens on black-budget projects that boded ill for the common person. By way of contrast, Twiggs and Twiggs 1992 was the story of the Twiggs' recovery not only of abduction memories, but also memories of having alien spouses and children with whom they were happily reunited during each abduction experience.

117. Greenleaf Publications, P.O. Box 8152, Murfreesboro, Tennessee 37133; Wild Flower Press, P.O. Box 190, Mill Spring, North Carolina 28756. It should be noted that the "granddaddy" of UFO book distributors (founded in 1980) is Arcturus Books, Inc., 1443 S.E. Port St. Lucie Blvd., Port St. Lucie, Florida 34952. The fact that the market for UFO books can support three such enterprises indicates the magnitude of the surge in popularity that the subject of UFOs and alien abductions have enjoyed since the late 1980s, though as Robert Girard, owner of Arcturus Books, points out, the continuing growth of the large chain bookstores poses a real threat to the survival of small, independent, specialty booksellers.

118. *Contact Forum,* c/o Wild Flower Press, P.O. Box 190, Mill Spring, North Carolina 28756. Kaye Kizziar's *The Superstition Chronicles: Adventures in the Paranormal,* AZ-Tex Publishing, P.O. Box 5903, Apache Jct., Arizona 85278.

119. On the value of having contact with other abductees as a means to "integrate these experiences [in order] to resume a coherent, productive life," see Collings and Jamerson 1996, 92 (quote), 347–50.

120. See Lowry 1995, 21–25. As the story developed in *The X-Files,* the main character, Fox Mulder, had witnessed the abduction of his little sister when he was still a preteen. She, however, had never been returned by the aliens, and the ensuing sense of responsibility and guilt had driven him into a career with the Federal Bureau of Investigation in order to try to learn the truth about what had happened.

121. Rogo 1980, 17. On the idea that the UFO phenomenon adjusts itself to the individual percipient, see also Vallee 1990a, 145–46.

122. Vallee 1979, 1975, esp. 194–206, and 1991a, esp. 224–37.

123. Bullard's results were published in abbreviated form as "UFO Abduction Reports: The Supernatural Kidnap Narrative Returns in Technological Guise," *Journal of American Folklore* 102 (April–June 1989): 147–70, and in a slightly more elaborated form in Bullard 1987a. Also see Bullard 1991.

124. Not everyone agreed with Bullard's analysis. Vallee thought that the possibly unsolvable mystery of the UFOs combined with their continued manifestation might produce a "new mythological movement." (See Vallee 1969, 155, 157.) Others were absolutely certain that this was the case. Psychologist Robert A. Baker said that belief in alien abductions was a form of folklore easily accounted for by traditional folklore theory. He saw belief in folklore as quaint but detrimental to the long-term progress of humanity as a "race of intelligent and rational beings." (See Baker 1996, 34, 340, 356–57.) Also see Goss n.d.; Rimmer 1970; and Ellis 1988.

125. Bullard 1989b, 152–53, and 1987a, 14.

126. Alternatively, abductees may be driving at night when they see a UFO, become frightened or fascinated, then suddenly note that it has "jumped" to another area of the sky and flown away. A check of the clock may reveal that it is much later than they thought it should be.

127. Personal communication, T. K., 16 May 1997.

128. One of my personal correspondents remarked, with just a hint of good-humored jealousy, that she didn't know anything about that levitating and passing through solid objects, because her abductors always made her walk!

129. Fowler 1979, 28–31.

130. See R. Haines and, more ominously, David M. Jacobs 1998, 116.

131. Whitley Strieber, private communication, 19 April 1998.

132. Personal communication, M. F., 11 October 1996. Also see the account of Beth Collings's confrontation with her own father over this issue (Collings and Jamerson 1996, 55–60).

133. Some consideration has been given to the special needs of child abductees. See G. Dean 1994. Budd Hopkins gave a similar presentation at the 1995 Tampa UFO Conference, which I attended. Coincidentally, while riding on the shuttle bus from the airport to the hotel conference site, I met a woman from Minnesota whose sole reason for attending the conference was to hear Hopkins's lecture. As we talked later over supper, "Polly" was obviously upset — at times her eyes welled up with tears — as she described the fear and trauma her five-year-old had been suffering as a result of his abduction experiences. At the First Annual Greenville (S.C.) Alien Abduction and UFO Conference in 1994, a woman in the audience, her voice quavering with emotion, asked Hopkins (a featured speaker) what she could say when her young daughter angrily accused her of having stood by as the child was forcibly taken away by alien abductors.

134. Conroy n.d., 47, 78. Compare David M. Jacobs 1992, 25.

135. See Turner 1994b, 36–37, 40, 58–59, 71–73, 77, 82–83, 167; Turner 1994a, 229–38; Haley 1993, 84–87; K. Wilson 1993, 170; Robinson 1997, 32–36, 126-27; David M. Jacobs 1998, 76–88; and Wright 1996, 11–12. Rogo initially interpreted some incidents reported in alien encounters as "rape fantasies." See Rogo 1980, 236–37. Also see "Reptoid Rape: A Multi-Part Series," by Blue Resonant Human, Ph.D., at <www.brotherblue.org/libers/intro.htm>.

136. Mack 1993, 17.

137. See, for instance, Strieber and Strieber 1997, 204; Hopkins 1987b, 221–68, 282. There have been several claims by different abductees that they have medical proof that they were pregnant and then suddenly not pregnant. Under scrutiny by a sympathetic physician, however, none of the claims that were investigated could be indisputably verified. See Miller and Neal 1994. Also see David M. Jacobs 1998, 61–75.

138. Hopkins 1987b, 283. For corroboration of this hypothesis, see David M. Jacobs 1998, 242, 245.

139. Hopkins 1987b, 273–74. See also David M. Jacobs 1992, 153–86, and 1998, 70.

140. Robinson 1997, 88; cf. David M. Jacobs 1998, 101.

141. One writer reports having seen a secret paper estimating that one out of forty people on Earth have received such implants. (See Cooper 1991, 233.) Hynek himself reportedly estimated that one out of forty people may have been abducted. (See Preston Dennett 1990.) This figure may well be unreliable, but in spirit it is of a piece with the quest to know how many people may have been abducted by aliens.

142. Some ufologists and abductees felt that implants might also be used by the aliens to control their subjects. See, for instance, the lengthy discussion of this possibility in Strieber 1998, 233–47.

143. See, for instance, Leir 1996 and 1998; Fenwick 1995; and Basterfield 1992. For an early piece on the implant issue and a possible relationship of

implants to an anomalous find in genetics research, see John Schuessler 1990. Also note Strieber 1998, 159–261. Jacobs reports that he knows of about twenty implants that have come out spontaneously. See David M. Jacobs 1998, 71–72, 113.

144. David M. Jacobs 1992, 95–96, and 1998, 64–69.

145. See the Communion Foundation web site at <www.strieber.com/implant .html>.

146. Haley 1993, 158. Haley agreed to undergo a lie detector test about her experiences for The Learning Channel's show "UFOs Uncovered," broadcast on 1 March 1999. According to the examiner, she failed the test. In a private conversation with me, Haley's husband pointed out a number of factors in the test procedure that had contributed to the outcome. For instance, he said, the examiner neglected to tell Haley in advance what his "test" question would be, to which she was supposed to lie. Thus, when asked whether she drank coffee (the test question), Haley replied truthfully that she did not. The examiner presumed she was knowingly lying, and used that response to help him determine the truthfulness of her responses to his other questions.

147. Among whom see Turner 1994b; K. Wilson 1993; Collings and Jamerson 1996.

148. Fowler 1993, 338.

149. See Bryan 1995, 133.

150. See Blum 1990, 41. Also see chapter 1, this volume.

151. An entire subelement of the military involvement in abductions concerns just such a betrayal. According to John Lear, the government has negotiated a secret treaty with alien forces in which the United States was to get limited technological assistance from the aliens in exchange for permission for abductions and the alien use of secret government facilities. For the gist of John Lear's statements, see Good 1991, 39–40, 110, 169–71.

152. M. Cannon n.d. and Kanon 1997, 91–114.

153. K. Wilson 1993, 90, 174, 198, 215, 283–85.

154. David M. Jacobs 1998, 187–88.

155. Lammer 1996, 1997, and 1999.

156. Bullard 1987a, 18.

157. Along with this apocalypse, many abductees report being told that some humans will be taken from Earth by the aliens and moved to a place where they (and the human race) can continue to grow. See, for example, Mack 1994, 40.

158. Jacobs does a particularly good job in elaborating upon the reproductive (or as he suggests, the simply *productive* [305]) aspects of the abduction phenomenon, as well as the child presentation element included in so many abduction narratives. See David M. Jacobs 1992, 107–31 and 153–86. The latest development in his theory about the alien purposes behind the procedures are set forth in *The Threat*.

159. David M. Jacobs 1992, 96–106, 136–50.

160. Ibid., 312, 315.

161. On close friendship, see Collings and Jamerson 1996, and also Bryan 1995, 32, 51–64, 201–30, 282–333, 339–415; Emmons 1997, 71; and Strieber

and Strieber 1997, 162. On sexual attraction, see Hopkins 1996, 244, 286. Also see Robinson 1997, 96–99; David M. Jacobs 1998, 80–88.

162. Hopkins 1996, 186, 214.

163. Ibid., 379.

164. For an encounter model taking into account this and other features of the trope, see Nyman 1994a. One abductee reported remembering her own role as such a facilitator. She said that she had held and comforted another abductee who was sobbing hysterically during the abduction.

165. Hopkins 1996, 39–40, 97, 138, 148, 149, 180.

166. As part of a survey of abductees, I asked respondents how they had first become consciously aware of their abduction experiences, and 34 percent replied that they had always known about them (N = 215).

167. In my survey, 12 percent of respondents report beginning to remember their own abductions after reading a book on the subject or on UFOs; 7 percent report remembering after talking to another experiencer.

168. Again, 34 percent of survey respondents report this as the catalyst for the return of their memories.

169. Hopkins 1987b, 283–84. Since 1987 there have been several attempts to establish a set of criteria for evaluating whether an individual is a true abduction experiencer. Edith Fiore proposed a set of criteria in which the point is not understanding the phenomenon sui generis, but plumbing its (often transpersonal) psychological significance. (See Fiore 1989, 252–57.) For other sets of criteria, see Rodeghier 1994b; Rogo 1980, 3–4; Randles 1981, 25–26; Nyman 1988; "Possible Indications of an Abduction Experience," posted at <www.frii/com/~iufor/abduct.htm> and downloaded on 13 June 1997; and M. Leslie and Williams 1996.

170. Personal communication, S. F., 4 November 1996.

171. Turner 1992, 1.

172. For instance, see Jan Aldrich, e-mail of 30 September 1997, posted on <www.ufomind.com/ufo/updates/1997/oct/m01–003.shtml> and retrieved on 2 October 1997. See also Randle, Estes, and Cone 1999.

173. Appelle 1997.

174. Darren Gilmore <dgilmore@terracom.net>, a graduate student at Bowling Green State University in 1997, wrote his thesis on the ways in which "folklore has become popular culture in a postmodern/hypermediated society. To prove that, I am establishing that UFO stories (abductions, MIB, medical experimentation, aliens living among/observing us, etc.) can be classified folkloricly as legends. That is a point which Bullard contests. . . . Once proven as legends, I will trace those UFO legend subtypes into popular culture, specifically *Star Trek* and *Star Trek: The Next Generation*" (personal communication, 13 February 1997). University of Saskatchewan English professor Terry Matheson attempted to show how abduction narratives are simply raw material from the larger culture, reconfigured and manipulated by abduction researchers (unconsciously) into culturally pleasing myths (Matheson 1998). See also Randle, Estes, and Cone 1999.

175. "Interview: Strieber," *High Times* (August 1995): 61. On a survey of abductees that I conducted in 1995–1997, 32 percent of respondents said that

their abductions had felt threatening to them *as* they occurred (N = 192), but only 20 percent said that in retrospect their abductions still seemed threatening (N = 194). There is a debate in the UFO community — particularly among abductees — as to whether the alien abductors are good or bad. In my abduction survey, I asked respondents about this: 56 percent were not sure, 12 percent thought they were evil, and 31 percent thought they were good (N = 220).

176. See, for instance, Starr 1996. Also note Twiggs and Twiggs 1992.

177. The Stockholm Syndrome, named after a hostage situation that occurred in 1973, refers to the tendency of captives and people in otherwise impossible, coercive situations to take on the values, ideas, and attitudes of their captors as a way of relieving the stress of their predicament.

178. See Higbee 1995 and Donna Higbee, "New Abductee Trend," posted on <i-ufo-l@world.std.com> on 14 February 1996. Both of these articles are reproduced in *Flying Saucer Review* 41, no. 1 (spring 1996): 19–21 and 21–23, respectively.

179. David M. Jacobs 1998, 133, 229–30, 235, 251–54, 257.

180. Researcher Joe Nyman calls this feature of the abduction trope "dual reference." See Nyman 1994b. In my survey, 45 percent of respondents said that they felt they were in some way part alien. Another 27 percent were unsure.

181. For a critical rebuttal of the positive view of alien encounters — including the tendency to use mystical or religious lenses to view the situation — see David M. Jacobs 1998, 208–225.

182. Mannion 1998, 105.

183. Emmons 1997, 199–200.

3. UFOLOGY: ON THE CUTTING EDGE OR THE FRINGE OF SCIENCE?

1. The articles in question were Hynek 1953, 1966a, 1966b, 1967a, 1967b, and 1969.

2. Menzel 1972, 129.

3. Bauer 1992, 57–61. In the interest of fair play it should be pointed out that even scientists whose fields of research are thoroughly within the pale of mainstream science have resorted to popular presentations of their results before peer review or professional publication has been performed. See Perlman 1976, 251.

4. J. Allen Hynek to Michael Waters (pseudonym), personal correspondence, 6 May 1968.

5. Barclay and Barclay 1993, 16.

6. J. Gilbert 1997, 229.

7. Donald Menzel to Charles A. Maney, 14 February 1962, p. 1, box 8, file: M, Donald Menzel UFO Papers, American Philosophical Society, Philadelphia, Pennsylvania, and cited in J. Gilbert 1997, 233.

8. For the history of science in the United States, see R. Bruce 1987; Conser 1993; Kohlstedt 1976; Reingold 1979; LaFollette 1990, esp. 151–57 on science as a rival to religion; Shapin 1982; and Grabiner and Miller.

9. An excellent treatment of the cultural symbolism of science, and its evacu-

ation of content, is Tourney 1996. For the popularization of science see also Perlman 1976; Whalen 1981; Whitley 1985; McElheny 1985; and Nelkin 1987.

10. J. Gilbert 1997, 235.

11. Ibid., 236.

12. Ibid., 237.

13. Ruppelt 1956, 115.

14. Ibid., 204.

15. Anon. 1958.

16. Ruppelt 1956, 207. Also see Sturrock 1994a, 1994b, and 1994c. The findings of the survey of American Astronomical Society members were summarized in Sturrock 1977a and 1977b.

17. Ruppelt 1956, 199–209.

18. Rutledge 1981.

19. Ruppelt 1956, 216; David Michael Jacobs 1975, 82, cf. 234, 260, 300; and Hynek and Vallee 1975, 190ff.

20. Ruppelt 1956, 191.

21. David Michael Jacobs 1975, 85–86, 222, 259, 257. The most recent institution to review the scientific evidence for UFOs is the Society for Scientific Exploration (SSE), which announced the convening of a panel for that purpose. The SSE is "an interdisciplinary organization of scholars formed to support unbiased investigation of claimed anomalous phenomena." ("Society Convenes Science Panel to Review UFO Evidence," press release of the Society for Scientific Exploration, 6 October 1997.) Also see Sturrock 1999.

22. On the increasing numbers of scientists who investigated UFOs, see David Michael Jacobs 1975, 214. On the refusal to publish, see Vallee 1965, 129.

23. The periodicals surveyed were (or were published by) *Aeronautics and Astronautics*, American Association for the Advancement of Science, American Meteorological Society, American Society of Mechanical Engineers, *American Journal of Physics, Bulletin of the Atomic Scientist, Applied Optics, Icarus, Astronomy, Industrial Research, Scientific Research, Popular Science, Engineering Opportunities, Science and Mechanics, Technology Review, Nature, Journal of the Optical Society of America, Journal of Astronautical Sciences, Bio-Science, Science, Physics Today,* and *Popular Photography.* List taken from "UFOs in Scientific Literature," downloaded from <www.primenet.com/~bdzeiler/papers_a.htm> on 3 March 1997.

24. I. Scott 1990.

25. Strentz 1970, 57–58, 76, 94, 96–97. See also Hickman, McConkey, and Barrett 1995–1996.

26. Anon. 1971 and 1979.

27. Westrum, n.d.b, 7.

28. Rutledge 1981, 244.

29. Sturrock 1994a, 4.

30. F. Edwards 1966, 45–46; Keyhoe 1960, 99; Michel 1956, 60–64, 235.

31. Menzel and Boyd 1963, 269–70. Tombaugh passed away in 1997. It remains for a biographer to sort out the facts concerning his sighting and his interpretation thereof.

32. F. Edwards 1966, 36–49. C. Lorenzen 1966, 207.

33. F. Edwards 1966, 40.

34. Ruppelt 1956, 238. See also Oberth 1955.

35. One of the most notorious was eighteenth-century scientist-turned-mystic Emmanuel Swedenborg, whose visions of and conversations with the inhabitants of other planets were collected and published in 1758 as *De Telluribus in Universo*. For a modern English translation, see *The Worlds in Space,* trans. John Chadwick (London: The Swedenborg Society, 1997). For the exhaustive history of this debate, see Dick 1982 and Crowe 1986. For a discussion of the extraterrestrial intelligence question in the early decades of this century, especially in the years around World War II, see Swords 1992. Also see Dick 1996.

36. Crowe 1986, 475.

37. Dick 1996, 547.

38. Davies 1995a, 11–12.

39. See Sagan 1994.

40. For Drake's own work on these questions, see Drake 1961, 1954, and 1981, and Drake and Sobel 1992. For a brief presentation of the actual equation and a discussion of the larger scientific issues involved in the question of the existence of extraterrestrial life, see Swords 1989.

41. For example, see Menzel and Taves 1977, 199–209. For a discussion of extraterrestrial visitation based upon a negative evaluation of even the possibility of extraterrestrial life, see Sheaffer 1981, 129–38. Also see Carlson and Sturrock 1975, 63, cited in Fowler 1981, 224.

42. This argument is known as the Fermi Paradox, named after its originator. See Tipler 1980, cited in Swords 1989, 87–88. Yet another take on the visitation issue is proposed by Nickell, who says that for a space-faring civilization there must be myriads of interesting places to visit — so much so that they would be unlikely to spend any amount of time in just one location. The UFO sightings reported on Earth are far too numerous and have been taking place for too long a time to correspond to such a situation, which indicates that UFO sightings must not be of anything so exotic as extraterrestrial vehicles. (See Nickell 1995, 193–95.)

43. David M. Jacobs 1983, 220. See also Swords 1989, 89–90. On the likelihood that missionary concerns might motivate extraterrestrial travel to Earth, see Swords 1987a.

44. This is a major conclusion of M.I.T. physicist Philip Morrison when contemplating the reasons for people's fascination with "parascience," which to him includes ufology. See Morrison 1981, 361. For the dangers that scientific illiteracy presents to the "modern world view," see Holton 1993, excerpted in *The Skeptical Inquirer* 18:3 (spring 1994): 264; and for the public education potential of ufology, see Page 1972.

45. C. Mackay 1852.

46. Gardner 1952a.

47. Among those generalist books taking "pseudoscience" to task, see Gardner 1981; Cazeau and Scott 1979; Abell and Singer 1981; Gilovich 1991; Sagan 1996, esp. 210–16; Shermer 1997; and Nickell 1995.

48. However, debunker Robert Sheaffer pointed out that UFO sighting reports that gain a lot of media attention seldom receive as much attention later

when their prosaic cause(s) are determined. See Sheaffer 1981, 12. Menzel was also no fan of the media, which he felt had a pro-UFO bias and only helped to fuel UFO flaps while ignoring later, more rational explanations of UFO sightings. See Menzel and Taves 1977, 180, 186, 8; also see Sullivan 1972.

49. For other notable efforts, see Oberg 1982; Sheaffer 1981; Peebles 1994; and Matheson 1998. For a similar critique of the abduction phenomenon from within the UFO community, see Randle, Estes, and Cone 1999. On Klass and Oberg, see Friedlander 1995, 104, 107.

50. For a brief history of CSICOP and an analysis of its rhetorical practices in one scientific controversy, see Pinch and Collins 1984.

51. David M. Jacobs 1983. The adequacy of the ETH to account for UFOs has been a subject of debate among ufologists for many years. Hynek warned against a too-quick acceptance of the hypothesis, emphasizing that there was much about UFOs that remained unknown (Hynek 1983). Swords argued for the acceptability of the ETH, as long as it was considered alongside other acceptable possibilities (Swords 1989). Also see Vallee 1990b, 1991b, and 1992b; Wood 1991; Bramley 1992; and Jerome Clark's monograph on UFO hypotheses in Clark 1997b.

52. Menzel and Boyd 1963, 3, 228–89.

53. Skeptics pointed in particular to Ray Palmer, a science-fiction editor who published allegedly true stories of an underground space-faring civilization on Earth and later helped popularize the Kenneth Arnold sighting, and to Charles Fort, an early collector of scientific anomalies. Menzel and Boyd 1963, 1–30. Also see Peebles 1994, 3–7, 12–15.

54. Menzel and Boyd 1963, 3, 191, 196. Physicist Philip Morrison observed that it is not right to expect "large discoveries" in science — the kinds of discoveries of new laws of reality that are suggested by phenomena like UFOs. Instead, "truth enters more modestly, a little at a time." (See Morrison 1981, 359.)

55. Menzel and Boyd 1963, 277. Indeed, Menzel attributed the early pro-UFO stance of the air force investigation to the fact that "not one of the individuals chosen to study the observations had any training in the important and relevant field of meteorological optics." See Menzel and Taves 1977, 7. Bauer cautions scientists who are open to reasoned examination of anomalies against thinking that their expertise in one field makes them qualified to offer opinions on matters more closely allied to other fields (Bauer 1987).

56. Martin Gardner calls these amateurs "unorthodox scientists" who feed like parasites on the success of legitimate, mainstream science and are driven by paranoid and egomaniacal needs. See Gardner 1952a, 12–14.

57. Stiebing 1995, 5, and Randi 1981, 215.

58. Randi 1981, 210–11. Gardner was not so generous. He opined that legitimate scientists who supported fringe theories did so mostly out of a need for "an outlet for their own neurotic rebellions" (Gardner 1952a, 15).

59. Grinspoon and Perksy 1972.

60. Menzel and Taves 1977, 225.

61. Ibid., 228–229.

62. Ibid., 169–77.

63. Ibid., 142; Craig 1995, 95–96.

64. Menzel and Boyd 1963, 167–71. Ufologists placed great stock in sighting reports that involved simultaneous visual and radar observation. But Menzel cautioned that in no case can one ever "say with certainty that the source of the radar blip and the visual stimulus are identical" (123).

65. Menzel and Boyd 1963, 163. For other instances where multiple separate but simultaneous causes are invoked to explain UFO sightings, see Menzel and Boyd 1963, 6, 38, 48, 70–71, 80, 82–83, 183, 238, 239, 252, 253, and 282. Robert Moore named the "interaction of diverse rare mundane stimuli" the Mundane-synthesistic Hypothesis of UFOs. (See Robert Moore 1993, 90.) Charles Bowen, editor of the *Flying Saucer Review* in 1979, commented on this discrediting of visual and radar sightings:

> It is hard to avoid the impression either that radar equipment is given to malfunctions, or that the air controllers, and the pilots, who use various forms of that equipment, are incapable of distinguishing true signals from those spurious images like "angels" caused by various kinds of anomalous propagation due to temperature inversions, and so on. Indeed, if [debunkers are] to be believed, then it is remarkable that any reliance at all is placed on radar and other devices of the same *genre*, or on their operators. And yet every time we make a journey by plane we put our lives in the hands of operators like these, or pilots, and their "unreliable" tools.   (Bowen 1979, 1)

66. Menzel and Taves 1977, 142, 153; F. Drake 1972. Moore stated that there were more than 150 "mundane phenomena" that could generate a UFO report (Robert Moore 1993, 66). He recommended decreasing by half the number of accepted "unknowns" from UFO reports, on the assumption that even after extensive investigation, there were that many undetected instances of human misperception (90–91).

67. Menzel and Taves 1977, 14; Menzel 1953, 150; Barry Beyerstein, "How We Fool Ourselves: Anomalies of Perception and Interpretation," presentation given at the CSICOP conference, Seattle, Washington, 23–26 June 1994 and reported in *The Skeptical Inquirer* (March 1995), located at <www.csicop.org/si/9503/belief.html>. Emphasis on the unreliability of the powers of observation of even the experienced observer was a necessary rhetorical strategy for the debunkers, because ufologists (and the Battelle Institute report prepared in 1953) noted that the best UFO reports came from the most qualified and competent witnesses. See Maccabee 1979 and 1983; Zeidman and Rodeghier 1993, 19–20.

68. Menzel and Taves 1977, 186, cf. 116 and Menzel and Boyd 1963, 274, 275. Also see Nickell 1995, 193. This conclusion was questioned by the UFO Subcommittee of the American Institute of Aeronautics and Astronautics, who wondered if scientists were justified in extrapolating from the solved cases to the unsolved cases (Dick 1982, 305). Klass explained this reaction by claiming that the subcommittee had been filled with UFO believers. He proceeded to provide explanations for the cases that the subcommittee had studied (Klass 1975, 186–233). Menzel and Taves did the same for the unexplained cases from the Condon Report (see 1977, 89–116). Note, however, the circular reasoning involved: Unexplained sighting reports remained unexplained because there was inadequate data. Having enough data did not mean having certain kinds of data (like mutually confirming multiwitness testimony or instrumented readings of anomalous activity or information about extant meteorological conditions or the med-

ical history of a witness) or certain quantities of data, but having whatever kind of data would permit the case to be explained prosaically. If a case could not be explained prosaically, then it had, by definition, inadequate data.

69. Hoagland 1969, 625.

70. Menzel and Taves 1977, 114.

71. Menzel 1953, 150–51.

72. Menzel and Taves 1977, 145–53; also included in Menzel 1972, 155–61; Klass 1981.

73. Menzel and Boyd 1963, 205–218; Menzel and Taves 1977, 187–95. For a lengthier discussion of motion picture evidence, see R. M. L. Baker 1972.

74. Menzel and Boyd 1963, 219–37.

75. Menzel and Taves 1977, 212.

76. This maxim seems to be the unofficial mantra of the skeptical community. It has been used by Marcello Truzzi (Truzzi 1987), has often been attributed to Carl Sagan, and was invoked most recently by one of the codiscoverers of the Hale-Bopp comet, Alan Hale, in his "Personal Statement on UFOs" published in *The Skeptical Inquirer* (March 1997) located at <www.csicop.org/si/9703/ufo.html>.

77. For a discussion of kinds of hoaxes, see Menzel and Taves 1977, 211–23, which feeds into a discussion of the role of lying in the creation of UFO narratives in pp. 225–38.

78. Ibid., 214, 215.

79. Ibid., 239–49.

80. See Robert Baker 1988 and 1989; Nickell 1996. At a CSICOP conference Baker pointed out that hypnagogic and hypnopompic hallucinations afflict 4–5 percent of Americans and, "except for variations in the hallucinatory content, the descriptions given [by sufferers] are almost identical to the accounts of alleged alien abductees" (Genoni 1995a). For a rebuttal of the fantasy-prone hypothesis of abductions, see Basterfield 1994. For a rebuttal of the sleep paralysis hypothesis, see J. Carpenter 1995a.

81. For a comparison of the nightmare-prone personality with abductees, see Kottmeyer 1988.

82. The definitive study of hagging is Hufford 1982. Hufford reflected on the similarities and differences between being hagged and abduction experiences in his presentation at the Abduction Study Conference held at M.I.T. in 1992 and published in Hufford 1994.

83. On sadomasochistic tendencies, see Newman and Baumeister 1996. The entire issue of the *Journal* in which the Newman and Baumeister article was published focused on articles debating the reality of alien abductions and the psychological states of abductees. On Munchausen's Syndrome and dissociative states, see Jim Schnabel 1993.

84. Halperin 1995. Also see Robert Baker 1996, 337. A study by psychologist Kenneth Ring revealed that abductees have a higher incidence of reported childhood abuse, but the study does not posit that abduction memories are simply falsified renditions of those incidents. (See Ring 1992.) Also see Laibow 1989. On memories of birth trauma, see Alvin H. Lawson 1984.

85. Persinger 1983 and 1988; Persinger and Lafrenière 1977; Budden 1995a

and 1995b; and Pickover 1999. For a discussion of this theory and what is known as the tectonic strain theory (TST) in general, see the "Issues" section of the *Journal of UFO Studies*, n.s. 2 (1990).

86. Robert Baker 1988 and 1996, 141–80, 326–37; Bowers and Eastwood 1996; and David Gotlib 1993. Also note Randle, Estes, and Cone 1999.

87. Martin Orne, on *Extension 720*, WGN-Radio, Chicago, as transcribed in Martin Orne 1988, 277; and Robert Baker 1988, 159; also Martin T. Orne, et al. 1996. Klass characterized abductees as "little nobodies." See Rae 1993, 33.

88. Gleick 1994.

89. Robert Baker 1996, 327–28, 330; Gleick, 1994.

90. Carroll 2000, s.v. "Alien Abductions."

91. Robert Baker 1996, 330. See also Carl Sagan's summary of the skeptical viewpoint of various forms of evidence offered by ufologists in Sagan 1995, 180–88.

92. In many ways the UFO debate can be seen as the creation of certainty on an institutional level within science — especially the field of astronomy — in the face of anomalous evidence through the use of four techniques commonly (but largely unconsciously or uncritically) used by scientists: jettisoning the uncertainties, minimizing them, resolving them with reference to other certainties, or, least often, distributing the uncertainties so as to minimize their impact on the overall certainty of the discipline. For a description of these processes, see Star 1985. Star's article builds on earlier analyses describing the processes of managing uncertainties in laboratory work and in the public presentation of experimental results. Most important of these are Latour and Woolgar 1979 and Knorr-Cetina 1981.

93. Wilkins 1957a and 1957b, quoted in Swords 1992, 120. In all fairness to Wilkins, his own perspective on UFOs admitted that entirely competent scientists could also believe in the reality of UFOs through a study of the best reports and a feeling that they could honestly come to no other conclusion. This was not a view that was often shared — or at least spoken — in the mainstream scientific community. A study of MUFON consultants (those with advanced degrees in their fields) conducted by Charles Emmons in 1994 revealed that 48 percent had had some sort of UFO experience and another 8 percent thought they might have had one. Most of these individuals cited their experiences as the primary reason for their involvement in the UFO community. But, once in, having had a UFO experience made them no more or less active in the community than were the nonexperiencers. (See Emmons 1997, 48–54.)

94. Alan Hale, "An Astronomer's Personal Statement on UFOs," *The Skeptical Inquirer* (March 1997) located at <www.csicop.org/si/9703/ufo/html>. Condon stated that the only kind of evidence that would convince him of the reality of UFOs was for one "to land on the lawn of a hotel where a convention of the American Physical Society was in progress, and its occupants were to emerge and present a special paper to the assembled physicists, revealing where they came from, and the technology of how their craft operates. Searching questions from the audience would follow." (Condon and Gillmor 1969, 29). Similarly, astronomer William Markowitz stated, "As for me, I shall not believe that we

have ever been visited by any extraterrestrial visitor . . . until I am shown such a visitor" (Dick 1982, 296, citing Markowitz 1967).

95. Mullis 1998, 136.

96. Weber 1961. In 1985 Jenny Randles and Peter Warrington observed that it was "ufologists themselves to blame for the fact that they are not taken more seriously" (Randles and Warrington 1985, 67–68), a sentiment echoed yet again in 1996 by Bob Pratt, who wrote that science is still "the best hope for explaining the UFO phenomenon," but that "on the whole, ufologists have done a poor job of presenting their case" to the scientific world (Pratt 1996, 301). Randles and Warrington make insightful comments about the deficits of ufological research and the problem of scientific respectability (1985, 67–69, 81–82, 164–70). In 1994 Chris W. Brethwaite proposed seven ways to reform ufology and make it more scientific, including demanding minimum academic attainments for MUFON officers, a refusal to publicize sensational cases with little corroboration and cases from "anonymous" sources, and a renewed concentration on finding "that right front fender of a UFO" (Brethwaite 1994). Bernhard Haisch pointed out that at the public and the scientific levels there is a great deal of interest in understanding more about the universe and whether we are alone in it (Haisch 1996). He suggested that ufologists harness that interest by promoting grassroots lobbying efforts in government and by generating more truly scholarly articles for publication in professional journals, by which scientists' interest could be piqued through "'evidence of evidence,' credibly, soberly presented" (15). Also see Saul H. Goldstein's response to Haisch's article in Goldstein 1996. Finally, see Stuart Appelle's critical review of the interpretations given to statistical work on abductions, in which he castigates ufologists for "demanding acceptance from the scientific community" instead of earning it (Appelle 1996, 12), and see his follow-up article (Appelle 1997).

97. Maney 1956a.

98. Hynek and Vallee 1975, 73, 189.

99. Maney 1958; Sharp 1961. However, for twenty-five years, NASA engineer Paul Hill gathered and studied UFO sighting reports in order to understand the aerodynamic and physical properties UFOs appeared to follow. Far from finding that UFO maneuvers broke the laws of physics, Hill felt he could make sense of it all. The manuscript describing his findings was published posthumously. See P. Hill 1995.

100. Munro 1997.

101. Emmons 1997, 191–92.

102. Girvan 1960b and 1967.

103. B. Cannon 1983, 304; Clark 1996c, 3–4; Hynek and Vallee 1975, 3; J. Carpenter 1993a, 18–19 and 14–16, respectively. However, one ufologist pointed out that while the UFO community ridiculed scientists who pronounced "ex cathedra" on UFO matters without having done any noticeable fieldwork, they "heaped praises upon" those who spoke out in support of UFO reality though in terms of field experience they were "equally unqualified to make . . . pronouncements" (Sharp 1960, 11).

104. See Clark 1996c, 4.

105. Vallee 1965, 163.

106. Hynek described his own transformation from skeptic and debunker into believer as a decision to "quit calling all these people [UFO witnesses] liars" (Hynek and Vallee 1975, 202, 205).

107. B. Cannon 1983, 305; and Vallee 1965, 98, 113, 115, 124, 138, 149. The choice of relatively uninformed rather than well-informed committee members reflects the real nature of the topic under consideration in such venues. Uninformed participants might be considered appropriate when the issue is, at heart, belief in the object of study and the sponsoring group wants to weed out those whose previous exposure to it might bias them toward belief. Informed participants would be appropriate in a venue wherein the very existence of the subject matter was not at issue but its properties and their implications were.

108. Vallee 1968.

109. Hynek and Vallee 1975, 30.

110. Bullard 1989a.

111. Stacy 1993d, 12.

112. Hartmann 1972, 21.

113. Ruppelt 1956, 45, 201, 209.

114. Robert Low, quoted in Menzel and Taves 1977, 235.

115. Friedlander 1995, 107.

116. Hynek 1972a, 40, 50.

117. Hopkins 1996, 358. Attorney Peter Gersten made a similar statement about the quality of evidence released under the FOIA about UFOs. (See Gersten 1981, esp. 22.)

118. Craig 1995, 193.

119. Vallee 1965, 152; Sturrock 1974; also noted by Dick 1996, 311–13.

120. Menzel and Boyd 1963, 187–88.

121. For instance, the compilation of UFO evidence sponsored by NICAP and published in 1964 as The UFO Evidence (Richard Hall 1997), and McCampbell 1973.

122. Robert Moore 1993, 90.

123. Morrison 1972, 276–78. In this regard it is important to note how closely Morrison's criteria for the "chain of evidence" puts the focus of the evaluation on the witness as a private observer subject to nonobjective, irrational perceptions and interpretations. Pinch and Collins point out that focus on the private aspects of experimental science is one method used by hostile opponents in scientific debates. Discussion of the personal and private aspects of laboratory work, such as the motives, interests, failures, and financial problems of the researchers, serves to destroy "the privacy necessary for the predominance of fact-like accounts" and thus puts the one so depicted at a disadvantage in any debate over the scientific merit of their work (Pinch and Collins 1984). In like fashion, Morrison's evidential criteria tend to shift the primary focus onto the witness's private predilections and peccadilloes rather than allowing the focus to rest primarily on the witness's statement.

124. Morrison 1972, 282. For an extended critique of the idea that scientific progress relies on reproducibility see Travis 1981.

125. Vallee 1965, 108, 110, 155–56, 222.

126. Robert Low, quoted in Menzel and Taves 1977, 235.

127. Hynek 1972a, 50.

128. See G. Gilbert and Mulkay 1982; and G. Gilbert 1976. For a more extensive treatment of the social aspects of the scientific production of knowledge, see Fuchs 1992. Also see the critical essay on the peer review system in science in Gold 1989.

129. Menzel and Taves 1977, 273.

130. Randles and Warrington 1985, 68, 82; Hynek and Vallee 1975, 9, 71. Hynek observed, however, that the Condon Committee had proven that money alone was not enough to generate good UFO research. The subject also required intellectual support (85).

131. David Michael Jacobs 1975, 260–61, cf. 220; Peebles 1994, 193–94. For a lengthier treatment of McDonald's role in the promotion of ufology before government panels, see McCarthy 1975.

132. Law and Williams 1982, 537.

133. Ravetz 1981, 201.

134. Some skeptics would not even dignify ufology by calling it a pseudoscience, preferring to think of it, instead, as more of a cult. (See Emmons 1997, 96.) See also the summary of various proposed schemas in Bauer 1988 and 1989.

135. Friedlander 1995, ix–xii, 164.

136. Ibid., 159–72. For a discussion of peer reviewed publication and pseudoscience, see Bauer 1992. For other attempts to establish criteria for identifying pseudoscience, see Langmuir 1989, 36; Gardner 1952a, 11; and Bunge 1984, 36.

137. Support for this conjecture lies in the informal survey of astronomers conducted by Hynek in 1972, as mentioned previously. He found that a number of his respondents would have been interested in studying UFO phenomena if there had been no stigma and some professional scope and reward for doing so.

138. See Whitley 1972.

139. Ben-Yehuda 1985.

140. Ibid., 108, 114, 112.

141. Ibid., 141–44.

142. Ibid., 120. For a discussion of that incident and others in the history of science, see Mauskopf 1979. For a discussion of the discovery of meteorites, see Westrum 1978.

143. Ben-Yehuda 1985, 116. For a discussion of the processes whereby this support of high-status scientists is won or lost, see Fuchs 1992.

144. Ben-Yehuda 1985, 140.

145. Ibid., 117.

146. Ibid., 123. For an example of this self-redefinition at work, see Pinch and Collins 1984, wherein a CSICOP challenge to a researcher whose statistical findings tended to provide limited support for astrology resulted in CSICOP's having to reevaluate and restate its position on the character of legitimate scientific knowledge and its production.

147. Ben-Yehuda 1985, 141.

148. Ibid., 156, 161.

149. Ibid., 162.

150. Ibid., 165n.53; cf. Peters 1977, 78. Physicist Philip Morrison's under-

standing of the relevance of deviant science disagreed with Ben-Yehuda's more positive approach. Morrison felt that "We can be sure . . . that some valuable part of the fabric of science we now accept will be held naive and erroneous by those scientists who come after us. Just which part we are not given to know. To me it does not seem likely that it will come in one of the 'paranormal' fields" (Morrison 1981, 362).

151. L. Henry 1981.

152. Ibid., 7.

153. Ibid., 8.

154. Ibid., 12. The irony being, of course, that it is "explanation by scientific theory [that] is the essence of disenchantment."

155. Ibid., 12–13.

156. For more on the idea of deviant science as protoscience, see Truzzi 1971 and 1977.

157. Bauer points out that this use of the term *science* and its cognates is more a rhetorical device appealing to "Science" as a symbol of Truth than an appeal to any particular body of facts and principles that could be universally agreed upon as the substance of "science," and that the term is used for its rhetorical force within the scientific community just as often as it is outside of that community. (See Bauer 1987.)

158. Andrus 1995b. The first edition of the MUFON *Field Investigator's Manual* was published in 1971.

159. Hynek 1972b, 188. Also see Vallee 1975, esp. 46–47.

160. Rutkowski 1994; Alexander 1993.

161. Clark 1993b, 3; Vallee 1991a, 170–171; Garner 1993.

It should be noted that Vallee decries not just the abandonment of scientific methodology by UFO researchers, but also the abandonment of UFO research by qualified scientists. He considers the "visible part of American ufology today" (such as abduction research) to suffer from "crude methods of hypnotic regression" that are "worthless" because performed by "neocultists who are busy exploiting the public's fear of the unknown. They fill the vacuum science has left behind" (ibid.).

162. Hynek and Vallee 1975, 193.

163. Mack 1994.

164. Emery 1995; Honan 1995; Rae 1994; Internet post to UFO-L discussion list by William Hauck <DWHauck@aol.com> on 5 March 1995 quoting a letter from Mack's attorney, Daniel Sheehan; Internet post to UFO-L discussion list from William E. Pfleging <Billbeau@aol.com> on 6 March 1995; and Internet post to UFO-L discussion list by Stan Kulikowski II <stankuli@uwf.cc.uwf.edu> on 7 March 1995, also citing the letter from Daniel Sheehan. Kulikowski expressed the opinion that if Mack's activities had resulted in patients claiming injury, then such a review was entirely appropriate. If the review was motivated "on the grounds that his beliefs are strange to other doctors," he felt that the review was unwarranted. (None of Mack's abductee patients were claiming injury.) See also the statement of the psychiatric community's interest in alien abductions and the proceedings against Mack in Puhalski 1995 and the response to the statement in Nyman 1995.

165. Daly 1995, 1.

166. Press Release, "Society Convenes Science Panel to Review UFO Evidence," 6 October 1997. Friedlander, a skeptic of things paranormal, describes the SSE as composed of practitioners of science "concerned with careful scientific checking of claims for paranormal observations." Though he admits that the SSE is "somewhat more open to sympathetic evaluation of paranormal claims" than CSICOP, he nevertheless cites it as an example of scientists' "serious attempt[s] to cope with claims that cannot be dismissed out of hand" (Friedlander 1995, 167). The information considered by that panel and the group's conclusions and recommendations were later published. See Sturrock 1999.

167. "High Level French Government Report On UFOs and Defense," *CNI News* 5, no. 11 (1 August 1999) at <CNINews1@aol.com>.

168. Stiebing 1995, 4–5.

169. Barclay and Barclay 1993, 13. One abductee reported being advised by the aliens not to pursue science "in an orthodox academic setting and fashion," but rather to cultivate his intuitive skills (Mack 1994, 62). Another abductee also transmitted a warning against trying to find material, scientifically verifiable proof of abductions, such as implants, because anything that seemed to hold out such a promise would inevitably disappoint by its apparently prosaic nature (Mack 1994, 263).

170. Donderi 1993, 18.

171. Randles and Warrington 1985, 77; Hynek and Vallee 1975, 71.

172. Girvan 1960a and 1961.

173. Hynek and Vallee 1975, 226–27.

174. Ibid., 165, 215–16.

175. Randles and Warrington 1985, 176. The authors point out that, for all its concern to educate the public for a higher level of scientific literacy, when science decides to "tell members of the public what they have or have not 'really' seen . . . [the] attitude can only do harm to the scientific professions" (191).

176. Merrow 1960; also Maney 1956b; and Girvan 1962.

177. James 1961 and 1962a, quote from 1962a, 10.

178. James 1960.

179. James 1962b.

180. Bowen 1968. Also see Llewellyn 1969, and the article on the correlations between poltergeists and UFO sightings in Owen and Owen 1982. Also note Gratton-Buinness 1973; Bowen 1969a.

181. When I broached the subject of UFOs at the Foundation for Research on the Nature of Man in Durham, North Carolina (formerly the psychic research group founded by J. B. Rhine), I was told that they preferred not to get involved with such questionable subjects. Similarly, James A. Harder, a professor of civil engineering with ufological research interests, related a conversation between himself and a psychic researcher. Whereas the psi-researcher confessed that he was secretly interested in UFOs but would not let it be known for fear of ruining his credibility in the psychic research community, Harder confessed that he was secretly interested in psychic phenomena but was reluctant to mention it for fear of reducing his effectiveness as a UFO researcher! See Harder 1988. Note also the disclaimers of UFO interest made by contributors to Stoeber and Meynell 1996,

20n.6 and 81n.4. This dynamic was also at work among cryptozoologists, among whom having their field associated with ufology was a cause of considerable tension. See Allan Dowd, "For Hunters and Fans of Bigfoot, A Philosophical Divide," *Reuters News Service,* 27 September 1999.

182. See P. Edwards 1970; Bord and Bord 1979.

183. Hynek 1972b, 261.

184. For a list of these figures as of 1970, see Keel 1970, 34–39. For a description of Smith's paraphysical interpretations of UFO phenomena, see Craig 1995, 122–32.

185. Uriondo 1980.

186. Gardner 1952a, 7.

187. For a discussion of the viability of the ETH and the importance of (and history of) the SETI project, see Heidmann 1995, esp. 111–76 and 214–26.

188. Noble 1997, 126.

189. Ibid., 129, 131. Noble recounts one instance when repeated attempts to perfect a guidance system for a rocket booster had failed. Finally the designers wired a St. Christopher medal to the gyroscopic apparatus, noting their objective in the required specification form as "Addition of Divine Guidance" (136).

190. Ibid., 137–42.

191. J. Gilbert 1997, 235.

192. P. M. H. Edwards, quoted in "UFO Forum," in Schwarz 1983, 305.

193. See, for instance, Randles and Warrington 1985, 72, 75. For a discussion of the UFO controversy as it related to the fortunes of the ETH in the larger scientific community, see Dick 1982, 267–319.

194. Davenport 1992; V. Johnston 1993; Vesco 1971; Constable 1958 and 1976. The biologist Ivan T. Sanderson said that UFOs were most likely a life form or constructions of a life form and speculated that they could be or could contain robots, androids, or "living machines," among other options. See Sanderson 1967, 93–94, 110–111, 133–34. For other opinions about the origin of UFOs and their occupants, see Lindemann 1991.

195. See, for instance, Clark 1994a.

196. Dick 1982, 551–52.

197. Menzel and Taves 1977, 197–209, esp. 209.

198. Lamm 1965–1966, 12.

4. UFOLOGY AND THE IMAGINAL

1. Downing 1997b, 8.

2. Davenport 1994, 11.

3. The relationship between spiritualism and the UFO community has typically been considered by scholars as fairly unproblematic: The UFO community for them appears to consist in *toto* of the contactees. See Ellwood 1988, 717, and 1997, 93. A more complex analysis of that relationship is offered in Evans 1973, 137–75. Edward U. Condon expressed the opinion that belief in UFOs and belief in communication with the dead constituted the same kind of intellectual error (David Michael Jacobs 1975, 252). For a discussion of the relationship between contactees and Theosophy, see Stupple 1984 and 1994.

4. Hexham and Poewe describe a similar process of experience becoming story that becomes myth in the genesis of new religious movements based on "primal experiences" with the numinous, such experiences being "unexpected vivid encounters that are considered to be other than normal." See Hexham and Poewe 1997a, 55, 59.

5. For instance, they would cite Ezekiel's wheel-within-a-wheel vision (Ezekiel 1:4ff) or Paul's conversion experience on the road to Damascus (Acts 9:3ff). The irony of the situation is that it was Menzel, himself, who in 1953 pointed out parallels between UFO encounters and biblical texts, noting both as "superstitious imaginings" (Menzel 1953, 124–34). That he should have done so in the context of a book whose purpose was to disprove the reality of UFOs shows the extent to which a religion-versus-science mentality was at work in the early UFO debate.

6. J. Gilbert 1997, 232–33.

7. For example, see Trench 1960; W. Raymond Drake 1968 and 1974a; Von Daniken 1968; Dione 1969; Bergier 1970; Charroux 1971; Wilson 1972; Chatelain 1975a; Horn 1994; and Sitchin 1976, 1980, 1985, 1990, 1993, and 1995. For an excellent summary of some of the major works in the ancient astronauts genre, see Fitzgerald 1998, 9–68. For a summary of the diffusion of some of these ideas into the UFO world, see Clark 1997c.

8. Barranger 1998.

9. Freer 1998, 53. In a similar vein, D'Arc 2000 argues that the theory of evolution is a largely unproven belief system promoted to buttress Western materialism, but that it also serves to obscure the truth of humanity's cosmic ancestry.

10. Letter from G. L. Oliver, Jacksonville, Arkansas, reprinted in the *UFO Newsclipping Service,* Issue No. 338, September 1997, page 12.

11. Strieber and Strieber 1997, 180–81.

12. Rutledge 1981, 43, 47.

13. Ibid., 232–33, 236.

14. F. Edwards 1966, 274, 280. For more on UFO activity and research in the former Soviet Union, see Hobana and Weberbergh 1972; Migulin 1979; Vallee 1992c; and Bresh 1993.

15. Tickle 1997.

16. Peters 1977, 9, cf. 146–47.

17. Ibid., 8–9, cf. 155–56.

18. Hynek and Vallee 1975, xiv.

19. C. Lorenzen 1966, 102–3; C. Lorenzen and J. Lorenzen 1967, 124–25.

20. There is a small corpus of literature in the UFO community dealing with ways of coping with abduction experiences — including how to make them stop — though one group of abductees questions whether it is really desirable to try to put an end to abductions. For books on dealing with abductions, see Bryant and Seebach 1991; Mitchell 1994; and LaVigne 1995. For advice on resisting abductions, see Druffel 1988 and 1992a; a critical response to Druffel in Tilly 1992; and Druffel's response to Tilly in Druffel 1992b.

21. See, for instance, Hynek and Vallee 1975, 25. Barnes, Bloor, and Henry point out that scientists' tendency to adhere to previously established theories even in the face of new or disconfirming evidence can be understood sociologi-

cally as "a form of respect for the observational activity of the ancestors." See Barnes, Bloor, and Henry 1996, 92. Ufology, in this light, becomes a form of disrespect.

22. Gerald Holton points out that in many cases scientific thinking, particularly in the face of intractable problems, takes place first at the imaginative rather than at the rational level. He identifies three types of imagination commonly used by scientists, the third of which, thematic imagination, is both the most dangerous and yet potentially the most productive. Thematic imagination is "letting a fundamental presupposition . . . act for a time as a guide in one's own research when there is not yet good proof for it, and sometimes even in the face of seemingly contrary evidence." The danger is that this early stage in the analytical process may mislead the researcher, so it must be followed up by attention to standard scientific methods that can lead to more generally plausible theories (Holton 1996, 96–97). Ufologists' willingness to accept the reality of the UFO phenomenon in the absence of concrete physical evidence surely stands as an example of the exercise of the thematic imagination. Whether their eventual willingness to entertain psychic and occult theories about UFOs is an example of being misled by their presuppositions is debated within the UFO community. But if ufology, in the end, adds nothing to our fund of knowledge about the physical world, it will still have helped to illuminate the problem of twentieth-century "scientism" — an "addiction to science" that divides "all thought into two categories, up-to-date scientific knowledge and nonsense" (Holton 1996, 50).

23. Cahill 1996, xiv–xv.

24. See Bowen 1968 and 1969b; P. M. H. Edwards 1970; Bord and Bord 1979; Uriondo 1980; Wagner 1991; Kieffer 1979.

25. R. Moore 1977, 186–88.

26. Ibid., 192–95, 182.

27. Hynek and Vallee 1975, 206.

28. R. Moore 1977, 238–39, 242. Psi research in many ways blazed a trail through the hinterlands of the scientific establishment that UFO research was destined to follow just a few decades later. The rarity of the phenomena each was studying, the difficulty of producing the phenomena on command, the high value placed on scientific acceptance but the need to rely on popular support in lieu of having widespread institutional support for research — all were problems first encountered by parapsychologists and revisited by ufologists. See R. Moore 1977, 196–97, 208–10, 236–39, 242. On the history of investigation of psi phenomena and the relationship of that investigation to science, see Meynell 1996.

29. Kaneko 1983b.

30. Hynek and Vallee 1975, 29. Similar sentiments are at work among parapsychologists. See Griffin 1996, who says that one of the chief reasons why psi research is so important is precisely because it challenges the modern scientific paradigms to become larger and more comprehensive.

31. Hynek and Vallee 1975, 220–221.

32. Vallee 1969, 57. Note that "Secret Commonwealth" is a traditional name for the fairy kingdom.

33. Mesnard 1994, 4. See also Phillips 1993, 59.

34. I. Mackay 1970a and 1970b. See also E. Mackay 1973.

35. E. Mackay 1973, 28, 29. See also Essex 1988, wherein advances in theoretical physics were seen as confirmation of ideas that had been fostered for decades by an esoteric group. As an example of the kind of validation Mackay anticipated, he noted that ufologists had made an association between UFO sightings and geological fault areas. These, he said, were the material correlates of "weak spots" in the Earth's etheric envelope that served as gateways for "other orders of matter from other levels" to enter our world. (See I. Mackay 1970b; also mentioned in E. Mackay 1973.) The "gate" theory of UFO origins was echoed a short time later by Bernard E. Finch, an M.D. who theorized that gates in space-time were opened by certain gravitational fields, allowing entities from other dimensions to enter and leave our world (Finch 1980, 24). John Keel speculated that these gates were associated with anomalies in the Earth's electromagnetic energy field (Keel 1971, 92–96, and 1988, 57–59). On the relation between UFO sightings and geological faults, but in a more prosaic vein, see the *Journal of UFO Studies* n.s. 2 (1990), which devoted its "issues forum" section to a discussion of the tectonic stress theory.

36. See Ribera 1986 and 1987; Mesnard and Pavy 1968; Gregory 1971; Jansma 1981; and Creighton 1983.

37. See Branch 1979. Also note Murphy 1971.

38. Sitchin 1976, 1980, 1985, 1990, 1993, and 1995.

39. R. Thompson 1993.

40. Downing's most well-known work on the subject was *The Bible and Flying Saucers* (1968).

41. Holiday 1993.

42. Temple 1976. For critical reflections on Temple's work, see Van Beek 1991.

43. Gonzalez, 1975, esp. 347–86, 440–45; Barbour 1997, 63–72; Brooke 1991, 263–70.

44. Ezekiel 1:4ff.

45. See Blumrich 1974, 1–7, 146–47. In terms of the possible theological influences on Blumrich, it is interesting to note that he worked at the Huntsville, Alabama, NASA facilities, where there was a vibrant evangelical Christian subculture among many of the station's employees. See Noble 1997, 115–42.

46. See Capra 1975; Zukav 1979; Wolf 1981 and 1988; and Herbert 1985.

47. Talbot 1991, 46–55.

48. Ibid., 279–80. As a take-off on the idea that the universe is a holographic phenomenon, David Barclay asked in a provocative essay whether we were the cyberentities (the pawns in the UFO game) or the telepresences (the players of the game). If, as he suspected, both UFO entities and humanity were players in a cyberuniverse, he predicted that we could discover the parameters of the phenomenon by looking for patterns of repetition in it — a task, however, that only appropriate scientific investigation, not dabbling in the occult, could accomplish. See David Barclay, "Towards a Full Explanation," in Barclay and Barclay 1993, 185–89.

49. Davies 1983, 197–98. On the technological supernaturalism of abduction narratives, see Bullard 1989b, 168.

Much of the popular religious discussion of the New Physics has taken place in the context of the Eastern religions and mysticism. For discussions on the implications of the New Physics for Christian theology, see Needleman 1965; Worthing 1996; Polkinghorne 1988 and 1994; Russell 1988; and Hiebert 1986. There are, however, voices critical of the attempts to appropriate quantum theories for use outside the sciences. As Chetan Bhatt points out, "The tropes of quantum mystery, indeterminacy and holism are selectively appropriated in religious revivalist discourse as religious-natural metaphors while at the same time the rather complexly determinist and practical uses of quantum indeterminacy or holism are carefully ignored" (Bhatt 1997, 260).

50. Ring 1992, 210–22.

51. Corbin 1972.

52. See Chittick 1994, 70–72, 84–90. See also Chittick 1998, 303–307, 331–39.

53. Harpur 1994, 48, 124, 166–67, 195.

54. Strieber 1987, 245.

55. See Whitehead 1985, 1986a, and 1986b; Schonherr 1985; Swords 1987b.

56. Barrow and Tipler 1986; Dyson 1979a and 1979b.

57. For an example that makes the idea easier to grasp, think of what a sphere would look like as it passes through a two-dimensional universe. See Abbott 1952. Also see Kulikowski 1994.

58. Harvey-Wilson 1995; Davies 1995b; Whitehead 1987 and 1988; Uriondo 1980.

59. Lewels 1997b.

60. C. S. Lewis 1960, 89–90. See also Duffy 1980.

61. Vallee 1979, 209, and 1991a, 60, 236.

62. Vallee 1991a, 237.

63. Vallee 1969, 7, 40, 207; 1979, 209; and 1991a, 84, 165, 169, 178, 189, 236. Other ufologists indicated that it was not UFO behavior that caused belief in the ETH, but people's insistence on conceptualizing the "other" of UFOs in humanlike terms. According to these theorists, the ETH was a "dustbin" theory, allowing ufology to explain any peculiar experience by positing a sufficiently technologically advanced race to generate it. Under those conditions, the ETH lost all explanatory power (Rogerson 1984; Rimmer 1970). Even from a theological point of view, the ETH lacked plausibility. Presbyterian theologian Barry Downing opined that the ETH in ufology was "making a mole hill out of a mountain" (Downing 1997a).

64. Vallee 1969, 132, 150–51, 162; 1979, 157; and 1991a, 8, 10, 35–36.

65. Vallee 1975, 195, 201; 1991a, 10, 188; and 1979, 51. Vallee is not entirely clear from writing to writing on whether he feels that the consciousness behind the (genuine) UFOs is manipulative or not. At times he seems to believe that it is not. (See Vallee 1975, 201; and 1979, 195, 209, 222.)

66. Vallee 1975, 196–201, 204; and 1991a, 17–18.

67. Vallee 1979, 53, 208. Vallee does not intend to suggest that there is a vast governmental conspiracy. Indeed, he believes that for the most part world governments and military and intelligence agencies have all been kept in the dark

about the goings-on that are managed by a fairly small group of insiders (201). Also see 1991a, 166ff.

68. Vallee 1979, 51, 64, 200.

69. Ibid., 64, 194, and Vallee 1975, 205. See also Trench 1966, 149, citing the opinions of Wilbert B. Smith, former head of Project Magnet in Canada.

70. Vallee 1991a, 41, 70. Though the great mythographer Joseph Campbell never officially offered any statements about UFO phenomena, when asked about his views he replied:

> I really don't know what to think of it. . . . I'm interested also in these theories that men from outer space have come or beings from outer space have come and instituted civilizations. . . . I think this is a continuation of something that's at the core of our religious heritage, and it's not a very good aspect of our religious heritage. Namely, that the spiritual power is from the outside — it comes into us. . . . Whether there are UFOs or not, the fascination with the UFO I regard as a continuation of this notion. (Casteel 1992)

71. Vallee 1979, 192–94; and 1991a, 85, 192, 234–35. On the right-wing connections of some contactees, see Stupple 1984. The rhetoric linking science and rationality with democratic government was also used by one of the early UFO debunkers, Martin Gardner, but he felt that belief in UFOs was, itself, a social threat. Noting that "German quasi-science paralleled the rise of Hitler," Gardner feared that pseudoscience (such as belief in UFOs) could "receive the backing of politically powerful groups" in this country and facilitate the rise of a similarly totalitarian system. Gardner also cited the "cruder Biblicism" and "religious superstition" of fundamentalism as a threat to social order inherent in UFO beliefs. (See Gardner 1952b, 6, 7.) In the early 1990s concerns about the political ambitions of "alternative science" (aka pseudoscience) were voiced once again, this time by Gerald Holton in Holton 1993, 146–47, 178–84.

The correlation of unacceptable beliefs about UFOs with nondemocratic government was made again in the mid-1990s after publication of John Mack's book on abductions. A critical review pointed out that Mack's interpretation of the messages given to abductees by the aliens extolled all non-Western cultures while severely taking to task capitalism and Western culture and values for their lack of environmental sensitivity. The reviewer pointed out that while there was an active environmental movement in the West, it was in the former communist and in third-world countries that environmentalism was most conspicuous by its weakness or absence. Not only were "the world's most egregious ecological horrors" being perpetrated there, but two of the twentieth century's most notorious genocidal purges had occurred in those areas as well. That kind of totalitarian behavior, the critic noted, seemed eerily similar to the behavior of aliens abducting human beings against their will, and Mack's presentation of abductions as the intervention of benevolent entities in Earth's affairs in order to prevent environmental apocalypse sounded, to the reviewer, like just the kind of rhetoric so often used by tyrants to justify their brutalities. (See Clark 1994b, esp. 9–10; and the additional comments about liberals' denigration of the West in a response by Henry H. Bauer in Bauer 1994.)

72. Vallee 1969, 22, 49, 57, 81, 94–95, 163, and 67 (quotation), 110–111.

73. Vallee 1975, 209.

74. Vallee 1979, 67.

75. Ibid., 209, 210.

76. Ibid., 15–17; 222–23. The idea that Christianity was inimical to the rational thought of Greek intellectuals and hindered the progress of science has a long but contested history. For a more balanced presentation of the relationship of early Christianity to ancient science, see David C. Lindberg, "Science and the Early Church," in Lindberg and Numbers 1986, 19–48.

77. Keel 1970, 4, 243, 267, 272. It should be noted that in *Our Haunted Planet* (1971, 7) Keel dates his interest in UFOs from before 1952 and states that he had a UFO sighting while traveling in Egypt.

78. Keel 1970, 9, 14. After a time Keel's method of investigation was to look for evidence of UFO reality in the form of events occurring in different parts of the world but producing similar narrative details or physical aftereffects, and to correlate these details without regard to how they had been interpreted and categorized by the percipients or by previous investigators (see 125, 190, 241–42).

79. Ibid., 14; cf. 162, 172, 195, 241; Keel 1991, 44–45, 157–58.

80. Keel 1971, 17, 22, 62, 69, 76, 102. Keel also discusses the idea, popular in the UFO community, that humanity was not an evolutionary development from lower animals but was seeded or genetically engineered by nonhuman intelligences. See 1971, 132–43. Also see Keel 1988, 106–107, 117–19, 122, 146, 156.

81. Keel 1970, 45, 51, 54, 56, 123, 170–71. Keel postulated that there were a variety of inhabitants of the universe who existed outside our space-time location, some on slightly "lower" frequencies than humanity, others on varying degrees of higher frequencies (Keel 1970, 47, 171, 200).

82. Ibid., 47, 150, 190–91, 210–13, 219, 239–42.

83. Ibid., 172, 192; Keel 1971, 90–91, 144ff; Keel 1991, 42–43. For a brief discussion of the possibility that Joseph Smith, founder of the Church of Jesus Christ of Latter Day Saints, had an encounter with an ultraterrestrial, see Keel 1971, 116–17; for Mohammed, 117–18; and for St. Paul, 118. Also on the possible link between UFOs and Joseph Smith, see C. Bord 1972 and Clyde Lewis 1998. One paranormalist, reflecting on the fact that "the only revealed teachings in which there is a specific allusion to extraterrestrials are those that God conveyed to Joseph Smith," commented: "Scientific discoveries have had some curious and unforeseen consequences, but all precedents of the kind would be surpassed if the discovery of extraterrestrials resulted in the conversion of the peoples of the Earth to Mormonism" (Holroyd 1979, 221).

84. Keel 1991, 185, 220; also see Keel 1988, 100, 159, 161.

85. Keel 1971, 49, 172; 1988, 162. For Keel, the protean nature of ultraterrestrial manifestations throughout human history suggested that they were engaged in a form of psychological warfare (1988, 159). He was willing to speculate more benevolently that deception might have been used only as a tool in order to support certain beliefs useful to human culture on a temporary basis. Though in themselves erroneous, these beliefs might have served as "stepping-stones to the higher, more complex truth" that humanity would have been unable to cope with if exposed to it too soon (Keel 1970, 149, 174). On the whole, however, Keel mistrusted the ultraterrestrials.

86. Keel 1971, 144–51, 161, 212–13. Keel reported that a number of abductees, contactees, and ufologists came to feel that pseudohuman hybrids with alien loyalties were living on Earth and that some had infiltrated the government (1988, 131–33).

87. David M. Jacobs 1998, 251–253. The idea that reported human-alien sexual encounters presaged a future infiltration of human society by "people" with thoroughly alien sympathies appeared soon after the Antonio Villas-Boas case became known. See Anon. 1965.

88. Keel 1971, 144–70; 1988, 138.

89. Keel 1971, 171. This appeal to the early centuries of Christian influence in the West as the dawn of a long Age of Darkness and the model for what is wrong in the world has been wielded also by UFO debunkers. Both Holton and Keel, citing E. R. Dodds's *The Greeks and the Irrational,* see the problems of the period as rooted in an intellectual chasm that grew between elites and the masses. Without the intellectual guidance of the elites, the masses increasingly embraced superstitious and irrational ideas while holding at the same time some of the more rational beliefs of which they were the cultural heirs. The coexistence of these "opposing kinds of consciousness" in the body politic was the unstable soil in which the Christian religion took root and eventually blossomed into the Age of Darkness. (See Holton 1993, 148–51.) While Holton sees this development as in itself an evil, Keel elaborates upon the nature of that evil by attributing it to ultraterrestrials once more controlling humanity through religion.

90. Keel 1971, 97–98.

91. Keel 1988, 100, 143–44, 161, 170–74.

92. Ibid., 159, 162.

93. Ibid., 169.

94. Keel 1970, 270, 273.

95. Keel 1971, 219; 1988, 163.

96. Keel 1971, 217–19; 1991, 168.

97. Keel 1971, 116–17, 221.

98. Keel 1988, 117, 121–22, 141–42, 148, 165. The connection Keel draws between spiritualism and UFOs is not simply for the sake of his argument. If not in the nineteenth century then at least in the modern UFO era, some spiritualists reported UFO encounters. See St. George 1975.

99. Keel 1991, 168. Keel's theory is internally inconsistent in places. For instance, despite his fear that false "illuminations" produced by UFO encounters would lead to a greater belief in the ETH and the threat of more direct ultraterrestrial intervention in human affairs, he also observed that "many of the people attracted to the [UFO] subject . . . gradually drift into the study of psychic phenomena, abandoning the extraterrestrial theory along the way" (1991, 116).

100. Keel 1971, 220–21.

101. Keel 1988, 171.

102. Ibid., 166.

103. Ibid., 173–74. A similar attitude of caution toward the return of the "Sky People" was expressed by Israeli ufologist Barry Chamish, who observed, "I believe the ancient giants may be coming home. . . . The Biblical giants were God's enemy, and Israel's armies were the means to their destruction. There is a

legitimate reason to contemplate the recent re-arrival of giants in Israel with a good measure of dread" (Chamish 1999, 4).

104. One critical ufologist remarked that Vallee's idea of UFOs being a sort of "control system . . . was in fact merging the notion of a divine providence behind history with popular feelings of manipulation and loss of autonomy" (Rogerson 1981).

105. The scientific worldview grew out of the religious worldview not as a decisive break but as a manifestation of the medieval commitment to understanding the work of God in the world. Specifically, early scientists sought to read God's Book of Nature by using specific methods and by systematizing the knowledge gained thereby into general principles describing how the world works. By the twentieth century the religious roots of science and its continuing relationship to religion had become all but invisible. Further, the obvious explanatory and technological successes of science forced religion to rethink its relationship to science, the natural world, and the production of knowledge in ways that could scarcely have been foreseen by the natural philosophers of the Enlightenment. The gist of this rethinking was the rationalization of theology (if not of the actual practice of religion for many people). For a study of the interpenetration of science and religion in the discoveries and revolutions of the Enlightenment, see Shapin 1996. For the ongoing relationship between science and religion in the twentieth century, see J. Gilbert 1997; LaFollette 1990, 151–57; Noble 1997; and Goldberg 1999.

106. R. Moore 1994, 9.

107. Wuthnow 1988, 300–301.

108. Casteel 1993, 12.

5. UFOLOGY, GOD-TALK, AND THEOLOGY

1. See G. Davis 1967; M. Smith 1978; Goodes 1979.

2. Jansma 1981, 68. Other books in this genre were C. Wilson 1974; Weldon and Levitt 1975; D. Lewis and Shreckhise 1991; J. Thompson 1993; Dailey 1995, 44–100; Fox 1996; Alnor 1997; and Larson 1997.

3. Strieber and Strieber 1997, 135. Also note the letter on pages 172–73, where an experiencer describes being plunged from a world of light and beauty into a world of demonic horrors, and the letter from a person who reported seeing a "hooded figure that emanated pure evil" (230). Also note the story of Sandy and Jackie Larson in Clark 1980, esp. 144.

4. Turner 1994b, 258–259.

5. For example, see Marystone 1996a and 1996b.

6. Ruth Gledhill, "Defense Chief Warns of 'Satanic UFOs,'" *The Times of London* (ca. 1 March 1997), as posted in AUFORA News Update of March 1, 1997, at <www.aufora.org>. Anon. 1996b; Paul Inglesby, personal communication, 8 February 1997. This group disbanded in 1998.

7. Wes Clark, personal electronic communication, 2 March 1997. CE4 Research Group, Inc. can be reached at 6845 Anecia Ave., Cocoa, FL 32927, Tel: (407) 631–4393, Joe Jordan (407) 268–0352.

8. "Woman Believes Aliens Present," *Labor News,* Rockford, Illinois, 21 November 1997, reprint in *UFO Newsclipping Service* 342 (January 1998), 8.

9. Fowler 1990, 334, 338.

10. The story of Luca's abductions was meticulously chronicled by ufologist Raymond Fowler in a series of books: Fowler 1979, 1982, 1990, 1995, and 1997.

11. Fowler 1979, 24–27. As the story developed, the aliens miraculously replicated Luca's Bible and examined it while she watched. She was allowed to keep the blue book, she said, for ten days, after which she could not find it anywhere. In that period, however, her oldest daughter also saw it.

12. Fowler 1979, 95–105. It was clear to Fowler that Luca's own faith commitments may have colored her interpretation of the messages she reported receiving from her abductors. He speculated that, wanting to reward her for her cooperation, the entities had provided her with a religious experience using the symbol of the phoenix — a symbol with which Luca was not immediately familiar, but which would have been well known in the first centuries of Christian history (203). Compare an experience reported by abductee Jeanne Marie Robinson in which she was told that a bird she had drawn was a phoenix and that it symbolized the rebirth of the aliens' formerly dying species as it interbred with the human race (Robinson 1997, 54–55).

13. Casteel 1993, 12.

14. Sam, personal communication, 16 February 1997. See also Mack 1994, 121.

15. Ted, personal communication, 17 July 1996.

16. P. M. H. Edwards 1996, 23; Phillips 1993, 59–60, 63. According to Phillips, these belief systems were the primary reason why no human civilization had ever "survived to go on to greater things."

17. See, for instance, Downing 1968 and 1998a; Ujvarosy 1977; Andrews 1989; and Moyer 1970.

18. P. M. H. Edwards 1996, 23.

19. Freixedo 1992, 151. It should be noted that according to Freixedo, "alien" interference in human affairs was only secondary to their real interest, which was a battle against other aliens. In that battle, humans served as pawns, not players. See Freixedo and Taboas 1973, reviewed in Boyd 1975. Also note Jim Swartzmiller, "Whose Side Are You On?" <www.cybergate.com/~ufonline/editor8.htm>.

20. Freixedo 1992, 149, 126.

21. P. M. H. Edwards 1996, 23.

22. Creighton 1983. See also Creighton 1997c in response to Martín 1997a.

23. Ephesians 6:12.

24. "πρὸς τὰ πνευματικα τῆς πονηρίας ἐν τοῖς ἐπουρανίοις." Creighton 1997b.

25. Gillman 1967. Also see Misraki 1965.

26. Downing 1994, 9. Also see Downing 1997a.

27. Downing 1994, 10.

28. Ibid., 9. Cf. Moyer 1970, 305–29, 353–68, wherein the author specu-

lates that extraterrestrials once had direction of our planet and human civilization but neglected their duties for a number of centuries. The modern-day reap-
pearance of UFOs, he suggested, was contemporary evidence of the return of this
extraterrestrial intelligence to "reorient" human science and religion. In regard to
the latter, he said, the "Great Incarnation was performed" two thousand years
ago.

29. Downing 1994, 10.

30. Downing 1990.

31. Ibid., 11.

32. The Institute of Noetic Sciences (IONS) was founded in 1973 with a
"cautiously optimistic vision . . . to expand knowledge of the nature and potentials of the mind and spirit, and apply that knowledge to advance health and
well-being for humankind and our planet." They consider the "noetic sciences"
to be science, mind-body health, psychology, healing arts, philosophy and ethics,
and spirituality. IONS publishes *Noetic Sciences Review* and *Connections*, spon-
sors research projects, has community groups scattered around the world, holds
conferences, and conducts special tours. They report approximately fifty thousand members.

33. White 1992, 7. White does not cite specific scriptures in his rebuttal.

34. White 1996, 65. Another author who considered the UFO phenomenon
in conjunction with spiritualist manifestations, artificial intelligence, and idiosyncratic writings such as the *Book of Mormon* reached substantially the same
conclusions, noting the continuum of "communicators" with humanity who
appear to exist at various levels of spiritual development (Holroyd 1979, 210).

35. White 1996, 69.

36. Ibid., 66–69.

37. Ibid., 69.

38. There were, however, others in the UFO community who analyzed the
UFO evidence and determined that formal contact was just around the corner.
Edwards predicted in 1966 that this should occur within two to three years (F.
Edwards 1966, 314). Abductee Sergeant Charles Moody reported that in 1975
his abductors told him they would reveal themselves openly within three years
(C. Lorenzen and J. Lorenzen 1977, 42, 49). Similarly, an abductee in the early
1970s said that according to the information he had been given, the entities
planned a worldwide contact in about 1987 (Rogo 1980, 177).

39. Green 1967, 126.

40. Keyhoe 1960, 277–80. On the "warfare" explanation for lack of contact, see also Michel 1956, 240, and skeptic Craig 1995, 265–66.

41. Trench 1966, 84–88, 104–106, 129–30, 175. Trench's optimistic view
in the 1960s of technology's role in "subduing the earth" can be contrasted with
the 1990s' more pessimistic view as reported in Tenner 1996.

42. Hopkins 1981, 36, 191.

43. Bryan 1995, 51, 151; Carlsberg 1995, 131, 242.

44. C. Lorenzen and J. Lorenzen 1967, 40.

45. An exception to this was psychologist R. Leo Sprinkle, who wrote in
1967 that it was "useful" to speculate that witness reports of mental (telepathic)
communications with UFO occupants were true and that "UFO occupants have

the powers to bring about, in the long run, either man's destruction or man's perfection. . . . In the short run, further information about UFO occupants will only serve to increase man's understanding of himself and the universe in which he lives" (Sprinkle 1967, 182–83).

46. Hopkins 1981, 215–16.

47. For an account of the manifestation of this ideological divide at the M.I.T. abduction conference in 1992, see Bryan 1995, 125–33. Also see Vallee 1990a, 153–55, and David M. Jacobs 1998, 208–25.

48. D. Scott Rogo, "Conclusion: A Theory of Abductions," in Rogo 1980, 228.

49. Rogo 1980, introduction, 14, 170; cf. Strieber and Strieber 1997, 156.

50. D. Barclay 1993, 179, 181–182. See also Rogo 1980, 170. In Harpur's study of the imaginal world, he noted that "Daimonic events are nothing if not theatrical. They like to leave enigmatic pieces of evidence which turn out to confuse the issue further, to deepen rather than prove the mystery" (Harpur 1994, 66, 139ff, 148, 178). In a similar vein, Vallee noted that UFOs encountered at close range acted as "reality transformers . . . triggering for the witness a series of symbolic displays that are indistinguishable from reality . . . [and which] induce a state of intense confusion for the subjects" (Vallee 1990a, 142). Vallee went on to lament the tendency of ufologists to take these displays at face value instead of critically examining them (142–43). An abductee, however, had a rather different appraisal of the whole situation. "I came to the startling realization that many apparently intensely real contacts with visitors and their craft are indeed effects of a crossover into a living and universal spiritual dimension, no less real than anything imaginable in the material world and experience, but rather infinitely more so" (Strieber and Strieber 1997, 69, cf. 192, 206).

51. Hopkins 1981, 204.

52. C. Lorenzen and J. Lorenzen 1977, 15, 18–20, 23, 66, 127; Rogo 1980, 158, 202–203; David M. Jacobs 1992, 96–99, 136–53; Fiore 1989, 137, 155, 239–40; Carlsberg 1995, 162.

53. Hopkins 1987b, 278; David M. Jacobs 1992, 236; Fiore 1989, 45; Turner 1994b, 124, 149, 172; Carlsberg 1995, 78. It is interesting to note that the theologian C. S. Lewis speculated that an unfallen race of beings, if space-faring humanity ever met them, would have "godlike wisdom, selfless valour, and perfect unanimity" (C. S. Lewis 1960, 89).

54. Mack 1994, 311; Collings and Jamerson 1996, 289. For those with a bent toward critical theory, the implications of abductees' encounters with a coldly rational, instrumental "other" speaks volumes about late-twentieth-century comfort with our own technoscientific world.

55. Strieber and Strieber 1997, 34, cf. 251.

56. Hopkins 1981, 204–205, 208. Although presenting a negative picture of alien interactions with abductees, Hopkins admitted that in some ways their behavior showed a "consistent ethical position" of trying to make the experiences pain-free for their subjects. This kind of caring about the physical welfare of abductees while ignoring the long-term psychological and emotional damage suffered by abductees puzzled him. But in this moral ambiguity Hopkins saw evidence of the authenticity of abduction stories. This inconsistent morality, he

pointed out, bore little resemblance to what one would expect if abduction narratives were the products of "popular fantasy and imagination" (Hopkins 1987b, 277–79). See also David M. Jacobs 1992, 230, 236, 310.

57. C. Lorenzen and J. Lorenzen 1977, 13. See also Hopkins 1987b, 286; Fiore 1989, 57–8, 67, 119–20, 166–71, 235; and Mack 1994, 153, 156, 303. One abductee reported confronting her captors with the statement that they did not really care about their human subjects, that they did not know what "care" meant. She was told, she said, "'No, we know. We just don't feel it as intensely as you do'" (Mack 1994, 163).

58. Hopkins 1981, 209.

59. Ibid., 213–15; Rogo 1980, 26; Hopkins 1987b, 258; David M. Jacobs 1992, 107–31, 153–86, 310–11; Fiore 1989, 32–33, 38, 100–101, 132–33; and Collings and Jamerson 1996, 303. One abductee reported being told that the reason for some of the medical procedures performed by the aliens was to "reproduce some problems that they've got, so that they can study ways to treat it." These problems were immune-related and were part of the reason for the hybridization program (Fiore 1989, 143–44). Other abductees were told that alien medical procedures on both humans and animals were related to efforts at regeneration of the immune system (Turner 1992, 169).

60. David M. Jacobs 1998; Fiore 1989, 160, 173.

61. Turner 1994b, 219–22.

62. Turner 1992, 177; cf. Strieber and Strieber 1997, 240. Also see Armstrong 1988, esp. 138–43. Armstrong believes that some aliens are former guardians of Earth who abandoned their posts and, through the aeons of evolutionary development, lost their souls. They have now come back, he claims, to win human souls for themselves. (This basic idea was also reported by an abductee as information he received from his abductors. See Mack 1994, 312–13.) In contrast, another abductee reported that when he frantically tried to wake his wife just as he was about to be abducted one night, it occurred to him that what was happening to him might be demonic possession. "At that exact moment," he said, "all the activity around me abruptly halted," and he returned to normal consciousness (Strieber and Strieber 1997, 40–41). Another abductee rejected the notion that his abductors might be demonic, noting that "if they were evil, I'd probably be dead by now. I really don't think that a demon would treat a person with gentle respect, nor help them achieve a better understanding of themselves" (Strieber and Strieber 1997, 226).

63. Strieber 1987, 89; cf. 225, 245; cf. Strieber and Strieber 1997, 73. Bryan 1995, 42.

64. Strieber and Strieber 1997, 156; cf. 47.

65. Strieber 1988, 142, 190, 193, 216.

66. Strieber and Strieber 1997, 41; cf. 223; cf. Carlsberg 1995, 56; Bryan 1995, 148.

67. Strieber and Strieber 1997, 60.

68. Mack 1994, 144, 167, 171. Coming to terms with — and overcoming — fear was a central feature of the change that abductees made (or attempted to make) in changing the nature of their experiences. In retrospect they said that the whole point of the fear-inducing features of the experiences was to force

abductees to confront and deal constructively with that emotion as a part of the unfolding of human consciousness. See Mack 1994, 47, 173, 259, 308, 364, 370, 381, 383; Carlsberg 1995, 256. Nevertheless, at an abduction conference at M.I.T. in 1992, Mack cautioned against accepting that abductions are "ultimately good" without more evidence to back up that evaluation (see Bryan 1995, 133).

69. Strieber and Strieber 1997, 59.

70. Not all abductees, however, report undergoing the medical procedures. See Mack 1994, 45, 260, 369–86.

71. Turner 1994b, 17.

72. Turner 1992, 183, and 1994b, 28, 160–61; Strieber 1988, 158, 209, 240–41; Carlsberg 1995, 184–87; Mack 1994, 283.

73. Strieber 1987, 5. Abductee Kim Carlsberg emphasized, however, that it seemed the aliens were a manifestation of the "self" of the universe that was trying to "reconnect on a biological, as well as spiritual, level" (Carlsberg 1995, 237).

74. Turner 1994b, 66; Haley 1993, 93, 129; Strieber 1987, 173. Some abductees feel that they are supposed to communicate something to the "outside" world, but they remain unsure of just what it is. See Mack 1994, 376.

75. Martín 1997b, 17; Fiore 1989, 136; Carlsberg 1995, 238–39; Rogo 1980, 93–94. One theory about UFO contact, suggested psychologist Leo Sprinkle, was that those who pass from being mere "observers" of UFO phenomena to being "witnesses" of or for them also tend to have more successful life outcomes. (See Sprinkle 1980, 64–65, 68.) As for the idea that the aliens wanted to live openly among humans, one abductee reported being told that the aliens did want to live here, but *without* humans, unless, of course, humanity changed its ways. (See Mack 1994, 104–105. But see 250. Also see David M. Jacobs 1998, esp. 230–50.)

76. Haley 1993, 158; Turner 1994b, 120; Fiore 1989, 126, 148; Rogo 1980, 162, 167; Mack 1994, 60–61, 323–25.

77. Fiore 1989, 75, 85; Turner 1994b, 67; Collings and Jamerson 1996, 279, 300–303, 305, 342–43; Andrews 1989; Mack 1994, 135, 186, 213, 276, 294, 306.

78. Turner 1994b, 207.

79. Mack 1994, 128, cf. 308.

80. Turner 1994b, 155, 195, and 1992, 169; Fiore 1989, 88, 123, 144, 173, 221; Carlsberg 1995, 82; Mack 1994, 91ff, 116, 182; Bryan 1995, 29, 149, 199. One abductee described alien identity as an awareness that he was a "lighter" being who had put on a "denser existence" that could get "stuck" on you. "You begin to believe what your body tells you and you forget . . . that you're vaster than it" (Mack 1994, 188–95; see also 209–210, 224–26, 258). Following this line of thought, one abductee wondered: "How did we get our butts strapped down onto the physical plane? Is *this* the actual abduction?" (Kent Steadman, <Phikent@aol.com>, on IUFO <iufo@alterzone.com> on 18 July 1996).

81. Mandelker 1995. In a 1995 interview, Whitley Strieber stated that he thought there might be "visitors who appear entirely human here. My suspicion is that this is not the only human planet" (Whitley Strieber, "Interview with

Whitley Strieber," interview by Lynn Jennings [ISCNI Forum, 8 September 1995], posted on UFO-L <UFO-L@wilbur.protree.com>, downloaded on 26 December 1995). Strieber and Strieber 1997, 182, 281; Mack 1994, 223–25, 228–29, 257, 258, 325, 361.

82. Bryan 1995, 86; see also, for instance, Schneider 1998.

83. Turner 1994b, 147; Strieber and Strieber 1997, 94–95; Mack 1994, 320.

84. Collings and Jamerson 1996, 288, 303, 342–43, 345–46.

85. Strieber and Strieber 1997, 20; cf. 75, 240; Mack 1994, 79, 101–2, 367.

86. Strieber and Strieber 1997, 67, 71.

87. Haley 1993, 135–36; also note the entire Andreasson saga.

88. Turner 1994b, 194–95. Indeed, Italian abductee and stigmatist Georgio Bongiovanni decried the fact that religions "led to division, war and the quest for power" and, though a Christian, he claimed no formal church affiliation. See Wingfield 1995a. See also Andrews 1989, 82–83. For Andrews, one of the great deceptions of Christianity was the notion that one individual could pay the penalty for another's wrongdoing.

89. Fiore 1989, 249. One experiencer observed, however, "It may be (although I doubt it) that these creatures report to the same higher authority as believers here on earth do, . . . [but] I think we are on our own with this one" (Collings and Jamerson 1996, 280–81).

90. Strieber and Strieber 1997, 48; cf. Robinson 1997, 56.

91. Mack 1994, 167.

92. Fiore 1989, 226; Turner 1994b, 147; Mack 1994, 200.

93. Collings and Jamerson 1996, 301–3.

94. Turner 1994b, 161; Carlsberg 1995, 108.

95. Strieber and Strieber 1997, 149.

96. Mack 1994, 131, cf. 334.

97. Strieber and Strieber 1997, 76.

98. Sprinkle 1980, 54–70.

99. Sprinkle 1999, 139.

100. Mack 1994, 48–50.

101. Mack 1999.

102. Turner 1994b, 253. See also David M. Jacobs 1996, 21–25.

103. Turner 1994b, 267–69; cf. Carlsberg 1995, 133. Also note Sprinkle 1999, 140.

104. Dick Farley, "Exclusive One-on-One Interview with Budd Hopkins," 7 July 1996, as posted to <IUFO@alterzone.com> on 11 October 1996.

105. Turner 1994b, 259.

106. David M. Jacobs 1998, 252, 257.

107. Strieber and Strieber 1997, 46.

108. Roicewicz 1989.

109. Mack 1994, 3.

110. Bryan 1995, 273.

111. Downing 1994, 11.

112. Freixedo 1992, 159.

113. Ibid., *Visionaries,* 158–60.

114. Holroyd 1979, 225. Holroyd conceptualized God as the universe whose fundamental property is intelligence (223).

115. Wellman 1962.

116. J. Johnson 1990, 21.

117. Jan Aldrich, e-mail post of 30 September 1997.

118. Heaton 1994, 13; Donderi 1996, 20; Appelle 1989, 127; Pratt 1996, 308.

119. Druffel 1993, 6. British ufologist John Spencer, trying to fathom the distinction between contactees and abductees, offered the amusing hypothesis that "some people have a need to be God, while others have a need to be whipped" (Spencer 1989, 214).

120. Clark 1994a, 23.

121. See Randles 1981; Rogo 1980; Rodeghier 1994a; and Carlsberg 1995. Bullard 1994, 14; Clark 1994b, 8–9.

122. David M. Jacobs 1998, 256–57.

123. Clark 1990a, 1994a, and 1998a, 429–44; Puhalski 1994.

124. Richard Hall 1993a.

125. Mack 1994, 43.

126. The literature of postmodernism is galactic in size and most of it is labyrinthine in nature. Good, intelligible summaries of it can be found in Grenz 1996 and W. Anderson 1990.

127. Bryan 1995, 272.

128. Ring 1992, 243, citing Raschke 1989.

129. Hervieu-Léger 1998, 32.

130. Introduction to Peter Rogerson, "Blood, Vision and Brimstone," *Magonia* 53 (August 1995), at <www.netkonect.co.uk/d/dogon/magonia/arc/90/blood/htm>.

131. Downing 1997b, 8; Gerner 1992, 19; also Anon. 1992, 20.

132. Biersdorf 1975, 123. For a critique of this tendency to subsume the traditional insights of faith to the scientific worldview, see Goldberg 1999 and Hick 1999.

133. Carlsberg 1995, 113.

134. Collings and Jamerson, 347–50.

135. Lewels 1997a, 6, cf. 97.

136. Lewels felt that the Judeo-Christian viewpoint made those who held it too prone to "a heightened state of paranoia" (ibid., quote on 21, 61).

137. Ibid., 7, 17, 59, 82.

138. Ibid., quote on 163, 231, 295.

139. Ibid., 299.

140. Ibid., 53.

141. Ibid., 54–55.

142. Ibid., 311, 82, cf. 278.

143. Ibid., 261.

144. Ibid., 262–63, citing Galatians 4:9.

145. Ibid., 288.

146. Ibid., 289.

147. The conference was not totally welcomed within the Native American community. There were protests by dissenting groups during each day of the conference. See Beresford 1996 and Meyer 1996. The resistance among Native Americans to the promulgation of their traditions outside their own culture has also occurred in other situations. See the case of Sun Bear and the Bear Tribe, described in Albanese 1990, 162.

148. Those familiar with the history of Native Americans in the United States will be reminded of the vision reported by Wovoka, a member of the Paiute tribe of the Pawnee, which led during the late nineteenth century to the Ghost Dance Religion that swept through the Native American community. See Lesser 1978.

149. Boylan 1996a, 1. Also see Beresford 1996, 8. Years before the Star Knowledge Conference — years, even, before the boom of interest in abductions — another Lakota Sioux shared a similar message. Wallace Black Elk described his own encounter with what Anglo culture calls "the aliens," the place of these beings in his tribe's traditions, and the tribal expectation that "at the seventh whistle" the Star Nation people would come down in "countless numbers" from the sky. See Black Elk 1990, 91, 145.

150. Boylan 1996a, 4, quoting Standing Elk.

151. Ibid., quoting Floyd Hand. For further information on the prophecies that Hand says he was given, see Shapiro 1996.

152. Boylan 1996a, 6, quoting Rod Shenandoah and Standing Elk.

153. Boylan 1996b, 12. One of the principals in this thirteen-person team has told me that the group has met and attempted to establish contact on two occasions as of this writing. As for the Star Knowledge conferences, they continue to be held periodically in different locations around the United States, and several of the Native speakers have become honored guests at "prophets'" conferences and other New Age–oriented events.

154. Crissey 1996, 7.

155. Beresford 1996, 8.

156. Ibid., 9.

157. Stockbauer 1997; Boylan 1997a and 1997b; Standing Elk 1997; Huayta 1997a and 1997b. The one issue lacking an overtly Native American emphasis contained an article by Willis Morel on "The Creating Intelligences of Insects," which sought to explain the beauty and wisdom of the collective intelligence of the insect world. (See Morel 1997.) This article was extremely relevant to the abduction phenomenon, as many abductees described the typical gray aliens as looking like "bugs" — usually praying mantises — and the working hypothesis about alien society was that it had a hive-like cognitive structure.

158. Boylan 1996a, 4.

159. Boylan 1996b, 12.

160. Boylan 1998, 25.

161. The shape of the emergent abductee-based religious sensibility was also very much like other "denominations" of what Catharine Albanese has called "religions of nature." See Albanese 1990.

162. Marty 1989, 9. For a larger socioreligious context for this modern "Transformation," see Lucas 1992. For history and analysis of the New Age movement, see Kyle 1995; J. Lewis and Melton 1992; and Heelas 1996. For an

excellent study of one facet of the New Age movement, see M. Brown 1997. For small-group religion in America, see Wuthnow 1994.

163. Walter 1996, 69.

164. Needleman 1965, 131; Bloom 1996, 144.

165. Biersdorf 1975, 25, 26. Also Hexham and Poewe 1997a, 59.

166. Gilkey 1993, 63.

167. Roszak 1976, 27. It is this project of discrimination that has largely been refused by religion when it comes to helping UFO witnesses and abductees make sense of and integrate their experiences. For religion, as for science, the reality of UFO phenomena is unproven, which makes it a nonissue. But within a belief system in which reality could manifest through other than our five physical senses, UFO experiences might be more amenable to consideration. Terry J. Tekippe issued a call for a rapprochement between an intuitive style of knowing (perhaps more suitable to UFO phenomena) and conceptual styles of knowing, pointing out that conceptual knowledge alone is "incommensurate with the mystery of life or of reality" (Tekippe 1996, 473). See also Gilkey 1993, 63, 86–87.

168. Biersdorf 1975, 135.

169. Thavis 1996. A similar caution was urged by Rabbi Norman Lamm (Lamm 1965–1966, 18).

170. Jennings 1980, 9.

171. Hamilton 1976, 25, 26.

172. Downing 1998c, 42–43.

173. Ibid., 39–40.

174. Alexander 1994b, 4. For the full survey, see Alexander 1994a.

175. Anon. 1999a.

176. Downing 1998b.

177. Brookings Institute 1961, 225n.34, excerpted in Durrant 1995. Also see GIFS of the relevant pages from the report at <www.enterprisemission.com/brooking.html>.

178. Clapp 1983.

179. Waddell 1996.

180. Holroyd 1979, 220–21. (Clearly Holroyd was unfamiliar with Calvin's thought!)

181. Jennings 1980, 12; Davies 1983, 71; and J. Davis 1997, 28.

182. Pittenger 1956.

183. See, for instance, Milne 1952, esp. 151–54; Mascall 1956, esp. 36–46; C. S. Lewis 1960; Lamm 1965–1966; Puccetti 1969; Hamilton 1976, 24–26; McMullin 1980, 69–89; Jaki 1980; Clapp 1983, 10; J. Davis 1997, 21–34.

184. Scully 1950, 137. This dismissive attitude was echoed by a number of theologians in the 1950s and 1960s. See also Keyhoe 1960, 206–7.

185. Scully 1950, 181. This opinion was confirmed in an article by the Rev. D. Grassi in the November 7, 1952 issue of *Civilta Cattolica*. It was substantially repeated thirty-five years later when Father George Coyne, head of the Vatican Observatory, noted (on the occasion of the announcement that microbial fossils had been found in a meteorite from Mars) that discovery of alien life would provide a "beautiful opening in which to reconsider the rich theological tradition of God as goodness" (Thavis 1996).

186. Anon. 1955, 2. Also note an article in the Catholic magazine *America* by Rev. L. C. McHugh, S.J., which stated that he believed that intelligent life was in fact common throughout space (cited in C. Lorenzen 1966, 208).

187. Gerhard Jacobi, in *Unsere Kirche* (27 October 1954), cited in Michel 1965, 259.

188. Connell 1956. See also Anon. 1952.

189. Anon. 1985.

190. Skip Porteous, "Robertson Advocates Stoning for UFO Enthusiasts," *Freedom Writer Press Release*, Great Barrington, Massachusetts (28 July 1997).

191. The posting of Monsignor Balducci's statements to IUFO (<iufo@world.std.com>) elicited a flurry of responses from list members. Some asked for the source that the original poster had used for his information, precipitating yet another lengthy online debate about the propriety of demanding proof for statements others made, the circumstances thereof, and so on. Others debated whether such a statement could possibly come from the Vatican itself, and discussed the politics of Vatican announcements. Many, however, expressed surprise combined with a mixture of mild skepticism and quiet hope — and adopted a wait-and-see attitude. Balducci, quoted in Strieber 1998, 273, 274.

192. Strieber 1998, 273.

193. Ibid., 272, also 265–66, 267, 273.

194. Post from Joseph Polanik <jpolanik@mindspring.com> to the Starfriends Discussion List <starfriends@eosoft.com> on 17 March 1998. Also see Rita Elkins, "Spiritual Warfare? Some Look to Bible for Answers to Alien Abductions," *Florida Today*, 17 August 1997, at <www.flatoday.com/space/explore/stories/1997b/081797b.html>.

195. Timothy Heaton pointed out that given the diverse religious backgrounds of the UFO community, a thorough-going investigation of the religious implications of UFOs conducted within the UFO community might prove divisive. See Heaton 1994, 15. The history of the UFO movement does not indicate that there would be nearly as much divisiveness over specific doctrinal points as there has already been over the ethical issues raised around the topic of abductions.

196. Downing 1981, 41.

197. Jennings 1978, 189.

198. Peters 1979.

199. Peters 1977, 160–66.

200. A. Hill 1994. Hill also listed the social cohesion offered by UFO organizations (and their "complex status hierarchy") as a factor contributing to the religiousness of the UFO movement. Although UFO organizations play an important part in making the UFO movement a visible and viable social actor, I find the degree of cohesion of the broader movement rather less compelling than does Hill, and the stability (and general, long-term effectiveness) of the status hierarchy in UFO organizations very much subject to question. I do agree to some extent with his assessment that for many in the UFO community, belief is more important than evidence or critical questioning. On the UFO and abduction discussion lists to which I subscribe, the issue of standards of proof is a recurring point of contention among discussants. For another observation, see Bryan 1995,

133, regarding the "almost revival-meeting fervor" after John Mack's address at the M.I.T. Abduction Conference.

201. Saliba 1995, 55. I am unconvinced by Saliba's suggestion that Christianity is a religion with a terrestrial focus or that the UFO myth could add a "cosmic dimension" to it.

202. Ibid., 74. Saliba notes in an aside that his estimation of the abduction phenomenon as an essentially religious one has had to bracket the reports of alien genetic tampering and the presentation to abductees of hybrid children because "the religious significance of these episodes is by no means clear" (82n.2).

203. Donald E. Ehler, "Letters," *New York Times* (27 January 1969): 32, cited in David Michael Jacobs 1975, 248.

204. Hynek 1972b, 10–11.

205. *Time Magazine* poll, downloaded from <cgi.pathfinder.com/@@$x4vmg . . . Xe7Z/cgi-bin/gdm12x/game/time/cult> on 9 April 1997. Of course, a certain amount of self-interest may be reflected in that response. When asked if they believed in extraterrestrial life, a nearly identical number of respondents said yes.

206. Davies 1995a, 135–36. Davies's assertion that conventional religion is in sharp decline is debated and considerably nuanced among sociologists and scholars of American religion. See, among others, Roof 1993; Hoge, Johnson, and Luidens 1994; Wentz 1998; S. Bruce, esp. chapter 6; and Greeley 1989.

207. Shweder 1997. The changes — even the scientific ones — had their critics, however. See especially Midgley 1992.

208. Davies 1995a, 137–38.

209. See Hebrews 11:1.

AFTERWORD. FINAL THOUGHTS ON SCIENCE,
RELIGION, AND UFOS

1. Olson 1994, 18.
2. Vallee 1975, 204.
3. Ibid., 205.
4. Peters 1976, 60.
5. Clapp 1983, 10.
6. Phillips Brooks quoted in Jennings 1978, 189.
7. L. Henry 1981.
8. E. Barker 1981, 273–75.

9. For a critique of the quest for the Theory of Everything see Trigg 1993, esp. 180–84. For a discussion of the relationship of scientific theory to reality, see Barnes, Bloor, and Henry 1996, esp. the chapter titled "Beyond Experience," which the ufologically informed reader can apply usefully to the historically problematic relationship of ufology to mainstream science.

10. Critics say that this popular theory is a species megalomania that draws more on metaphysics than on scientific fact and that makes essentially salvific statements about humanity's significance and future in the cosmos. Philosopher Mary Midgley traces the popularity of this idea to a lack of "sane and reasonable" praise for science, caused at least in part by minimal scientific literacy among most people, combined with a deep-seated need to restore meaning to

human life. The Anthropic Principle in particular, she writes, is a glorification "both of science itself and of human beings practicing it" that betrays a profound reluctance to ground both in "normal life on earth." See Midgley 1992, 32–33, 224. Other scientists attempt to maintain the centrality of the development of an intelligence in the universe, without resorting to what they feel is "a nostalgia for the Absolute," even if that absolute be conceived in the form of humanity as the "omega point" of the forces of creation (Smolin quoted in Holt 1997, 20). See Smolin 1997.

    11. Needleman 1965, 2–3.

    12. See, for instance, Duerr 1985.

    13. Hynek and Vallee 1975, 263.

APPENDIX. A PICTURE OF THE UFO COMMUNITY

    1. "Gallup Poll Results" from NACOMM, <www.nacomm.org/> on 5 May 1997. Belief in the reality of UFOs peaked in 1978 when 57 percent of those surveyed responded in the affirmative.

    2. In 1956 Edward Ruppelt, former head of Project Blue Book, wrote that the number of UFO reports remaining unknowns was 15–20 percent (Ruppelt 1956, 10). Since the 1960s the more frequently cited figure for the number of unexplainable UFO sightings has been roughly 10 percent. This means that of the 23 million Americans who have sighted a UFO, only 2.3 million sightings would probably be unexplainable by conventional means if every case could be investigated. That breaks down to approximately 125 unexplainable sightings per day for the last fifty years.

    3. Andrus 1997, 24.

    4. In addition to the major UFO study groups already described, there were several UFO hotlines in operation in the late 1990s. Among the better-known was the National UFO Reporting Center at (206) 722–3000, online at <www.nwlink.com/~ufocntr/>.

    5. Strentz 1970, 117.

    6. Ibid., 128.

    7. Friedman 1989, 10.

    8. Westrum n.d.a, 8, 10, 15.

    9. See Festinger, Riecken, and Schachter 1956; Stupple and McNeece 1979 (about "The Two," aka "Bo and Peep," later known as the Heaven's Gate cult); Balch 1980; Balch and Taylor 1977; Wallis 1974 (about contactee George King's group); Jackson 1966 (about the Aetherius Society); and Buckner 1965 (about a contactee group with a more "open door" approach to the propagation of its ideas). Other more generally focused scholarly treatments of contactee groups are Ashworth 1980; Hexham 1986; Saliba 1990; Sanarov 1981; Schwarz 1976; Stupple 1984; and Stupple and Dashti 1977.

    10. Stupple 1994, 94–95.

    11. Lawson and McCall 1978 and 1982; Lawson 1984; Clamar 1988; Parnell 1988; Parnell and Sprinkle 1990; Ring 1992; Rodeghier, Goodpaster, and Blatterbauer 1991.

    12. McIver 1985, 21–22.

13. Ibid., 1.

14. Local reading and discussion groups surveyed were the Houston UFO Network (1996), the Full Story Group of Greensboro, North Carolina (1996), and the UFO Awareness Study Group of Greensboro and Durham, North Carolina (1996). Conferences surveyed were the Gulf Breeze UFO Conference (October 1995 and March 1996), the Greenville, South Carolina, Alien Abduction and UFO Conference (May 1996), the MUFON UFO Symposium (July 1996 and July 1997), and the Tampa, Florida, UFO Conference (September 1996).

15. Though the response rates when personally handing out surveys at conferences was best, it tended to generate anxiety among some conference-goers. There was a general suspicion that I might be a government surveillance agent (probably CIA) infiltrating the conference, despite the fact that I was careful to provide respondents with more personal identifying information about myself than what I was asking of them. My willingness to be available to talk helped, gradually, to dispel the suspicions that I was a CIA agent. The information I provided included the fact that I was studying the alien abduction movement. Some conference-goers took the term *movement* as potentially pejorative and grilled me about my ideas and how I intended to portray the UFO community. Only when they were satisfied that I was not a "debunker" and did not intend to portray them as religious fanatics did they begin to relax and become more friendly and open.

This response should be expected by any participant-observer in the UFO community — at least initially. McIver reports that when she identified herself as a sociologist, other members of her UFO group became anxious about her intentions. "But this anxiety seemed to be alleviated when I explained that it was my dissatisfaction with previous sociological research on the UFO movement which prompted my research and that I intended to present a more complete picture; following this I appeared to be treated as a novice ufologist once again. Gradually I became known as the 'sociological ufologist' and was accepted as a participant with yet another point of view" (McIver 1985, 215).

16. "The Nation: Demographics" in *The Chronicle of Higher Education* as posted at <chronicle.merit.edu/.almanac/.almdem2.html>, downloaded on 10 April 1997.

17. Cited by Strentz 1970, 134.

18. Alan Scher Zagier, "Durham Wreck Writes Tragic End to Outing," *The Raleigh News and Observer*, 2 July 1997. This group became the focus of media attention in the summer of 1999 when armed guards denied a building inspector and the local sheriff access to the community's property near Eatonton, Georgia. See "Georgia Sect Alarms Neighbors," Associated Press (27 July 1999). Though small, the group draws supporters from a wide geographic area. See "Thousands Gather for Nuwaubian Event," Associated Press (28 June 1998) and "United Nuwaubian Nation of Moors," posted 30 July 1998 on <www.wanonline.com/blackhistory/blackhistory3564.html>. For the Nuwaubians' web site, see <www.netgenius.com/ amom/rizq.htm>.

19. Druffel 1980a.

20. Martin and Wann 1995.

21. For instance, abductee Betty Andreasson Luca's daughter, Becky, reported

being taken on board a UFO when she was three years old and allowed to play with another child, a black girl about her own age. See Fowler 1997, 12–26.

22. The only ufologist I have found who has attempted to use race as a category for analysis of UFO events is C. B. Scott Jones, "Push My Buttons: Color and Sex," in C. Jones 1995, 52–75. Jones suggests that the typical abduction scenario involving the capture and reproductive manipulation of women (most of whom are white) by small gray aliens contains an "underlying sub-conscious racial theme" strongly reminiscent of the capture and subjugation of West Africans for the slave trade in the Americas.

23. U.S. Bureau of the Census 1996, Table 14, "Resident Population by Age and Sex."

24. Pritchard et al., 622–28.

25. A survey of 423 articles, book reviews, columns, and letters to the editor in the *Flying Saucer Review,* the *Mutual UFO Network UFO Journal,* and the *International UFO Reporter* from 1995 through 1996 revealed that 87 percent of the pieces were written by men, 8 percent were written by women, and 5 percent were written by individuals whose names did not clearly indicate gender.

26. A question about abductee status on my short survey of UFO community members revealed that, of probable or certain abductees, 41 percent were men and 59 percent were women. The longer survey designed specifically for abductees returned figures of 42 percent men and 58 percent women. This figure for the gender distribution differs from that found by Rodeghier, Goodpaster, and Blatterbauer, whose sample of abductees was 74 percent female (Rodeghier, Goodpaster, and Blatterbauer 1991, 69). In another study by folklorist Thomas E. Bullard of 270 abduction stories published through the year 1985, 67 percent of the accounts were from men and only 33 percent were from women (Bullard 1987a, 4). Of abduction researcher David Jacobs's subjects in his 1992 book, 54 percent were women (David M. Jacobs 1992, 327–28). A report by psychologist Richard Boylan on forty-four of his abductee-clients had 55 percent women to 45 percent men (Boylan and Boylan 1994, 55). An analysis of HUMCAT, a database of humanoid UFO occupant sighting reports, revealed that the approximately 375 reports involving abductionlike encounters were provided by men and women in equal numbers (Webb 1994, 198–200). But Harvard psychiatrist John Mack reported in 1994 that 62 percent of his abduction cases were women (Mack 1994, 2). Finally, researcher Richard Hall reports that in a five-year project on abductions, 72 percent of the project participants were women and only 28 percent were men (Richard Hall 1993b, 1). In a cross-cultural study of abduction accounts from England, Brazil, the United States, and Australia, 52.5 percent of the subjects were women and 47.5 percent were men (see Richard Hall 1994, 191).

The different figures reported by various researchers may well reflect sampling biases among the various studies. While some such as Rodeghier, Goodpaster, and Blatterbauer set criteria for what counted as an abduction and then used those criteria to select a sample, my own study is a self-selected sample of individuals who identify in one way or another, and to one degree or another, with the label "abductee."

27. Zack Van Eyck, "Extraterrestrials Capture Imagination of Utahns," *Dese-*

ret News (Salt Lake City) 18 August 1996, reprinted in the *UFO Newsclipping Service,* 327 (October 1996): 8. In contrast, Charles Emmons comments favorably on the increasing visibility of women in the UFO movement but does not document the ways in which that visibility has been achieved (Emmons 1997, 71).

28. Five of the most well-known abduction researchers who have written books about their investigations are John Mack, David Jacobs, Budd Hopkins, Richard Boylan, and Raymond Fowler. All but Fowler have written about many different abductees, Fowler alone having concentrated almost exclusively on a single case — that of Betty Andreasson Luca. (Fowler has written two other single-case books as well, but the bulk of his work has been to chronicle the Andreasson case.) Michael Craft chose to explore the mysterious, abductionlike events in his own past not by writing a book about them, but by writing a book about the UFO and abduction phenomenon in general terms (Craft 1996). The most recent abduction report by a man, however, is once again a personal narrative (Krapf 1998). In England, Jenny Randles has written one book on numerous abduction cases. In the United States, the late Karla Turner wrote her second book about several abductees and her third about the case of one particular abductee, Ted Rice.

29. Among the better-known women abductees who have written their own stories are the late Karla Turner, Leah Haley, Beth Collings and Anna Jamerson, Katharina Wilson, Jeanette Robinson, Debbie Jordan, Mia Adams, Joy Gilbert, Lyssa Royall, and Kim Carlsberg. Of these, only Turner and Jordan negotiated contracts with larger publishers; neither got the same degree of national media coverage as did the two men who also published their abduction accounts with major houses. The only two men to have written their own, personal abduction accounts before 1998 — Whitley Strieber and Travis Walton — were published by major houses.

30. Robert Girard, Arcturus Books Inc., Catalogue 1997–10, October, page 8 and Catalogue 1997–11, November, page 6.

31. Personal correspondence, [Identity Protected] to Brenda Denzler, 19 October 1996.

32. Stacy 1992b, 20.

33. Douglass 1992, 20–21. For the second letter, which expressed appreciation for Douglass's letter and pointed out that one locus of discrimination against women ufologists was in the more technical areas of research, see M. Jones 1993.

34. Greenfield 1976; and Greenfield 1977, quoted in Sheaffer 1981, 21.

35. Denzler 1996.

36. For a more scholarly analysis of the gendered aspects of ufology and especially of abduction narratives, see J. Dean 1996 and 1998.

37. U.S. Bureau of the Census 1996, Table 712, "Money Income of Households — Aggregate and Average Income, by Race and Hispanic Origin: 1993." The UFO survey did not specify whether household or personal and individual information was being requested when asking about income levels. In this analysis I have presumed that the data reflect household incomes. Ibid., Table 243, "Educational Attainment, by Selected Characteristic: 1995."

38. Ibid., Table 711, "Money Income of Households — Percent Distribution, by Income Level and Selected Characteristics: 1994."

39. The modal household income level is fifteen to thirty-five thousand dollars on the UFO survey.

40. U.S. Bureau of the Census 1996, Table 243, "Educational Attainment, by Selected Characteristics: 1995," reports 15.2 percent with a bachelor's level degree; the 1993 *General Social Survey* (GSS), 1993, Question 15D, "Highest Year of School Completed," reports 15.8 percent; and *The Chronicle of Higher Education Almanac* in 1996 reported 13.1 percent.

41. GSS 1993, Question 15D, "Highest Year of School Completed."

42. *Chronicle of Higher Education Almanac,* 1996, and U.S. Bureau of the Census 1996, Table 243, "Educational Attainment," respectively.

43. Warren 1970, 600.

44. Ibid., 603, 600 (that is, UFO sightings as an "appropriate link" between social alienation and its individual expression). When Warren included women and African-American men in his sample, the results did not support his hypothesis that status frustration led to UFO sighting reports that reflected an effort to break out of an unrewarding social order. He attributed this to the "special inconsistency associated with racial and sex roles" which skewed the over-all sample (601).

45. Ibid., 602. By way of comparison, a study of the geographic distribution of UFO sighting reports found that more reports came from counties with higher educational levels than from counties with lower levels (Saunders 1975, cited in Rodeghier, Goodpaster, and Blatterbauer 1991, 68).

46. For instance, Warren states on page 600 that "UFO sightings are linked to status frustration." On page 603 he writes that he seeks to establish that "status inconsistents who see saucers do so in response to their position of ambiguity and marginality" (Warren 1970).

47. Westrum 1978, 4.

48. Ibid., 10. Also see Strentz's perceptive analysis of the psychology of reporting UFO sightings in Strentz 1970, 117–38.

49. Warren 1970, 603, 601. Social alienation is a popular theory. Other scholars have suggested it as the reason why some people join contactee groups. See Wallis 1974; Buckner 1965; and Glock and Stark 1973, 254.

50. On the prevalence of the ETH in UFO circles, see Clark 1996d, esp. 4: "The evidence indicates that far from rushing to embrace visitation (or salvation) from space, even those who had directly experienced the UFO phenomenon embraced the ETH only slowly and reluctantly. . . . The ETH became a popular interpretation only when the perceived failure of other explanations to account for the phenomenon's persistence, its appearance, and its behavioral characteristics became apparent to all but the most committedly hostile." Also see Swords 1989 and note the exhaustive study of the debates on the extraterrestrial life question among educated elites chronicled in Crowe 1986.

51. Zimmer 1985. The theory that UFO believers are psychologically disturbed was proposed in Meerloo 1968 and by Lester Grinspoon and Alan D. Persky in 1969 at the annual symposium of the American Association for the Advancement of Science (Grinspoon and Perksy 1972). However, the Condon Report failed to find any significant levels of psychiatric disturbance in UFO believers (Condon and Gillmor 1969, 4), and studies of UFO believers since that

time have failed to find signs of any significant psychological disturbance. A study of 225 UFO experiencers conducted at the University of Wyoming in the mid-1980s found "no overt psychopathology" (Parnell and Sprinkle 1990). A study in the early 1990s also failed to find psychopathology in two groups of UFO believers, though among the group reporting more intense UFO experiences there was a higher degree of fantasy-proneness and unusual sensory experiences (Spanos et al. 1993).

52. See Resta 1975, which found that there was no correlation between anomie and belief in UFOs.

53. GSS 1993, Item 55, "Political Party Affiliation."

54. U.S. Bureau of the Census 1996, Table 459, "Resident Population of Voting Age and Percent Casting Votes—States: 1986 to 1996." The cited 55 percent represents the best voter participation figure available. The percentages of those who vote in congressional and in local elections is significantly smaller. GSS 1987, Item 352, "Has Respondent Given Money to Candidate or Cause."

55. Ibid., Item 343, "Has Respondent Worked for Parties or Candidates."

56. U.S. Bureau of the Census 1996, Table 610, "Charity Contributions— Percent of Households Contributing, by Dollar Amount, 1987 to 1993, and Type of Charity, 1993." Ibid., Table 608, "Percent of Adult Population Doing Volunteer Work: 1993." For a lengthier treatment of volunteerism in America, see Wuthnow 1991.

57. GSS 1993, Item 104, "Respondent's Religious Preference."

58. See Roof 1993, esp. 30–31, 41, and 76–80. See also Hoge, Johnson, and Luidens 1994, 211.

59. GSS 1991, Item 606, "How Often Respondent Attends Religious Services."

60. In support of this conclusion, see A. Hill 1994 and Saliba 1995, 55.

61. U.S. Bureau of Census 1996, Table 608, "Percent of Adult Population Doing Volunteer Work: 1993." David Sheff, "Portrait of a Generation," *Rolling Stone* (5 May 1988): 55.

62. To the statement that the condition of the average person is getting worse, 59 percent of this subset agreed, 21 percent disagreed, and 20 percent were unsure. To the statement that officials don't really care about the condition of the average person, 68 percent agreed, 18 percent disagreed, and 14 percent were unsure.

63. Average educational level among this subset of the UFO community is, once again, a bachelor's degree: 33 percent have a high school degree (and many have some college education); 9 percent have an associate's degree; 24 percent have at least a bachelor's degree; 17 percent have a master's degree; and 7 percent have a Ph.D. The 5 percent who have gone through some sort of professional certification program may reasonably be added to those who have at least a high school diploma. This respondent subset has an average annual income of between thirty-six thousand and fifty thousand dollars.

64. Of this group, 82 percent vote, 19 percent contribute financially to political campaigns, and 9 percent do campaign work. Also, 80 percent of the group make charitable contributions, and 38 percent have done work for charities.

65. Hynek 1972b, 31–34.

66. For a more elaborated version of Hynek's typology, see J. Johnson 1995.

67. Greer and CSETI members have been actively involved not only in trying to establish regular contact with UFO aliens but also in pressing the government to permit "full disclosure" of its UFO interests and involvements by allowing individuals bound by national security oaths to speak freely about what they know, without fear of reprisal. CSETI claims to have more than one hundred witnesses to government involvement in UFO matters who would willingly come forward if permitted to do so.

68. By way of comparison with the perception that most of the abductees are women, see note 26. In this regard, one must keep in mind the tendency for men to underreport illness and psychological or emotional problems in Western society.

69. For a collection of these kinds of accounts, see Preston E. Dennett 1996 and Aronson 1999. A more general catalog of physical aftereffects of UFO encounters is John F. Schuessler 1996. However, UFOs are also reported to cause physical harm to some percipients. For the most focused treatment of this topic, see Pratt 1996; Vallee 1990a; and John Schuessler 1998.

70. For an example of the lengths to which experiencers will go to get proof of abductions (and to prevent them from happening), see Collings and Jamerson 1996, 121–29. Some abductees report having had a pregnancy that suddenly terminated (without miscarriage) for reasons that their doctors could not determine. There has been an effort to document these missing pregnancies. See Neal 1992. Finally, there have recently been a number of anomalous objects (which abductees identify as alien implants) removed from their hosts and subjected to laboratory analysis. See Leir 1996 and 1998. After Canadian abductee Betty Stewart Dagenais passed away, an unknown object behind her left ear was finally removed and analyzed. See Vankerkom 1996.

71. H. Smith 1989, 120 and 94.

Bibliography

ABBREVIATIONS

FSR = *Flying Saucer Review*

JUFOS = *Journal of UFO Studies*

IUR = *International UFO Reporter*

MUJ = *MUFON UFO Journal*

Abbott, Edwin A. 1952. *Flatland: A Romance of Many Dimensions.* New York: Dover Publications.

Abell, George O., and Barry Singer, eds. 1981. *Science and the Paranormal: Probing the Existence of the Supernatural.* New York: Charles Scribner's Sons.

Abrahamson, Reverend Charles. 1965, "Introduction." In *The Day the Gods Came* by George King, 9–14. Los Angeles: The Aetherius Society.

Adamski, George. 1955. *Inside the Flying Saucers.* New York: Warner Paperback Library. Reprint, *Inside the Space Ships.*

Albanese, Catharine L. 1990. *Nature Religion in America: From the Algonkian Indians to the New Age.* Chicago: University of Chicago Press.

Aldrich, Jan. 1998a. "Top-Secret 1949 Document." *IUR* 23, no. 1 (spring): 3–6, 31.

———. 1998b. "Investigating the Ghost Rockets." *IUR* 23, no. 4 (winter): 9–14.

———. 1999. "Aerial Phenomena Research Organization Files Located." *MUJ* 370 (February): 8.

Alexander, Victoria. 1993. "New Protocol for Abduction Research." *MUJ* 307 (November): 7–10.

———. 1996. *The Alexander UFO Religious Crisis Survey: The Impact of UFOs and Their Occupants on Religion.* Dublin, Ohio: MidOhio Research Associates.

———. 1994b. "The Alexander UFO Religious Crisis Survey: The Impact of UFOs and Their Occupants on Religion." *MUJ* 317 (September): 3–7, 13.

Allan, Christopher D. 1998. "The Mantell Case — Fifty Years Later." *IUR* 23, no. 1 (spring): 7–9, 31–32.

Alnor, William M. 1997. *UFOs in the New Age.* Grand Rapids, Mich.: Baker Book House.

Anderson, Bruce. 1995–1996. *UFO Update Arizona* (winter).

Anderson, Walter Truett. 1990. *Reality Isn't What It Used to Be: Theatrical Politics, Ready-to-Wear Religion, Global Myths, Primitive Chic, and Other Wonders of the Postmodern World.* New York: HarperSanFrancisco.

Andrews, John H. 1989. *The Extraterrestrials and Their Reality.* Prescott, Ariz.: JACO.

Andrus, Walter H., Jr. 1992. "UFOLOGY: The Emergence of a New Science." *MUJ* 295 (November): 3.

———. 1995a. "Roswell's Smoking Gun?" *MUJ* 325 (May): 16–17.

———. 1997. "Director's Message." *MUJ* 353 (September): 24.

———, ed. 1995b. *MUFON Field Investigator's Manual.* 4th ed. Seguin, Tex.: Mutual UFO Network.

Angelucci, Orfeo. 1955. *The Secret of the Saucers.* Amherst, Wisc.: Amherst Press.

Anon. 1952. "The Theology of Saucers." *Time* (18 August): 62.

———. 1955. "Let's Talk Space: German Priest Says: 'We're Being Watched.'" *FSR* 1, no. 2 (May–June): 2.

———. 1958. "Jet Propulsion Laboratory has UFO Club." *FSR* 4, no. 3 (May): 30.

———. 1962. "The Brazilian Abduction." *FSR* 8, no. 6 (November): 10–12.

———. 1964. "What Happened At Fatima?" *FSR* 10, no. 2 (March–April): 12–14.

———. 1965. "Mail Bag: The Brazilian Farmer's Story." *FSR* 11, no. 3 (May–June): 24–25.

———. 1971. "UFOs Probably Exist." *Industrial Research* (April): 75.

———. 1976. "New Time Lapse Case from England Uncovered." *MUJ* 107 (October): 17–18.

———. 1977. "Papua: Father Gill Revisited." *IUR* 2, no. 11 (November): 4–7, and 2, no. 12 (December): 4–7.

———. 1979. "Good Chance UFOs Exist in Some Form." *Industrial Research/Development* 21 (July): 139–40.

———. 1984. "Abductees Are 'Normal' People." *IUR* (July–August): 10–12.

———. 1985. "A Turkish Religious Leader Speaks on UFOs." *FSR* 30, no. 6 (August): 25.

———. 1992. "Letters: UFOs — the Religious Dimension." *MUJ* 291 (July): 20.

———. 1994a. *Project Blue Book Special Report No. 14.* Evanston, Ill.: Center for UFO Studies.

———. 1994b. "What MacArthur Really Said." *MUJ* 320 (December): 8, 10.

———. 1995. "The GAO Report: Results of a Search for Records Concerning the 1947 Crash Near Roswell, New Mexico." *IUR* 20, no. 4 (July–August): 3–6.

———. 1996a. "Former NATO Staffer Robert Dean Speaks Out on UFOs." *ISCNI Flash* 2, no. 5 (16 May).

———. 1996b. "Lord Hill-Norton Speaks Again." *FSR* 41, no. 3 (autumn): 26.

———. 1996c. "The Rockefeller Briefing Report." *Unsolved UFO Sightings* (fall): 15–25.

———. 1997. "Popular Science UFO Poll Results." Posted to I-UFO (4 July). <iufo@world.std.com>.

———. 1999a. "Scientists, Theologians Ponder ET Impact on Religion." *CNI News* 5:5 (1 May) at <CNINews1@aol.com>.

———. 1999b. "Joe Firmage Enters UFO Scene with Nationwide Publicity." *MUJ* 370 (February): 11.

Appelle, Stuart. 1989. "Reflections on the Reports of Being Abducted by UFOs." *JUFOS* n.s. 1: 127–29.

———. 1996. "Abduction Report Consistency and Statistical Inference." *MUJ* 341 (September): 9–13.

———. 1997. "Abduction Report Consistencies as Scientific Evidence of Alien Abductions." *MUJ* 347 (March): 12–16.

Armstrong, Virgil. 1988. *The Armstrong Report: "They Need Us, We Don't Need Them."* Oak Creek, Ariz.: Entheos Publishing.

Arnold, Kenneth, and Ray Palmer. 1952. *The Coming of the Saucers.* Boise, Id.. Privately published.

Aronson, Virginia. 1999. *Celestial Healing: Close Encounters That Cure.* New York: Signet Books.

Ashworth, C. E. 1980. "Saucers, Spoon-Bending, and Atlantis: A Structural Analysis of New Mythologies." *Sociological Review* 18: 353–76.

Baker, R. M. L., Jr. 1972. "Motion Pictures of UFO's." In Sagan and Page 1972, 190–210.

Baker, Robert A. 1988. "The Aliens among Us: Hypnotic Regression Revisited." *The Skeptical Inquirer* 12, no. 2: 148–62.

———. 1989. "Q: Are UFO Abduction Experiences For Real? A: No, No, A Thousand Times No!" *JUFOS*, n.s. 1: 104–110.

———. 1996. *Hidden Memories: Voices and Visions from Within.* Amherst, N.Y.: Prometheus Books.

Balch, Robert. 1980. "Looking behind the Scenes in a Religious Cult: Implications for the Study of Conversion." *Sociological Analysis* 41 (summer): 137–43.

Balch, Robert, and David Taylor. 1977. "Seekers and Saucers: The Role of the Cultic Milieu in Joining a UFO Cult." *American Behavioral Scientist* 20, no. 6: 839–60.

Balch, Robert W., Gwen Farnsworth, and Sue Wilkins. 1983. "When the Bombs Drop: Reactions to Disconfirmed Prophecy in a Millennial Sect." *Sociological Perspectives* 26: 137–58.

Barbour, Ian G. 1997. *Religion and Science: Historical and Contemporary Issues.*

San Francisco: Harper Collins. Revision and reprint of *Religion in an Age of Science,* 1990.

Barclay, David. 1993. "Towards a Full Explanation." In Barclay and Barclay 1993, 172–89.

Barclay, David, and Therése Marie Barclay, eds. 1993. *UFOs: The Final Answer? Ufology for the Twenty-First Century.* London: Blandford/Villiers House.

Barker, Eileen. 1981. "Science as Theology: The Theological Functioning of Western Science." In *Science and Theology in the Twentieth Century,* ed. A. R. Peacocke, 262–80. Notre Dame: University of Notre Dame Press.

Barker, Gray. 1956. *They Knew Too Much about Flying Saucers.* New York: Tower Books/University Books.

Barnes, Barry, David Bloor, and John Henry. 1996. *Scientific Knowledge: A Sociological Analysis.* Chicago: University of Chicago Press.

Barranger, Jack. 1998. *Past Shock: The Origin of Religion and Its Impact on the Human Soul.* Escondido, Calif.: The Prometheus Project.

Barrow, John D., and Frank J. Tipler. 1986. *The Anthropic Cosmological Principle.* Oxford: Oxford University Press.

Bartlett, Jenna. 1995. "Letter to the Editor." *Contact Forum* 3, no. 3 (May–June): 2.

Bascom, William. 1965. "The Forms of Folklore: Prose Narratives." *Journal of American Folklore* 78, no. 307 (January–March): 3–20.

Basiago, Andrew D. 1992. "Dreamland and the CIA." *MUJ* 291 (July): 10–12.

Basterfield, Keith. 1992. "Implants." *IUR* 17, no. 1 (January–February): 18–20.

———. 1994. "Fantasy-Prone Personality Hypothesis." *MUJ* 309 (January): 16–18.

Basterfield, Keith, and Robert E. Bartholomew. 1988. "Abductions: The Fantasy-Prone-Personality Hypothesis." *IUR* 13, no. 3 (May–June): 9–11, 22.

Bauer, Henry H. 1986. *The Enigma of Loch Ness: Making Sense of a Mystery.* Urbana: University of Illinois Press.

———. 1987. "What Do We Mean by 'Scientific'?" *Journal of Scientific Exploration* 1, no. 2: 119–27.

———. 1988. "Commonalities in Arguments over Anomalies." *Journal of Scientific Exploration* 2, no. 1: 1–11.

———. 1989. "Arguments over Anomalies: 2. Polemics." *Journal of Scientific Exploration* 3, no. 1: 1–14.

———. 1992. *Scientific Literacy and the Myth of the Scientific Method.* Urbana: University of Illinois Press.

———. 1994. "Letters: Antagonism toward Science." *IUR* 19, no. 3 (May–June): 18.

Baxter, Marla. 1958. *My Saturnian Lover.* New York: Vantage Press.

Beckley, Timothy Green. 1993. "Jackie Gleason and the Little 'Men from Mars.'" *UFO Universe* (summer): 32–39.

Bender, Albert K. 1962. *Flying Saucers and the Three Men.* New York: Paperback Library.

Ben-Yehuda, Nachman. 1985. *Deviance and Moral Boundaries: Witchcraft, the Occult, Science Fiction, Deviant Sciences, and Scientists.* Chicago: University of Chicago Press.

Beresford, John. 1996. "Report on the Star Knowledge Conference." *Contact Forum* 4, no. 4 (July–August): 8–9.

Bergier, Jacques. 1970. *Extraterrestrial Visitations from Prehistoric Times to the Present*. Reprint, Chicago: Henry Regnery.

Berlitz, Charles, and William L. Moore. 1980. *The Roswell Incident: The Classic Study of UFO Contact*. New York: Berkley.

Bethurum, Truman. 1954. *Aboard a Flying Saucer*. Los Angeles: DeVorss and Co.

Bhatt, Chetan. 1997. *Liberation and Purity: Race, New Religious Movements, and the Ethics of Postmodernity*. London: UCL Press.

Biersdorf, John E. 1975. *Hunger for Experience: Vital Religious Communities in America*. New York: Seabury Press.

Binder, Otto. 1967. *What We Really Know about Flying Saucers*. New York: Fawcett Gold Medal Books.

Binder, Otto O. 1968. *Flying Saucers Are Watching Us*. New York City: Belmont Tower Books.

Black Elk, Wallace, and William S. Lynn. 1990. *Black Elk: The Sacred Ways of a Lakota*. San Francisco: HarperSanFrancisco.

Blevins, David. 1996. *International UFO Directory*. 4th ed. San Bruno, Calif.: Phaedra Enterprises.

Bloecher, Ted. 1975. "A Catalog of Humanoid Reports for 1974." In *MUFON 1975 UFO Symposium Proceedings: UFOs: Searching for a Scientific Breakthrough*, ed. N. Joseph Gurney and Walter H. Andrus Jr., 50–76. Seguin, Tex.: Mutual UFO Network.

———. 1978. "A Survey of CE3K Reports for 1977." In *MUFON 1978 UFO Symposium Proceedings: UFOs: A Historical Perspective on Close Encounters*, ed. Walter H. Andrus Jr., 12–50. Seguin, Tex.: Mutual UFO Network.

Blomqvist, Hakan. 1988. "At Last: A Verdict on Adamski!" *Focus* 3, no. 3 (March): 1, 3, 6.

Bloom, Harold. 1996. *Omens of Millennium: The Gnosis of Angels, Dreams, and Resurrection*. New York: Riverhead Books.

Blum, Howard. 1990. *Out There*. New York: Pocket Books.

Blumrich, Josef F. 1974. *The Spaceships of Ezekiel*. New York: Bantam Books.

Bolle, Kees. W. 1987. "Myth." In Vol. 10 of *The Encyclopedia of Religion*, ed. Mircea Eliade. New York: Macmillan Publishing.

Bord, Colin. 1972. "Angels and UFOs." *FSR* 18, no. 5 (September–October): 17–19.

Bord, Janet, and Colin Bord. 1979. "More Evidence for the Psychic Link?" *FSR* 24, no. 5 (March): 19–21.

Bourdais, Gildas. 1998a. "American Documents: What Do They Reveal/Hide?" *MUJ* 357 (January): 17–19.

———. 1998b. "The Twining Letter." *MUJ* 358 (February): 19–20.

Bowen, Charles. 1968. "Strangers about the House." *FSR* 14, no. 5 (September–October): 10–12.

———. 1969a. "UFOs and Psychic Phenomena." *FSR* 15, no. 4 (July–August): 22–24.

———. 1979. "Disservices Rendered," *FSR* 25, no. 1 (May): 1.

———, ed. 1969b. *The Humanoids: A Survey of Worldwide Reports of Landings of Unconventional Aerial Objects and Their Alleged Occupants.* Chicago: Henry Regnery.

Bowers, Kenneth S., and John D. Eastwood. 1996. "On the Edge of Science: Coping with UFOlogy Scientifically." *Psychological Inquiry* 7, no. 2: 136–39.

Boyd, Mary. 1975. "Demonology and UFO's: A Book Review." *FSR* 20, no. 4: 28, 32.

Boylan, Richard J. 1992. "Secret 'Saucer' Sites." *MUJ* 292 (August): 14–15.

———. 1996a. "Native Elders Reveal Centuries of ET Contact Lore." *Contact Forum* 4, no. 4 (July–August): 1, 4–6.

———. 1996b. "Worlds in Transition: Report on the Star Visions Conference, Part 1." *Contact Forum* 4, no. 6 (November–December): 1, 8–9, 11–13.

———. 1997a. "Star Nations-Earth Direct Contact Process Underway." *Contact Forum* 5, no. 2 (March–April): 1, 10–11.

———. 1997b. "Red Road to the Stars: Star Family Gathering of Native American Elders." *Contact Forum* 5, no. 3 (May–June): 18–22.

———. 1998. "Transition from Fourth to Fifth World: The 'Thunder Beings' Return." *Contact Forum* 6, no. 2 (March–April): 23–26.

Boylan, Richard J., and Lee K Boylan. 1994. *Close Extraterrestrial Encounters: Positive Experiences With Mysterious Visitors.* Tigard, Ore.: Wildflower Press.

Bramley, William. 1989. *The Gods of Eden.* New York: Avon Books.

———. 1992. "Can the UFO Extraterrestrial Hypothesis and Vallee Hypotheses Be Reconciled?" *Journal of Scientific Exploration* 6, no. 1: 3–9.

Branch, Clare. 1979. "Mail Bag: Elemental Rather Than ET?" *FSR* 25, no. 4 (July–August): 31.

Bresh, Bryan. 1993. "Soviet UFO Secrets." *MUJ* 306 (October): 3–7.

Brethwaite, Chris W. 1994. "What MUFON Can Do to Change the Public's Perception of Ufology: One Man's Opinion." *MUJ* 312 (April): 19–20.

Brooke, John Hedley. 1991. *Science and Religion: Some Historical Perspectives.* Cambridge: Cambridge University Press.

Brookesmith, Peter. 1995. *UFO: The Complete Sightings.* New York: Barnes and Noble Books.

Brookings Institute. 1961. *The Brookings Report. House Reports,* Vol. 2, *Miscellaneous Reports on Public Bills,* II, 87th Congress, 1st Session, 3 January– 27 September.

Brown, Courtney. 1996. *Cosmic Voyage: A Scientific Discovery of Extraterrestrials Visiting Earth.* New York: Dutton Books.

Brown, Michael F. 1997. *The Channeling Zone: American Spirituality in an Anxious Age.* Cambridge: Harvard University Press.

Bruce, Robert V. 1987. *The Launching of American Science, 1846–1876.* New York: Knopf.

Bruce, Steve. 1996. *Religion in the Modern World: From Cathedrals to Cults.* New York: Oxford University Press.

Bryan, C. D. B. 1995. *Close Encounters of the Fourth Kind: Alien Abduction, UFOs, and the Conference at M.I.T.* New York: Alfred A. Knopf.

Bryant, Alice, and Linda Seebach. 1991. *Healing Shattered Reality: Understanding Contactee Trauma.* Tigard, Ore.: Wildflower Press.

Buckner, H. Taylor. 1965. "The Flying Saucerian Books: A Lingering Cult." *New Society* (9 September): 14–16.

Budden, Albert. 1995a. "Aliens, Electricity, and Allergies: A New Theory about Alien Abductions Proves to Be Both Shocking and Controversial." *MUJ* 322 (February): 10–15.

———. 1995b. *UFOs: Psychic Close Encounters: The Electromagnetic Indictment.* New York: Blandford Books/Sterling Publishing.

Bullard, Thomas. 1987a. *On Stolen Time: A Summary of a Comparative Study of the UFO Abduction Mystery.* Mt. Rainier, Md.: Fund for UFO Research.

———. 1987b. "Klass Takes on Abductions; Abductions Win." *IUR* 12, no. 6 (November–December): 9–13, 20.

———. 1989a. "Never to Have Reasoned at All: Robert Basil and the Skeptics' Silence." *IUR* 14, no. 1 (January–February): 13–15.

———. 1989b. "UFO Abduction Reports: The Supernatural Kidnap Narrative Returns in Technological Guise." *Journal of American Folklore* 102, no. 404 (April–June): 147–70.

———. 1991. "Why Abduction Reports Are Not Urban Legends." *IUR* 16, no. 4 (July–August): 15–20, 24.

———. 1994. "Epistemological Totalitarianism: The Skeptical Case against Abductions." *IUR* 19, no. 5 (September–October): 9–16.

Bunge, Mario. 1984. "What Is Pseudoscience?" *The Skeptical Inquirer* 9, no. 1: 36–47.

Burleson, Donald R. 1999. "Update on Deciphering Gen. Ramey Letter." *MUJ* 371 (March): 17.

Cahill, Kelly. 1996. *Encounter.* Sydney, Australia: HarperCollinsAustralia.

Campagna, Palmiro. 1997. *The UFO Files: The Canadian Connection Exposed.* Toronto: Stoddart.

Campbell, Glenn. 1994. "Robert Lazar as a Fictional Character." *MUJ* 310 (February): 11–14.

Cannon, Brian C. 1983. "UFO Forum." In Schwarz 1983, 303–313.

Cannon, Martin. N.d. *The Controllers: A New Hypothesis of Alien Abduction.* Privately published. Reprint, *MindNet Journal* 1, no. 3a–f, archived at </www.mk.net/~mcf/mind_net/mn13a.htm>.

Capra, Fritjof. 1975. *The Tao of Physics: An Exploration of the Parallels between Modern Physics and Eastern Mysticism.* Boulder: Shambhala Press.

Carlsberg, Kim. 1995. *Beyond My Wildest Dreams: Diary of a UFO Abductee.* Santa Fe: Bear and Co.

Carlson, J. B., and P. A. Sturrock. 1975. "Stanford Workshop on Extraterrestrial Civilization: Opening a New Scientific Dialog." *Astronautics and Aeronautics* (June): 63.

Carpenter, Donald G., Major USAF. 1968. "Unidentified Flying Objects." In *Introductory Space Science*, 461ff. Department of Physics, USAF Academy.

Carpenter, John. 1993a. "Explanations: 'Healthy Skepticism vs. Psychological Denial.'" *MUJ* 304 (August): 18–19.

———. 1993b. "Explanations: 'Healthy Skepticism vs. Psychological Denial.'"
   MUJ 306 (October): 14–16.
———. 1994. "Review of Symptomatology." *MUJ* 312 (April): 16, 18.
———. 1995a. "Does Sleep Paralysis Explain Abductions?" *MUJ* 327 (July):
   18–19.
———. 1995b. "Alien Autopsy Film: Discrepancies with Research." *MUJ* 330
   (October): 16–17.
———. 1995c. "Alien Autopsy, Part 2: More Doubts." *MUJ* 330 (October):
   11–12.
———. 1996. "Alien Autopsy Bodies." *MUJ* 334 (February): 13–14.
Carroll, Robert Todd. 2000. *The Skeptic's Dictionary.* <http://www.skepdic
   .com>.
Cassirer, Manfred. 1994. *Dimensions of Enchantment: The Mystery of UFO
   Abductions, Close Encounters, and Aliens.* London: Breese Books.
Casteel, Sean. 1992. "Jacques Vallee and Joseph Campbell." *MUJ* 287 (March):
   13.
———. 1993. "Whitley Strieber Breaks His Silence." *MUJ* 305 (September): 12.
Cazeau, Charles J., and Stuart D. Scott Jr. 1979. *Exploring the Unknown: Great
   Mysteries Reexamined.* New York: Plenum Press.
Chalker, Bill. 1996. *The Oz Files: The Australian UFO Story.* Potts Point, NSW:
   Duffy and Snellgrove.
Chamish, Barry. 1999. "Israel: Return of the Biblical Giants? — Nothing to Cel-
   ebrate!" *FSR* 44, no. 4 (winter): 4–7.
Charroux, Robert. 1971. *Forgotten Worlds: Scientific Secrets of the Ancients and
   Their Warning for Our Time.* New York: Popular Library.
Chatelain, Maurice. 1975a. *Our Ancestors Came from Outer Space.* New York:
   Dell Books.
———. 1975b. *Our Cosmic Ancestors.* Paris: Robert Laffont. Reprint, Sedona,
   Ariz.: Temple Golden Publications, 1987.
Chittick, William C. 1994. *Imaginal Worlds: Ibn al-'Arabī and the Problem of
   Religious Diversity.* Albany: State University of New York Press.
———. 1998. *The Self-Disclosure of God: Principles of Ibn al-'Arabī's Cosmol-
   ogy.* Albany: State University of New York Press.
Chorost, Michael. 1993. "Project Argus Report." *MUJ* 304 (August): 4–5.
Clamar, Aphrodite. 1988. "Is It Time for Psychology to Take UFOs Seriously?"
   Psychotherapy in Private Practice 6: 143–49.
Clapp, Rodney. 1983. "Extraterrestrial Intelligence and Christian Wonder."
   Christianity Today 27, no. 7 (8 April): 10.
Clark, Jerome. 1965. "A Contact Claim." *FSR* 11, no. 1 (January–February):
   30–32.
———. 1980. "UFO Abduction in North Dakota." In Rogo 1980, 138–159.
———. 1987. "Abductions: The Case for a Rational Approach." *IUR* 12, no. 1
   (January–February): 3.
———. 1990a. "The Thickets of Magonia." *IUR* 15, no. 1 (January–February):
   4–11.
———. 1990b. *UFOs in the 1980s.* Vol. 1 of *The UFO Encyclopedia.* Detroit:
   Apogee Books.

———. 1992. *The Emergence of a Phenomenon: UFOs from the Beginning through 1959*. Vol. 2 of *The UFO Encyclopedia*. Detroit: Omnigraphics.

———. 1993a. "A Catalog of Early Crash Claims." *IUR* 18, no. 4 (July–August): 11–18.

———. 1993b. "Into the Mystic." *IUR* 18, no. 5 (September–October): 3.

———. 1994a. "Wagging the Dog." *IUR* 19, no. 1 (January–February): 1, 22–24.

———. 1994b. "Big (Space) Brothers." *IUR* 19, no. 2 (March–April): 7–10.

———. 1994c. "Circles." *IUR* 19, no. 6 (November–December): 13–14, 24.

———. 1996a. *High Strangeness: UFOs from 1960 through 1979*. Vol. 3 of *The UFO Encyclopedia*. Detroit: Omnigraphics.

———. 1996b. "The Pancakes of Eagle River." *IUR* 21, no. 1 (spring): 1–8.

———. 1996c. "Carl Sagan's Demons." *IUR* 21, no. 2 (summer): 3–4.

———. 1996d. "The Salvation Myth." *IUR* 21, no. 4 (winter): 3–4.

———. 1997b. *Spacemen, Demons, and Conspiracies: The Evolution of UFO Hypotheses*. Mt. Rainier, Md.: Fund for UFO Research.

———. 1997c. "Vimanas Have Landed: Ancient Astronautics in Ufology." *IUR* 22, no. 3 (fall): 23–30.

———. 1998a. "Paranormal and Occult Theories about UFOs." In Clark 1998b, 429–44.

———. 1998b. *The UFO Book: Encyclopedia of the Extraterrestrial*. Detroit: Visible Ink Press.

Cleary-Baker, John. 1965. "Obituary: George Adamski." *BUFORA Journal and Bulletin* 1, no. 4 (spring): 18–19.

Collings, Beth, and Anna Jamerson. 1996. *Connections: Solving Our Alien Abduction Mystery*. Tigard, Ore.: Wild Flower Press.

Collins, H. M., and T. J. Pinch. 1982. *Frames of Meaning: The Social Construction of Extraordinary Science*. London: Routledge and Kegan Paul.

Colvin, Terry. 1995. *CSICOP as Religion*. UFO-List <misc@interport.net> (24 July).

Condon, Edward U., and Daniel S. Gillmor, eds. 1969. *Final Report of the Scientific Study of Unidentified Flying Objects*. New York: Bantam Books.

Connell, Father Francis J. 1956. "Flying Saucers and Theology." In Michel 1956, 256–58.

Conroy, Ed. N.d. "The Aliens That Aren't: An Interview with Whitley Strieber." *Magical Blend* 46: 47, 78.

Conser, Walter H., Jr. 1993. *God and the Natural World: Religion and Science in Antebellum America*. Columbia: University of South Carolina Press.

Constable, Trevor James. 1958. *They Live in the Sky*. Los Angeles: New Age Publishing.

———. 1976. *The Cosmic Pulse of Life: The Revolutionary Biological Power behind UFOs*. Bayside, Calif.: Borderland Sciences Research Foundation.

Cooper, Milton William. 1991. *Behold a Pale Horse*. Sedona, Ariz.: Light Technology Publishing.

Corbin, Henry. 1972. *Mundus Imaginalis or the Imaginal and the Imaginary*. Ipswich, England: Golgonooza Press.

Cordova, Henry. 1999. "Astronomers and UFOs." *IUR* 24, no. 3 (fall): 13–14.

Corso, Col. Philip J. (Ret.), with William J. Birnes. 1997. *The Day after Roswell.* New York: Pocket Books.

Cousineau, Phil. 1995. *UFOs: A Manual for the Millennium.* New York: Harper-Collins West.

Craft, Michael. 1996. *Alien Impact.* New York: St. Martin's Press.

Craig, Roy. 1995. *UFOs: An Insider's View of the Official Quest for Evidence.* Denton: University of North Texas Press.

Creighton, Gordon. 1965a. "The Most Amazing Case of All: Part 1 — A Brazilian Farmer's Story." *FSR* 11, no. 1 (January–February): 13–17.

———. 1965b. "The Most Amazing Case of All: Part 2 — Analysis of the Brazilian Farmer's Story." *FSR* 11, no. 2 (March–April): 5–8.

———. 1969. "The Amazing Case of Antonio Villas Boas." In Bowen 1969a, 200–238.

———. 1983. "A Brief Account of the True Nature of the 'UFO Entities.'" *FSR* 29, no. 1 (October): 2–6.

———. 1997a. "The Extraordinary Affair of the U.S. Air Force Academy's Own Text-Book on UFOs in the 1960s." *FSR* 42, no. 1 (spring): 23–26.

———. 1997b. "What St. Paul Is Actually Reported to Have Said." *FSR* 42, no. 2 (summer): 11–13.

———. 1997c. "Additional Notes by Editor, FSR." *FSR* 42, no. 3 (autumn): 22–23.

———. 1999. "Did Presidents Have Meetings with Aliens?" *FSR* 44, no. 3 (autumn): 2.

Crissey, Brian "Blue Water." 1996. "Notes from the Center of the Universe." *Contact Forum* 4, no. 4 (July–August): 1, 7.

Crowe, Michael J. 1986. *The Extraterrestrial Life Debate, 1750–1900: The Idea of a Plurality of Worlds from Kant to Lowell.* Cambridge: Cambridge University Press.

Cybulski, Capt. Joseph A. 1995. "How the Air Force Investigated UFOs." *IUR* 20, no. 5 (winter): 11, 30–32.

Dailey, Timothy J. 1995. *The Millennial Deception: Angels, Aliens, and the Antichrist.* Grand Rapids, Mich.: Chosen Books.

Daly, Christopher B. 1995. "Harvard Clears Abduction Researcher John Mack." *The Washington Post* (4 August): 1.

Daniels, Pat. 1987. *The UFO Phenomenon.* Alexandria, Va.: Time-Life Books.

D'Arc, Joan. 2000. *Space Travelers and the Genesis of the Human Form: Evidence of Human Contact in the Solar System.* Escondido, Calif.: The Book Tree.

———. ed. 1996. *Paranoid Women Collect Their Thoughts.* 1:1. Paranoia Annual. Providence, R.I.: Paranoia Publishing.

Darrach, H. Bradford, and Robert Ginna. 1952. "Have We Visitors from Space?" *Life* (7 April): 80–82.

Davenport, Marc. 1992. *Visitors from Time: The Secret of the UFOs.* Tigard, Ore.: Wild Flower Press.

———. 1994. "Interview with Raymond E. Fowler." *Contact Forum* 2, no. 6 (November–December): 1, 7–12.

Davies, Paul. 1980. *Other Worlds: Space, Superspace, and the Quantum Universe.* New York: Simon and Schuster, Touchstone.

———. 1983. *God and the New Physics.* New York: Simon and Schuster.

———. 1995a. *Are We Alone? Philosophical Implications of the Discovery of Extraterrestrial Life.* New York: Basic Books.

———. 1995b. *The Cosmic Blueprint.* New York: Penguin.

Davis, G. L. O. 1967. "Mail Bag: The Mystery of Iniquity?" *FSR* 13, no. 2 (March–April): 18.

Davis, Isabel L. 1957. "Meet the Extraterrestrial." *Fantastic Universe* 8, no. 5 (November): 40–43.

Davis, John Jefferson. 1997. "Search for Extraterrestrial Intelligence and the Christian Doctrine of Redemption." *Science and Christian Belief* 9, no. 1: 21–34.

Dean, Gwen L. 1994. "Trauma and Treatment of Children Who Are Alleged Abductees." In Pritchard et al. 1994, 513–19.

Dean, Jodi. 1996. "Coming Out as Alien: Feminists, UFOs, and the 'Oprah Effect.'" In *Bad Girls, Good Girls: Women, Sex, and Power in the 1990s,* ed. Nan Bauer Maglin and Bonna Perry, 90–105. New Brunswick: Rutgers University Press.

———. 1998. *Aliens in America: Conspiracy Cultures from Outerspace to Cyberspace.* Ithaca: Cornell University Press.

Deetken, Chad. 1993. "Comparison of British and Canadian Crop Circle Lays." *MUJ* 304 (August): 9–13.

Delgado, Pat, and Colin Andrews. 1991. *Circular Evidence.* Grand Rapids, Mich.: Phanes Press.

Dennett, Preston. 1990. "One in Forty." *MUJ* 266 (June): 9–10.

Dennett, Preston E. 1996. *UFO Healings: True Accounts of People Healed by Extraterrestrials.* Mill Spring, N.C.: Wild Flower Press.

Denzler, Brenda. 1996. "Rape and the Feminization of Consciousness in the Alien Abduction Movement." Paper presented at the American Academy of Religion, San Francisco, 25 November.

Dick, Steven J. 1982. *Plurality of Worlds: The Origins of the Extraterrestrial Life Debate from Democritus to Kant.* Cambridge: Cambridge University Press.

———. 1996. *The Biological Universe: The Twentieth-Century Extraterrestrial Life Debate and the Limits of Science.* Cambridge: Cambridge University Press.

Dickson, Malcolm. 1969. "UFOs and Signs of the Times." *FSR* 15, no. 5 (September–October): 30–32.

Dione, R. L. 1969. *God Drives A Flying Saucer.* New York: Bantam Books.

Donderi, Don C. 1993. "The Small Picture." *IUR* 18, no. 1 (January–February): 18, 24.

———. 1994. "Validating the Roper Poll: A Scientific Approach to Abduction Evidence." In Pritchard et al. 1994, 224–31.

———. 1996. "The Scientific Context of the UFO/Abduction Phenomenon." *IUR* 21, no. 1 (spring): 13–21.

Doty, William G. 1986. *Mythography: The Study of Myths and Rituals.* University: University of Alabama Press.

Douglass, Elaine. 1992. "No Discrimination?" *MUJ* 296 (December): 20–21.

Downing, Barry. 1968. *The Bible and Flying Saucers.* New York: Avon Books.

———. 1981. "Faith, Theory, and UFOs." In *MUFON 1981 UFO Symposium Proceedings: UFOs: The Hidden Evidence,* ed. Walter H. Andrus Jr. and Dennis W. Stacy, 34–42. Seguin, Tex.: Mutual UFO Network.

———. 1990. "The Rock of Ages Principle." *MUJ* 265 (May): 11–12.

———. 1994. "Exodus as a Paradigm of UFO Strategy." *MUJ* 318 (October): 8–11.

———. 1997a. "*The God Hypothesis:* A Review." *MUJ* 348 (April): 10–11, 16.

———. 1997b. "The Second Coming of Marshall Applewhite." *MUJ* 349 (May): 8.

———. 1998a. "The Bible and UFO Abductions." *MUJ* 357 (January): 3–5.

———. 1998b. "The Balducci Interview and Religious Certainty." *MUJ* 365 (September): 16–17.

———. 1998c. "UFOs: Four Questions for Theological Seminaries." In *MUFON 1988 International UFO Symposium Proceedings: The UFO Cover Up: A Government Conspiracy?* ed. Walter H. Andrus Jr., 37–57. Seguin, Tex.: Mutual UFO Network.

Drake, Frank. 1954. *Intelligent Life in Space.* New York: MacMillan Publishers.

———. 1961. "Project Ozma," *Physics Today* 14: 40.

———. 1972. "On the Abilities and Limitations of Witnesses of UFO's and Similar Phenomena." In Sagan and Page 1972, 247–57.

———. 1981. "Intelligent Life in the Universe." In Abell and Singer 1981, 329–348.

Drake, Frank, and Dava Sobel. 1992. *Is Anyone Out There?* New York: Delacorte.

Drake, W. R. 1963. "UFOs Over Ancient Rome." *FSR* 9, no. 1 (January): 11–13.

———. 1964a. "Spacemen in Antiquity." *FSR* 10, no. 1 (January): 21–23.

———. 1964b. "Spacemen in Saxon Times." *FSR* 10, no. 5 (September): 10–12.

Drake, W. Raymond. 1968. *Gods and Spacemen in the Ancient East.* New York: Signet Books.

———. 1974a. *Gods and Spacemen in the Ancient West.* New York: Signet Books.

———. 1974b. *Gods and Spacemen of the Ancient Past.* New York: Signet Books.

———. 1976. *Gods and Spacemen in Greece and Rome.* New York: Signet Books.

Druffel, Ann. 1980a. "Harrison Bailey and the 'Flying Saucer Disease.'" In Rogo 1980, 122–37.

———. 1980b. "Hypnotic Regression of UFO Abductees." *FSR* 25, no. 5 (March): 28–31.

———. 1988. "Abductions: Can We Battle Back?" *MUJ* 247 (November): 17–21.

———. 1992a. "Resisting Alien Abductions: An Update." *MUJ* 287 (March): 3–7.

———. 1992b. "Response to Virginia Tilly's Letter." *MUJ* 292 (August): 13.

———. 1993. "Remembering James McDonald." *IUR* 18, no. 5 (September–October): 4–6, 23–24.

Druffel, Ann, and D. Scott Rogo. 1980. *The Tujunga Canyon Contacts.* Update edition, New York: Signet Books, 1988.

Duerr, Hans Peter. 1985. *Dreamtime: Concerning the Boundary between Wilderness and Civilization.* Trans. Felicitas Goodman. New York: Basil Blackwell.

Duffy, Maureen. 1980. "What Shall We Do If They Come?" *Second Look* (January–February): 15–17.

Durant, Robert J. 1993. "Evolution of Public Opinion on UFOs." *IUR* 18, no. 6 (November–December): 11–12.

Durrant, Robert. 1995. "The Brookings Report: Proposed Studies on the Implications of Peaceful Space Activities for Human Affairs." *MUJ* 326 (June): 3–6.

Dyson, Freeman J. 1979a. *Disturbing the Universe.* New York: Harper and Row.

———. 1979b. "Time without End: Physics and Biology in an Open Universe." *Reviews of Modern Physics* 51, no. 3 (July): 447–60.

Eberhart, George M. 1999. "Astronomers and UFOs: Some Other Examples." *IUR* 24, no. 3 (fall): 15, 32.

Eberlein, Gerald L. 1993. "Mainstream Sciences vs. Parasciences: Toward an Old Dualism?" *Journal of Scientific Exploration* 7, no. 1: 39–48.

Edwards, Frank. 1966. *Flying Saucers: Serious Business.* Secaucus, N.J.: Citadel Press.

———. 1967. *Flying Saucers: Here and Now!* New York: Bantam Books.

Edwards, P. M. H. 1970. "UFOs and ESP." *FSR* 16, no. 6 (November–December): 18–20, 26.

———. 1996. "Supernatural Biblical Visions and Present-Day Sightings." *FSR* 41, no. 2 (summer): 19–25.

Eliade, Mircea, ed. *The Encyclopedia of Religion.* Vol. 10. New York: Macmillan Publishing. S.v. "Myth."

Ellis, Bill. 1988. "The Varieties of Alien Experience." *The Skeptical Inquirer* 12, no. 3 (spring): 263–69.

Ellwood, Robert S. 1988. "Occult Movements in America." In *Encyclopedia of the American Religious Experience: Studies of Traditions and Movements,* vol. 2, ed. Charles H. Lippy and Peter W. Williams. New York: Charles Scribner's Sons.

———. 1997. *The Fifties Spiritual Marketplace: American Religion in a Decade of Conflict.* New Brunswick: Rutgers University Press.

Emenegger, Robert. 1974. *UFOs: Past, Present, and Future.* New York: Ballantine Books.

Emery, C. Eugene, Jr. 1995. "Harvard Launches John Mack Attack: Abduction Psychiatrist's Scholarship Questioned." *The Skeptical Inquirer* 19, no. 5 (September–October): 3.

Emmons, Charles F. 1997. *At the Threshold: UFOs, Science, and the New Age.* Mill Spring, N.C.: Wild Flower Press.

Epstein, Michael S. 1995. "The Critical Role of Analytical Science in the Study of Anomalies." *Journal of Scientific Exploration* 9, no. 1: 71–78.

Essex, Laurence R. 1988. "Mail Bag: 'Parallel Universes.'" *FSR* 33, no. 1: 23.

Evans, Christopher. 1973. *Cults of Unreason.* London: Harrap.

Farish, Lucius. 1973. "The E.T. Concept in History." *FSR* 19, no. 4: 14–15, 26.

Fawcett, Lawrence, and Barry J. Greenwood. 1984. *Clear Intent: The Government Coverup of the UFO Experience.* Englewood Cliffs: Prentice-Hall.

Felber, Ron. 1994. *Searchers: A True Story of Alien Abduction.* New York: St. Martin's Paperbacks.

Fenwick, Lawrence J. 1995. "Implant Probed in Canada." *FSR* 40, no. 4 (winter): 20–21.

Ferris, L. M. 1963. "Mailbag: UFOs over Ancient Rome." *FSR* 9, no. 2 (March): 26.

Festinger, Leon, Henry W. Riecken, and Stanley Schachter. 1956. *When Prophecy Fails: A Social and Psychological Study of a Modern Group That Predicted the Destruction of the World.* New York: Harper Torchbooks.

Filer, George. 1998. "Work Continues on Message that Gen. Ramey Holds in Hand." *MUJ* 367 (November): 15.

Finch, Bernard E. 1980. "The UFO 'Gate' Theory." *FSR* 26, no. 1 (spring): 24.

Fiore, Edith. 1989. *Encounters: A Psychologist Reveals Case Studies of Abductions by Extraterrestrials.* New York: Ballantine Books.

Fitzgerald, Randall. 1998. *Cosmic Test Tube: Extraterrestrial Contact, Theories and Evidence.* Los Angeles: Moon Lake Media.

Flammonde, Paris. 1976. *UFO Exist!* New York: Ballantine Books.

Fowler, Raymond E. 1974. *UFOs: Interplanetary Visitors: A UFO Investigator Reports on the Facts, Fables, and Fantasies of the Flying Saucer Conspiracy.* New York: Bantam Books.

———. 1979. *The Andreasson Affair: The Documented Investigation of a Woman's Abduction Aboard a UFO.* Englewood Cliffs: Prentice-Hall. Reprint, Newberg, Ore.: Wild Flower Press, 1994.

———. 1981. *Casebook of a UFO Investigator: A Personal Memoir.* Englewood Cliffs: Prentice-Hall.

———. 1982. *The Andreasson Affair, Phase Two: The Continuing Investigation of a Woman's Abduction by Extraterrestrials.* Englewood Cliffs: Prentice-Hall. Reprint, Newberg, Ore.: Wild Flower Press, 1994.

———. 1990. *The Watchers: The Secret Design behind UFO Abduction.* New York: Bantam Books.

———. 1993. *The Alagash Abductions: Undeniable Evidence of Alien Intervention.* Tigard, Ore.: Wild Flower Press.

———. 1995. *The Watchers II: Exploring UFOs and the Near-Death Experience.* Newberg, Ore.: Wild Flower Press.

———. 1997. *The Andreasson Legacy.* New York: Marlowe and Company.

Fox, B. 1996. *The Agenda: The Real Reason They're Here.* Kearney, Nebr.: Morris Publishers.

Freer, Niel. 1998. *God Games: What Do You Do Forever?* Escondido, Calif.: The Book Tree.

Freixedo, Salvador. 1992. *Visionaries, Mystics, and Contactees.* Trans. Scott Corrales. Avondale Estates, Ga.: Illuminet Press.

———. 1994. "Contacts between U.S. Presidents and Aliens: Part 1." *FSR* 39, no. 4 (December): 1–7.

———. 1995. "Contacts between U.S. Presidents and Aliens: Part 2." *FSR* 40, no. 1 (March): 2–4.

Freixedo, Salvador, and Alfonso Taboas. 1973. *El Diabolico Inconsciente: Parapsychology and Religion*. Mexico: Editorial Isla.

Friedlander, Michael W. 1995. *At the Fringes of Science*. Boulder: Westview Press.

Friedman, Stanton. 1989. "Who Believes in UFOs?" *IUR* 14, no. 1 (January–February): 6–10.

———. 1996. *Top Secret/Majic*. New York: Marlowe and Co..

Fuchs, Stephan. 1992. *The Professional Quest for Truth: A Social Theory of Science and Knowledge*. Albany: State University of New York Press.

Fuller, John G. 1966a. *Incident at Exeter: Unidentified Flying Objects over America Now*. New York: G. P. Putnam's Sons, Berkley Medallion Book.

———. 1966b. *The Interrupted Journey*. New York: Berkley Publishing.

Galganski, Robert A. 1995. "The Roswell Debris: A Quantitative Evaluation of the Project Mogul Hypothesis." *IUR* 20, no. 2 (March–April): 3–6, 23–24.

Gardner, Martin. 1952a. *Fads and Fallacies in the Name of Science*. New York: G. P. Putnam's Sons. Reprint, New York: Dover Publications, 1957.

———. 1981. *Science: Good, Bad, and Bogus*. Buffalo: Prometheus Books.

Garner, W. L., Jr. 1993. "MUFON versus the New Age." *MUJ* 308 (December): 13–14.

General Accounting Office. 1995. *Results of a Search for Records Concerning the 1947 Crash Near Roswell, New Mexico*. GOA/NSIAD-95–187. General Accounting Office (July).

Genoni, Tom, Jr. 1995a. "Exploring Mind, Memory, and the Psychology of Belief." *The Skeptical Inquirer* 19, no. 1 (January–February): 10–13.

———. 1995b. "Science Literacy: The Good News and the Bad." *The Skeptical Inquirer* 19, no. 1 (January–February): 5–6.

Geremia, Peter R. 1997. "Astronaut Gordon Cooper." *MUJ* 356 (December): 10.

Gerner, Connie. 1992. "Letters." *MUJ* 288 (April): 19.

Gersten, Peter. 1981. "What the Government Would Know about UFOs If They Read Their Own Documents." In *MUFON 1981 UFO Symposium Proceedings: UFOs: The Hidden Evidence*, ed. Walter H. Andrus, 20–33. Seguin, Tex.: Mutual UFO Network.

Gieryn, Thomas F. 1983. "Boundary-Work and the Demarcation of Science from Non-Science: Strains and Interests in Professional Ideologies of Scientists." *American Sociological Review* 48 (December): 781–95.

Gilbert, G. Nigel. 1976. "The Transformation of Research Findings into Scientific Knowledge." *Social Studies of Science* 6: 281–306.

Gilbert, G. Nigel, and Michael Mulkay. 1982. "Warranting Scientific Belief." *Social Studies of Science* 12: 383–408.

Gilbert, James. 1997. *Redeeming Culture: American Religion in an Age of Science*. Chicago: University of Chicago Press.

Gilkey, Langdon. 1993. *Nature, Reality, and the Sacred: The Nexus of Science and Religion*. Minneapolis: Fortress Press.

Gills, J. R. 1998. "Pascagoula's Charlie Hickson Still Interested in UFOs." *MUJ* 362 (June): 16–18.

Gilman, Peter. 1967. "Do the Cherubim Come from Mars? A Preliminary Study Based on the Gary Wilcox Contact Story." *FSR* 13, no. 5 (September–October): 19–21, 29.

Gilovich, Thomas. 1991. *How We Know What Isn't So: The Fallibility of Human Reason in Everyday Life.* New York: The Free Press.

Girvan, Waveney. 1960a. "The Scientific Approach." *FSR* 6, no. 3 (May–June): 1–2.

———. 1960b. "Science and Scepticism." *FSR* 6, no. 6 (November): 30.

———. 1961. "Science and Authority." *FSR* 7, no. 5 (September–October): 1–2.

———. 1962. "The 'Outsider' and Scientific Resistance." *FSR* 8, no. 1 (January): 30.

———. 1967. "Scientists and Saucers." *FSR* 13, no. 5 (September–October): 1–2.

Gleick, James. 1994. "The Doctor's Plot." *The New Republic* (22 May): <www.around.com/abduct.html>.

Glock, C., and R. Stark. 1973. *Religion and Society in Tension.* Chicago: Rand McNally and Co.

Gold, Thomas. 1989. "New Ideas in Science." *Journal of Scientific Exploration* 3, no. 2: 103–12.

Goldberg, Steven. 1999. *Seduced by Science: How American Religion Has Lost Its Way.* New York: New York University Press.

Goldstein, Saul H. 1996. "MUFON Forum: Scientific Ufology." *MUJ* 340 (August): 20.

Gonzalez, Justo L. 1975. *A History of Christian Thought: From the Protestant Reformation to the Twentieth Century.* Nashville, Tenn.: Abingdon Press.

Good, Timothy. 1988. *Above Top Secret: The Worldwide UFO Cover-Up.* New York: William Morrow.

———. 1991. *Alien Contact: Top-Secret UFO Files Revealed.* Great Britain: Random Century Group. Reprint, New York: William Morrow and Company, 1993.

———, ed. 1993. *Alien Update: The Contact Continues . . . .* New York: Avon Books.

Goodes, J. W. 1979. "Mail Bag: Do UFOs Feature in Biblical Prophecy?" *FSR* 24, no. 4 (January–February): 32.

Goodstein, David. 1994. "Pariah Science." *The American Scholar* (autumn): 527-54.

Goss, Michael. N.d. "The Lessons of Folklore." *Magonia* 38 <http://www.netkonect.co.uk/d/dogon/magonia/>.

Gotlib, David. 1993. "False Memory Syndrome." *MUJ* 303 (July): 12–14.

Gotlib, David A. 1992. "Abductions: Imagined or Imaginal?" *IUR* 17, no. 4 (July–August): 16–20.

Grabiner, Judith V., and Peter D. Miller. 1974. "Effects of the Scopes Trial." *Science* 185 (6 September): 832–37.

Granchi, Irene. 1994. *UFOs and Abductions in Brazil.* Madison, Wisc.: Horus House Press.

Gratton-Buinness, I. 1973. "Rationality and Its Limitations." *FSR* 19, no. 5 (September–October): 22–23.

Greeley, Andrew W. 1989. *Religious Change in America*. Cambridge: Harvard University Press.

Green, Gabriel. 1967. *Let's Face the Facts about Flying Saucers*. New York: Popular Library.

Greenfield, Allen H. 1976. *Saucers and Saucerers*. Privately published.

———, ed. 1977. *UFOlogy Notebook* 3, no. 6 (May).

Gregory, Janet. 1971. "Similarities in UFO and Demon Lore." *FSR* 17, no. 2 (March–April): 32, iii.

Grenz, Stanley J. 1996. *A Primer on Postmodernism*. Grand Rapids, Mich.: William B. Eerdmans Publishing.

Griffin, David Ray. 1996. "Why Critical Reflection on the Paranormal Is So Important — and So Difficult." In Stoeber and Meynell 1996, 87–117.

Grim, Patrick, ed. 1982. *Philosophy of Science and the Occult*. Albany: State University of New York Press.

Grinspoon, Lester, and Alan D. Persky. 1972. "Psychiatry and UFO Reports." In Sagan and Page 1972, 233–46.

Haines, Gerald K. 1997. "A Die-Hard Issue: CIA's Role in the Study of UFOs, 1947–1990." *Studies in Intelligence [Unclassified]*: 67–84.

Haines, Richard F. 1994. "Searching for Bloodline Linkage in Alleged Abductees." In Pritchard et al. 1994, 106–16.

Haisch, Bernhard. 1996. "UFO's and Mainstream Science." *MUJ* 335 (March): 14–16.

Haley, Leah A. 1993. *Lost Was the Key*. Tuscaloosa: Greenleaf Publications.

Halford, Larry J., C. Leroy Anderson, and Robert E. Clark. 1981. "Prophecy Fails Again and Again: The Morrisites." *Free Inquiry in Creative Sociology* 9, no. 1: 5–10.

Hall, Michael D., and Wendy Connors. 2000. *Captain Edward J. Ruppelt: Summer of the Saucers — 1952*. Alburquerque, N. Mex.: Rose Press International.

Hall, Richard. 1988. *Uninvited Guests: A Documented History of UFO Sightings, Alien Encounters, and Coverups*. Santa Fe: Aurora Press.

———. 1993a. "The Future of Ufology." *IUR* 18, no. 5 (September–October): 7, 24.

———. 1993b. *Testing Reality: A Research Guide for the UFO Abduction Experience*. Mt. Rainier, Md.: Fund for UFO Research.

———. 1994. "Are UFO Abductions a Universal or a Culturally-Dependent Phenomenon?" In Pritchard et al. 1994, 191–93.

———. 1995. "Fact vs. Fiction in the Pentagon." *IUR* 20, no. 5 (winter): 7–8.

———. 1998. "Signals, Noise, and UFO Waves." *IUR* 23, no. 4 (winter): 16–20.

———, ed. 1964. *The UFO Evidence*. National Investigations Committee on Aerial Phenomena. Reprint, New York: Barnes and Noble Books, 1997.

Hall, Robert L., Donald A. Johnson, and Mark Rodeghier. 1993. "UFO Abduction Survey: A Critique." *MUJ* 303 (July): 9–11, 14.

Halperin, David. 1995. "UFO Abduction Narratives and Religious Traditions of Heavenly Ascent: A Comparative Study." Paper presented at the American Academy of Religion in Philadelphia, Pa., November.

Hamilton, William. 1976. "The Discovery of Extraterrestrial Intelligence: A Religious Response." *The Humanist* 36, no. 3 (May–June): 24–26.

Hamilton, William F. III. 1991. *Cosmic Top Secret: America's Secret UFO Program*. New Brunswick, N.J.: Inner Light Publications.

Hanlon, Donald B. 1970. "The Airship . . . Fact and Fiction." *FSR* 16, no. 4 (July–August): 20–21.

Harder, James A. 1988. "Mainstream Science and the Strangeness of the Universe." *FSR* 33, no. 1: 10–14.

Hardyck, Jane Allyn, and Marcia Braden. 1962. "Prophecy Fails Again: A Report of a Failure to Replicate." *Journal of Abnormal and Social Psychology* 65, no. 2: 136–41.

Harpur, Patrick. 1994. *Daimonic Reality: A Field Guide to the Otherworld*. New York: Viking/Arkana.

Harrold, Francis B., and Raymond A. Eve, eds. 1995. *Cult Archaeology and Creationism: Understanding Pseudoscientific Beliefs about the Past*. Iowa City: University of Iowa Press.

Hartmann, William K. 1972. "Historical Perspectives: Photos of UFO's." In Sagan and Page 1972, 11–22.

Harvey-Wilson, Simon. 1995. "Dimensions, Consciousness, and Non-Locality." *MUJ* 321 (January): 3–9.

Heaton, Timothy H. 1994. "The UFO Press: *Abduction: Human Encounters with Aliens*, by John E. Mack, M.D." *MUJ* 315 (July): 13–15.

Heelas, Paul. 1996. *The New Age Movement: The Celebration of the Self and the Sacralization of Modernity*. Cambridge, Mass.: Blackwell Publishers.

Heiden, Richard W. 1975. "The Pascagoula UFO and Occupant Incident." *FSR* 20, no. 6 (April–May): 23–24.

———. 1996. "The Word 'Ufology.'" *IUR* 21, no. 1 (spring): 11–12.

Heidmann, Jean. 1995. *Extraterrestrial Intelligence*. Trans. Storm Dunlop. Cambridge: Cambridge University Press.

Henry, Lyell D., Jr. 1981. "Unorthodox Science as a Popular Activity." *Journal of American Culture* 4, no. 2 (summer): 1–22.

Henry, Richard C. 1988. "UFOs and NASA." *Journal of Scientific Exploration* 2, no. 2: 93–142.

Herbert, Nick. 1985. *Quantum Reality: Beyond the New Physics*. New York: Anchor Books.

Hervieu-Léger, Danièle. 1998. "Secularization, Tradition, and New Forms of Religiosity: Some Theoretical Proposals." In *New Religions and New Religiosity*, eds. Eileen Barker and Margit Warburg. Oakville, Conn.: Aarhus University Press.

Hesemann, Michael. 1995. *The Cosmic Connection: Worldwide Crop Formations and ET Contacts*. Baltimore, Md.: Gateway Press.

———, Producer. 1992. *UFOs: The Secret Evidence*. 105 min. Lightworks Audio and Video, Los Angeles. Videocassette.

Hexham, Irving. 1986. "Yoga, UFOs, and Cult Membership." *Update: A Quarterly Journal on New Religious Movements* 10, no. 3 (September): 3–17.

Hexham, Irving, and Karla Poewe. 1997a. *New Religions as Global Cultures: Making the Human Sacred*. Boulder: Westview Press.

———. 1997b. "UFO Religion: A Science Fiction Tradition." *Christian Century* (7 May): 439–40.

Hick, John. 1999. *The Fifth Dimension: An Exploration of the Spiritual Realm.* Boston: Oneworld Publications.

Hickman, John C., E. Dale McConkey II, and Matthew A. Barrett. 1995–1996. "Fewer Sightings in the National Press: A Content Analysis of UFO News Coverage in *The New York Times, 1947–1995.*" *JUFOS* n.s. 6: 213–25.

Hiebert, Erwin N. 1986. "Modern Physics and Christian Faith." In Lindberg and Numbers 1986, 424–47.

Higbee, Donna. 1995. "Abductee Brainwashing?" *MUJ* 329 (September): 10–13.

Hill, Alan G. 1994. "The UFO Abduction Movement as a Religious Movement." Paper presented at the Annual Meeting of the American Sociological Association, August; available at <www.delta-edu/~cri/ ufopaper.html> (6 March 1997).

Hill, Paul R. 1995. *Unconventional Flying Objects: A Scientific Analysis.* Charlottesville, Va.: Hampton Roads Publishing.

Hind, Cynthia. 1996. *UFOs over Africa.* Madison, Wisc.: Horus House Press.

Hines, Terrence. 1988. *Pseudoscience and the Paranormal: A Critical Examination of the Evidence.* Buffalo: Prometheus Books.

Hinfelaar, Henk J. 1965. "Mail Bag: The Brazilian Farmer's Story." *FSR* 11, no. 3 (May–June): 24.

Hoagland, Hudson. 1969. "Beings from Outer Space: Corporeal and Spiritual." *Science* 163, no. 3868 (14 February): 625.

Hobana, Ion, and Julien Weverbergh. 1972. *UFO's from behind the Iron Curtain.* New York: Bantam Books.

Hoge, Dean R., Benton Johnson, and Donald A. Luidens. 1994. *Vanishing Boundaries: The Religion of Mainline Protestant Baby Boomers.* Louisville, Ky.: Westminster/John Knox Press.

Holiday, F. W. 1993. *Serpents of the Sky, Dragons of the Earth.* Madison, Wisc.: Horus House Press. Reprint of *The Dragon and the Disc,* New York: W. W. Norton, 1973.

Holroyd, Stuart. 1979. *Alien Intelligence.* London: David and Charles.

Holt, Jim. 1997. "Space Race." *Lingua Franca* (June–July): 19–20.

Holton, Gerald. 1993. *Science and Anti-Science.* Cambridge: Harvard University Press.

———. 1994. "The Antiscience Problem." *The Skeptical Inquirer* 18, no. 3 (spring): 264ff.

———. 1996. *Einstein, History, and Other Passions: The Rebellion against Science at the End of the Twentieth Century.* Reading, Mass.: Addison-Wesley.

Holton, Gerald, and William A. Blanpied, eds. 1976. *Science and Its Public: The Changing Relationship.* Boston: D. Reidel Publishing.

Honan, William H. 1995. "Harvard Investigates Tenured Professor Who Wrote of Aliens." *New York Times News Service* (4 May).

Honey, C. A. 1964. "A Need to Face Facts." *Cosmic Science Newsletter* 28: 3–8.

Hopkins, Budd. 1981. *Missing Time.* New York: Ballantine Books.

———. 1987a. "Contact Fantasies and Abduction Realities." *IUR* 12, no. 1 (January–February): 4–7.

———. 1987b. *Intruders: The Incredible Visitations at Copley Woods.* New York: Bantam Books.

———. 1991. "UFO Abductions at the Event Level." *IUR* 19, no. 4 (July–August): 9–14.

———. 1994. "The Roper Poll on Unusual Personal Experiences." In Pritchard et al. 1994, 215–18.

———. 1996. *Witnessed: The True Story of the Brooklyn Bridge UFO Abductions.* New York: Pocket Books.

Hopkins, Budd, David Michael Jacobs, and Ron Westrum, eds. 1992. *Unusual Personal Experiences: An Analysis of the Data from Three National Surveys.* Las Vegas: Bigelow Holding Corporation.

Horn, Arthur David. 1994. *Humanity's Extraterrestrial Origins: ET Influences on Humankind's Biological and Cultural Evolution.* Mt. Shasta, Calif.: A. and L. Horn.

Hough, Peter, and Moyshe Kalman. 1997. *The Truth about Alien Abductions.* London: Blandford.

Howe, Linda Moulton. 1989. *An Alien Harvest.* LMH Productions.

———. 1992. "1992 Animal Mutilation Update." *MUJ* 294 (October): 3–9.

———. 1993. *Facts and Eyewitnesses.* Vol. 1 of *Glimpses of Other Realities.* Jamison, Pa.: LMH Productions.

———. 1998. *High Strangeness.* Vol. 2 of *Glimpses of Other Realities.* New Orleans, La.: Paper Chase Press.

Huayta, Willaru, Chasqui Sun Messenger of the Incas. 1997a. "Planetary Mission of the Extraterrestrials." *Contact Forum* 5, no. 4 (July–August): 1, 4–5.

———. 1997b. "Awakening." *Contact Forum* 5, no. 5 (September–October): 18–19.

Hubbell, Webster. 1997. *Friends in High Places.* New York: William Morrow.

Hufford, David J. 1982. *The Terror That Comes in the Night: An Experience-Centered Study of Supernatural Assault Traditions.* Philadelphia: University of Pennsylvania Press.

———. 1994. "Awakening Paralyzed in the Presence of a Strange 'Visitor.'" In Pritchard et al. 1994, 348–54.

Human Potential Foundation. 1996. *When Cosmic Cultures Meet: An International Conference Presented by the Human Potential Foundation.* Falls Church, Va.: Human Potential Foundation.

Huyghe, Patrick. 1996. *The Field Guide to Extraterrestrials: A Complete Overview of Alien Lifeforms — Based on Actual Accounts and Sightings.* New York: Avon Books.

Hynek, J. Allen. 1953. "Unusual Aerial Phenomena." *Journal of the Optical Society of America* 43 (April): 311–14.

———. 1966a. "UFOs Merit Scientific Study." *Science* (21 October): 329.

———. 1966b. "Are Flying Saucers Real?" *Saturday Evening Post* (17 December): 17–21.

———. 1967a. "White Paper on UFOs." *Christian Science Monitor* (23 May): 9.

———. 1967b. "The UFO Gap." *Playboy* (December): 143–46.

———. 1969. "The Condon Report and UFOs." *Bulletin of the Atomic Scientists* 25 (April): 39–42.

———. 1972a. "Twenty-One Years of UFO Reports." In Sagan and Page 1972, 37–51.

———. 1972b. *The UFO Experience: A Scientific Inquiry.* Chicago: Henry Regnery.

———. 1977. *The Hynek UFO Report.* New York: Dell Books.

———. 1983. "The Case against E.T." In the *MUFON 1983 UFO Symposium Proceedings: UFOs: A Scientific Challenge,* ed. Walter H. Andrus Jr. and Dennis W. Stacy, 119–26. Seguin, Tex.: Mutual UFO Network.

Hynek, J. Allen, and Jacques Vallee. 1975. *The Edge of Reality: A Progress Report on Unidentified Flying Objects.* Chicago: Henry Regnery.

Imbrogno, Philip J., and Marianne Horrigan. 1997. *Contact of the Fifth Kind: The Silent Invasion Has Begun.* St. Paul, Minn.: Llewellyn Publications.

Jackson, John A. 1966. "Two Contemporary Cults." *Advancement of Science* 23, no. 108 (June): 60–64.

Jacobs, David M. 1975. *The UFO Controversy in America.* Bloomington: Indiana University Press.

———. 1983. "UFOs and the Search for Scientific Legitimacy." In *The Occult in America: New Historical Perspectives,* ed. Howard Kerr and Charles L. Crow, 218–32. Urbana: University of Illinois Press.

———. 1992. *Secret Life: Firsthand Accounts of UFO Abductions.* New York: Simon and Schuster.

———. 1996. "Are Abductions Positive?" *IUR* 21, no. 2 (summer): 21–25.

———. 1997. "UFOs at Fifty: Some Personal Observations." In *The 50th Anniversary of Ufology: MUFON 1997 International UFO Symposium Proceedings,* ed. Walter H. Andrus and Irena Scott, 17–30. Seguin, Tex.: Mutual UFO Network.

———. 1998. *The Threat—The Secret Agenda: What the Aliens Really Want . . . and How They Plan to Get It.* New York: Simon and Schuster.

Jaki, Stanley L. 1980. *Cosmos and Creator.* Edinburgh: Scottish Academic Press.

James, Trevor. 1960. "Scientists, Contactees, and Equilibrium." *FSR* 6, no. 1 (January): 19–20.

———. 1961. "The Case for Contact: Part 1." *FSR* 7, no. 6 (November): 6–8.

———. 1962a. "The Case for Contact: Part 2." *FSR* 8, no. 1 (January): 9–11.

———. 1962b. "UFOLOGY: Something More Than a Science." *FSR* 8, no. 4 (July): 7–9.

Jansma, Sidney J., Sr. 1981. *UFOs and Evolution.* N.p.

Jeffers, Joan L. 1996. "MUFON Forum: UFO Cycles." *MUJ* 334 (February): 20.

Jeffrey, Kent. 1995. "The Purported 1947 Roswell Film." *MUJ* 326 (June): 7–10.

———. 1996. "Santilli's Controversial Autopsy Movie." *MUJ* 335 (March): 3–13.

———, 1997. "Roswell: Anatomy of a Myth." *MUJ* 350 (June): 3–17.

Jennings, Jack A. 1978. "UFOs: The Next Theological Challenge?" *The Christian Century* 95, no. 6 (22 February): 184–89.

———. 1980. "Impact of Contact on Religion." *Second Look* (January–February): 11–14, 41.

Jessup, M. K. 1955. *The Case for the UFO: Unidentified Flying Objects.* New York: Bantam Books.

Johnson, Jerold R. 1990. "Letters." *MUJ* 270 (October): 21.

———. 1995. "Vallee Classification of Reports by Type." In Andrus 1995b, 210–13.

Johnson, Miller. 1996. "Roswell 'Debris' Jeweler's Cast-Off." *MUJ* 343 (November): 3–6, 9.

Johnson, Vince. 1993. "Time Travelers: An Alternative to the ET Hypothesis." *MUJ* 297 (January): 4–5.

Johnson, Wayne B., and Kenn Thomas. 1998. *Flying Saucers over Los Angeles.* Kempton, Ill.: Adventures Unlimited Press.

Jones, C. B. Scott. 1995. *Phoenix in the Labyrinth.* Falls Church, Va.: Human Potential Foundation.

Jones, Marie. 1993. "Sexism." *MUJ* 297 (January): 20.

Jordan, Debbie, and Kathy Mitchell. 1994. *Abducted! The Story of the Intruders Continues.* New York: Carroll and Graf Publishers/Richard Gallen.

Jung, C. G. 1978. *Flying Saucers: A Modern Myth of Things Seen in the Skies.* Trans. R. F. C. Hull. Princeton: Princeton University Press.

Kaneko, Julian H. 1983a. "God: The Supreme Illusionist." *FSR* 28, no. 4: 28.

———. 1983b. "Mail Bag: The UFO Phenomenon Is Not Amenable to Scientific Study." *FSR* 29, no. 2: iii.

Kanon, Gregory M. 1997. *The Great UFO Hoax: The Final Solution to the UFO Mystery.* Lakeville, Minn.: Galde Press.

Keel, John A. 1970. *Operation Trojan Horse.* New York: Putnam. Reprint, Lilburn, Ga.: IllumiNet Press, 1996.

———. 1971. *Our Haunted Planet.* New York: Fawcett Gold Medal Books.

———. 1988. *Disneyland of the Gods.* New York: Amok Press. Reprint, Lilburn, Ga.: IllumiNet Press, 1995.

———. 1991. *The Mothman Prophecies.* Avondale Estates, Ga.: IllumiNet Press.

Keith, Jim. 1997. *Casebook on the Men in Black.* Lilburn, Ga.: IllumiNet Press.

Keyhoe, Donald. 1950. *The Flying Saucers Are Real.* New York: Fawcett Publications.

———. 1953. *Flying Saucers from Outer Space.* New York: Holt.

———. 1955. *The Flying Saucer Conspiracy.* New York: Holt.

———. 1960. *Flying Saucers: Top Secret.* New York: G. P. Putnam's Sons.

———. 1973. *Aliens from Space: The Real Story of Unidentified Flying Objects.* New York: Signet Books, New American Library.

Kieffer, Gene. 1979. "UFOs and Kundalini." In *Kundalini, Evolution, and Enlightenment,* ed. John White, 380–85. Garden City: Anchor Books.

King, Jon. 1996. "Ex-Sgt. Major Robert O. Dean Speaks Out." *UFO Reality* (October–November): 20–23.

Kirby, John. 1993. "An Interview with Robert Lazar." *MUJ* 306 (October): 8–13, 16.

Klass, Philip J. 1968. *UFO's: Identified.* New York: Random House.

———. 1975. *UFOs Explained.* New York: Random House.

———. 1981. "UFOs." In Abell and Singer 1981, 313–34.

———. 1983. *UFOs: The Public Deceived.* Buffalo: Prometheus Books.

————. 1987–1988. "The MJ-12 Crashed Saucer Documents." *Skeptical Inquirer* (winter): 137–46, and (spring): 279–89.

————. 1989. *UFO Abductions: A Dangerous Game.* Rev. ed. New York: Prometheus Books.

————. 1993. *The Crashed Saucer Cover-Up.* Buffalo: Prometheus Books.

————. 1997. "UFOlogist Robert Dean Claims 'It's Quite Easy to Lie to the American Public,' and Demonstrates This Claim to Be True." *Skeptics UFO Newsletter* (November): 1–3.

Knorr-Cetina, Karin. 1981. *The Manufacture of Knowledge: An Essay on the Constructivist and Contextual Nature of Science.* Oxford: Pergamon Press.

Kohlstedt, Sally Gregory. 1976. "The Nineteenth-Century Amateur Tradition: The Case of the Boston Society of Natural History." In Holton and Blanpied 1976, 173–90.

Kor, Peter. 1977. "Is There a Plot to Promote the Saucers?" *Search Magazine* (winter).

Kottmeyer, Marvin. 1988. "Abductions: The Boundary Deficit Hypothesis." *Magonia* 32 (March): n.p. <http://www.netkonect.co.uk/d/dogon/magonia/arc/80/ boundary.htm>.

————. 1990. "Entirely Unpredisposed: The Cultural Background of UFO Abduction Reports." *Magonia* (January): n.p.

————. "UFO Flaps." 1995–1996. *The Anomalist* 3 (winter): 64–89.

Krapf, Phillip H. 1998. *Contact Has Begun: The True Story of a Journalist's Encounter with Alien Beings.* Carlsbad, Calif.: Hay House.

Kulikowski, Stan II. 1994. "Infernal UFOs: Bigger Inside Than Out?" *MUJ* 313 (May): 9–12, 14.

Kyle, Richard. 1995. *The New Age Movement in American Culture.* Lanham: University Press of America.

LaFollette, Marcel. 1990. *Making Science Our Own: Public Images of Science, 1910–1955.* Chicago: University of Chicago Press.

Lagrange, Pierre. 1998. "A Moment in History: An Interview with Bill Bequette." *IUR* 23, no. 4 (winter): 15, 20.

Laibow, Rima E. 1989. "Dual Victims: The Abused and the Abducted." *IUR* 14, no. 3 (May–June): 4–9.

————. 1993. *Clinical Discrepancies between Expected and Observed Data in Patients Reporting UFO Abductions: Implications for Treatment.* <alt.alien.visitors> (9 February).

Lamarche, Sebastián Robiou. 1996. "UFOs and Deaths of Animals in Puerto Rico (1975)." *FSR* 41, no. 3 (autumn): 14–20.

Lamm, Norman. 1965–1966. "The Religious Implications of Extraterrestrial Life." *Tradition — Journal of Orthodox Jewish Thought* 7, no. 4, to 8, no. 1 (winter–spring): 5–56.

Lammer, Helmut. 1996. "Preliminary Findings of Project MILAB: Evidence for Military Kidnappings of Alleged UFO Abductees." *MUJ* 344 (December): 3–8.

————. 1997. "More Findings of Project MILAB." *MUJ* 355 (November): 5–12.

————. 1999. *MILABS: Military Mind Control and Alien Abduction.* Lilburn, Ga.: IllumiNet Press.

Langmuir, Irving. 1989. "Pathological Science: The Science of Things That Aren't So." *Physics Today* 42 (October): 36.

Lankford, John. 1981. "Amateurs and Astrophysics: A Neglected Aspect in the Development of a Scientific Specialty." *Social Studies of Science* 11: 275–303.

Larson, Bob. 1997. *UFO's and the Alien Agenda*. Nashville: Thomas Nelson Publishers.

Latour, Bruno, and Steve Woolgar. 1979. *Laboratory Life*. Beverly Hills: Sage.

LaVigne, Michelle. 1995. *The Alien Abduction Survival Guide*. New Berg, Ore.: Wild Flower Press.

Law, John, and R. J. Williams. 1982. "Putting Facts Together: A Study of Scientific Persuasion." *Social Studies of Science* 12: 535–58.

Lawrence, David. 1950. "Flying Saucers — The Real Story: U.S. Built First One in 1942." *U.S. News and World Report* (7 April): 13–15.

Lawson, Alvin. 1978. "Hypnosis of Imaginary UFO 'Abductees.'" *IUR* 3, no. 10–11 (October–November): 20.

———. 1980. "Archetypes and Abductions." *Frontiers of Science* (September–October): 32–36.

———. 1982. "Birth Trauma and the UFO Abduction." *Frontiers of Science* 4 (May–June): 19–24, 39–40.

———. 1984. "Perinatal Imagery in UFO Abduction Reports." *Journal of Psychohistory* 12: 211–39.

Lawson, Alvin H., and W. C. McCall. 1978. "Hypnosis of Imaginary UFO Abductees." Paper presented at the meeting of the American Psychological Association, Toronto, August.

———. 1982. "The Abduction Experience: A Testable Hypothesis." *Magonia* 10: 3–18.

Leir, Roger K. 1996. "In Search of Hard Evidence." *MUJ* 336 (April): 9–12, 15.

———. 1998. *The Surgeon and the Scalpel*. Columbus, N.C.: Granite Publishing.

Leslie, Desmond, and George Adamski. 1953. *Flying Saucers Have Landed*. New York: The British Book Centre.

Leslie, Melinda, and Mark Williams. 1996. "Have YOU Had Alien Encounters?" <http://www.anw.com/ML/index.htm>.

Lesser, Alexander. 1978. *The Pawnee Ghost Dance Hand Game: Ghost Dance Revival and Ethnic Identity*. Madison: University of Wisconsin Press.

Lévy-Bruhl, Lucien. 1966. *Primitive Mentality*. Boston: Beacon Press.

Lewels, Joe. 1997a. *The God Hypothesis: Extraterrestrial Life and Its Implications for Science and Religion*. Mill Spring, N.C.: Wild Flower Press.

———. 1997b. "The Holographic Universe and the UFO Phenomenon." *MUJ* 356 (December): 3–5.

Lewis, C. S. 1960. "Religion and Rocketry." In *The World's Last Night and Other Essays by C. S. Lewis*, 83–92. New York: Harcourt, Brace and Company.

Lewis, Clyde. 1998. "The New Alien Religion?" <http://www.xzone.org/clyde1. html> (6 April).

Lewis, David Allen, and Robert Shreckhise. 1991. *UFO: End-Time Delusion*. Green Forest, Ark.: New Leaf Press.

Lewis, James R., ed. 1995. *The Gods Have Landed: New Religions From Other Worlds*. Albany: State University of New York Press.

Lewis, James R., and J. Gordon Melton, eds. 1992. *Perspectives on the New Age*. Albany: State University of New York Press.

Lieb, Michael. 1998. *Children of Ezekiel: Aliens, UFOs, the Crisis of Race, and the Advent of the End Time*. Durham: Duke University Press.

Lindberg, David C., and Ronald L. Numbers, eds. 1986. *God and Nature: Historical Essays on the Encounter between Christianity and Science*. Berkeley: University of California Press.

Lindemann, Michael, ed. 1991. *UFOs and the Alien Presence: Six Viewpoints*. Newberg, Ore.: Wild Flower Press.

Llewellyn, John D. 1969. "UFOs and OSC." *Orbit* 4, no. 3.

Lloyd, Dan. 1992. "The Battle against Spiritual Powers of Hindrance." *FSR* 37, no. 3 (autumn): 1–6.

Lopez, John William. 1992. "Ufology in Crisis: Six Views." *IUR* 17, no. 1 (January–February): 21.

Lorenzen, Coral. 1962. *The Great Flying Saucer Hoax: The UFO Facts and Their Interpretation*. New York: Signet Books.

———. 1966. *Flying Saucers: The Startling Evidence of the Invasion from Outer Space — An Exposure of the Establishment's Flying Saucer Cover-Up*.

———. 1969. *UFOs: The Whole Story*. New York: Signet Books.

Lorenzen, Coral, and Jim Lorenzen. 1967. *Flying Saucer Occupants*. New York: Signet Books.

———. 1977. *Abducted! Confrontations with Beings from Outer Space*. New York: Berkley Books.

Lorenzen, Jim, and Coral Lorenzen. 1968. *UFOs over the Americas*. New York: Signet Books.

Lowry, Brian. 1995. *The Truth Is Out There: The Official Guide to* The X-Files. New York: HarperPrism.

Lucas, Philip C. 1992. "The New Age Movement and the Pentecostal/Charismatic Revival: Distinct Yet Parallel Phases of a Fourth Great Awakening." In Lewis and Melton 1992, 189–212.

MacArthur, General Douglas. 1964. *Reminiscences*. New York: McGraw-Hill.

Maccabee, Bruce. 1979. "Scientific Investigation of Unidentified Flying Objects: Part 1." *JUFOS* 1: 70–92.

———. 1983. "Scientific Investigation of Unidentified Flying Objects: Part 2." *JUFOS* 3: 24–52.

———. 1995a. "The Arnold Phenomenon: Part 1." *IUR* 20, no. 1 (January–February): 14–17.

———. 1995b "The Arnold Phenomenon: Part 2." *IUR* 20, no. 2 (March–April): 10–3, 24.

———. 1995c. "The Arnold Phenomenon: Part 3." *IUR* 20, no. 3 (May–June): 6–7.

———. 1996. "The White Sands Films." *IUR* 21, no. 1 (spring): 22–25.

———. 1997. "CIA's UFO Explanation Is Preposterous." *MUJ* 354 (October): 3–6.

Mack, John E. 1993. "Stirring Our Deepest Fears." *IUR* 18, no. 2 (March–April): 17, 21.

———. 1994. *Abduction: Human Encounters with Aliens.* New York: Charles Scribner's Sons.

———. 1999. *Passport to the Cosmos: Human Transformation and Alien Encounters.* New York: Crown Publishers.

Mackay, Charles. 1852. *Memoirs of Extraordinary Popular Delusions and the Madness of Crowds.* 2nd ed. London: Office of the National Illustrated Library.

Mackay, E. A. I. [Ivar]. 1973. "UFO Entities: Occult and Physical." *FSR* 19, no. 2 (March–April): 26–29.

Mackay, Ivar. 1970a. "UFOs and the Occult: Part 1." *FSR* 16, no. 4 (July–August): 27–29.

———. 1970b. "UFOs and the Occult: Part 2." *FSR* 16, no. 5 (September–October): 24–26.

Mandelker, Scott. 1995. *From Elsewhere: Being E.T. in America: The Subculture of Those Who Claim to Be of Non-Earthly Origins.* New York: Birch Lane Press/Carol Publishing Group.

Maney, Charles A. 1956a. "Saucers and Science." *FSR* 2, no. 1 (January): 16–19, 29–30.

———. 1956b. "An Open Letter to Scientists." *FSR* 2, no. 5 (September): 14–15.

———. 1958. "Scientific Aspects of UFO Research." *FSR* 4, no. 5 (September): 10–12, 30.

Mannion, Michael. 1998. *Project Mindshift: The Re-education of the American Public Concerning Extraterrestrial Life, 1947–Present.* New York: M. Evans and Co.

Mantle, Philip. 1995. "An Interview with Ray Santilli." *MUJ* 328 (August): 3–7.

Mantle, Philip, and Stanton Friedman. 1995. "Open Letters to Ray Santilli and the Merlin Group." *MUJ* 325 (May): 17–18.

Margolis, Howard. 1993. *Paradigms and Barriers: How Habits of Mind Govern Scientific Beliefs.* Chicago: University of Chicago Press.

Markowitz, William. 1967. "The Physics and Metaphysics of UFOs." *Science* 157: 1274–79.

Marrs, Jim. 1997. *Alien Agenda: Investigating the Extraterrestrial Presence among Us.* New York: HarperCollins Publishers.

Martín, Jorge. 1997a. "Healed by 'ETs' in Puerto Rico." *FSR* 42, no. 3 (autumn): 18–22.

———. 1997b. "A UFO Base beneath the Sierra Bermeja Range in S.W. Puerto Rico?" *FSR* 42, no. 4 (winter): 14–17.

Martin, Riley L., and O-Qua Tangin Wann. 1995. *The Coming of Tan.* New Hope, Pa.: Historicity Productions.

Marty, Martin E. 1989. "The Sacred and the Secular in American History." In *Transforming Faith: The Sacred and the Secular in Modern American History,* ed. M. L. Bradbury and James B. Gilbert, 1–9. New York: Greenwood Press.

Marystone, Cyril. 1996a. "A List of Suggested Delusions Created or Promoted by the Aliens." *FSR* 41, no. 4 (winter): 19–20.

———. 1996b. "Wishful-Thinking and Self-Deception of Abductees and Ufolo-gists." *FSR* 41, no. 4 (winter): 15–19.

Mascall, E. L. 1956. *Christian Theology and Natural Science: Some Questions on Their Relations.* London: Longmans, Green and Co.

Matheson, Terry. 1998. *Alien Abductions: Creating a Modern Phenomenon.* Amherst, N.Y.: Prometheus Books.

Mauskopf, Seymour H., ed. 1979. *The Reception of Unconventional Science.* Boulder: Westview Press.

McAndrew, J. 1997. *The Roswell Report: Case Closed.* Washington, D.C.: U.S. General Publications Office.

McCall, W. D. 1978. "What Can We Learn from the Emotional Reactions of UFO Abductees?" *IUR* 3, no. 10–11 (October–November): 21.

McCampbell, James M. 1973. *UFOlogy: New Insights from Science and Common Sense.* N.p.

McCarthy, Paul E. 1975. "Politicking and Paradigm Shifting: James E. McDonald and the UFO Case Study." Ph.D. diss., University of Hawaii.

McElheny, Victor E. 1985. "Impacts of Present-Day Popularization." In *Expository Science: Forms and Functions of Popularization,* ed. T. Shinn and R. Whitley, 277–82. Boston: Reidel.

McIver, Shirley. 1985. "The UFO Movement: A Sociological Study of Unidentified Flying Object Groups." Master's thesis. University of York, North Yorkshire, England. Self-published.

McMullin, Ernan. 1980. "Persons in the Universe." *Zygon* 15, no. 1 (March): 69–89.

———. 1988. "The Shaping of Scientific Rationality: Construction and Constraint." In *Construction and Constraint: The Shaping of Scientific Rationality,* ed. Ernan McMullin, 1–47. Notre Dame: University of Notre Dame Press.

———. 1993. "Rationality and Paradigm Change in Science." In *World Changes: Thomas Kuhn and the Nature of Science,* ed. Paul Horwich, 55–78. Cambridge: The MIT Press.

———, ed. 1992. *The Social Dimensions of Science.* Notre Dame: University of Notre Dame Press.

Meerloo, J. A. M. 1968. "The Flying Saucer Syndrome and the Need for Miracles." *JAMA: Journal of the American Medical Association* 170: 501–40.

Meheust, Bertrand. 1978. *Science fiction et soucoupes volantes.* Paris: Mercure de France.

———. 1985. *Soucouples volantes et folklore.* Paris: Mercure de France.

Melton, J. Gordon. 1992. "New Thought and the New Age." In Lewis and Melton 1992, 15–29.

Mendez, William, and Charles Hickson. 1983. *UFO Contact at Pensacola.* Privately published.

Menger, Howard. 1959. *From Outer Space.* New York: Pyramid Books.

Menzel, Donald. 1953. *Flying Saucers.* Cambridge: Harvard University Press.

———. 1972. "UFO's: The Modern Myth." In Sagan and Page 1972, 146–53.

Menzel, Donald H., and Lyle G. Boyd. 1963. *The World of Flying Saucers: A Sci-*

entific Examination of a Major Myth of the Space Age. Garden City: Doubleday.

Menzel, Donald H., and Ernest H. Taves. 1977. *The UFO Enigma: The Definitive Explanation of the UFO Phenomenon.* Garden City: Doubleday.

Merrow, Alexander. 1960. "Is the Scientific Approach the Best Way to the Truth?" *FSR* 6, no. 4 (July): 9–10.

Mesnard, Joël. 1994. "The French Abduction File." *MUJ* 309 (January): 3–13.

Mesnard, Joël, and Claude Pavy. 1968. "Encounter with 'Devils.'" *FSR* 14, no. 5 (September–October): 7–9.

Meyer, Pamela. 1996. "Experiencing Star Knowledge." *Contact Forum* 4, no. 4 (July–August): 3.

Meynell, Hugo. 1996. "On Investigation of the So-Called Paranormal." In Stoeber and Meynell 1996, 23–45.

Michel, Aimé. 1956. *The Truth about Flying Saucers.* New York: Pyramid Books.

Midgley, Mary. 1992. *Science As Salvation: A Modern Myth and Its Meaning.* New York: Routledge.

Migulin, Vladimir. 1979. "UFOs: The Soviet Point of View." *Second Look* (November–December): 6–8.

Miller, John, and Richard Neal. 1994. "Lack of Proof for Missing Embryo/Fetus Syndrome." In Pritchard et al. 1994, 262–69.

Milne, E. A. 1952. *Modern Cosmology and the Christian Idea of God.* London: Clarendon Press.

Misraki, M. Paul. 1965. *Flying Saucers through the Ages.* London: Spearman. Reprint, London: Tandem Press, 1973.

Mission Control and Zoev Jho. 1990. *E.T. 101: The Cosmic Instruction Manual for Planetary Evolution — An Emergency Remedial Earth Edition.* Reprint, San Francisco: HarperSanFrancisco, 1995.

Mitchell, Karyn K. 1994. *Abductions: Stop Them, Heal Them, Now!* St. Charles, Ill.: Mind Rivers Publication.

Moore, R. Laurence. 1977. *In Search of White Crows: Spiritualism, Parapsychology, and American Culture.* New York: Oxford University Press.

———. 1994. *Selling God: American Religion in the Marketplace of Culture.* New York: Oxford University Press.

Moore, Robert. 1993. "Science v. Saucery?" In Barclay and Barclay 1993, 65–96.

Moore, William L. 1985. "The Adamski Photos: Models or Scout Ships from Venus?" *Focus* 1, no. 8 (31 October): 1, 3–4.

Morel, Willis. 1997. "The Creating Intelligences of Insects." *Contact Forum* 5, no. 6 (November–December): 15.

Morrison, Philip. 1972. "The Nature of Scientific Evidence: A Summary." In Sagan and Page 1972, 276–290.

———. 1981. "On the Causes of Wonderful Things: A Perspective." In Abell and Singer 1981, 349–362.

Moseley, James W. 1991. *UFO Crash Secrets.* Abelard Productions.

———. 1997. "Tidbits of Miscellaneous Trash." *Saucer Smear* 44, no. 2 (10 February): 4.

Moyer, Ernest P. 1970. *God, Man, and the UFOs.* New York: Carlton Press.

Müller, Max. 1885. "The Savage." *Nineteenth Century* 17: 109–32.

Mullis, Kary. 1998. *Dancing Naked in the Mind Field.* New York: Pantheon Books.

Munro, Scott Allen. 1997. "Mainstream Scientists and Ufology." *Internet UFO Skeptics Site.* <http://www.geocities.com/Area51/7595/serious.html> (7 May).

Murphy, William M. 1971. "Mail Bag: Ultra-terrestrial, Infra-terrestrial." *FSR* 17, no. 3 (May–June): 31.

Neal, Richard M., Jr. 1992. "The Missing Embryo-Fetus Syndrome." In *MUFON 1992 International UFO Symposium Proceedings: The Ultimate Mystery of the Millennia,* ed. Walter H. Andrus Jr., 214–29. Seguin, Tex.: Mutual UFO Network.

Needleman, Jacob. 1965. *A Sense of the Cosmos: The Encounter of Modern Science and Ancient Truth.* New York: E. P. Dutton and Co.

Neeley, Robert G., Jr. N.d.a. *The Airship Chronicle.* Mount Rainier, Md.: Fund for UFO Research.

———. N.d.b. *UFOs of 1896–1897: The Airship Wave.* Mount Rainier, Md.: Fund for UFO Research.

Nelkin, Dorothy. 1987. *Selling Science: How the Press Covers Science and Technology.* New York: Freeman Publishers.

Newald, Alec. 1996. *Co-Evolution: The True Story of a Man Taken for Ten Days to an Extraterrestrial Civilisation.* Mapleton, Queensland: Nexus Publishing.

Newman, H. Kent. 1978. "How Can Hypnosis Be Used in UFO Abduction Cases?" *IUR* 3, no. 10–11 (October–November): 19.

Newman, Leonard S., and Roy F. Baumeister. 1996. "Toward an Explanation of the UFO Abduction Phenomenon: Hypnotic Elaboration, Extraterrestrial Sadomasochism, and Spurious Memories." *Psychological Inquiry* 7, no. 2: 99–126.

Newman, Robert P. 1995. "American Intransigence: The Rejection of Continental Drift in the Great Debates of the 1920s." In *Science, Reason, and Rhetoric,* ed. Henry Krips, J. E. McGuire, and Trevor Melia, 181–210. Pittsburgh, Pa.: University of Pittsburgh.

Nickell, Joe. 1995. *Entities, Angels, Spirits, Demons, and Other Alien Beings.* Amherst, N.Y.: Prometheus Books.

———. 1996. "Investigative Files: A Study of Fantasy Proneness in the Thirteen Cases of Alleged Encounters in John Mack's *Abduction.*" *The Skeptical Inquirer* (May). <http://www.csicop.org/si/9605/mack.html>.

Noble, David F. 1997. *The Religion of Technology: The Divinity of Man and the Spirit of Invention.* New York: Alfred A. Knopf.

Nyman, Joe. 1988. "The Latent Encounter Experience: A Composite Model." *MUJ* 242 (June): 10–12.

———. 1994a. "A Composite Encounter Model." In Pritchard et al. 1994, 83–85.

———. 1994b. "Dual Reference in the UFO Encounter." In Pritchard et al. 1994, 142–48.

———. 1994c. "Follow-up of Diagnostic Positives." In Pritchard et al. 1994, 218–23.

———. 1995. "MUFON Forum: More on the Fall." *MUJ* 326 (June): 17–18.

Oberg, J. E. 1977. "Astronauts and UFOs: The Whole Story." *Spaceworld* N-2–158 (February): 4–28.

Oberg, James. 1982. *UFOs and Outer Space Mysteries*. Norfolk, Va.: Donning.

Oberth, Hermann. 1955. "They Come from Outer Space." *FSR* 1, no. 2 (May–June): 12–15.

O'Flaherty, Wendy Doniger. 1988. *Other People's Myths*. New York: Macmillan Publishing.

Olson, Geoff. 1994. "Letters to *MUFON UFO Journal*: Ufology as Theology." *MUJ* 316 (August): 18.

———. 1995. "Truth Can Be Selective for the Skeptics Who Probe the Paranormal." 23 August [List message]. Terry Colvin on UFO-L at <misc@interport.net>.

Orne, Martin. 1988. "Alien-Abduction Claims and Standards of Inquiry." *The Skeptical Inquirer* (spring): 270–78.

Orne, Martin, Wayne G. Whitehouse, Emily Carota Orne, and David F. Dinges. 1996. "'Memories' of Anomalous and Traumatic Autobiographical Experiences: Validation and Consolidation of Fantasy Through Hypnosis." *Psychological Inquiry* 7, no. 2: 168–72.

Owen, George, and Iris Owen. 1982. "The UFO Phenomenon and Its Relationship to Parapsychological Research." In *MUFON Symposium Proceedings 1982: UFOs — Canada: A Global Perspective,* ed. Walter H. Andrus Jr. and Dennis W. Stacy, 26–32. Seguin, Tex.: Mutual UFO Network.

Page, Thornton. 1972. "Education and the UFO Phenomenon." In Sagan and Page 1972, 3–10.

Paris, S. A. 1965. ."Mailbag: Spacemen in Saxon Time and Some Notes on Fireballs." *FSR* 11, no. 2 (March): 22–23.

Parnell, June. 1988. "Measured Personality Characteristics of Persons Who Claim UFO Experiences." *Psychotherapy in Private Practice* 6: 159–65.

Parnell, June, and Leo Sprinkle. 1990. "Personality Characteristics of Persons Who Claim UFO Experiences." *JUFOS* n.s. 2: 45–58.

Peebles, Curtis. 1994. *Watch the Skies! A Chronicle of the Flying Saucer Myth*. Washington: Smithsonian Institution Press.

Perlman, David. 1976. "Science and the Mass Media." In Holton and Blanpied 1976, 245–60.

Persinger, M. A. 1978. "What Factors Can Account for UFO Experiences?" *IUR* 3, no. 10–11 (October–November): 21.

———. 1983. "Geophysical Variables and Human Behavior." *Perceptual and Motor Skills* 56: 184–88.

———. 1988. "Neuropsychological Aspects of the Visitor Experience." *MUJ* 247 (November): 10–14.

———. 1992. "Neuropsychological Profiles of Adults Who Report 'Sudden Remembering' of Early Childhood Memories: Implications for Claims of Sex Abuse and Alien Visitation/Abduction Experiences." *Perceptual and Motor Skills* 75, no. 1 (August): 259–66.

Persinger, M. A., and G. F. Lafrenière. 1977. *Space Time Transients and Unusual Events*. Chicago: Nelson Hall.

Peters, Ted. 1976. "Heavenly Chariots and Flying Saucers." In *MUFON 1976 UFO Symposium Proceedings: New Frontiers in UFO Research*, ed. N. Joseph Gurney and Walter H. Andrus Jr., 53–64. Seguin, Tex.: Mutual UFO Network.

———. 1977. *UFOs: God's Chariots? Flying Saucers in Politics, Science, and Religion*. Atlanta: John Knox Press.

———. 1979. "The Religious Dimensions of the UFO Phenomenon." In *MUFON 1979 UFO Symposium Proceedings: Intensifying the Scientific Investigation of the UFO Surveillance*, ed. Walter H. Andrus Jr., 37–45. Seguin, Tex.: Mutual UFO Network.

———. 1995. "Exo-Theology: Speculations on Extraterrestrial Life." In J. Lewis 1995, 187–206.

Pflock, Karl T. 1994. "Roswell, the Air Force, and Us." *IUR* 19, no. 6 (November–December): 3–5, 24.

Phillips, K. W. C. 1993. "The Psycho-Sociology of Ufology." In Barclay and Barclay 1993, 40–64.

Pickover, Clifford. 1999. "The Vision of the Chariot: Transcendent Experience and Temporal Lobe Epilepsy." *Science and Spirit* 10, no. 3 (September–October): 38–39.

Pinch, T. J., and H. M. Collins. 1984. "Private Science and Public Knowledge: The Committee for the Scientific Investigation of Claims of the Paranormal and Its Use of the Literature." *Social Studies of Science* 14: 521–46.

Pope, Nick. 1997. *The Uninvited: An Exposé of the Alien Abduction Phenomenon*. New York: Simon and Schuster.

Powers, W. T. 1969. "The Landing at Socorro: New Light on a Classic Case." In Bowen 1969a, 130–42.

Pratt, Bob. 1996. *UFO Danger Zone: Terror and Death in Brazil — Where Next?* Madison, Wisc.: Horus House Press.

Pritchard, Andrea, David E. Pritchard, John E. Mack, Pam Kasey, and Claudia Yapp, eds. 1994. *Alien Discussions: Proceedings of the Abduction Study Conference Held at MIT, Cambridge, MA*. Cambridge, Mass.: North Cambridge Press.

Puccetti, Roland. 1969. *Persons: A Study of Possible Moral Agents in the Universe*. New York: Herder and Herder.

Puhalski, Roberta. 1994. "Abductions: State of Siege — or Mind?" *MUJ* 313 (May): 15, 17.

———. 1995. "Fall from Grace." *MUJ* 324 (April): 9–16.

Pursglove, Paul David. 1995. *Zen in the Art of Close Encounters: Crazy Wisdom and UFOs*. Berkeley: The New Being Project.

Quintanilla, Hector, Jr. 1966. "The Investigation of UFOs." *Studies in Intelligence* 10, no. 4 (February). 95 110.

Rae, Stephen. 1994. "John Mack's Abductees." *New York Times Magazine* (20 March): 30–33.

Rak, Charles, and Jack Weiner. 1993. *The Allagash Incident*. Northampton, Mass.: Tundra Publishing.

Raloff, Janet. 1996. "When Science and Beliefs Collide: A Large and Growing

Share of the Population Rejects Aspects of Science." *Science News* 149 (8 June): 360–61.

Randi, James. 1981. "Science and the Chimera." In Abell and Singer 1981, 209–22.

Randle, Kevin D. 1991. *UFO Crash at Roswell*. New York: Avon Books.

———. 1994. "The Project Mogul Flights and Roswell." *IUR* 19, no. 6 (November–December): 6–7, 23.

———. 1996a. "Does Pop Culture Affect Our Views?" In *MUFON 1996 International UFO Symposium Proceedings: Ufology: A Scientific Enigma,* ed. Walter H. Andrus Jr., 17–25. Seguin, Tex.: Mutual UFO Network.

———. 1996b. "The MJ-12 Operations Manual: Another Forgery?" *IUR* 21, no. 1 (spring): 9–10.

———. 1997. "Randle Responds to Jeffrey on Roswell." *MUJ* 351 (July): 7–10.

———. 1999. "Ramey Message May Be 'Face In the Clouds.'" *CNI News* 5, no. 3 (1 April).

Randle, Kevin D., Russ Estes, and William P. Cone. 1999. *The Abduction Enigma*. New York: Tom Doherty Associates.

Randle, Kevin D., and Donald R. Schmitt. 1991. *UFO Crash at Roswell*. New York: Avon Books.

———. 1994. *The Truth about the UFO Crash at Roswell*. New York: Avon Books.

Randles, Jenny. 1981. "Research Report — 4: Close Encounters of the Fourth Kind." *FSR* 26, no. 5 (January): 25–26.

———. 1986. "Anatomy of a UFO Wave." *IUR* 11, no. 2 (March–April): 4–8, 19.

———. 1988. *Alien Abductions: The Mystery Solved*. New Brunswick, N.J.: Inner Light Publications.

———. 1993. *Alien Contacts and Abductions: The Real Story from the Other Side*. New York: Sterling Publishing.

———. 1994. *Star Children: The True Story of Alien Offspring among Us*. London: Robert Hale Limited. Reprint, New York: Sterling Publishing, 1994.

———. 1995. *UFO Retrievals: The Recovery of Alien Spacecraft*. London: Blandford Books.

———. 1997. *The Truth behind Men in Black: Government Agents — or Visitors from Beyond*. New York: St. Martin's Press.

Randles, Jenny, and Peter Warrington. 1985. *Science and the UFOs*. New York: Basil Blackwell.

Rardin, T. Patrick. 1982. "A Rational Approach to the UFO Problem." In Grim 1982, 256–66.

Raschke, Carl. 1989. "UFOs: Ultraterrestrial Agents of Cultural Deconstruction." In *Cyberbiological Studies of the Imaginal Component in the UFO Contact Experience,* ed. D. Stillings, 21–32. St. Paul, Minn.: Archaeus Project.

Ravetz, J. R. 1981. "The Varieties of Scientific Experience." In *The Sciences and Theology in the Twentieth Century,* ed. A. R. Peacocke. Notre Dame: University of Notre Dame Press.

Rayl, A. J. S. 1994. "Inside the Military UFO Underground." *Omni Magazine* (April): 48–59.

Reeve, Bryant, and Helen Reeve. 1957. *Flying Saucer Pilgrimage*. Amherst, Wisc.: Amherst Press.

Reid, Frank John. 1999. "Astronomers and UFOs: An Epilogue." *IUR* 24, no. 3 (fall): 14–15.

Reingold, Nathan. 1979. "Reflections on 200 Years of Science in the United States." In *The Sciences in the American Context*, ed. N. Reingold, 9–20. Washington, D.C.: Smithsonian Institution Press.

Resta, Stephen P. 1975. "The Relationship of Anomie and Externality to Strength of Belief in Unidentified Flying Objects." Master's thesis, Loyola College, Baltimore, Md.

Ribera, Antonio. 1964. "What Happened At Fatima?" *FSR* 10, no. 2 (March–April): 12–14.

———. 1986. "The Jinn and the Dolmen: The Most Amazing Case of Abduction Yet." *FSR* 31, no. 4 (May–June): 2–12.

———. 1987. "The Jinn and the Dolmen." *FSR* 32, no. 2 (February–March): 20–21.

Rimmer, John. 1970. "The UFO Is Alive and Living in Fairy Land." *Merseyside UFO Bulletin* n.v. (December): n.p. <http://www.magonia.demon.co.uk/arc/70/fairy.htm>.

Ring, Kenneth. 1992. *The Omega Project: Near-Death Experiences, UFO Encounters, and Mind at Large*. New York: William Morrow and Company.

Ritrovato, Joseph W. 1995. "Analyzing UFO Waves." *MUJ* 323 (March): 3–7, 17.

———. 1996. "The Importance of UFO Waves and a Cyclic Connection with Some Curious Links." *MUJ* 338 (June): 7–12.

Rivas, Juan A. Lorenzo. 1999. "President Eisenhower's 'E.T.' Encounter: What *Really* Happened at Muroc Base?" *FSR* 44, no. 3 (autumn): 2–6.

Robinson, Jeanne Marie. 1997. *Alienated: A Quest to Understand Contact*. Murfreesboro, Tenn.: Greenleaf Publications.

Rodeghier, Mark. 1994a. "Hypnosis and the Hill Abduction Case." *IUR* 19, no. 2 (March–April): 4–6, 23–24.

———. 1994b. "A Set of Selection Criteria for Abductees." In Pritchard et al. 1994, 22–23.

———. 1997. "The CIA's UFO History." *IUR* 22, no. 3 (fall): 3–6, 36.

Rodeghier, Mark, and Mark Chesney. 1994. "The Air Force Report on Roswell: An Absence of Evidence." *IUR* 19, no. 5 (September–October): 3, 20–24.

———. 1995a. "What the GAO Found: Nothing about Much Ado." *IUR* 20, no. 4 (July–August): 7–8, 24.

———. 1995b. "The Final(?) Air Force Report on Roswell." *IUR* 20, no. 5 (winter): 5–6.

Rodeghier, Mark, Jeff Goodpaster, and Sandra Blatterbauer. 1991. "Psychological Characteristics of Abductees: Results from the CUFOS Abduction Project." *JUFOS* n.s. 3: 59–90.

Rogerson, Peter. 1981. "Where Have All the UFOs Gone?" *Magonia* 7. <http://www. netkonect.co.uk/d/dogon/magonia/arc/80/why.htm>.

————. 1984. "People of a Different Shape." *Magonia* 17 (October). <http://www.netkonect.co.uk/d/dogon/magonia/arc/80/shape.htm>.

Rogo, D. Scott, ed. 1980. *UFO Abductions: True Cases of Alien Kidnappings.* New York: Signet Books.

————. 1985a. "Birth Traumas from Outer Space." *IUR* (May–June): 4–5, 16.

————. 1985b. "Secret Language of UFO Abductions: A Speculation." *IUR* (July–August): 8–11.

Roicewicz, Peter M. 1989. "Signals of Transcendence: The Human-UFO Equation." *JUFOS* n.s. 1: 111–26.

Rojas, Carlos A. Guzman. 1996. "A Chronology of Ufology in Mexico." In *MUFON 1996 International UFO Symposium Proceedings: Ufology: A Scientific Enigma,* ed. Walter H. Andrus, Jr., 72–86. Seguin, Tex.: Mutual UFO Network.

Roof, Wade Clark, 1993. *A Generation of Seekers: The Spiritual Journeys of the Baby Boom Generation.* New York: HarperSanFrancisco.

Roszak, Theodore. 1976. "The Monster and the Titan: Science, Knowledge, and Gnosis." In Holton and Blanpied 1976, 17–32.

Rothenberg, Marc. 1981. "Organization and Control: Professionals and Amateurs in American Astronomy, 1899–1918." *Social Studies of Science* 11: 305–25.

Royal, Lyssa, and Keith Priest. 1992. *Visitors from Within.* Scottsdale, Ariz.: Royal Priest Research Press.

Ruppelt, Edward J. 1956. *The Report on Unidentified Flying Objects.* Garden City: Doubleday.

Russell, R. J. 1988. "Quantum Physics in Philosophical and Theological Perspective." In *Physics, Philosophy, and Theology: A Common Quest for Understanding,* ed. J. Robert John Russell, William F. Stoeger, S.J., and George V. Coyne, S.J., 343–74. Vatican City State: Vatican Observatory.

Rutkowski, Chris. 1993. "Will the Circles Be Broken?" *IUR* 18, no. 1 (January–February): 11–12, 23.

————. 1994. "Scientific Studies of Unidentified Flying Objects." *IUR* 19, no. 1 (January–February): 21–22.

Rutledge, Harley D. 1981. *Project Identification: The First Scientific Study of UFO Phenomena.* Englewood Cliffs: Prentice-Hall.

Rydeen, Paul. 1995. "The Circular File." *MUJ* 326 (June): 15–16.

Sachs, Margaret. 1980. *The UFO Encyclopedia.* New York: Putnam and Sons.

Sagan, Carl. 1994. *Pale Blue Dot: A Vision of the Human Future in Space.* New York: Random House.

————. 1995. "Wonder and Skepticism." *The Skeptical Inquirer* 19, no. 1: 24–30.

————. 1996. *The Demon-Haunted World: Science as a Candle in the Dark.* New York: Random House.

Sagan, Carl, and Thornton Page, eds. 1972. *UFO's: A Scientific Debate.* Ithaca: Cornell University Press. Reprint, New York: Barnes and Noble, 1996.

Salas, Robert L. 1997. "Minuteman Missiles Shutdown." *MUJ* 345 (January): 15–17.

Saliba, John A., ed. 1990. *Flying Saucer Contactees: A Sociopsychological Perspective*. Detroit: Apogee Books.

———. 1995. "Religious Dimensions of UFO Phenomena." In J. Lewis 1995, 15–64.

Samuel, Raphael, and Paul Thompson. 1990. *The Myths We Live By*. London: Routledge University Press.

Sanarov, Valerii I. 1981. "On the Nature and Origin of Flying Saucers and Little Green Men." *Current Anthropology* 22: 163–76.

Sanderson, Ivan T. 1967. *Uninvited Visitors: A Biologist Looks at UFOs*. New York: Cowles Education Corporation.

Saunders, David R. 1975. "Extrinsic Factors in UFO Reporting." AIAA paper presented at the Thirteenth Aerospace Sciences Meeting, Pasadena, Calif., 20–22 January.

Saunders, David R., and R. Roger Harkins. 1968. *UFOs? Yes! Where the Condon Committee Went Wrong*. New York: Signet Books.

Schick, Theodore, Jr. 1997. "The End of Science?" *The Skeptical Inquirer* (March). <http://www.csicop.org/si/9703/end.html>.

Schmidt, Roger. 1988. *Exploring Religion*. 2nd ed. Belmont, Calif.: Wadsworth Publishing.

Schnabel, James. 1992. "Confessions of a Crop Circle Spy!" *MUJ* 295 (November): 4–8.

———. 1993. "Deception, Dissociation, and Alien Abductions." *MUJ* 301 (May): 14–19.

———. 1994a. "Chronic Claims of Alien Abduction and Some Other Traumas as Self-Victimization Syndromes." *Dissociation Progress in the Dissociative Disorders* 7, no. 1 (March): 51–62.

———. 1994b. *Dark White: Aliens, Abductions, and the UFO Obsession*. London: Hamish Hamilton.

———. 1994c. *Round in Circles: Poltergeists, Pranksters, and the Secret History of Cropwatchers*. Amherst, N.Y.: Prometheus Books.

Schneider, Eri-Ka. 1998. "Dorothy's Journal: Time to Remember." *Contact Forum* 6, no. 2 (March–April): 27–32.

Schoen, Walter T. 1997. "MUFON Forum: Disgruntled." *MUJ* 354 (October): 16–17.

Schonherr, Luis. 1985. "UFOs and the Fourth Dimension: A Re-Examination." *FSR* 31, no. 1 (October): 4–7.

Schuessler, John. 1990. "The Implant Enigma." *MUJ* 266 (June): 18, 23.

———. 1996. *UFO-Related Human Physiological Effects*. LaPorte, Tex.: GeoGraphics.

———. 1998. *The Cash-Landrum Incident*. LaPorte, Tex.: GeoGraphics.

Schwarz, Berthold Eric. 1976. "UFO Contactee Stella Lansing: Possible Medical Implications of Her Motion Picture Experiments." *Journal of the American Society for Psychosomatic Dentistry and Medicine* 23: 60–68.

———. 1983. *UFO Dynamics: Psychiatric and Psychic Aspects of the UFO Syndrome*. Moore Haven, Fla.: Rainbow Books.

Scott, I. 1990. "UFO Studies in the Scientific Literature." *IUR* 15 (July–August): 16–18.

Scott, Irena, and William E. Jones. 1995. "Wright-Patterson AFB Historian Investigates Roswell Saucer Crash Story." *MUJ* 331 (November): 3–8.

Scully, Frank. 1950. *Behind the Flying Saucers.* New York: Henry Holt and Company.

Shapin, Steven. 1982. "History of Science and Its Sociological Reconstructions." *History of Science* 20: 157–211.

———. 1996. *The Scientific Revolution.* Chicago: University of Chicago Press.

Shapiro, Joshua. 1996. "Star Knowledge UFO Conference Update." *Contact Forum* 4, no. 5 (September–October): 8–9.

Sharp, Peter F. 1960. "Saucers and Science." *FSR* 6, no. 5 (September): 10–12.

———. 1961. "An Appraisal of the Present UFO Position." *FSR* 7, no. 2 (March): 19–22.

Sheaffer, Robert. 1981. *The UFO Verdict: Examining the Evidence.* Buffalo: Prometheus Books.

———. 1987–1988. "Psychic Vibrations." *The Skeptical Inquirer* 12 (winter): 134.

Sherman, Dan. 1997. *Above Black: Project Preserve Destiny — Insider Account of Alien Contact and Government Cover-Up.* Tualatin, Ore.: OneTeam Publishing.

Shermer, Michael. 1997. *Why People Believe Weird Things: Pseudoscience, Superstition, and Other Confusions of Our Time.* New York: W. H. Freeman and Company.

Shils, Edward. 1976. "Faith, Utility, and the Legitimacy of Science." In Holton and Blanpied 1976, 1–15.

Shirley, Elsie. 1997–1998. "Out of the Sky? A Curious Story of 1911." *IUR* 22, no. 4 (winter): 13, 27.

Shweder, Richard A. 1997. "How We Down Here View What's Out There." *New York Times* (24 August).

Singelenberg, Richard. 1988. "It Separated the Wheat from the Chaff: The 1975 Prophecy and Its Impact among the Dutch Jehovah's Witnesses." *Sociological Analysis* 50: 23–40.

Sitchin, Zechariah. 1976. *The Twelfth Planet.* New York: Avon Books.

———. 1980. *The Stairway to Heaven.* New York: Avon Books.

———. 1985. *The Wars of Gods and Men.* New York: Avon Books.

———. 1990. *Genesis Revisited: Is Modern Science Catching Up with Ancient Knowledge?* New York: Avon Books.

———. 1993. *When Time Began: The First New Age.* New York: Avon Books.

———. 1995. *Divine Encounters: A Guide to Visions, Angels, and Other Emissaries.* New York: Avon Books.

Skow, Brian, and Terry Endres. 1995. "The 4602d Air Intelligence Service Squadron and UFOs." *IUR* 20, no. 5 (winter): 9–10.

Smith, Huston. 1989. *Beyond the Post-Modern Mind.* Wheaton, Ill.: Theosophical Publishing House.

Smith, Malcolm. 1978. "Mail Bag: UFOs and the Bible." *FSR* 24, no. 2 (September–October): 32.

Smolin, Lee. 1997. *The Life of the Cosmos.* New York: Oxford University Press.

Spanos, Nicholas P., Patricia A. Cross, Kirby Dickson, and Susan C. DuBreuil.

1993. "Close Encounters: An Examination of UFO Experiences." *Journal of Abnormal Psychology* 102, no. 4: 624–32.

Spencer, John. 1989. *Perspectives: A Radical Examination of the Alien Abduction Phenomenon*. London: Macdonald and Co.

———, ed. 1991. *The UFO Encyclopedia*. New York: Avon Books.

Sprinkle, R. Leo. 1967. "Psychological Implications in the Investigation of UFO Reports." In C. Lorenzen and J. Lorenzen 1967, 160–86.

———. 1978. "What Are the Implications of UFO Experiences?" *IUR* 3, no. 10–11 (October–November): 19–20.

———. 1980. "UFO Contactees: Captive Collaborators or Cosmic Citizens?" In *MUFON 1980 UFO Symposium Proceedings: UFO Technology: A Detailed Examination*, ed. Walter H. Andrus Jr. and Dennis W. Stacy, 53–70. Seguin, Tex.: Mutual UFO Network.

———. 1999. *Soul Samples: Personal Explorations in Reincarnation and UFO Experiences*. Columbus, N.C.: Granite Publishing.

St. George, George. 1975. "Mail Bag: Spiritualists and UFO Experiences." *FSR* 20, no. 5: 30.

Stacy, Dennis. 1992a. "Letters . . . UFOs: The Religious Dimension." *MUJ* 291 (July): 20.

———. 1992b. "Editor's Column." *MUJ* 294 (October): 20.

———. 1992c. "Cover-Up: What Governments Do." *MUJ* 296 (December): 3–4.

———. 1993a. "Flying Saucers vs. UFOs." *MUJ* 303 (July): 3.

———. 1993b. "Crop Circles: Suspect or Merely Circumspect?" *MUJ* 304 (August): 3.

———. 1993c. "Loneliness of the Long Distance Runner: Part 1." *MUJ* 307 (November): 3.

———. 1993d. "The Long Distance Runner: Part 2." *MUJ* 308 (December): 12, 14.

Standing Elk. 1997. "Rods on the Yankton." *Contact Forum* 5, no. 3 (May–June): 22–23.

Stanton, L. Jerome. 1966. *Flying Saucers: Hoax or Reality?* New York: Belmont Books.

Star, Susan Leigh. 1985. "Scientific Work and Uncertainty." *Social Studies of Science* 15: 391–427.

Starr, Renata. 1996. "Encounters with Beloved Entities." *Contact Forum* 4, no. 2 (May–June): 3–5.

Steinmetz, Ken, ed. 1970. *Science and the UFO: A Supplement to the Proceedings of the Third Nationwide Amateur Astronomers Convention*. Denver: National Amateur Astronomers.

Stiebing, William H., Jr. 1995. "The Nature and Dangers of Cult Archeology." In Harrold and Eve 1995, 1–10.

Stockbauer, Bette. 1997. "Native American Prophecies, UFOs, and the Coming of a Messiah." *Contact Forum* 5, no. 1 (January–February): 1, 6–8.

Stoeber, Michael, and Hugo Meynell, eds. 1996. *Critical Reflections on the Paranormal*. Albany: State University of New York Press.

Stone, Clifford E. 1991. *UFO's: Let the Evidence Speak for Itself*. California: Image Colors Graphic.

———. 1997. *UFOs Are Real: Extraterrestrial Encounters Documented by the U.S. Government*. New York: SPI Books.

Strainic, Michael. 1993. "Canadian Cut-Ups and Crop Circles." *MUJ* 301 (May): 3–10.

Strentz, Herbert. 1970. "A Survey of Press Coverage of Unidentified Flying Objects, 1947–1966." Ph.D. diss., Northwestern University.

Strieber, Whitley. 1987. *Communion: A True Story*. New York: Avon Books.

———. 1988. *Transformation: The Breakthrough*. New York: Avon Books.

———. 1995. *Breakthrough: The Next Step*. New York: HarperCollins.

———. 1997. *The Secret School: Preparation for Contact*. New York: Harper-Collins.

———. 1998. *Confirmation: The Hard Evidence of Aliens among Us*. New York: St. Martin's Press.

Strieber, Whitley, and Anne Strieber. 1997. *The Communion Letters*. New York: HarperPrism.

Stringfield, Leonard. 1977. *Situation Red: The UFO Siege!* New York: Fawcett Crest Book.

———. 1978. *Retrievals of the Third Kind: A Case Study of Alleged UFOs and Occupants in Military Custody*. Seguin, Tex.: Mutual UFO Network.

———. 1980. *The UFO Crash/Retrieval Syndrome: New Sources, New Data, Status Report 2*. Seguin, Tex.: Mutual UFO Network.

———. 1982. *UFO Crash/Retrievals: Amassing the Evidence, Status Report 3*. Seguin, Tex.: Mutual UFO Network.

———. 1991. *UFO Crash/Retrievals: The Inner Sanctum, Status Report 6*. Seguin, Tex.: Mutual UFO Network.

———. 1994. *UFO Crash/Retrievals: Search for Proof in a Hall of Mirrors, Status Report 7*. Seguin, Tex.: Mutual UFO Network.

Stupple, David. 1979a. "The Man Who Talked with Venusians." *Fate* 32, no. 1 (January): 30–39.

———. 1979b. "Report from the Readers: The Author Replies." *Fate* 32, no. 5 (May): 119–20.

———. 1984. "Mahatmas and Space Brothers: The Ideologies of Alleged Contact with Mahatmas and Space Brothers." *Journal of American Culture* 7: 131–39.

———. 1994. "Historical Links between the Occult and Flying Saucers." *JUFOS* n.s. 5: 93–108.

Stupple, David, and Abdollah Dashti. 1977. "Flying Saucers and Multiple Realities: A Case Study in Phenomenological Theory." *Journal of Popular Culture* 11: 479–93.

Stupple, David, and William McNeece. 1979. "Contactees, Cults, and Culture." In *MUFON 1979 UFO Symposium Proceedings: Intensifying the Scientific Investigation of the UFO Surveillance*, ed. Walter H. Andrus Jr., 47–61. Seguin, Tex.: Mutual UFO Network.

Sturrock, Peter A. 1974. "Evaluation of the Condon Report on the Colorado

UFO Project." Stanford University Institute for Plasma Research Report No. 599, October.

―――. 1977a. "Astronomers and UFO's: A Survey." *IUR* 2, no. 3 (March): 3–4.

―――. 1977b. "Astronomers and UFO's: A Survey." *IUR* 2, no. 4 (April): 3–4.

―――. 1994a. "Report on a Survey of the Membership of the American Astronomical Society Concerning the UFO Problem: Part 1." *Journal of Scientific Exploration* 8, no. 1: 1–45.

―――. 1994b. "Report on a Survey of the Membership of the American Astronomical Society Concerning the UFO Problem: Part 2." *Journal of Scientific Exploration* 8, no. 2: 153–95.

―――. 1994c. "Report on a Survey of the Membership of the American Astronomical Society Concerning the UFO Problem: Part 3." *Journal of Scientific Exploration* 8, no. 3: 309–46.

―――. 1999. *The UFO Enigma: A New Review of the Physical Evidence.* New York: Warner Books.

Sullivan, Walter. 1972. "Influence of the Press and Other Mass Media." In Sagan and Page 1972, 258–62.

Swords, Michael. 1985. "Close Encounters: Mind or Matter?" *IUR* 10, no. 5 (September–October): 13–14.

―――. 1987a. "The Third Option: How They Got Here, and Why." *IUR* 12, no. 1 (January–February): 12–19.

―――. 1987b. "Are There Parallel Universes?" *IUR* 12, no. 6 (November–December): 17–20.

―――. 1989. "Science and the Extraterrestrial Hypothesis in Ufology." *JUFOS* n.s. 1: 67–102.

―――. 1992. "Astronomers, the Extraterrestrial Hypothesis, and the United States Air Force at the Beginning of the Modern UFO Phenomenon." *JUFOS* n.s. 4: 79–130.

―――. 1995. "The Lost Words of Edward Ruppelt." *IUR* 20, no. 2 (March–April): 14–15.

Swords, Michael D., Walter W. Walker, and Robert W. Johnson. 1992. "Analysis of Alleged Fragments from an Exploding UFO Near Ubatuba, Brazil." *JUFOS* n.s. 4: 1–38.

Talbot, Michael. 1991. *The Holographic Universe.* New York: Harper Collins.

Tekippe, Terry J. 1996. *Scientific and Primordial Knowing.* Lanham: University Press of America.

Temple, Robert. 1976. *The Sirius Mystery.* New York: St. Martin's Press. Reprint Rochester, Vt.: Destiny Books, 1987.

Tenner, Edward. 1996. *Why Things Bite Back: Technology and the Revenge of Unintended Consequences.* New York: Alfred A. Knopf.

Thavis, John. 1996. "E.T., Phone Home: The Church Wants to Talk to Your Fellow Aliens." *CNI News* 17, no. 3–4 (8 April). <CNINews1@aol.com>.

Thompson, James L. 1993. *Aliens and UFOs: Messengers or Deceivers?* Bountiful, Utah: Horizon Publishers.

Thompson, Keith. 1991. *Angels and Aliens: UFOs and the Mythic Imagination.* Reading, Mass.: Addison-Wesley Publishing.

Thompson, Richard L. 1993. *Alien Identities: Ancient Insights into Modern UFO Phenomena.* San Diego, Calif.: Govardhan Hill Publishing.

Tickle, Phyllis A. 1997. *God-Talk in America.* New York: Crossroad Publishing.

Tilly, Virginia M. 1992. "Resisting Resisting." *MUJ* 292 (August): 11–12.

Tipler, Frank J. 1980. "Extraterrestrial Intelligent Beings Do Not Exist." *Quarterly Journal of the Royal Astronomical Society* 21: 267–81.

Tobin, Clive H. 1995a. "MUFON Forum: Roswell Film." *MUJ* 328 (August): 19.

———. 1995b. "Dating the Santilli Film." *MUJ* 330 (October): 17–19.

Toumey, Christopher P. 1996. *Conjuring Science: Scientific Symbols and Cultural Meanings in American Life.* New Brunswick: Rutgers University Press.

Travis, G. D. L. 1981. "Replicating Replication? Aspects of the Social Construction of Learning in Planarian Worms." *Social Studies of Science* 11: 11–32.

Trench, Brinsley Le Poer. 1960. *The Sky People.* New York: Award Books.

———. 1962. *Temple of the Stars.* New York: Ballantine Books.

———. 1966. *The Flying Saucer Story.* New York: Ace Books.

———. 1971. *Mysterious Visitors: The UFO Story.* New York: Day Books/Stein and Day Publishers.

Trigg, Roger. 1993. *Rationality and Science: Can Science Explain Everything?* Cambridge, Mass.: Blackwell Publishers.

Truzzi, Marcello. 1971. "Definition and Dimensions of the Occult: Toward a Sociological Perspective." *Journal of Popular Culture* 5: 635–46.

———. 1977. "Editorial." *Zetetic Scholar* 1: 2, 3–8.

———. 1979. "Discussion: On the Reception of Unconventional Scientific Claims." In Mauskopf 1979, 125–37.

———. 1987. "Zetetic Ruminations on Skepticism and Anomalies in Science." *Zetetic Scholar* 12, no. 13: 7–20.

Turner, Karla. 1992. *Into the Fringe: A True Story of Alien Abduction.* New York: Berkley Books.

———. 1994a. *Masquerade of Angels.* Roland, Ark.: Kelt Works.

———. 1994b. *Taken: Inside the Alien-Human Abduction Agenda.* Roland, Ark.: Kelt Works.

Twiggs, Denise Rieb, and Bert Twiggs. 1992. *Secret Vows: Our Lives with Extraterrestrials.* New York: Berkley Books.

Tylor, E. B. 1883. *Primitive Culture: Researches into the Development of Mythology, Philosophy, Religion, Language, Art, and Customs.* 2 vols. New York: H. Holt and Company.

Ujvarosy, Kazmer. 1977. *The UFO Connections of Jesus Christ: Extracts from Ancient Texts Combined into One Story.* New York: Vantage Press.

Uriondo, Oscar. 1980. "Paranormal Features in UFO Phenomenology." *FSR* 26, no. 3: 8–10.

U.S. Bureau of the Census. 1996. *Statistical Abstract of the United States: 1996.* 116th ed. Washington, D.C.: Government Printing Office.

Vallee, Jacques. 1965. *Anatomy of a Phenomenon.* New York: Ace Books.

———. 1968. "Mail Bag: From Jacques Vallee." *FSR* 14, no. 4 (July–August): 19.

———. 1969. *Passport to Magonia: From Folklore to Flying Saucers.* Chicago: Henry Regnery.

———. 1975. *The Invisible College: What a Group of Scientists Has Discovered about UFO Influences on the Human Race.* New York: E. P. Dutton.

———. 1979. *Messengers of Deception: UFO Contacts and Cults.* Berkeley: And/Or Press.

———. 1990a. *Confrontations: A Scientist's Search for Alien Contact.* New York: Ballantine Books.

———. 1990b. "Five Arguments against the Extraterrestrial Origin of Unidentified Flying Objects." *Journal of Scientific Exploration* 4, no. 1: 105–17.

———. 1991a. *Revelations: Alien Contact and Human Deception.* New York: Ballantine Books.

———. 1991b. "Toward a Second-Degree Extraterrestrial Theory of UFOs: A Response to Dr. Wood and Prof. Bozhich." *Journal of Scientific Exploration* 5, no. 1: 103–11.

———. 1992a. *Forbidden Science: Journals 1957–1969.* Berkeley: North Atlantic Books.

———. 1992b. "The Hybridization Question," *MUJ* 290 (June): 11–13.

———. 1992c. *UFO Chronicles of the Soviet Union.* New York: Ballantine Books.

Vallee, Jacques, and Janine Vallee. 1966. *Challenge to Science: The UFO Enigma.* Chicago: Henry Regnery.

Van Tassel, George. 1952. *I Rode a Flying Saucer! The Mystery of the Flying Saucers Revealed.* Los Angeles: New Age Publishing.

Van Beek, Walter E. A. 1991. "Dogon Restudies." *Current Anthropology* 32 (April): 139–67.

Vankerkom, Tin. 1996. "Tall Tales in Flatland: Abductions in the Netherlands." *IUR* 21, no. 4 (winter): 6–8.

Vesco, Renato. 1971. *Intercept UFO: The True Story of the Flying Saucers!* New York: Pinnacle Books.

Vick, Karl. 1995. "UFO Abduction Tales Not Quite So Alien: Mainstream Society Finds Space for Supernatural Storytellers." *Washington Post* (9 May): final edition.

Von Daniken, Erich. 1968. *Chariots of the Gods: Unsolved Mysteries of the Past.* New York: Bantam Books.

Waddell, John S. 1996. "The Glass Ceiling." *MUJ* 339 (July): 15–16.

Wagner, Mahlon W. 1991. "What Can Ufologists Learn from Parapsychology?" *IUR* (September–October): 16–18.

Wallis, Roy. 1974. "The Aetherius Society: A Case Study in the Formation of a Mystagogic Congregation." *Sociological Review* 22 (February): 27–44.

Walter, Tony. 1996. *The Eclipse of Eternity: A Sociology of the Afterlife.* New York: St. Martin's Press.

Walton, Travis. 1977. *The Walton Experience.* New York: Berkley Books.

———. 1996. *Fire in the Sky: The Walton Experience.* New York: Marlowe and Company.

Warren, Donald I. 1970. "Status Inconsistency Theory and Flying Saucer Sightings." *Science* 170 (6 November): 599–603.

Watts, Alan. 1996. *UFO Visitation: Preparing for the Twenty-First Century.* London: Blandford.

Weaver, Col. Richard L., and 1st Lt. James McAndrew, eds. 1995. *The Roswell Report: Fact vs. Fiction in the New Mexico Desert.* Washington, D.C.: U.S. General Publications Office.

Webb, David. 1976a. *1973 — Year of the Humanoids: An Analysis of the Fall 1973 UFO/Humanoid Wave.* 2nd ed. Evanston, Ill.: Center for UFO Studies.

———. 1976b. "Analysis of Humanoid Reports." In *MUFON 1976 Symposium Proceedings: New Frontiers in UFO Research,* ed. N. Joseph Gurney and Walter H. Andrus Jr., 29–35. Seguin, Tex.: Mutual UFO Network.

———. 1994. "The Use of Hypnosis in Abduction Cases." In Pritchard et al. 1994, 198–202.

Weber, Rolf. 1961. "Why the Scientist Stands Aside." *FSR* 7, no. 1 (January): 15–16.

Weldon, John, and Zola Levitt. 1975. *UFOs: What on Earth Is Happening?* Irvine, Calif.: Harvest House Publishers.

Wellman, Wade, 1962. "Mail Bag: Science and Religion." *FSR* 8, no. 5 (September): 32.

Wentz, Richard E. 1998. *The Culture of Religious Pluralism.* Boulder: Westview Press.

Wertheim, Margaret. 1994. "Science and Religion: Blurring the Boundaries." *Omni* 17, no. 1 (October): 36–43, 104–107.

Westrum, Ron. 1978. "Science and Social Intelligence about Anomalies: The Case of Meteorites." *Social Studies of Science* 8, no. 4 (November): 461–93.

———. 1979. "Witnesses of UFOs and Other Anomalies." *UFO Phenomena and the Behavioral Scientist.* Metuchen, N.J.: The Scarecrow Press.

———. N.d.a. *Social Intelligence about UFOs: An Essay in the Sociology of Knowledge.* Institute for the Study of Social Change, Purdue University, Working Paper No. 48.

———. N.d.b. "UFO Sightings among Engineers and Scientists: A Report on the Anomaly Project's Industrial Research and Development UFO Sighting Poll." N.p.

Whalen, Matthew D. 1981. "Science, the Public, and American Culture: A Preface to the Study of Popular Culture." *Journal of American Culture* 4, no. 2: 14–26.

White, John. 1992. "Aliens Among Us: A UFO Conspiracy Hypothesis in a Religious Mode." *MUJ* 286 (February): 1992): 7–13.

———. 1996. "UFOs: In Search of an Overview." In *MUFON 1996 International UFO Symposium Proceedings — Ufology: A Scientific Enigma,* ed. Walter H. Andrus Jr. Seguin, Tex.: Mutual UFO Network.

Whitehead, Paul. 1985. "From Atoms to Tachyons and Hyperspace — and Back Again!" *FSR* 31, no. 1 (October): 8–10.

———. 1986a. "Science Comes under Attack — and the 'Hologram Universe' Is Proposed." *FSR* 31, no. 4 (August): 13–14.

———. 1986b. "Other Worlds: Fact, Fiction, or Beyond Human Comprehension?" *FSR* 31, no. 6 (October): 14–18.

———. 1987. "From Dust, Alien Consciousness May Arise! From Afar, Aliens

May Be Here! From Other Dimensions, UFOs May Emanate!" *FSR* 32, no. 2: 17–20.

———. 1988. "The Debate on Extraterrestrial Life 'Hots Up' and Scientist Claims Our Galaxy Is Dominated by a Superior Civilization." *FSR* 33, no. 1: 14–16.

———. 1996. "Bob Dean Speaks Again: Aliens Are Here." *FSR* 14, no. 1 (spring): 26.

Whitley, Richard. 1972. *Black Boxism and the Sociology of Science.* Sociological Review Monograph 18.

———. 1985. "Knowledge Producers and Knowledge Acquirers: Popularization as a Relation between Scientific Fields and Their Publics." In *Expository Science: Forms and Functions of Popularization,* ed. T. Shinn and R. Whitley, 3–30. Boston: Reidel.

Wilkins, H. Percy. 1957a. "The Known and the Unknown." *FSR* 3, no. 5 (September–October): 10–13.

———. 1957b. "Unidentified Flying Objects." *FSR* 3, no. 6 (November–December): 10–14.

Wilson, Clifford. 1972. *Crash Go the Chariots.* New York: Lancer Books.

———. 1974. *UFOs and Their Mission Impossible.* New York: Signet Classics.

———. 1975. *The Chariots Still Crash.* New York: Signet Books.

Wilson, James. 1992. "Are Memories of Alien Abductions Recollections of Surgical Experiences?" *Journal of Scientific Exploration* 6, no. 3: 291–92.

Wilson, Katharina. 1993. *The Alien Jigsaw.* Portland, Ore.: Puzzle Publishing.

Wingfield, George. 1995a. "Crop Circles and Stigmata: Symbols of Divine Origin?" *FSR* 40, no. 3 (autumn): 5–11.

———. 1995b. "Pathologist Says Santilli 'Alien' Appears Human." *MUJ* 328 (August): 18.

Winthrop, Robert H., ed. 1991. *Dictionary of Concepts in Cultural Anthropology.* New York: Greenwood Press. S.v. "Myth."

Wolf, Fred Alan. 1981. *Taking the Quantum Leap: The New Physics for Nonscientists.* San Francisco: Harper and Row.

———. 1988. *Parallel Universes: The Search for Other Worlds.* New York: Simon and Schuster.

Wolverton, Keith, and Thom Danenhower. 1995. "Montana Mutilations on the Rise?" *MUJ* 323 (March): 8–11.

Wood, Robert M. 1991. "The Extraterrestrial Hypothesis Is Not That Bad." *Journal of Scientific Exploration* 5, no. 1: 103–11.

Worthing, Mark William. 1996. *God, Creation, and Contemporary Physics.* Minneapolis: Fortress Press.

Wright, Dan. 1996. "Sexuality, Aliens, Hybrids, and Abductions." *MUJ* 334 (February): 11–12.

Wuthnow, Robert. 1988. *The Restructuring of American Religion: Society and Faith Since World War II.* Princeton: Princeton University Press.

———. 1991. *Acts of Compassion: Caring for Others and Helping Ourselves.* Princeton: Princeton University Press.

———. 1994. *"I Come Away Stronger": How Small Groups Are Shaping American Religion.* Grand Rapids, Mich.: William B. Eerdmans Publishing.

Zeidman, Jennie, and Mark Rodeghier. 1993. "The Pentacle Letter and the Battelle UFO Project." *IUR* 18, no. 3 (May–June): 4–12, 19–21.

Zimmer, Troy A. 1985. "Belief in UFOs as Alternative Reality, Cultural Rejection, or Disturbed Psyche." *Deviant Behavior* 6, no. 4: 405–19.

Zukav, Gary. 1979. *The Dancing Wu Li Masters: An Overview of the New Physics*. New York: William Morrow and Co.

Index

Compositor: BookMatters, Berkeley
Text: 10/13 Sabon
Display: Sabon
Printer and Binder: Haddon Craftsmen